SYBASE TRANSACT SQL GUIDELINES BEST PRACTICES

FOR DEVELOPERS AND DBAS

WITH COVERAGE TO ASE 12.5.2

MICH TALEBZADEH

RYAN THOMAS PUTNAM

Graphics design by Ryan Thomas Putnam
Book design by Mich Talebzadeh and Ryan Thomas Putnam

ISBN 0-9759693-0-7

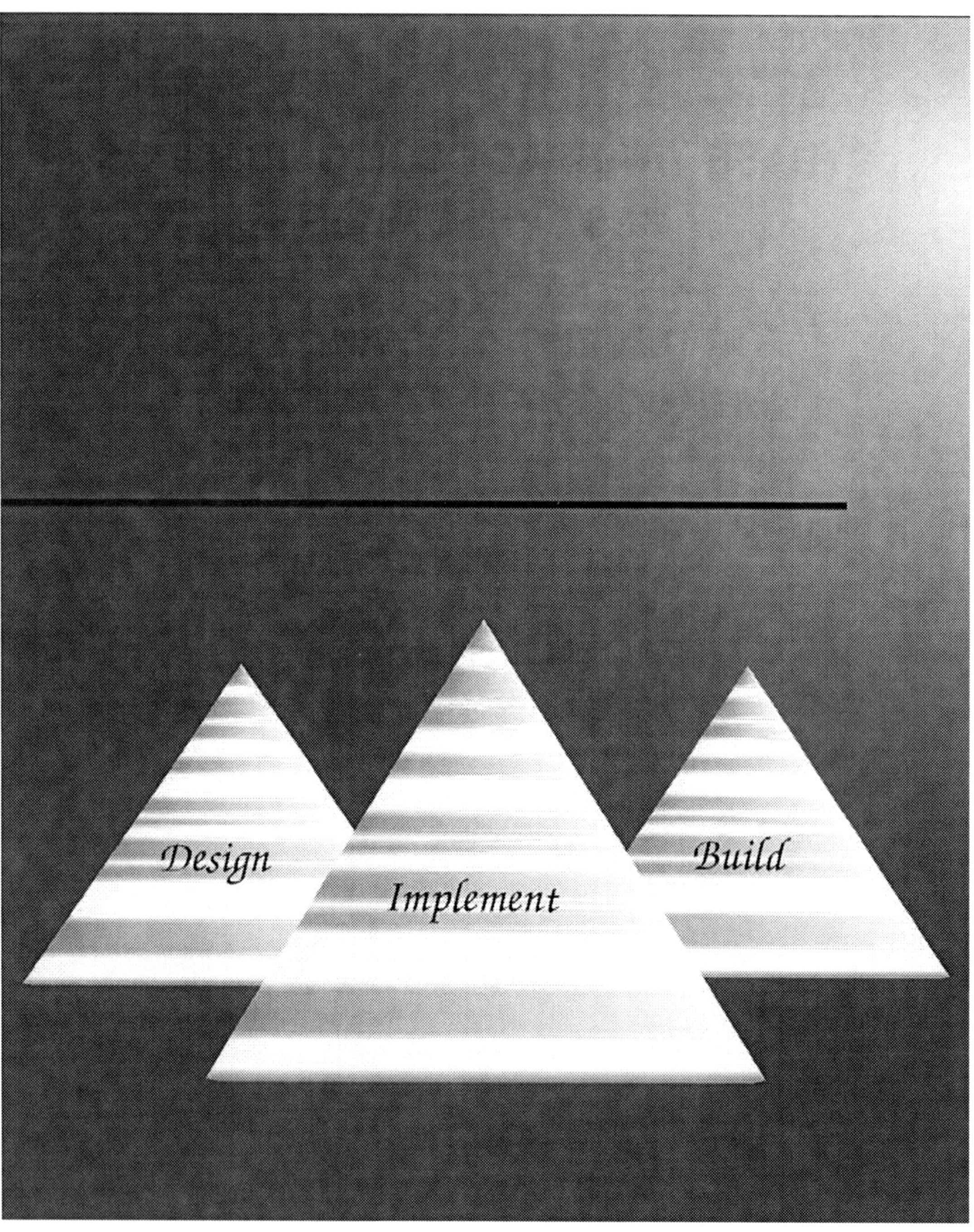
Design
Implement
Build

Table of Contents

About ISOSF

The International Sybase Open Source Forum (ISOSF) was formed one year ago by a group of Sybase(R) practitioners in the Sybase Future Forum sybase-product-future@isug.com[†] with the mission:

“Sybase Open Source Forum aims to work closely with Sybase Inc on products offered in the RDBMS area. This forum's development effort uses an open source environment to create from new or enhance the existing Sybase products with emphasis on ease of use, functionality, portability and open architecture. We strive to ensure that the products developed work on diverse environments and extend the features of the new and existing products in cooperation with Sybase Inc, members of ISUG, and the Sybase User Community at large – to satisfy the user demands. Our goal is to make Sybase a more cost effective and feature rich RDBMS to deploy and maintain."

Since its inception, there have been numerous discussions in ISOSF, with regard to the current and future Sybase products. ISOSF has members who are some of the World’s most prominent Sybase specialists, and who passionately discuss and argue on issues related to Sybase at large. It is clear to everyone that there is no substitute for experience, and it is impossible for a single person to experience everything. That is why ISOSF was formed – to openly share, discuss, and exchange ideas and solutions.

Among a number of discussions in ISOSF, there were topics on Sybase Transact-SQL(R) that the authors felt could benefit developers and DBAs. Where appropriate, these discussions are included in our write-ups. We hope you will find them helpful.

[†] ISOSF now hosts its own website: www.isosf.com

Preface

There were a number of reasons to write this book. First and foremost, it was written out of necessity. Indeed, it was not our intention to write this book. However, the demand from the developer community and DBAs who were looking for a practical modern guide convinced us that it was a good idea to write a book on Sybase T-SQL.

Unlike the majority of books on Transact-SQL, which cover many vendor products, we wrote this book specifically for the Sybase user community. As such, this book is intended for writing and tuning Sybase Transact-SQL, and where applicable it incorporates ideas about tuning your server. However, this is not a comprehensive Sybase tuning book.

With more and more emphasis on providing a 24x7 service, the pressure to write code and tune the server to perform well in production is becoming ever more critical. As Sybase practitioners, we tune many large Sybase sites. Many of these sites, such as banks and other large financial institutions are incredibly sensitive to poor performance. Any new code written and introduced to production is expected to perform well without impairing other applications. When a new index is added, we have to be certain that it will not be used inappropriately by the existing code. This book addresses these issues.

Traditionally, many Sybase sites utilize third party packages such as Imagine, Summit, Murex, Gloss, and others. Tuning SQL for these applications must be done without placing overrides on SQL statements. This is because we may not be authorized to touch the application code. Even if there are valid reasons for code changes, these changes must be requested from the vendor and released via application patches, which most often results in delays. However, there are many tips and ideas in this book that will assist you when tuning packaged software.

In this book, we cover the most practical aspects of Sybase Transact-SQL. Where applicable, we provide real-world examples. These examples cover the most commonly addressed issues. Sybase's new releases from Adaptive Server(R) Enterprise 12.5 onwards, include many new features that provide additional utilities and functionalities. This book will assist you in learning and deploying these new capabilities.

We do not believe that improving code can be done in isolation without understanding other areas of equal importance (such as tempdb databases). Where appropriate, we make suggestions to improve and fine tune ASE's configuration in these areas. Indeed, through our experience, we have concluded that a relatively small percentage of code (10-20%) is responsible for 80% of performance issues. To address these areas of concern, the DBAs and developers need to work closely and quickly to remedy the performance bottlenecks. In other words, more often than not, tuning the code must be a joint operation.

Through these writings we would like to portray the message, and our belief, that there are always ways of improving the performance of your applications – be they OLTP applications, reports, or other, to make them acceptable to the business community.

Audience

Sybase ASE is an elegant, powerful, and modern database management system. Compared to the other leading RDBMSs in its class, ASE possesses the advantage of flexibility and at the same time avoids esotericism. However, in order to design powerful applications based on ASE, it is necessary to understand Sybase Transact-SQL and how ASE manipulates the data stored within the system. Sybase Transact-SQL is an important tool that is designed for a variety of tasks, including data manipulation, both internally within ASE and externally in your own applications.

We believe there is something in this book for everyone: programmers, database administrators, database designers, data modelers, and other technically-inclined Sybase ASE users. If you work with ASE on a daily basis, and if you use Sybase Transact-SQL in your work, then you need to know what is in this book. Sybase Transact-SQL is a multi-faceted product, and can be used for a wide variety of tasks. If you are contemplating upgrading to the latest ASE releases and you would like to get that extra bit from your new server, and add value, then this book is a perfect guide.

About the Authors

Mich Talebzadeh is a Database expert with considerable DBA and Architecture experience with special interests in Sybase and Oracle. Mich started working on databases when he was a post graduate and has worked on Sybase since the early 1990s.

Mich specializes in creating database architectures for large global trading systems involving heterogeneous databases. He spends a good deal of his time working with Sybase and, more specifically, helping people who are using Sybase both as a DBA and developer.

Mich works directly with customers, either in specifying and helping them build their systems, or more frequently helping them to rebuild or tune their applications and databases. Mich serves as a Board member of the Sybase Future Forum. He is a frequent speaker at Sybase Technical Forums and other international database conferences, and is the resident Sybase specialist at www.searchdatabase.com.

Mich holds a PhD in Particle Physics from Imperial College, University of London and C.E.R.N., Geneva, Switzerland.

Ryan Putnam has been working with Sybase products since 1998, and is certified as a Sybase Developer, Associate, and Professional. He also holds certifications in Replication Server(R), Oracle, Database Design, ANSI SQL, Korn Shell Programming, IBM AIX Administration, and IBM AIX Support.

Ryan works mainly with high transaction rate distribution systems in a 24x7 operation, which performs over 300 million business and system transactions daily.

Ryan is an application DBA, backup and recovery DBA, and Replication Server expert. He is a frequent contributor to the Sybase Future forum. Ryan's passions are music, mathematics, and information systems.

Ryan thanks his family Alicia, Anna, and Justine for their love, understanding, and patience as he spent many long hours working on this book.

Acknowledgements

It is hard to thank everyone who helped us with this book. At a minimum, we owe:

1. Thanks for members of Sybase Future Forum sybase-product-future@isug.com for their lively discussions which we benefited a lot. We also thank the members of this forum for all their help and advice for the structure and content of this book.
2. Thanks to Mark Hughes, Eric Miner, Luke Woods-McConville, Eddie Bahari, Firoz Mahomedali, Elaine Carter and Mark Hudson for helping to review the material and providing feedbacks.
3. A very special thanks to Fred Cathey and Joseph Leighly for painstaking page-by-page reviews of the whole book.
4. Our thanks to the engineers in the Data Server Technology of Sybase Inc. for their advice and guidance. Special thanks to Sethu Meenakshisundara, the Technical Director of ASE.
5. Much gratitude to our main sponsors Sybase Inc. and Peridale Ltd. for getting this book to the print.

Without your help, this book would not have contained the current contents, and may not have made it to print.

From Mich:

I wish to personally acknowledge Johan McDonald and Chris M Driver in providing me with valuable feedbacks in writing sections on optimizing tempdb databases. They answered numerous emails, which contributed significantly to the accuracy of the text, as well as ensuring all the key points were made.

Chris Young, Rob Verschoor, Jason L. Froebe, Peter Thawley and Mark Hudson deserve an additional note of thanks for their notes and general comments.

I owe a debt of gratitude to David Hardy of Peridale Ltd. Which goes way beyond his support for this work. His guidance and friendship in the past few years have had a profound impact on my development at Peridale as a consultant.

I would like to thank Irfan Khan and Dr Raj Nathan of Sybase Inc. who took the idea of Sybase Inc. sponsoring this book on board.

I would like to thank Ian Gillies, Eddie Bahari, and Luke Woods-Mcconville for their friendship and advice over the years that I worked as a consultant at Deutsche Bank. My special thanks to Elaine Carter and Firoz Mahomedali of Bank of America who encouraged me to write this book. I also like to acknowledge expert comments and advice from Mark Hughes of Barclays Capital.

Last, but certainly not least, comes the family acknowledgement. I would like to thank my parents for their help and support throughout my years as a student in Switzerland and London and my later life as a Consultant. Without their love, sacrifice and support, I would not have been able to get where I am now.

Mich Talebzadeh

mich@peridale.co.uk

London, England

August 2004

From Ryan:

I would like to thank myself and Mich for finding the time to spend many hours writing, reading, and organizing this book. Secondly, my wife and family for their enduring love and support. And lastly, my parents who raised me to work hard on every aspect of my life.

Ryan Putnam

ultradad2002@yahoo.com

Grand Rapids, Michigan
United States

August 2004

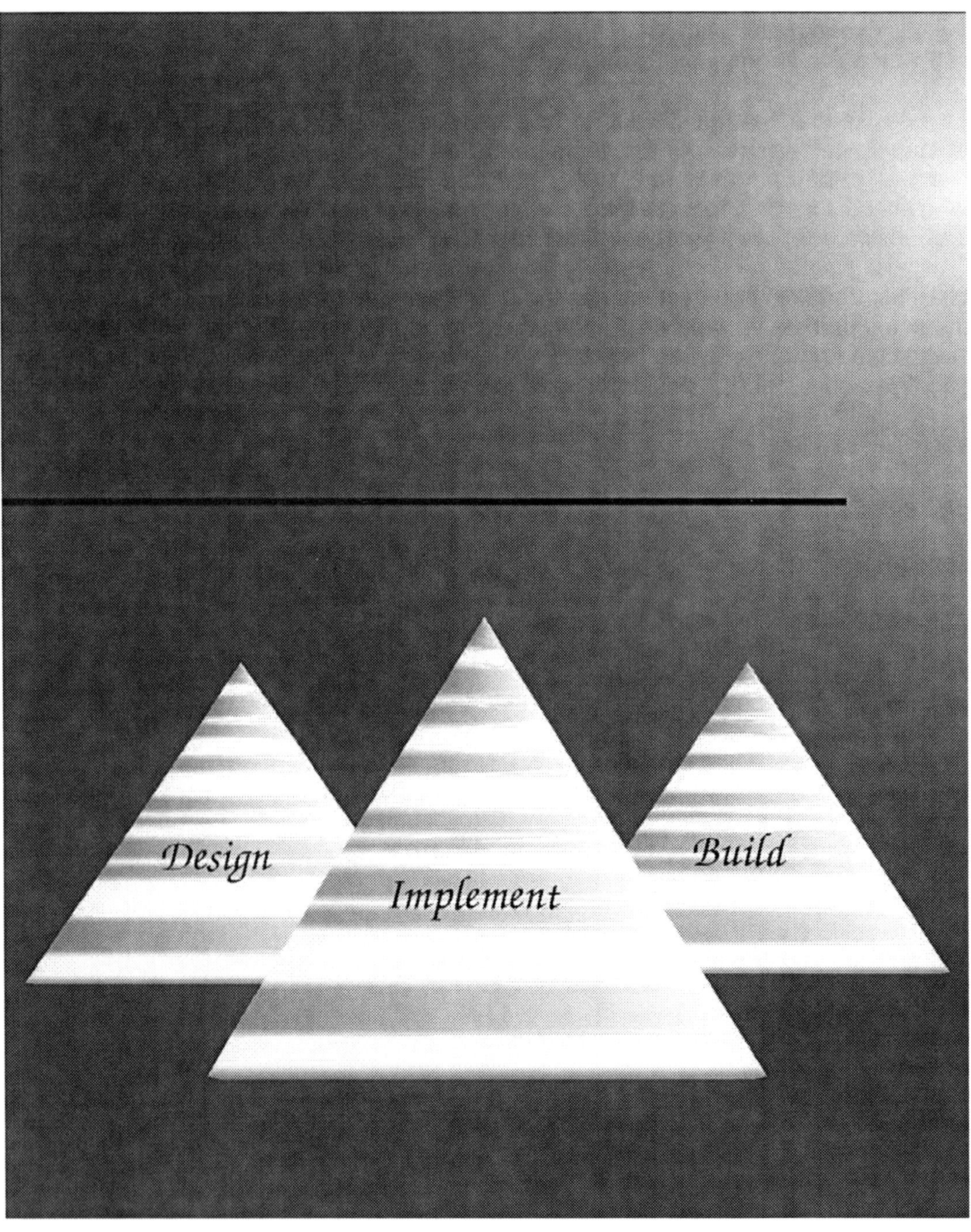
Design
Implement
Build

Chapter 1. SQL Batches

When SQL is executed in Adaptive Server(R) Enterprise, it is done so within a command batch. A command batch is the code that is submitted to ASE before or between batch separators. By default, the command batch separator is the Transact-SQL(R) keyword "go".

Example:

```
SELECT c1
  FROM table
go
----------------------------------------------------------------
123
```

In the previous example, the batch was composed of the following:

```
SELECT c1
  FROM table
go
```

Procedures and Triggers

A stored procedure is a named set of Transact-SQL (T-SQL) commands that may be invoked in an ASE database by name. A trigger is a special type of stored procedure that can be created to fire upon an insert, update, and/or delete to a table.

If you execute a stored procedure named proc_1, then the entire execution of proc_1 is considered to be part of the same batch. Thus, if proc_1 calls proc_2, and proc_2 runs an update which fires trigger trig_1, then the batch is composed of proc_1, proc_2, and trig_1.

Batches and Transactions

While a batch and a transaction may both perform database modifications, a batch which fails may not roll back all of the work that was performed by the batch.

Whereas, all database modifications performed within a transaction are guaranteed to be committed or rolled back.

A transaction may span multiple batches. However, you should *not allow* any transactions to span multiple batches as this may lead to lock contention, "BLOCKING".

Transactions

A transaction is both a unit of work and a unit of recovery. It is an all or nothing operation. Partial results cannot be seen outside of the transaction, and each transaction is independent of all other transactions. Changes made by an incomplete transaction are not available to other users until the transaction has committed. Before committing a transaction, the user may rollback the transaction and the state of the database will be as if the transaction never occurred.

In ASE, multiple T-SQL statements can be grouped and treated as a transaction. Each transaction is assumed to take the data from one valid state to another. Hence, if each and every transaction has been executed in full, or not at all, the database is considered to contain consistent data. Transactions can be aborted because a user decides the change would be invalid, or because ASE is unable to guarantee that the transaction would operate independent of other transactions.

Transaction Tips

Transactions that include many statements or take a long time to run may result in increased lock contention (see the chapter on Locking). As such, try to keep transactions as short as possible, and avoid holding locks (especially exclusive or update locks), while waiting for user interaction.

Write transactions to acquire locks in the same order on the system. This will help to reduce both lock contention and deadlocks.

Write only those statements which must be committed or rolled back as a group within a transaction. This will help reduce lock contention and deadlocks.

Check the transaction state using the global variable @@transtate. @@transtate contains the current state of a transaction after a statement executes in the current user session. However, unlike @@error, @@transtate does not get cleared for each batch.

@@transtate may take on the following values:

0 - Transaction in progress: an explicit or implicit transaction is in effect; the previous statement executed successfully.

1 - Transaction succeeded: the transaction completed and committed its changes.

2 - Statement aborted: the previous statement was aborted; no effect on the transaction.

3 - Transaction aborted: the transaction aborted and rolled back any changes.

Note: @@transtate only changes due to execution errors. Syntax and compile errors do not affect the value of @@transtate.

Check that a transaction is committed or the current nesting level using the global variable @@trancount.

@@trancount has the following properties:

- An initial implicit or explicit BEGIN TRANSACTION sets @@trancount to 1.
- Each BEGIN TRANSACTION increments @@trancount by 1.
- A COMMIT TRANSACTION decrements @@trancount by 1.
- Firing a trigger increments @@trancount by 1.
- Nested transactions are not committed unless @@trancount equals 0.
- A ROLLBACK TRANSACTION reverts all modifications that were made by the transaction to the state before the transaction occurred and sets @@trancount to 0.

Example:

```
BEGIN TRAN
go
SELECT @@trancount,
       @@transtate
-------------------------------------------------
1      0

BEGIN TRAN
go
SELECT @@trancount,
       @@transtate
-------------------------------------------------
2      0

BEGIN TRAN
BEGIN TRAN
COMMIT TRAN
go
SELECT @@trancount,
       @@transtate
-------------------------------------------------
3      0

ROLLBACK TRAN
SELECT @@trancount,
       @@transtate
-------------------------------------------------
0      3
```

Since the value of @@trancount is 0, we know that we do not have a transaction in progress. We also know that from the value of @@transtate "3" that our previous transaction aborted and all modifications were rolled back.

Transaction Example:
Update the c1 column of table and set it to 5 where c2 is 123 and c3 is 186.

```
BEGIN TRAN
go
SELECT @@trancount,
       @@transtate,
       @@rowcount
go
-------------------------------------------------
1      0      0
```

```
UPDATE table
   SET c1 = 5
go

SELECT @@trancount,
       @@transtate,
       @@rowcount
go
-----------------------------------------------
1      0      32222
```

What did I do wrong? I forgot to include the "WHERE" clause as part of the update and updated all of the table's records, some 32222 of them. Oops! but I am okay. Do you know why? I have not committed the transaction yet and can rollback my modifications.

So I Enter:

```
ROLLBACK TRAN
go
SELECT @@trancount,
       @@transtate,
       @@rowcount
go
-----------------------------------------------
0      3      0
```

Named Transactions

You should always assign your transactions a name. This name can be used for troubleshooting, auditing, replicating, and potentially other purposes. When you name a transaction, only the outermost named transaction will be visible in master..sysprocesses. In addition, names can be duplicated without any issues.

A good naming standard for stored procedures and triggers is to use the stored procedure name or trigger name.

Example:

```
DECLARE @TRNAME VARCHAR(30)

SELECT @TRNAME = OBJECT_NAME(@@PROCID)

BEGIN TRAN @TRNAME
```

The name of the transaction does not matter when you are going to ROLLBACK or COMMIT your modifications. As such, you do not need to include the name in the ROLLBACK or COMMIT.

Example:
```
DECLARE @TRNAME VARCHAR(30)

SELECT @TRNAME = OBJECT_NAME(@@PROCID)

BEGIN TRAN @TRNAME

SELECT @@TRANCOUNT

COMMIT TRAN

SELECT @@TRANCOUNT
go
----------------------------------------------------------------------
1
0
```

Dynamic T-SQL or Embedded T-SQL which uses transactions should name transactions according to the function of the T-SQL statements. This means that someone needs to create a Matrix of values to be assigned to these T-SQL batches.

Savepoints

ASE supports transaction savepoints. A savepoint allows for transactional units to be defined within a transaction. These transactional units may be rolled back without rolling back the entire transaction.

Example:
```
BEGIN TRANSACTION

UPDATE table1
   SET c1 = "ABC"
 WHERE c2 = "DEF"

SAVE TRANSACTION after_table1

UPDATE table2
```

```
   SET c1 = "ABC"
 WHERE c2 = "DEF"

IF ( @@ROWCOUNT > 2 )
BEGIN
   ROLLBACK TRANSACTION after_table1
END

COMMIT TRAN
go
```

In the previous example, we modified table1 and defined a savepoint for the modifications to table2. Our conditional statement states that if our update of table2 exceeds two records, we rollback to the defined savepoint. Thus, the modifications to table2 would not take effect. However, the modifications to table1 will be committed and made available.

When mixing SAVEPOINTS and named transactions, you need to be sure that each named transaction for a user session uses a unique SAVEPOINT name.

Example:

```
DECLARE @TRNAME VARCHAR(30)
SELECT @TRNAME = OBJECT_NAME(@@PROCID)

BEGIN TRANSACTION @TRNAME

SELECT @TRNAME = "S1" + OBJECT_NAME(@@PROCID)

SAVE TRANSACTION @TRNAME

ROLLBACK TRANSACTION @TRNAME

COMMIT TRAN
go
```

In ASE, you can define multiple SAVEPOINTS. As such, you need to determine which label or SAVEPOINT to roll back your transaction.

Example:

```
DECLARE @TRNAME VARCHAR(30)
SELECT @TRNAME = OBJECT_NAME(@@PROCID)

BEGIN TRANSACTION @TRNAME

SELECT @TRNAME = "S1" + OBJECT_NAME(@@PROCID)

SAVE TRANSACTION @TRNAME

SELECT @TRNAME = "S2" + OBJECT_NAME(@@PROCID)

SAVE TRANSACTION @TRNAME

/* Let's rollback to the first SAVEPOINT */
SELECT @TRNAME = "S1" + OBJECT_NAME(@@PROCID)

ROLLBACK TRANSACTION @TRNAME

/* Let's Commit our changes now */
COMMIT TRAN
go
```

Chapter 1. SQL Batches

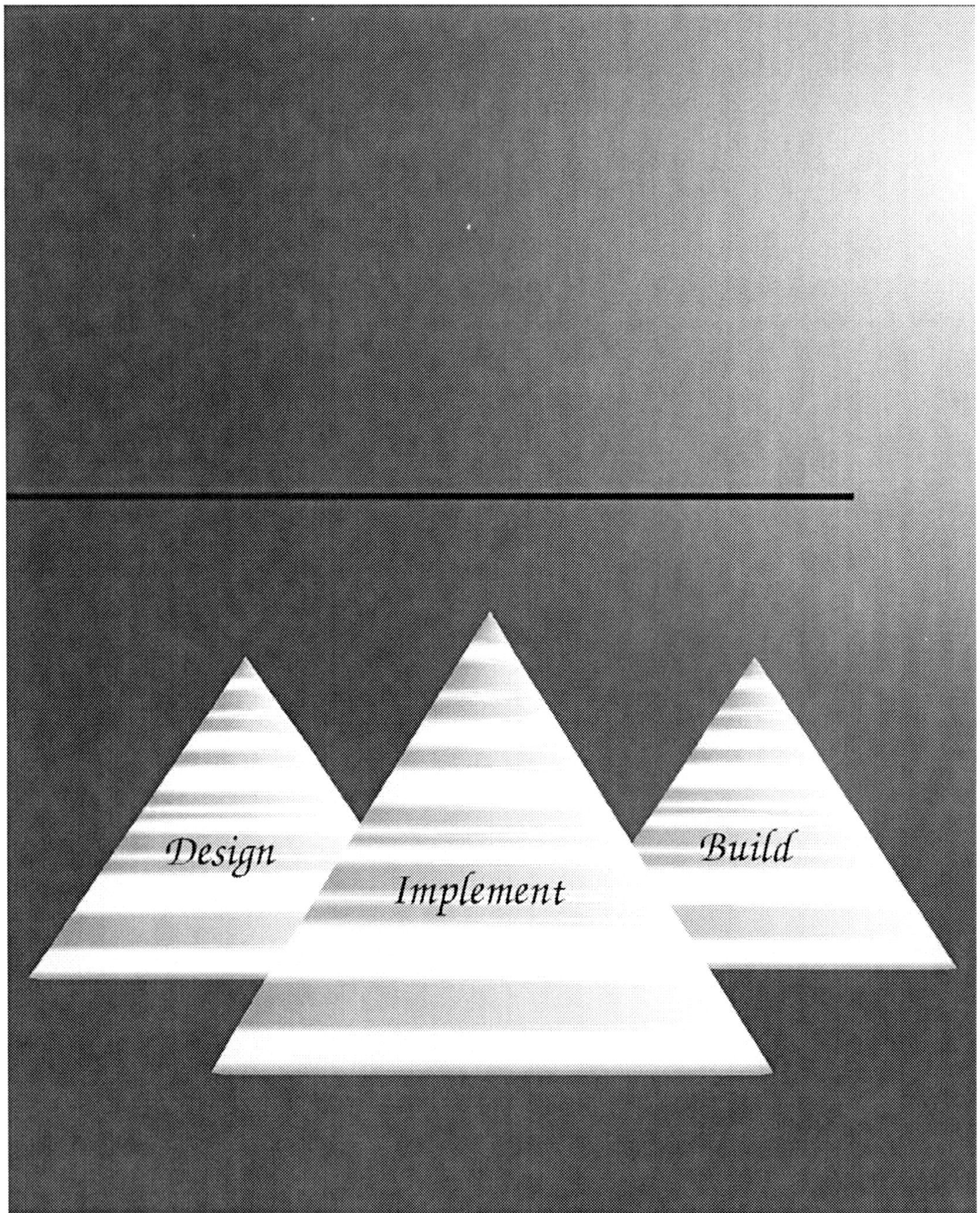
Design
Implement
Build

Chapter 2. Data Access

There are numerous ways in which data may be retrieved from a table. The most typical retrieval methods are via:

1. Table Scan
2. Clustered Index (Contains table data sorted by index keys)
3. Non-Clustered Index Access and Table Lookups
4. Non-Clustered Index Only (Index contains all columns)

The most efficient access method is almost always through the use of an index. The most efficient method of index access is typically a covered Non-Clustered Index. The least efficient method is a full table scan.

Note: On medium to large sized tables, let's say any table which has more than 500 records, full tables scans should almost always be avoided.

However, before going any further it is important to understand some relevant terminologies used in this chapter.

Useful terminologies

Index

An index is a database object that can be created for a table – to enhance the speed of direct access to specific data rows.

Allocation Units and Extents

When you initialize a database device, the **disk init** command divides the new space into **allocation units** of 256 2K data pages by default. The first page of each allocation unit is known as the **allocation page**. The allocation page tracks the use of all pages in the allocation unit.

When a table or an index requires space, ASE allocates a block of 8 2K pages to the object by default. This 8-page block is called an **extent**. Each 256-page allocation unit contains 32 extents. ASE uses extents as a unit of space management to allocate and deallocate space as follows:

1. When you create a table or an index, ASE allocates an extent for the object.

2. When you add rows to an existing table, and the existing pages are full, ASE allocates another page. If all pages in an extent are full, ASE allocates an additional extent.

3. When you drop a table or an index, ASE deallocates the extents it occupied.

4. When you delete rows from a table so that it shrinks by a page, ASE deallocates the page. If the table shrinks off the extent, ASE deallocates the extent.

Every time space is allocated or deallocated on an extent, ASE records the event on the allocation page that tracks the extents for that object. This provides a fast method for tracking space allocations in the database, since objects can shrink or grow without excessive overhead.

Types of ASE tables

When a table is created, by default the locking scheme is the server-wide setting for the configuration parameter ***lock scheme***. The default value for this parameter is "allpages" or APL. In addition, ASE allows you to set the table locking scheme to "datapages" DPL or "datarows DOL. These are explained below:

1. In APL, the data page and the index pages are locked during the operation.

2. In DPL, only the data page is locked, no index page locking.

3. In DOL, only the rows are locked , no index page locking.

Database Cache

One of the main tools used by Sybase to reduce disk I/O is the data cache. ASE acquires a segment of shared memory and typically sets aside the largest proportion of it to hold data or index pages. When a transaction requires a page, it reads the page from disk and stores it in the data cache; subsequent transactions requesting the same page can then retrieve it from memory rather than from disk.

LRU/MRU Chain and Wash Marker

In practice, there is rarely enough memory in the data cache to accommodate every data page required by transactions, so pages cannot be held in memory indefinitely. Each ASE data cache is managed as an MRU/LRU (most recently used/least recently used) chain of buffers. As buffers age in the cache, they move from the MRU end toward the LRU end.

When changed pages in the cache pass a point called the wash marker, on the MRU/LRU chain, ASE initiates an asynchronous write on any pages that changed while they were in cache. This helps ensure that when the pages reach the LRU end of the cache, they are clean and can be reused. LRU replacement strategy is usually used for pages that a query needs to access more than once or pages that must be updated. On the other hand, MRU, or fetch-and-discard replacement strategy is used for pages that a query needs to read only once.

Indexes

An index is a structure in the database used by the system to effectively access rows of data meeting certain criterion. There are multiple types of indexes implemented in Sybase ASE, and each type is optimized for different operations. In general, each instance of an index is specific to a single table, and a table can have multiple indexes.

An index stores an ordered replica of a subset of the information stored in the rows of a table, as well as a pointer to the source row. In other words, it contains copies of certain columns from the row as well as a pointer to the row. The table is said to have an index on those columns. A query requesting rows from a table that has an index which meets a restriction criterion of the query, will potentially use the index to determine specifically which data pages contain the requested information.

Indexes are the most important physical design element in improving database performance.

Indexes:

- Help to prevent table scans. Instead of reading hundreds of data pages, a few index pages and data pages can satisfy many queries.
- For some queries, data can be retrieved from a non-clustered index without ever accessing the data rows.
- Clustered indexes can randomize data inserts, and avoid "hot spots" on the last page of a table.
- Indexes can help avoid sorts, if the index order matches the order of columns in an order by clause.

In addition to their performance benefits, indexes can enforce the uniqueness of data.

Although indexes speed data retrieval, too many indexes on the same table can slow down data modifications, since changes to the data often times require updating the indexes.

Optimal indexing demands:

- An understanding of the behaviour of queries that access un-indexed heap tables, tables with clustered indexes, and tables with non-clustered indexes.
- An understanding of the mix of queries that run on your server.
- An understanding of the ASE optimizer.

Types of Indexes

Adaptive Server provides two types of indexes:

1. **Clustered Indexes** - Where the table data is physically stored in the order of the keys on the index. You can create only one clustered index on a table because there is only one possible physical ordering of the data rows.

   - For allpages-locked tables (APL), rows are stored in key order on pages, and pages are linked in key order.

   - For data-only-locked tables (DOL), indexes are used to direct the storage of data on rows and pages, but strict key ordering is not maintained.

2. **Non-Clustered Indexes** - Where the storage order of data in the table is not related to index keys. You can create up to 249 non-clustered indexes per table.

Indexes are used to support Primary Key (PK) and Foreign Key (FK) constraints in the database.

Index pages

Index entries are stored as rows on index pages in a format similar to the format used for data rows on data pages. Index entries store the key values and pointers to lower levels of the index, to the data pages, or to individual data rows.

ASE uses B-tree indexing, where each node in the index structure can have multiple children (other nodes).

Index entries are usually limited to one or few columns and are usually much smaller than a data row in a data page, and index pages are much more densely populated than data pages. If a data row has 200 bytes (including row overhead), there are 10 rows per page.

An index on a 15-byte field has about 100 rows per index page (the pointers require 4-9 bytes per row, depending on the type of index and the index level).

Indexes can have multiple levels:

- Root level
- Leaf level
- Intermediate level

Root level

The root level is the highest level of the index. There is only one root page. If an allpages-locked table is very small, so that the entire index fits on a single page, there are no intermediate or leaf levels, and the root page stores pointers to the data pages.

Data-only-locked tables always have a leaf level between the root page and the data pages.

For larger tables, the root page stores pointers to the intermediate level index pages or to leaf-level pages.

Leaf level

The lowest level of the index is the leaf level. At the leaf level, the index contains a key value for each row in the table, and the rows are stored in sorted order by the index key:

- For clustered indexes on allpages-locked tables, the leaf level is the data. No other level of the index contains one index row for each data row.
- For non-clustered indexes and clustered indexes on data-only-locked tables, the leaf level contains the index key value for each row, a pointer to the page where the row is stored, and a pointer to the rows on the data page.

The leaf level is the level just above the data; it contains one index row for each data row. Index rows on the index page are stored in key value order.

Intermediate level

All levels between the root and leaf levels are intermediate levels. An index on a large table or an index using long keys may have many intermediate levels. A very small allpages-locked table may not have an intermediate level at all; the root page points directly to the leaf level.

Index Size

The following table describes the new limits on index size for APL and DOL tables:

Page size	User-visible index row-size limit	Internal index row-size limit
2K (2048 bytes)	600	650
4K (4096bytes)	1250	1310
8K (8192 bytes)	2600	2670
16K (16384 bytes)	5300	5390

Because you can create tables with columns wider than the limit for the index key, these columns become non-indexable. For example, if you perform the following on a 2K page server, then try to create an index on c3, the command fails and Adaptive Server issues an error message because column c3 is larger than the index row-size limit (600 bytes).

Example:

```
CREATE
 TABLE t1(
      c1 INT NOT NULL,
      c2 INT NOT NULL,
      c3 CHAR(700) NOT NULL
)
go

CREATE NONCLUSTERED INDEX ix01_t1
ON t1 (c3)
go
```

"Non-indexable" does not mean that you cannot use these columns in search clauses. Even though a column is non-indexable (as in c3, previous), you can still create statistics for it. Also, if you include the column in a **where** clause, it will be evaluated during optimization.

Clustered Indexes on Allpages-Locked Tables

With clustered indexes on allpages-locked tables, leaf-level pages are also the data pages, and all rows are kept in physical order by the keys.

Physical ordering means that:

- All entries on a data page are in index key order.
- By following the "next page" pointers on the data pages, Adaptive Server reads the entire table in index key order.

On the root and intermediate pages, each entry points to a page on the next level.

Clustered Indexes and select operations

To select a particular last name using a clustered index, ASE first uses *sysindexes* to find the root page. It examines the values on the root page and then follows page pointers, performing a binary search on each page it accesses as it traverses the index.

See the following figure.

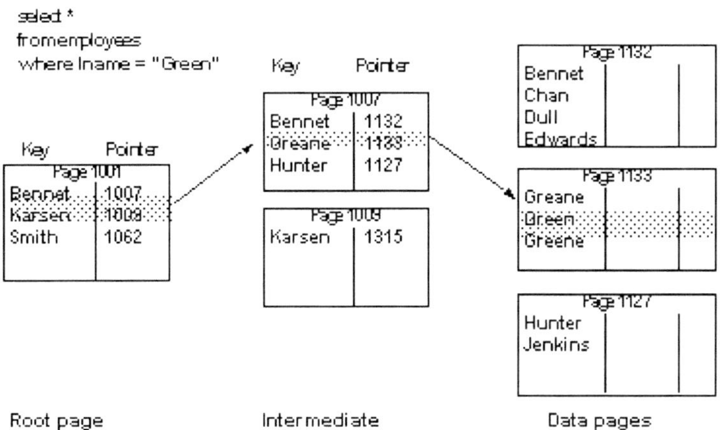

On the root level page, "Green" is greater than "Bennet," but less than "Karsen", so the pointer for "Bennet" is followed to page 1007. On page 1007, "Green" is greater than "Greane", but less than "Hunter", so the pointer to page 1133 is followed to the data page, where the row is located and returned to the user.

This retrieval via the clustered index requires:

1. One read for the root level of the index

2. One read for the intermediate level

3. One read for the data page

These reads may come either from the cache (called a logical read) or from disk (called a physical read). On tables that are frequently used, the higher levels of the indexes are often found in the cache, with lower levels and data pages being read from disk.

Clustered Indexes and Insert Operations

When you insert a row into an allpages-locked table with a clustered index, the data row must be placed in the physical order according to the key value on the table.

Other rows on the data page move down on the page, as needed, to make room for the new value. As long as there is room for the new row on the page, the insert does not affect any other pages in the database.

The clustered index is used to find the location for the new row.

The following figure shows a simple case where there is room on an existing data page for the new row. In this case, the key values in the index do not change.

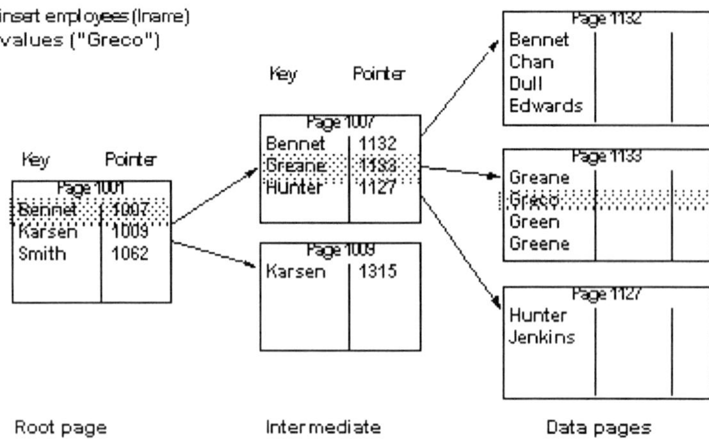

Page Splitting on Full Data Pages

If there is not enough room on the data page for the new row, a page split must be performed.

- A new data page is allocated on an extent already in use by the table. If there is no free page available, a new extent is allocated.

- The next and previous page pointers on adjacent pages are changed to incorporate the new page in the page chain. This requires reading those pages into memory and locking them.
- Approximately half of the rows are moved to the new page, with the new row inserted in order.
- The higher levels of the clustered index change to point to the new page.
- If the table also has non-clustered indexes, all pointers to the affected data rows must be changed to point to the new page and row locations.

In some cases, page splitting is handled slightly differently.

Overflow Pages

Overflow pages are created for non-unique clustered indexes on allpages-locked tables, when a newly inserted row has the same key as the last row on a full data page. A new data page is allocated and linked into the page chain, and the newly inserted row is placed on the new page.

The only rows that will be placed on this overflow page are the additional rows with the same key value. In a non-unique clustered index with many duplicate key values, there can be numerous overflow pages for the same value.

The clustered index does not contain pointers directly to overflow pages. Instead, the next page pointers are used to follow the chain of overflow pages until a value is found that does not match the search value.

Clustered Indexes and Delete Operations

When you delete a row from an allpages-locked table that has a clustered index, other rows on the page move up to fill the empty space so that the data remains contiguous on the page.

If you delete the last row on a data page, the page is deallocated and the next and previous page pointers on the adjacent pages are changed.

The rows that point to that page in the leaf and intermediate levels of the index are removed.

If the deallocated data page is on the same extent as other pages belonging to the table, it can be used again when that table needs an additional page.

If the deallocated data page is the last page on the extent that belongs to the table, the extent is also deallocated and becomes available for the expansion of other objects in the database.

If you delete a pointer from an index page, leaving only one row on that page, the row is moved onto an adjacent page, and the empty page is deallocated. The pointers on the parent page are updated to reflect the changes.

Non-Clustered Indexes

The B-tree works much the same for non-clustered indexes as it does for clustered indexes, but there are some differences.

In non-clustered indexes:

- The leaf pages are not the same as the data pages.
- The leaf level stores one key-pointer pair for *each row* in the table.
- The leaf-level pages store the index keys and page pointers, plus a pointer to the row offset table on the data page. This combination of page pointer plus the row offset number is called the row ID.
- The root and intermediate levels store index keys and page pointers to other index pages. They also store the row ID of the key's data row.

With keys of the same size, non-clustered indexes require more space than clustered indexes.

Leaf Pages Revisited

The leaf page of an index is the lowest level of the index where all of the keys for the index appear in sorted order.

In clustered indexes on allpages-locked tables, the data rows are stored in order by the index keys, so by definition, the data level is the leaf level. There is no other level of the clustered index that contains one index row for each data row. Clustered indexes on allpages-locked tables are sparse indexes.

The level above the data contains one pointer for every data *page*, not data *row*.

In non-clustered indexes and clustered indexes on data-only-locked tables, the level just above the data is the leaf level: it contains a key-pointer pair for each data row. These indexes are dense. At the level above the data, they contain one index row for each data row.

Non-Clustered Index Structure

The table in the following figure shows a non-clustered index on *lname*. The data rows at the far right show pages in ascending order by *employee_id* (10, 11, 12, and so on) because there is a clustered index on that column.

The root and intermediate pages store:

1. The key value
2. The row ID
3. The pointer to the next level of the index

The leaf level stores:

1. The key value
2. The row ID

The row ID in higher levels of the index is used for indexes that allow duplicate keys. If a data modification changes the index key or deletes a row, the row ID positively identifies all occurrences of the key at all index levels.

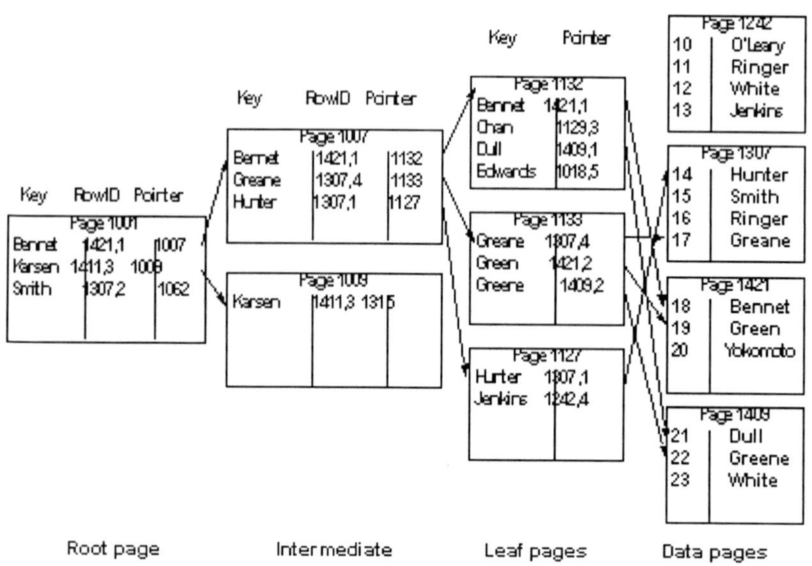

Non-Clustered Indexes and Select Operations

When you select a row using a non-clustered index, the search starts at the root level. *sysindexes.root* stores the page number for the root page of the non-clustered index.

In the previous figure, "Green" is greater than "Bennet", but less than "Karsen", so the pointer to page 1007 is followed.

"Green" is greater than "Greane", but less than "Hunter", so the pointer to page 1133 is followed. Page 1133 is the leaf page, showing that the row for "Green" is row 2 on page 1421. This page is fetched, the "2" byte in the offset table is checked, and the row is returned from the byte position on the data page.

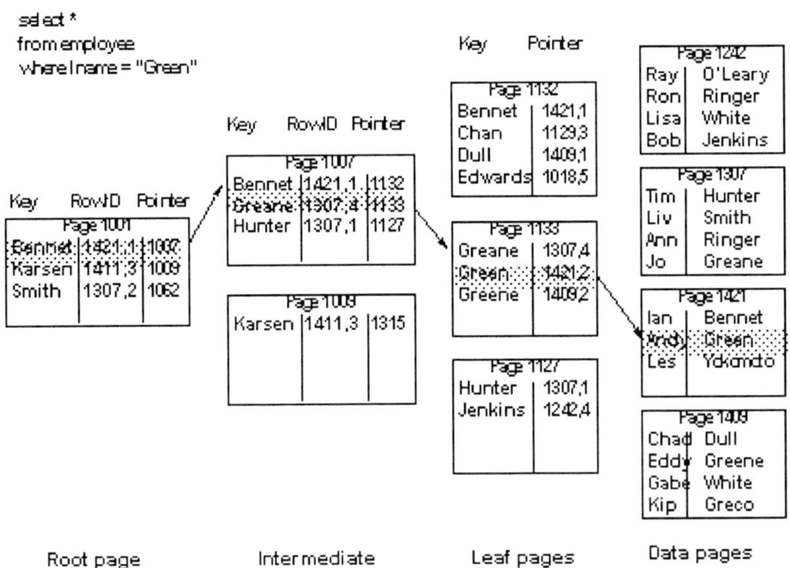

Non-Clustered Index Performance

The query in the previous figure requires the following I/O:

- One read for the root level page.
- One read for the intermediate level page.
- One read for the leaf-level page.
- One read for the data page.

Note: If your applications use a particular non-clustered index frequently, the root and intermediate pages will probably be in cache, so only one or two physical disk I/Os need to be performed.

Non-Clustered Indexes and Insert Operations

When you insert rows into a heap table (a table without a clustered index) that has a non-clustered index, the insert goes to the last page of the table.

If the heap table is partitioned, the insert goes to the last page on one of the partitions. Then, the non-clustered index is updated to include the new row. Thus, partitioned heap tables can improve the performance of insertions.

If the table has a clustered index, it is used to find the location for the row. The clustered index is updated, if necessary, and each non-clustered index is updated to include the new row as described under inserts with clustered indexes.

The figure which follows, shows an insert into a heap table with a non-clustered index. The row is placed at the end of the table. A row containing the new key value and the row ID is also inserted into the leaf level of the non-clustered index.

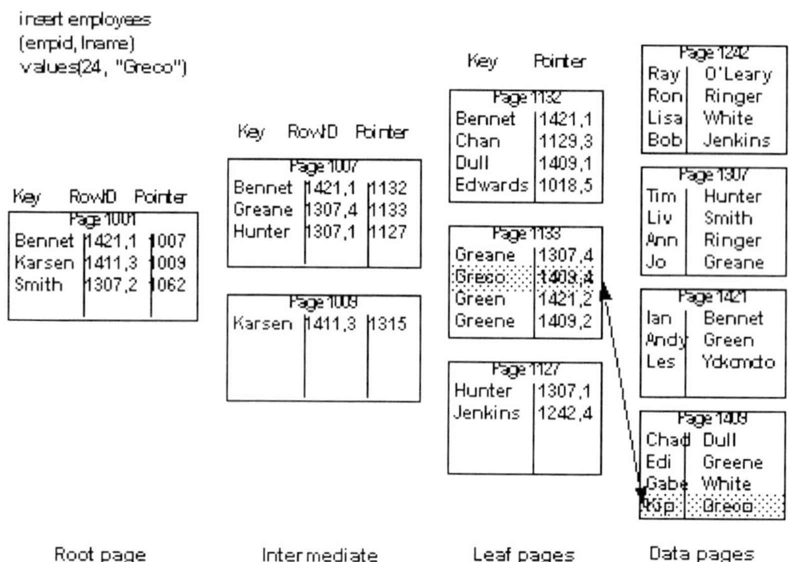

Non-Clustered Indexes and Delete Operations

When you delete a row from a table, the query can use a non-clustered index on the columns in the **where** clause to locate the data row to delete, as shown in the figure that follows.

The row in the leaf level of the non-clustered index that points to the data row is also removed. If there are other non-clustered indexes on the table, the rows on the leaf level of those indexes are also deleted.

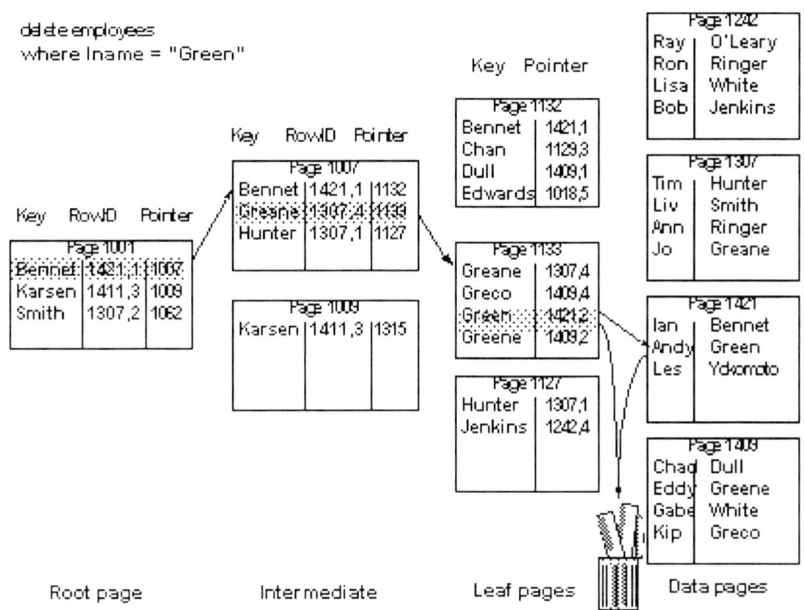

If the delete operation removes the last row on the data page, the page is deallocated and the adjacent page pointers are adjusted in allpages-locked tables. Any references to the page are also deleted in higher levels of the index.

If the delete operation leaves only a single row on an index intermediate page, index pages may be merged, as with clustered indexes.

There is no automatic page merging on data pages, so if your applications make many random deletes, you may end up with data pages that have only a single row, or a few rows, on a page. This can result in fragmentation. See Chapter 3 for more details on fragmentation.

Clustered Indexes on Data-Only-Locked Tables

Clustered indexes on data-only-locked tables are structured like non-clustered indexes. They have a leaf level above the data pages. The leaf level contains the key values and row ID for each row in the table.

Unlike clustered indexes on allpages-locked tables, the data rows in a data-only-locked table are not necessarily maintained in exact order by the key. Instead, the index directs the placement of rows to pages that have adjacent or nearby keys.

When a row needs to be inserted in a data-only-locked table with a clustered index, the insert uses the clustered index key just before the value to be inserted. The index pointers are used to find that page, and the row is inserted on the page if there is room. If there is not room, the row is inserted on a page in the same allocation unit, or on another allocation unit already used by the table.

To provide nearby space for maintaining data clustering, during inserts and updates to data-only-locked tables, you can set space management properties to provide space on pages (using **fillfactor** and **exp_row_size**) or on allocation units (using **reservepagegap**).

Index Covering

Index covering can produce dramatic performance improvements when all columns needed by the query are included in the index.

You can create indexes on more than one key. These types of indexes are called *composite indexes*. Composite indexes can have up to 31 columns adding up to a maximum specified by your ASE page size.

If you create a composite non-clustered index on each column referenced in the query's select list and in any **where**, **having**, **group by**, and **order by** clauses, the query can be satisfied by accessing the index only.

Since the leaf level of a non-clustered index or a clustered index on a data-only-locked table contains the key values for each row in a table, queries that access only the key values can retrieve the information by using the leaf level of the non-clustered index as if it were the actual table data. This is called index covering.

There are two types of index scans that can use an index that covers the query:

- matching index scan
- non-matching index scan

For both types of covered queries, the index keys must contain all the columns named in the query. Matching scans have additional requirements.

Covering Matching Index Scans

These let you skip the last read for each row returned by the query, the read that fetches the data page.

For point queries that return only a single row, the performance gain is slight – just one page.

For range queries, the performance gain is larger, since the covering index saves one read for each row returned by the query.

For a covering matching index scan to be used, the index must contain all columns named in the query. In addition, the columns in the **where** clauses of the query must include the leading column of the columns in the index.

For example, for an index on columns A, B, C, and D, the following sets can perform matching scans: A, AB, ABC, AC, ACD, ABD, AD, and ABCD. The columns B, BC, BCD, BD, C, CD, or D do not include the leading column and can be used only for non matching scans.

When performing a matching index scan, Adaptive Server uses standard index access methods to move from the root of the index to the non-clustered leaf page that contains the first row.

In the following figure, the non-clustered index on *lname, fname* covers the query. The **where** clause includes the leading column, and all columns in the select list are included in the index, so the data page does not need to be accessed.

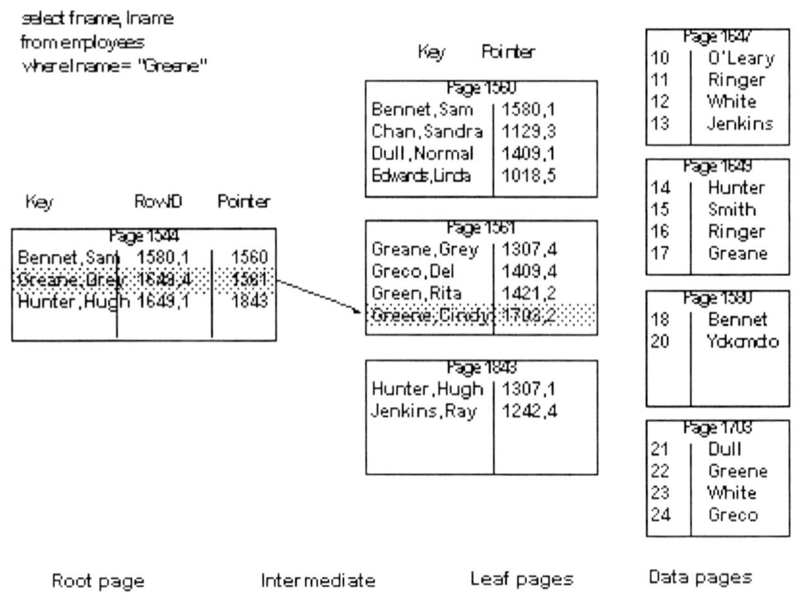

Covering Non-matching Index Scans

When the columns specified in the **where** clause do not include the leading column in the index, but all columns named in the select list and other query clauses (such as **group by** or **having**) are included in the index, ASE saves I/O by scanning the entire leaf level of the index, rather than scanning the table.

It cannot perform a matching scan because the first column of the index is not specified.

The query and figure below shows a non-matching index scan. This query does not use the leading columns on the index, but all columns required in the query are in the non-clustered index on *lname, fname, emp_id.*

The non-matching scan must examine all rows on the leaf level. It scans all leaf level index pages, starting from the first page. It has no way of knowing how many rows might match the query conditions, so it must examine every row in the index. Since it must begin at the first page of the leaf level, it can use the pointer in *sysindexes.first* rather than descending the index.

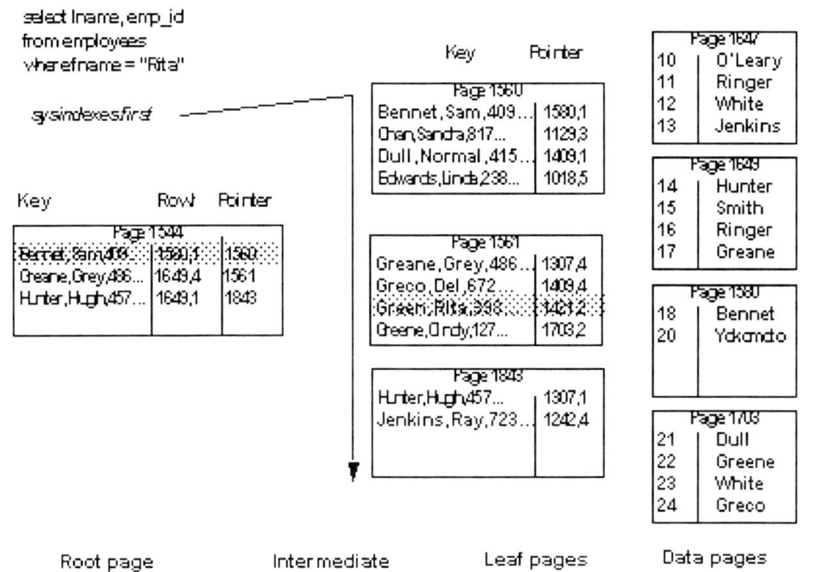

Indexes and Caching

Index pages get special handling in the data cache, as follows:

- Root and intermediate index pages always use an LRU strategy.
- Index pages can use one cache while the data pages use a different cache, if the index is bound to a different cache.
- Covering index scans can use a fetch-and-discard strategy.
- Index pages can cycle through the cache many times, if **number of index trips** is configured.

When a query that uses an index is executed, the root, intermediate, leaf and data pages are read in that order. If these pages are not in the cache, they are read into the MRU end of the cache and are moved toward the LRU end as additional pages are read in.

Each time a page is found in the cache, it is moved to the MRU end of the page chain, so the root page and higher levels of the index tend to stay in the cache.

Using Separate Caches for Data and Index Pages

Indexes and the tables they index can use different caches. A System Administrator or table owner can bind a clustered or non-clustered index to one cache and its table to another.

Index Trips Through the Cache

A special strategy is developed to keep index pages in cache for a longer duration. Data pages make only a single trip through the cache: they are read in at the MRU end of the cache or placed just before the wash marker, depending on the cache strategy chosen for the query.

Once the pages reach the LRU end of the cache, the buffer for that page is reused when another page needs to be read into cache.

For index pages, a counter controls the number of trips that an index page can make through the cache.

When the counter is greater than 0 for an index page, and it reaches the LRU end of the page chain, the counter is decremented by 1, and the page is placed at the MRU end again.

By default, the number of trips that an index page makes through the cache is set to 0. To change the default, a System Administrator can set the **number of index trips** configuration parameter.

When to use Clustered Indexes

Operations that may benefit from a clustered index:

1. Selects, Inserts, Updates and Deletes on heavy utilized tables that demand high concurrency may benefit from a **clustered index that randomizes how the data is accessed by point queries**. This is because we are spreading the I/O for the table across more of its page ranges and thus reducing and/or preventing any "hot spots" on the table. **Hot spots are those points in the data or index where many queries access.** If too many queries are accessing the same pages for Selects and DML operations, then lock contention and/or frequent deadlocks could result.

2. Range queries can benefit from a clustered index if we are retrieving a medium to large set of data by the ordering of how the index keys are defined. This benefit comes from the ability of ASE to position the query access about the leaf level pages and scan the next and previous page pointers linking these pages. Be careful though, as creating a clustered index that orders the data by the frequently accessed values, may lead to "hot spots".

A table that does not have a clustered index is called a heap table. Data that is inserted into a heap table is inserted into the empty space on the last page of the table. If the last page is full, a new page is allocated and linked to the last page. The data will then be inserted into the new last page. So, essentially, **data is always inserted into the last page of a heap table**.

There are some operations that may benefit by using a heap table.

1. Large multiple row inserts into a table and large BCP operations will benefit from a heap table assuming lock contention will not be an issue. This is because ASE does not have to position each record for insertion into the table. Instead, ASE can start the insert on the last page of the table and allocate additional last pages for data insertion as necessary. Hence, for a large insert into a heap table, ASE only needs to locate the last page of the table.

2. Heap tables are usually avoided as they may cause many issues including:
   - A "hot spot" on the last page of the table leading to lock contention and frequent deadlocks.

3. Space reclamation. A clustered index may help reduce the space used by a table by:

4. Keeping insertions and deletions random such that space is continually freed and used by these operations.

5. Continually allocating new last pages and continually de-allocating the first page of the table. This is typical of a clustered index that is created with a datetime column as the leading column in the index.

A Note on the Heap Tables

"Q." Does one get much benefit from having a heap table around even as a DOL table?

"A." For DOL heap tables, and even for DOL tables with a clustered index, **ASE maintains an in-memory non-disk-resident hint list of target pages.** These provide multiple insertion points to the online inserters. When these target pages become full, or are found to be not very useful for space, they are replaced with other target hint pages. Inserts are directed to different 'spots' in the table for randomizing the inserts.

The expected behaviour is that in a stable system these hints will direct the insert traffic to sufficiently randomize inserts. Also, if the hint page did not have sufficient space, these hint pages provide start pages to start the search for page allocations.

If you have a clustered index, the clustered index B-tree is first consulted to try and improve locality of rows with near-by key values. Then, these in-memory hints of target pages are consulted to see where else there might be a candidate page with space to store the to-be- inserted row.

"Q." Is it true that the server keeps an in-memory hint list of target pages for every DOL table? Obviously this will help performance although I assume there will be an overhead with regard to memory consumption. Does this help the bulk loading of data into a table?

"A." Yes, it's maintained for all DOL tables. The in-memory list is small and does not require too much additional memory. Yes, this helps the bulk loading of data into a table. However, if you do BCP into a table other schemes of page allocation (such as extent allocation in chunks of 2 or more extents) are employed to improve page allocation for newly inserted rows.

"Q." If we maintain DOL heap tables in such a way is there any performance gain from partitioning this type of table?

"A." For partitioned DOL heap tables, an in-memory list is stored for each partition. Thus, you benefit from both partitioning (multiple insertion points into randomly chosen partitions) and multiple insertion points within the chosen partition.

When to use Non-Clustered Indexes

Operations that may benefit from a non-clustered index:

1. Point queries that typically return few data rows.

2. Range queries if they are covered by non-clustered index. A non-clustered index is covered by a query if the index contains all columns that are accessed by the query. When an index is covered, ASE locates all of the data in the index. In this case, ASE does not have to traverse the row ids of the leaf level pages to locate the associated data rows. In this sense, a covered index is similar to a clustered index.

3. Referential integrity checks are typically much faster and consume less I/O when performed against a non-clustered index. This is because a non-clustered index is much denser compared to a clustered index. A clustered index contains the data in the leaf level pages and a non-clustered index contains only row ids that point to the data.

Considerations:

- DOL Clustered indexes have structure like non-clustered indexes so they can be used in referential integrity

- Use table partitioning to provide multiple insertion points for a heap table

Checking for Indexes

Before you run any SQL statement you should check what indexes exist on the objects you are querying. Sybase ASE provides several stored procedures to check objects for the existence of indexes.

You can use the system stored procedure sp_helpindex.
Syntax: sp_helpindex <table name>

Or, you can use the system stored procedure sp_help.
Syntax: sp_help <table name>

Example:
```
EXEC sp_helpindex table
go
```

index_name	index_description	index_keys
ix01_table	clustered, unique located on sg01	c1, c2
ix02_table	non-clustered located on sg03	c3, c4
ix03_table	non-clustered located on sg05	c5, c9
ix04_table	non-clustered located on sg02	c8, c7
ix05_table	non-clustered located on sg04	c12
ix06_table	non-clustered located on sg08	c15
ix07_table	non-clustered located on sg07	c10, c11, c18, c19
ix08_table	non-clustered located on sg06	c24

To minimize the number of index pages accessed and to help influence the optimizer's decision about an index, you should code most queries such that for each table a reference is made to one of the leading index columns for the table. From our previous example, a query against table should almost always contain reference(s) to c1, c3, c5, c8, c12, c15, c10, and/or c24.

Having lots of indexes on a table will usually have only a small impact on OLTP systems, because only a few rows are processed in a single transaction, and the impact of updating many indexes is small.

Having lots of indexes can be detrimental for batch processing with its typically high number of inserts, updates and deletes.

Up until ASE 12.5, it was not possible to positively determine if the indexes were used frequently. However, if you are running ASE 12.5 or above, you should be able to identify when an index was last used, and the number of times the index has been used. Using this method, you can get rid of the indexes which are not required. You are strongly advised to discuss this matter with your DBA and developers.

The bottom line is that all SQL statements must run acceptably. There is always a way of achieving this. If it requires having 14 indexes on a table, then you should put 14 indexes on the table.

Indexes and Small Tables

Yet another common problem that we see is small tables which do not have an index. Our experience has been that every table should be indexed. The two reasons for the index are that the uniqueness of the rows in the table can be enforced by the primary or unique key, and more importantly, the optimizer has the opportunity to work out the optimal execution plan for queries against the table. Lastly, these so-called small tables have a tendency to outgrow their projected size.

SQL Searches and Indexes

Check that there are indexes that qualify for the SARG or join clauses in the query. Keep in mind that, at minimum, the lead column of the index must be referenced in the SARG or join clauses. If the lead column of the index is not referenced in the SARG (**where** clause), the distribution page of the index cannot be used for the query.

For a join clause, if the lead column is not used in the join clause, the density information stored on the index's distribution page cannot be used. Additionally, if the index is composite, column references must be sequential. For example, if the index consists of three columns and the first and third columns are in the join clause only, the density value stored for the first column can be used. Since density information is stored on multiple columns, they must be referenced sequentially in order for the optimizer to take full advantage of the density information.

Index Key Sort Order

You can use the ASC (ascending) and DESC (descending) keywords to assign a sort order to each column in an index. By default, sort order is ascending. This is typically useful for queries which only sort by using one column or multiple columns in only one direction. That is because the index can be read backwards just as easily as it can be read forwards for the DESC order queries.

Now, where this may provide huge benefits is when queries need to mix ASC and DESC columns in and ORDER BY clause.

Example:

Consider Index on (column01 ASC, column02 ASC, column03 ASC)

```
SELECT t1.column01,
              t1.column02,
              t1.column03,
              t1.column04
  FROM test_table t1
WHERE t1.column04 = 5
 ORDER
    BY t1.column01 ASC,
       t1.column02 DESC,
       t1.column03 DESC
go
```

ASE will read out all records sorted by t1.column01 and perform sorts on each different set defined by column01. This can cause serious performance degradation in some cases.

Instead, if possible, create your index as follows:
Index on (column01 ASC, column02 DESC, column03 DESC)

Now, with the previous index, ASE will not have to perform any sorts and can read the data from the index already sorted thus avoiding a lot of potential overhead.

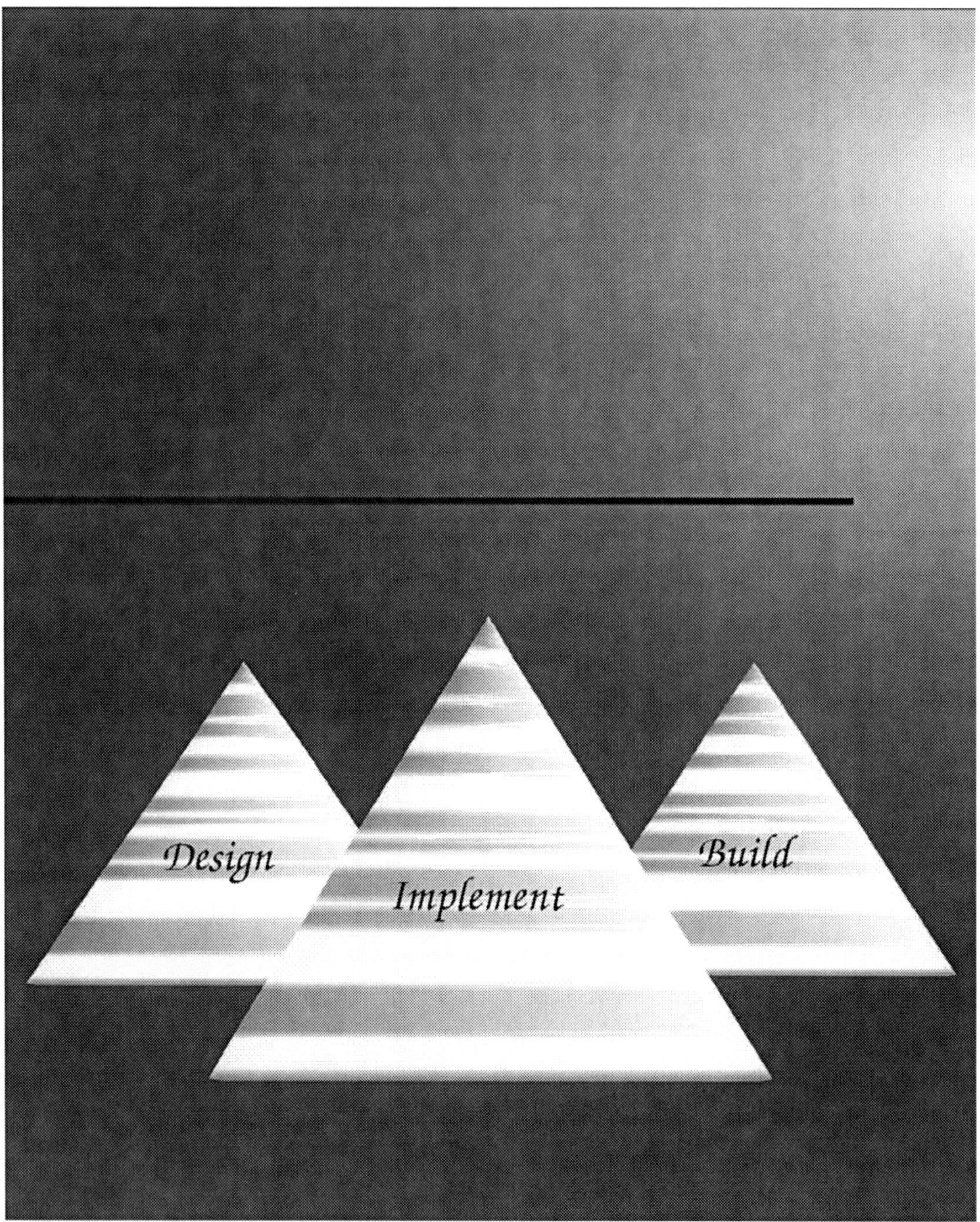
Design
Implement
Build

Chapter 3. Index Fragmentation

Table and Index fragmentations occur as a result of heavy activities, especially deletes and updates. As tables grow in size, this problem becomes more acute.

There is no doubt of the benefits of adding indexes to tables, and for the most part we have to do little work to keep the indexes maintained. However, some maintenance is required as indexes can become fragmented during data modifications, especially deletes and updates. This fragmentation can become a source of performance issues with queries.

So what exactly is index fragmentation? Index fragmentation actually comes in two different forms: external fragmentation and internal fragmentation. These two forms of fragmentation result in the inefficient use of pages within an index. This inefficient use may be because the logical order of the pages are wrong (external fragmentation) or because the amount of data stored within each page is less than the data page can contain (internal fragmentation). Whichever type of fragmentation occurs in the index, we could face performance issues with our queries because of the fragmentation.

External Fragmentation

External fragmentation occurs when an index leaf page is not in logical order. When an index is created, the index keys are placed in a logical order on a set of index pages. As new data is inserted into the index, it is possible for the new keys to be inserted in between existing keys. This may cause new index pages to be created to accommodate any existing keys that were moved so that the new keys can be inserted in correct order. These new index pages usually will not be physically adjacent to the pages the moved keys were originally stored in. It is this process of creating new pages that causes the index pages to be out of logical order, i.e. non contiguous space.

The following example will explain this concept more clearly.

Example:

Assume this is the existing structure for an index on your table before any additional data inserts.

Existing Index Structure

2	4	6	8

10	12	14	16

18	20	22	24

An INSERT statement adds new data to the index. In this case we will add a 5. The INSERT will cause a new page to be created and 7 and 8 will be moved to the new page in order to make room for the 5 on the original page. This creation will cause the index pages to be out of logical order.

New Index Structure With Pages Out Of Order

2	4	5	

10	12	14	16

18	20	22	24

7	8		

In cases of queries that have specific searches or that return unordered result sets, the index pages being out of order do not pose a problem. For queries that return ordered result sets, extra processing is needed to search the index pages that are not in order. An example of an ordered result set would be a query that is returning everything from 4 to 10. This query would have to complete an extra page switch in order to return the 7 and 8. While one extra page switch is nothing in the long run, imagine this condition on a very large table with hundreds of pages out of order.

Internal Fragmentation

Internal fragmentation occurs when the index pages are not being used to their maximum volume. While this may be an advantage on an application with heavy data inserts, setting a fill factor causes space to be left on index pages, and severe internal fragmentation can lead to increased index size and cause additional reads to be performed to return needed data. These extra reads can lead to degradation in query performance.

Parameters to Check for the Degree of Index Fragmentation

ASE provides a number of parameters to indicate the level of fragmentation in the indexes:

- data-page-cluster-ratio, dpcr
- index-page-cluster-ratio, ipcr
- data-row-cluster-ratio, drcr
- space utilization, sput
- large I/O efficiency, lgio

For DOL tables with clustered indexes, dpcr indicates the level of data fragmentation. For DOL tables with non clustered indexes, both ipcr and sput figures are useful parameters. For APL tables with clustered indexes, both sput and lgio efficiency will be good indicators of data fragmentation. For APL and non-clustered indexes, look at the parameter "sput". The rule of thumb is that the lower these values, the higher the degree of fragmentation.

Working Out Index Fragmentation

In versions prior to ASE 12.5.1, we could get information about the fragmented indexes through the ASE utility ***optdiag***. The output from optdiag contains all sorts of information including "Derived statistics":

```
> OptDiag/12.0.0.8/P/EBF 11689 ESD1/Sun_svr4/OS 5.6/2047/32bit/OPT/Thu
> Feb 12 21:33:41 2004
> Adaptive Server Enterprise/12.0.0.8/P/EBF 11689 ESD1/Sun_svr4/OS
> 5.6/2047/32bit/FBO/Fri Feb 13 03:52:51 2004
>
> Server name:                          "PROD_SERVER"
>
> Specified database:                   "PROD"
> Specified table owner:                not specified
> Specified table:                      "op_services_log_detail_history"
> Specified column:                     not specified
>
```

```
> Table owner:                          "dbo"
> Table name:                           "op_services_log_detail_history"
>
> Statistics for index:
"op_services_log_detail_hst_idx"
> (clustered)
> Index column list:                    "op_services_run_id"
>      Data page count:                 877600
>      Empty data page count:           0
>      Data row count:                  31346435.0000000000000000
>      Forwarded row count:             0.0000000000000000
>      Deleted row count:               0.0000000000000000
>      Data page CR count:              111527.0000000000000000
>      OAM + allocation page count:     10561
>      First extent leaf pages:         0
>      Data row size:                   46.0000000000000000
>      Index height:                    3
>
>   Derived statistics:
>      Data page cluster ratio:         0.9976207839562443
>      Space utilization:               0.8150023207684015
>      Large I/O efficiency:            0.9836183166408136
>
```

For this example, we chose a fairly large APL table in excess of 31 million records. This table had a non-unique clustered index with a large number of overflow pages. The section under “Derived statistics” provides the information required to determine the level of fragmentation in this table. The two parameters that are important in this case are ***sput*** and ***lgio***.

The low "space utilization" figure is normally associated with an APL table with a non-unique clustered index. This can lead to lots of overflow pages as each key can have many rows. The non-unique clustered index is built on the column “op_services_run_id”. To find out the number of entries for each value of this column, you can run the following query:

```
SELECT op_services_run_id,
       COUNT(op_services_run_id)
  FROM op_services_log_detail_history
 GROUP
    BY COUNT(op_services_run_id)
HAVING COUNT(op_services_run_id) > 1
```

When we ran this query, not surprisingly we found a large number of entries for some rows. To reduce this problem, we changed the locking scheme of the table from allpages-locked to datapages-locked and performed a reorg rebuild on the table. That cured the problem.

Using DERIVED_STAT Function to Estimate Fragmentation

ASE 12.5.0.3 introduced the function:

DERIVED_STAT("table_name","index_name","option")

By using this function, one saves a good bit of time and effort in picking up a specific fragmentation indicator(s) without going into optdiag. The function derived_stat can provide a number of indicators. However, it is left to the DBA on how to go about identifying the tables and indexes that need to be defragged.

In general, the closer the value of these parameters to 1 (range 0-1), the better, and the less fragmentation you have. As explained earlier, for different table and index types, these parameters have different significance.

As a DBA, I wrote a shell script that carried out table and index "fragmentation analysis" for a given database. Note that if you have a pre ASE 12.5.0.3 database, as long as you have a test environment with ASE 12.5.0.3 or higher installed you can load your pre ASE 12.5.0.3 database there and run your analysis against the 12.5.0.3 loaded database.

We used the algorithm explained under section "Parameters to Check for the Degree of Index Fragmentation" to recommend which tables and indexes we need to defrag.

The parameters we look at are:

```
'table_type = DOL and index_type = clustered,     watch ====> dpcr'
'table_type = DOL and index_type = non-clustered, watch ====> ipcr &
sput'
'table_type = APL and index_type = clustered,     watch ====> sput &
lgio'
'table_type = APL and index_type = non-clustered  watch ====> sput'
```

The actions are twofold. If you have a DOL table, then carrying out "reorg rebuild" will do the trick. If you have an APL table with a clustered index, drop and recreate the clustered index. That action will rebuild all other indexes. If you have an APL table without a clustered index, then drop and recreate the index affected on that table.

The shell routine frag.ksh, in Appendix I, will help you in identifying the tables and indexes that need to be defragged. An example of summary output is shown below. In the example, I am considering only those objects that have more than 50,000 records for any table or index that has a ratio < 0.90.

Example (frag.ksh):

```
name                 table_type  row_size     index_name
        index_type      action
---------------------- ------------ ----------- ----------------------
        --------------- -------------------------------
sydeskvalues          DOL           35146215    sydeskvalues_idx1
        clustered        reorg
sbcnfevt              APL           18068242    sbcnfevt_idx2
        non-clustered    Rebuild the index
sycltrans             APL           17241872    sycltrans_idx6
        non-clustered    Rebuild the index
sycltrans             APL           17241872    sycltrans_idx7
        non-clustered    Rebuild the index
sylimviolsubamt       APL           14028379    sylimviolsubamt_pk
        clustered        Rebuild the index
syaudit               DOL           13035779    syaudit_idx1
        clustered        reorg
fa_fnx2t2             APL           12918331    fa_fnx2t2_pk
        clustered        Rebuild the index
fa_fnx2t2             APL           12918331    fa_fnx2t2_idx1
        non-clustered    Rebuild the index
sytrans_rel           DOL           11495007    sytrans_rel_indx4
        non-clustered    reorg
fa_stot2_status       APL            1702941    fa_stot2_status_idx1
        non-clustered    Rebuild the index
sylimviolate          APL            1328220    sylimviolate_idx1
        clustered        Rebuild the index
sylimviolate          APL            1328220    sylimviolate_pk
        non-clustered    Rebuild the index
sylimviolate          APL            1328220    sylimviolate_idx2
        non-clustered    Rebuild the index
sylimcashflowsum      DOL            1086273    sylimcashflowsum_pk
```

```
         clustered         reorg
sytrans                  DOL                 92232      sytrans_idx2
         clustered         reorg
sytrans                  DOL                 92232      sytrans_idx3
         non-clustered     reorg
sytrans                  DOL                 92232      sytrans_idx5
         non-clustered     reorg
sytrans                  DOL                 92232      sytrans_idx6
         non-clustered     reorg
sytrans                  DOL                 92232      sytrans_idx7
         non-clustered     reorg
sytrans                  DOL                 92232      sytrans_idx9
         non-clustered     reorg
sytrans                  DOL                 92232      sytrans_idx10
         non-clustered     reorg
sytrans                  DOL                 92232      sytrans_idx11
         non-clustered     reorg
sytrans                  DOL                 92232      sytrans_idx12
         non-clustered reorg
```

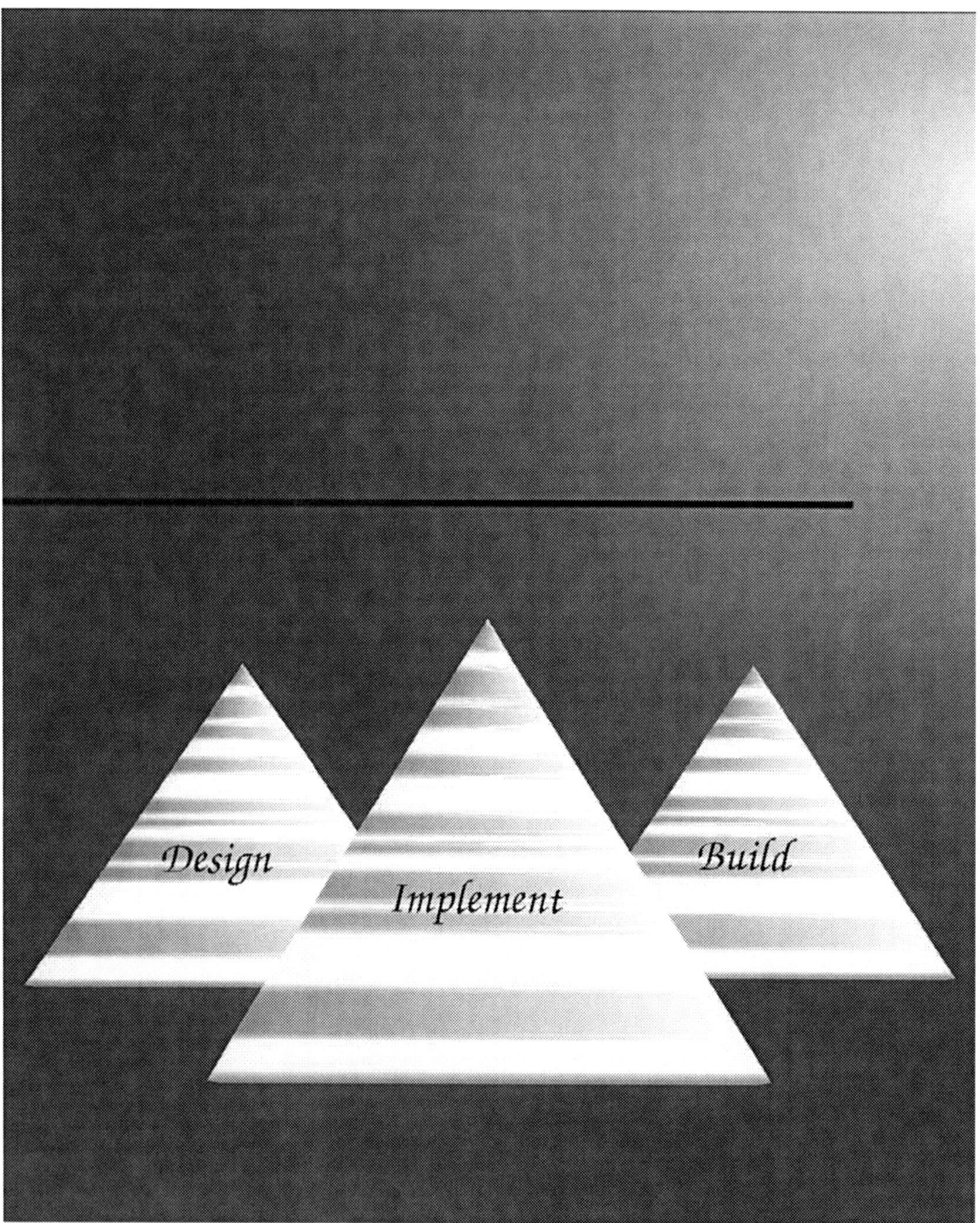
Design
Implement
Build

Chapter 4. Search Arguments

When writing SQL, you should be sure to code the **where** clause arguments such that they may be used as search arguments by the ASE optimizer. Search arguments are those columns, values, expressions, parameters and variables that compose the queries **where** clause and may be used by an index. Search arguments (SARGS) are those arguments that fall into one of the following forms:

<column> <operator> <expression>

Where the operator is one of the following:

=, >, <, >=, <=, !>, !<, <>, !=, is null, in, is not null, not in, between, like,

and where the expression is a constant value or evaluates to a constant value such as parameters that are passed to the query.

Example:

```
The expression ( 10 * 10 ) will evaluate as the constant 100.

In the proc (create proc pr_tproc (@a int)), the parameter @a will be
evaluated as a constant.
```

Declared variables are never considered to be constant by the optimizer. When variables are used the optimizer will use the density (aka distribution) statistics for the column when generating the query plan. If the data is not very distributed, a table scan may be performed on the table for a value that is very unique and is the leading column of an index.

The following query will return data if a variable is a bad option:

```
SET NOCOUNT ON

DECLARE @tbl_density INT

SELECT @tbl_density = count(*)
  FROM table

SELECT count(*) as col_density,
```

```
       @tbl_density as tbl_density,
       ( count(*) * 100 ) / @tbl_density as rough_pct,
       column
  FROM table
  GROUP
     BY column
HAVING COUNT(column) > ( .1 * @tbl_density )
```

Example:

```
SET NOCOUNT ON

DECLARE @tbl_density INT

SELECT @tbl_density = count(*)
  FROM table

SELECT count(*) as col_density,
       @tbl_density as tbl_density,
       ( count(*) * 100 ) / @tbl_density as rough_pct,
       c1
  FROM table
 GROUP
    BY c1
HAVING COUNT(c1) > ( .1 * @tbl_density )
go
```

Output:

col_density	tbl_density	rough_pct	c1
72928	73123	99	REG

From the previous output, we see that column c1 with a value of REG comprises greater than or equal to 99 percent of the table. Therefore, when querying upon table, based upon c1 alone, we should try to make sure that we either use a parameter or a constant for c1.

This query will only tell you if using a variable for the specified column is a bad option. It will not tell you that a variable is a good option.

Note: We recommend avoiding the use of variables in the **where** clause if possible.

Avoid performing operations, including SUBSTRING and ISNULL, on the columns in the WHERE clause if you want an index to be chosen on that column.

By performing operations on the column ASE must perform the operation on every value in the table for the column, unless other valid search arguments exist for a useful index, for the comparison.

Many times arguments can be converted to similar checks that are search arguments in order to perform the operation. This can be seen with **where** clause statements such as substring(value, 1, 3) = "abc". This statement can be written using the `like` operator.

Below are some examples of **where** clause statements to try to avoid and some possible solutions:

Avoid Using:	Instead Use:
value like "abc"	Value = "abc"
Substring(value, 1, 3) = "abc"	value like "abc%"
amount != 0	amount > 0
amount + 3000 < 5000	amount < 2000
last_name + ", " + first_name = "some, name"	last_name = "some" and first_name = "name"
< , >	<= , >=
value / 100 = 100	value = 100 * 100
or	UNION or UNION ALL

You should avoid all datatype mismatches and conversions. When ASE must perform a datatype conversion for a column in the **where** clause, any indexes that exist for that column are not considered for the query plan. This is true for joins, constants, parameters, expressions, functions, and values.

Look for Mismatched Datatypes

Using the query and **sp_help**, look for mismatched datatypes in join clauses. For example:

```
where tableA.col1=tableB.col1
```

A datatype mismatch on join optimization can lead to performance problems. When a join between mismatched columns occurs, the optimizer will only run a cost estimate (via **q_score_index**) on one table in the join. This eliminates consideration of indexes on one of the tables and will result, in most cases, in a table scan of the table that did not have a cost estimate run against it.

Problems involving mismatched datatypes usually involve mismatches between *int* and *float*, *char* and *varchar* and commonly between *char* null and *char* not null. A *char* null is stored internally as a *varchar*.

Note: The **char** data type is a fixed-length data type when the NOT NULL clause is specified. If a value shorter than the length of the column is inserted into a **char** NOT NULL column, the value is right-padded with blanks to the size of the column. For example, if a column is defined as **char(10)** and the data to be stored is "book", ASE stores this data as "book______", where "_" indicates a blank. If ANSI_PADDING is ON when a **char** NULL column is created, it behaves the same as a **char** NOT NULL column: values are right-padded to the size of the column. If ANSI_PADDING is OFF when a **char** NULL column is created, it behaves like a **varchar** column with ANSI_PADDING set OFF: trailing blanks are truncated.

A less common mismatch of datatypes occurs between numeric/decimal columns of differing precision and/or scale. For example, if a join of two identity columns (an identity column must be numeric with a scale of 0 like numeric(10,0)) with differing precisions will be handled as a datatype mismatch.

In addition, *binary*/*varbinary* and *float*/*int* mismatches are also a problem.

Most mismatched datatypes are easy to spot:

```
where col(char)=col(varchar)
where col(float)=col(int)
```

Others are less obvious:

```
where col(char NULL)=col(char NOT NULL)

where col(binary NULL)=col(binary NOT NULL)
```

char (null) and *binary* (null) are stored in SQL Server(R) as a *varchar* datatype.

Thus:

where col(char NULL)=col(varchar)

is not a mismatch and statistics will be used by the optimizer. However:

where col(char NULL)=col(char NOT NULL)

is a datatype mismatch. Be suspicious of columns with the same datatype but different handling of NULLs.

This does not apply to col(int NULL)=col(int NOT NULL). Datatype *int* NOT NULL and *int* NULL are not handled as a datatype mismatch.

If datatype mismatches are found, you can either rebuild and repopulate the tables with matching datatypes (this is often not a reasonable option) or use the **convert** function. The **convert** command may have detrimental effects on optimization. If the **convert** function is used, it is advisable to run a performance analysis with and without it. The cost of a datatype mismatch may be cheaper than the cost of incomplete optimization.

In the case where parameters are being passed into a stored procedure, you must make sure that the parameters are specified as the same datatype as the columns they will be used to search or join. It is easy to create a procedure with a *char* NOT NULL parameter that will be used against a *char* NULL column.

If the user-defined datatypes are used, run **sp_help** on the datatype name to ensure that there is not a datatype mismatch involved. If the same user-defined datatype name is used in a cross database join, make sure that they are defined the same way in both databases.

Some common datatype mismatches that result in conversion:

Comparison:	**Conversion:**
tinyint = smallint	tinyint is converted to a smallint
tinyint = integer	tinyint is converted to a integer
smallint = integer	smallint is converted to a integer
numeric = tinyint, smallint, int	tinyint, smallint, int are converted to numeric
smallmoney = money	smallmoney is converted to money
smalldatetime = datetime	smalldatetime is converted to datetime

If a conversion must be made and you are comparing a column to a value, then, if possible, you should convert the value to the datatype matching the column prior to the query.

Example:

```
Let column col_1 be a smallint and let value @value_1 be an int.

Suppose that @value_1 will only be used for comparisons to col_1.
Now, while although @value_1 is an integer, the possible return values
when making comparisons to col_1 are bounded by -32768 <= @value_1 <=
32767.

In addition, table_1{ PK(col_1), col_2, col_3} and that a unique index
exists on col_1.

From the chart, we quickly see that the below query will require a
table scan of table_1.  This is because col_1 is a smallint, and to
make the comparison to an integer ASE must convert every value in the
table for col_1 to an integer.

SELECT *
  FROM table_1
 WHERE col_1 = @value_1
go

Since, we know that @value_1 must fall in the range -32768 <= value_1
<= 32767, in order to return data, we could have written the query as
follows to qualify the unique index that exists for table_1 on col_1.

IF ( @value_1 BETWEEN -32768 AND 32768 )
BEGIN
   SELECT *
     FROM table_1
    WHERE col_1 = CONVERT(SMALLINT, @value_1)
END
ELSE
BEGIN
   SELECT *
     FROM table_1
    WHERE 1 = 2
END
go
```

For the previous query, ASE will rely upon the density/distribution statistics for the index, and since the index is unique on col_1 we know ASE will definitely choose the index because no value exceeds 20% of the table.

Bounding Results

Imagine if you will that someone tells you to find all results that are greater than a specific value from a sorted set. In order to fulfill this request you must first determine exactly where to start reading from the set.

Consider set: { 1, 2, 3, 4, 5, 6, 7, 8, 9 }

If we told you to locate all numbers which are greater than 6, you would first need to locate 6 and start your scan after 6. Thus, reading 6, 7, 8, and 9 and returning 7, 8, and 9. However, had we told you to locate numbers which are greater than or equal to 7, you could have started your scan immediately at position 7 and read 7, 8, and 9. Returning 7, 8, and 9.

Hence, when using greater than ">" or less than "<", consider how ASE must read the data in order to build the result set. And, use greater than or equal ">=" or less than or equal "<=" if you can modify your **where** predicate appropriately.

Functions on Columns

As stated earlier, you should avoid using functions on all columns which are intended to be used as search arguments.

Example (SUBSTRING):

```
SELECT *
  FROM TABLE
 WHERE SUBSTRING(COL01, 1, 5) = "ABCDE"
go
```

In the previous example, we have told ASE to compare the first five characters of the column COL01 to the string "ABCDE". In order to satisfy this request, ASE must perform the substring on every field in COL01 for every record in TABLE. This will negate the use of an index as a viable option. Thus, a table scan will be chosen.

Had we written the query as:

```
SELECT *
  FROM TABLE
 WHERE COL01 LIKE "ABCDE%"
go
```

ASE could have used the statistics for column COL01 and used an index if it were a viable option. Meaning that, ASE could return the query faster using the index versus performing a table scan.

ISNULL

When using the ISNULL function to compare a column to some value and alternate value, you must consider that ASE will choose the worst case scenario when building the query plan. Meaning that, the chosen plan may not be very efficient in most cases, but will be very efficient for the worst case scenario.

Note: This is a real world scenario which we frequently encounter.

Example (ISNULL):

```
SELECT *
  FROM TABLE
 WHERE COL01 = ISNULL(@PARM1, COL01)
go
```

Let's assume that in the previous example, an index on the column COL01 exists and COL01 is the leading column in this index. Now, despite there being index, ASE will choose a table scan of TABLE. This is because it has been told that @PARM1 could be NULL. In such a case, ASE needs to return every record of TABLE. Thus, a table scan would be the most optimal. However, @PARM1 may be passed nearly 100% of the time. Hence, we would like ASE to table scan only when @PARM1 is in fact null and use the index when @PARM is not null. We can easily modify our query so that this occurs.

Example (ISNULL):

```
IF ( @PARM1 IS NOT NULL )
BEGIN
   SELECT *
     FROM TABLE
    WHERE COL01 = @PARM1
END
ELSE
BEGIN
   SELECT *
     FROM TABLE
END
go
```

Datetimes

Note: When working with datetimes, you need to be concerned with all material in this chapter and not just this section.

We have often found that many people do not fully understand how datetimes are stored by ASE and how they are retrieved by queries.

For a datetime datatype, ASE stores data as a pair of 4 bytes. Where the first 4 bytes store the date component as a number of days from an internal base date, and the second 4 bytes store the time component to within 3 milliseconds of actual time. For a smalldatetime datatype, ASE stores data as a pair of 2 bytes. Where, the first 2 bytes store the date component as number of days from an internal base date, and the second 2 bytes store the time component to the minute.

Now, because of how ASE stores datetimes, querying datetimes becomes very efficient. This is due to the logical progression created by the growth of date or the first pair of bytes. The following table shows exactly how this progression works. For simplicity, we have listed the stored date and stored time as an integer.

Actual Date	*Actual Time*	*Stored Date*	*Stored Time*
x1	y1	1	100
x1 + 1	y2	2	200
x1 + 2	y3	3	150

Actual Date	*Actual Time*	*Stored Date*	*Stored Time*
x1 + 3	y4	4	30000
x1 + 4	y5	5	50

Now, when we use a datetime column in a where predicate without performing a conversion on the column, ASE will convert the value to be matched to the column to a pair of bytes for comparison.

Example:
```
SELECT *
  FROM TABLE
 WHERE COL01 >= "01/01/1900"
go
```

In the previous example, ASE will convert the specified datetime value to be matched against COL01 to a pair of bytes. Assume, date=100 and time=0. Thus, ASE will convert the value as PAD(100)PAD(0) to query against the stored PAD (date)PAD(time) and return the necessary results. This is very efficient as ASE can simply return all stored results which are >= (0...0)100(0...0).

The most common search operators we use when querying datetime columns are =, !=, >, >=, <, <=, and between. Also, when querying datetime columns, if the value which we supply does not include time, ASE will default the time to lowest possible value. Often referred to as midnight.

Now, if an application needs to determine all records newer than 24 hours of the current system time, we might write the question as follows:

```
DECLARE @FROM_DT DATETIME
SELECT @FROM_DT = DATEADD(DAY, -1, GETDATE())

SELECT *
  FROM table
 WHERE column >= @FROM_DT
go
```

The previous query while although correct, could cause issues or may not run with accurate times. This is because the T-SQL code uses a variable in the WHERE predicate to search for the specified conditions. Instead, you should write your query as follows:

```
SELECT *
  FROM table
 WHERE column >= DATEADD(DAY, -1, GETDATE())
go
```

If an application needs to determine all records bound to a specific datetime interval, such as within 48 hours and 24 hours ago, we might write our question as follows:

```
SELECT *
  FROM table
 WHERE column BETWEEN DATEADD(DAY, -2, GETDATE()) AND DATEADD(DAY, -1,
GETDATE())
go
```

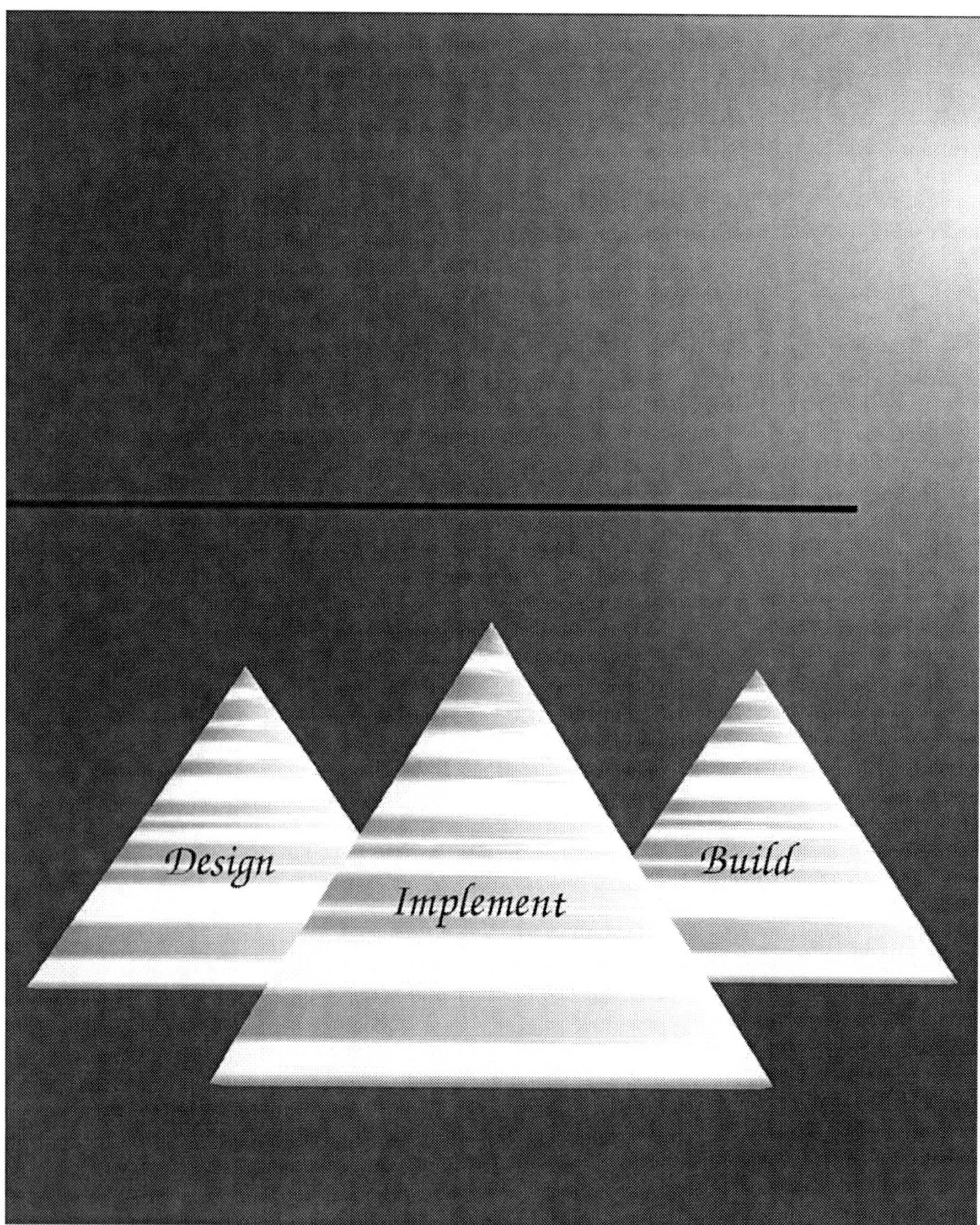
Design
Implement
Build

Chapter 5. Various Best Practices

Using MIN and MAX Aggregates

The function T-SQL function MIN(column) is used to get the single minimum column value for a list of values. MAX(column) is used to get the single maximum column value for a list of values.

When using the aggregate functions MIN and MAX, try not use them in the same query as it will cause either a table scan or a complete index scan. Instead, if you need to perform a MIN and MAX for a column, you should use two queries to perform the SELECT. However, there could be times when you need to perform both operations in the same command, in these cases nest either the MIN or MAX so that two index lookups are performed. That is, two index lookups will be performed if there is a qualifying index to perform the MIN or MAX lookups.

Never Do:

```
SELECT MIN(value_1),
       MAX(value_1)
  FROM table_1
```

Do:

```
SELECT MIN(value_1)
  FROM table_1

SELECT MAX(value_1)
  FROM table_1
```

Or Do:

```
SELECT MIN(value_1),
       ( SELECT MAX(value_1) FROM table_1 )
  FROM table_1
```

Or Do:
```
SELECT ( SELECT MIN(value_1) FROM table_1 ),
       ( SELECT MAX(value_1) FROM table_1 )
```

Example:
table_1

c1	*c2*	*c3*	*c4*	*c5*
1	*1*	*1*	*1*	*1*
2	*2*	*2*	*2*	*2*
3	*3*	*3*	*3*	*3*

Never Do This:
```
SELECT MIN(c1),
       MAX(c1)
  FROM table1
---------------------------------------------
1      3
```

Always Do These:
```
SELECT MIN(c1)
  FROM table1
go
---------------------------------------------
1
```

```
SELECT MAX(c1)
  FROM table1
go
---------------------------------------------
3
```

```
SELECT MIN(c1),
       ( SELECT MAX(c1)
           FROM table1 )
  FROM table1
go
---------------------------------------------
1      3
```

```
SELECT ( SELECT MIN(c1) FROM table_1 ),
       ( SELECT MAX(c1) FROM table_1 )
go
---------------------------------------------
1       3
```

Using the ORDER BY Clause

The ORDER BY clause determines the ordering of the records in the result set of a SELECT command. An ordering of ASC (ascending) or DESC (descending) may be specified for each column or expression that comprise the ORDER BY clause.

Example:

```
SELECT COL_1,
       COL_2,
       COL_3
  FROM TABLE
 ORDER
    BY COL_1 ASC,
       COL_2 DESC
```

Example:

```
SELECT c1
  FROM table
 ORDER
    BY c1 ASC
99778
146912
563775
950868
```

```
SELECT c1
  FROM table
 ORDER
    BY c1 DESC
950868
563775
146912
99778
```

Performance Considerations

To perform the sort for the table, an index must exist on the object with keys similar to the order in the ORDER BY clause, or a tempdb worktable will be created with the result set and a dynamic index will be created on the worktable.

Depending on the size of the result set, the performance impact of creating a giant tempdb worktable and creating a dynamic index can be disastrous for the overall throughput of the system. Therefore, unless an index exists where the order of the keys matches the order of columns in the ORDER BY clause, an ORDER BY should be avoided.

Using the GROUP BY Clause

When it is necessary to group data, usually so that aggregate functions may be performed against the group, one should use the GROUP BY command. In addition, if it is necessary to mix columns and aggregate functions one should be sure to always include the columns in the GROUP BY clause. A GROUP BY has the same performance considerations of an ORDER BY clause, except that a tempdb worktable will always be created to store the pre-aggregated result set.

Note: The result set will be in ascending order by the columns and expressions that compose the GROUP BY.

Suppose SELECT *
FROM table_1:

col_1	col_2	col_3
1	5	10
2	5	10
3	5	10
4	1	5
5	1	6

If it is necessary to determine the summation of col_3 on a grouping of the values in col_2, you should write the query as follows:

```
SELECT col_2,
       SUM(col_3) as 'summation'
  FROM table_1
 GROUP
    BY col_2

When executed yields:
      col_2          summation
      ----------------------------
       1               11
       5               30
```

Determine Data Distribution

A GROUP BY may be used to determine the distribution of data about a specific column.

Example:
```
SELECT COUNT(*) AS CNT,
       c1
  FROM table
 GROUP
    BY c1
go
CNT            c1
205020         N
413561         Y
```

Using the HAVING Clause

The HAVING clause for a query is used with the GROUP BY clause to specify search conditions for both aggregates and columns. If columns are included in the HAVING clause, the ASE optimizer will still consider those columns as potential search arguments. I recommend that when using the HAVING clause, unless necessary, do not include any columns. Putting columns in the HAVING clause can make the query harder to decipher. Instead, put the columns in the WHERE clause.

Adding to the previous GROUP BY examples:

```
SELECT col_2,
       SUM(col_3) as 'summation'
  FROM table_1
 GROUP
    BY col_2
HAVING SUM(col_3) > 20

When executed yields:
      col_2        summation
       5             30
```

Determine Data Distribution

Using the HAVING clause with the prior GROUP BY example, to determine the data distribution for the column c1 in table:

```
SELECT COUNT(*) AS CNT,
       c1
  FROM table
 GROUP
    BY c1
HAVING COUNT(*) > 300000
go
CNT           c1
41356         Y
```

Using the CASE Statement

ASE supports the use of conditional SQL through the CASE statement. This allows for various comparisons and responses to be made against the data. A CASE statement may be used anywhere that a value expression can be used. In addition, all responses for a CASE statement cannot return NULL.

The CASE statement has been one of the most overlooked commands in the database. The CASE statement allows in many cases, what would have required several passes of the data through various selects, updates, inserts, and/or deletes a SINGLE statement and a one time pass through of the data. This is tremendous as it reduces CPU, Memory, and I/O use. Thus mitigating and/or completely eliminating any potential resource constraints in the database.

Syntax for the CASE statement:

```
CASE
   WHEN expression_1
      THEN response_1
   WHEN expression_2
      THEN response_2
   .
   .
   .
   WHEN expression_X
```

```
      THEN response_X
   ELSE else_repsonse
END
```

Example:

```
SELECT CASE
         WHEN col_1 <= 25
           THEN "Between 0  % and 25%"
         WHEN col_1 <= 50
           THEN "Between 25% and 50%"
         WHEN col_1 <= 75
           THEN "Between 50% and 75%"
         WHEN col_1 <= 100
           THEN "Between 75% and 100%"
         ELSE "Percent Value Out Of Range: " + CONVERT(VARCHAR(10),
col_1) + "%"
       END
  FROM table_1
 WHERE col_2 = "name"
```

Example:

```
DECLARE @VAL_1 INT
SELECT @VAL_1 = 2

SELECT CASE
         WHEN @VAL_1 = 1
           THEN CONVERT(VARCHAR(10), @VAL_1) + " = 1"
         WHEN @VAL_1 = 2
           THEN CONVERT(VARCHAR(10), @VAL_1) + " = 2"
         WHEN @VAL_1 = 3
           THEN CONVERT(VARCHAR(10), @VAL_1) + " = 3"
         ELSE "Value of " + CONVERT(VARCHAR(10), @VAL_1) + " is out of
range"
       END
go
------------------------------------------------------------------------
2 = 2
```

Consider UNION ALL in Place of UNION

You are advised to use UNION ALL as opposed to UNION where you can. The UNION clause forces all rows returned by the different queries in the UNION to be sorted and merged in order to filter out duplicates before the first row can be returned to the calling module. A UNION ALL simply returns all rows, including duplicates, and does not have to perform any sort, merge, or filtering operations. Please bear in mind that if the return results expects no duplicate rows, then you have little choice but UNION.

When it is necessary to merge similar result sets, into one result set, you can use the UNION operator. ASE provides the UNION and UNION ALL unions to merge result sets. Union will remove duplicates from the merged result sets in a separate sort step using tempdb. Hence, the result set returned will contain only distinct records. A UNION ALL will not remove duplicates from the merged result sets nor will a sort be performed. Because of the performance overhead of using a UNION, UNION ALL should be used if it will suffice.

Example:

```
SELECT c1
  FROM table
 WHERE c1= 1

UNION

SELECT c1
  FROM table
 WHERE c1 = 5

/* Will always return the same as */
SELECT c1
  FROM table
 WHERE c1 = 1

UNION ALL

SELECT c1
  FROM table
 WHERE c1 = 5
```

This is because the two different sets that are being compared are disjoint.

In, Exists, Not In, Not Exists

You are probably wondering which is faster, NOT IN or NOT EXISTS. Should you choose IN, EXISTS, or a table join? The fact is that each can be faster than the other under certain circumstances. Even the dreaded NOT IN can be made to run fast with an appropriate hint inserted.

When a Join Outperforms a Subquery

As a general rule, table joins perform better than subqueries. My experience also suggests that, if you are forced to use a subquery, EXISTS outperforms IN in the majority of cases. However, there are always exceptions to the rule. The reason joins often run better than subqueries is that subqueries can result in full table scans, while joins are more likely to use indexes.

Which is Faster, IN or EXISTS?

The answer is that either can be faster depending on the circumstance. If EXISTS is used, the execution path is driven by the tables in the outer select; if IN is used, the subquery is evaluated first, and then joined to each row returned by the outer query. It is fair to say that in most cases, it is best to use EXISTS rather than IN. The exception is when a very small number of rows exist in the table in the subquery, and the table in the main query has a large number of rows that are required to be read to satisfy the query.

When only the existence of some records needs to be checked, you should use the EXISTS command. By using the EXISTS command instead of say a COUNT(*) you can eliminate potentially harmful reads. This is because a COUNT(*) will locate and count all records that match the search conditions. In contrast, an existence check will return true once the first record, that matches the search conditions, is located.

Example:

```
IF ( ( SELECT COUNT(*)
         FROM table ) > 0 )
BEGIN
   PRINT "YES"
END
```

Should be coded as an existence check.

Example:
```
IF EXISTS ( SELECT 1
              FROM table )
BEGIN
   PRINT "YES"
END
```

General Query Troubleshooting Tips

Problem:

The query I executed is taking a long time to execute. What steps should I perform to help ensure that the query runs more efficiently?

- Determine the showplan for the query you are executing. If the query is currently executing you can view the current query plan by using the stored procedure sp_showplan.

- Ensure that statistics are up to date by performing update statistics or update index statistics and sp_recompile. You may have to request your DBA to do this.

- Once, you have the query plan, review it. Try to determine the number of permutations that ASE had to perform in order to traverse the data by the query plan. Mostly, try to determine why ASE chose the path that it did.

- Verify that there are not any datatype mismatches. Use sp_help.

- Verify that you are using valid search arguments.

- Verify that indexes exist to support your query.

- Verify that the columns referenced in the index are chosen in the query plan.

- Modify the indexes if necessary to add additional columns referenced in the WHERE predicate.

- Use sp_help or sp_helpindex.

Sybase Transact SQL Guidelines and Best Practices

- Does your query contain a GROUP BY? If so, do all the non-aggregated columns appear in the GROUP BY clause?
- Does your query contain all the necessary search arguments? Did you forget any?
- Are you using an OR? If so, try a UNION or UNION ALL.
- Are you performing a sort, e.g. with ORDER BY? If so, what is the size of the set the sort is being performed on? Is it large? Do any indexes exist to support the sort?
- Are you running into lock contention? Use sp_who and sp_lock.
- What type of locks is your query trying to use? Use sp_lock.
- Are you using a variable or a parameter? What is the data distribution? Does a variable make sense to use?

Alignment Rules

To help enhance the readability and supportability of T-SQL code, we define the following the following rule.

Rule of Right

Certain SQL commands should be right-aligned for easy readability. These include, SELECT, UPDATE, DELETE, INSERT, FETCH, and DECLARATIONS. In addition, each new part of a command syntax should follow on its own line.

Example:

SELECT	*
FROM	Table
WHERE	column_1 = "ABC"
AND	column_2 = 5
UPDATE	Table
SET	column_2 = 6, column_124 = 99
FROM	Table
WHERE	column_1 = "ABC"
AND	column_2 = 5
AND	TSEQUAL(timestamp, @ts)
DELETE	Table
FROM	Table
WHERE	column_1 = "ABC"
OR	column_124 = 99
FETCH	named_cursor
INTO	@var_1,
	@var_2,
	@var_3
DECLARE	@var_1 INT,
	@var_c_1234 CHAR(1234)
INSERT	
INTO	table(
	column_1,

	column_2)
SELECT	column_1,
	column_2
FROM	table2 tb2
WHERE	tb2.col1 = "ABC"
OR	tb2.col_1234 = 1

Tabs vs. Spaces

Do not use tabs for indentation. Many products represent tabs differently and this can lead to code which is readable from one product and not so from another. Instead, use three spaces as a global indentation rule. That is for your procedures, triggers, Java, C, VB, etc.

Datatype Alignment

Many times I see developers and DBAs who align datatypes as part of a declaration list of variables. What do I mean?

Example:
```
DECLARE @VAR1          INT,
        @VAR_NUMBER_2  INT
```

We do not consider this as adding very much value to the readability of the code, and it causes wasted time trying to keep things aligned. Instead, just use a space.

Example:
```
DECLARE @VAR1 INT,
        @VAR_NUMBER_2 INT
```

Search Argument Alignment

Another area where I see developers and DBAs wasting time is trying to keep search arguments aligned.

What do I mean?

Example:
```
SELECT *
  FROM table
 WHERE c1                = 1
   AND another_column = 2
```

Again, we do not consider this as adding very much value to the readability of the code at the expense of maintaining the look. Instead, just use a single space as before.

Example:
```
SELECT *
  FROM table
 WHERE c1 = 1
   AND another_column = 2
```

Naming Standards

Many companies today have proven and adequate Enterprise-level naming standards in place. However, there are many companies which do not. We are not going to focus on the vocabulary or how to truncate words or their business meanings. Instead, we will simply give some examples of naming standards within an ASE database to help keep names unique and objects grouped together.

- Check Constraints – cc_<name>
- Defaults – df_<name>
- Foreign Keys – fk_<name>
- Groups – gr_<name>
- Indexes – ix##_<table name>
- Procedures – pr_<name>
- Roles – ro_<name>

- Rules – ru_<name>
- Tables – tb_<name>
- Triggers – tr<Action as u, i, or d>_<table name>
- Segments – sg##
- User Datatypes – ud_<name>
- Views – vw_<name>

Stored Procedures

Stored procedures represent a function that can be performed. They may be used by several different applications. Name a stored procedure after the function it performs and not after and application that needs it. Also, do not name a user defined stored procedure as “sp_<name>” as these should be reserved for system procedures like sp_who, sp_lock, etc.

Chapter 5. Various Best Practices

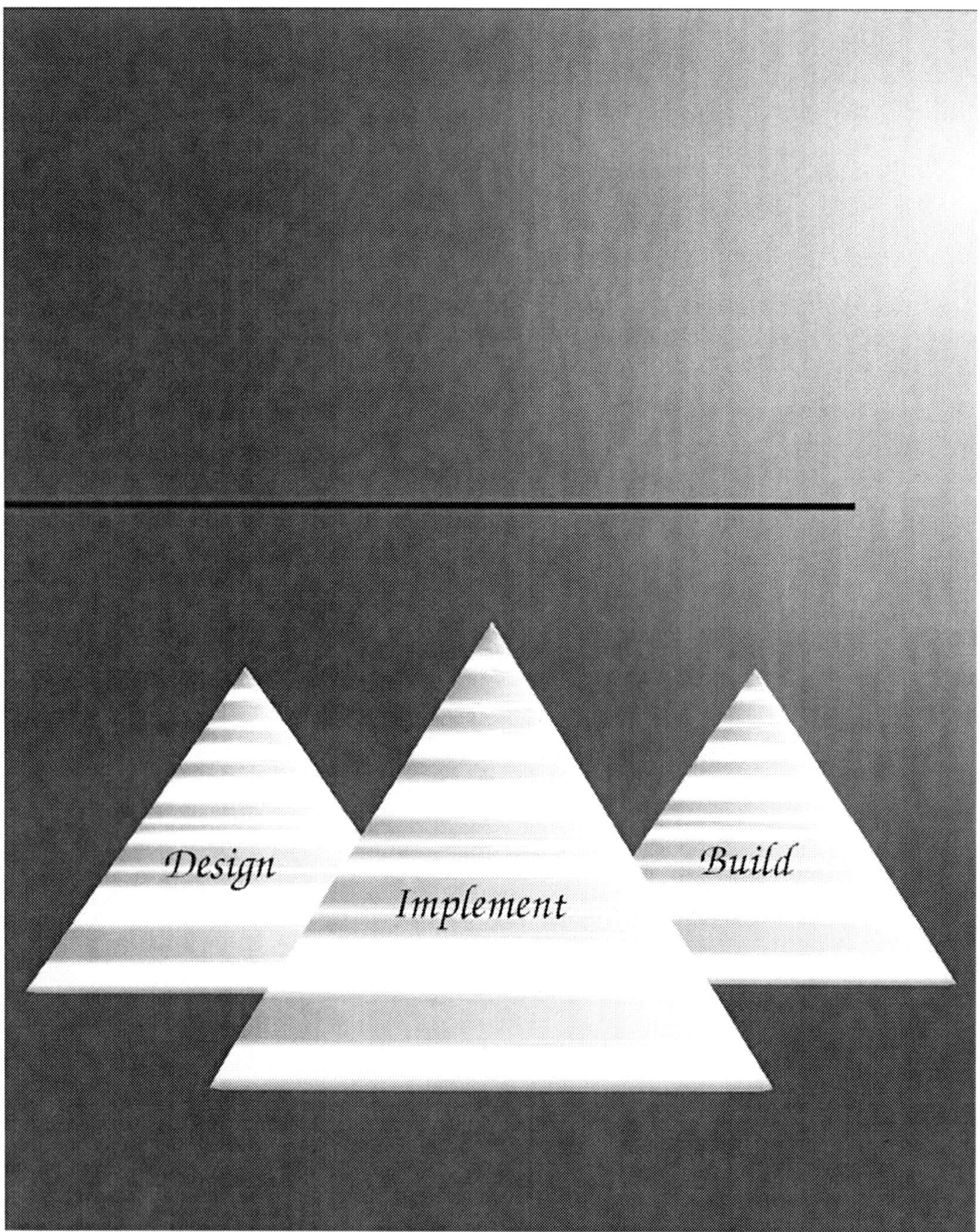
Design
Implement
Build

Chapter 6. Tempdb Usage Considerations

When ASE is installed, the setup program creates the **tempdb** database. The **tempdb** database is a system database used by ASE to store temporary tables and temporary stored procedures, for sorting, subqueries, and aggregates with GROUP BY, ORDER BY, for cursors, and so on. The **tempdb** database contains only temporary objects, so if you want to create a permanent object, do not create it in the **tempdb** database.

Note: The tempdb databases are recreated from the model database each time the server is restarted.

There are two primary ways for a user to create tables in tempdb. These tables are either #tables or private worktables. The #tables are session specific and are handled automatically by ASE when the session ends. #tables have the following properties:

Security: They can be created, on the fly, by any user query, without any CREATE TABLE, or other special privilege.

Simplicity: They are managed by the system, and are automatically dropped when the session that created them ends.

Functionality and Robustness: They avoid cross-session naming conflicts. Temp table names do not have to be unique inside a database, only inside a session. Two concurrent sessions, in the same database, can create temporary tables with the same name without any conflicts arising.

Transparency: They accomplish all these properties completely behind the scenes, without any participation by the developer.

For DBAs, good management of tempdb is critical to the overall performance of ASE. It is the most dynamic database on many servers and should receive special attention.

Types and Uses of Temporary Tables

The use or misuse of user-defined temporary tables can greatly affect the overall performance of ASE and your applications. Temporary tables can be quite useful, often reducing the work the server has to perform. However, temporary tables can add to the size requirement of tempdb. Some temporary tables are truly temporary, and others are permanent.

ASE allows three types of tables in tempdb:

1. Truly temporary tables

2. Regular user tables

3. Worktables

Truly Temporary Tables

You can create truly temporary tables by using "# " as the first character of the table name:

```
CREATE TABLE # temptable (...)

or:

SELECT columns
  INTO #temptable ...
```

Truly Temporary Tables:

- Exist only for the duration of the user session or for the scope of the procedure that creates them.

- Cannot be shared between user connections.

- Are automatically dropped at the end of the session or procedure (or can be dropped manually).

When you create indexes on temporary tables, the indexes are stored in tempdb:

Example:
```
CREATE INDEX tempix ON # temptable(col1)
```

Regular User Tables

You can create regular user tables in tempdb by specifying the database name in the command that creates the table:

```
CREATE TABLE tempdb..temptable (...)
or:
SELECT columns
  INTO tempdb..temptable ...
```

Regular User Tables in tempdb:

- Can persist across sessions.
- Can be used by bulk copy operations.
- By default can be accessed by everyone. This is because the owner of the table is typically "guest". Thus, try not to put sensitive data into a user table in the tempdb database.
- Must be explicitly dropped by the owner (otherwise, they are removed when Adaptive Server is restarted).
- You can create indexes in tempdb on permanent temporary tables.
- Beware! **If you specify tempdb..temptable in your code, that table will be created in the default tempdb database!** This is regardless of the fact that you may be assigned to another user defined tempdb database. If you want the table to be created in your user defined tempdb database, you have to explicitly refer to your specific tempdb in your code.

Worktables

Worktables are automatically created in tempdb or the user defined tempdb by ASE for merge joins, sorts, and other internal server processes.

These tables:

- Are never shared.
- Disappear as soon as the command completes.
- They are created in the tempdb database that the user assigned to
- Worktable have negative IDs and as such are not registered in tempdb..sysobjects.

To find out the size of tables and indexes in tempdb, you can use the following SQL:

```
USE tempdb
go
SELECT SO.name,
       SI.indid,
       CASE
         WHEN SI.indid > 1
            THEN DATA_PGS(SI.id, SI.ioampg)/512.0
         ELSE DATA_PGS(SI.id, SI.doampg)/512.0
       END AS "MB"
  FROM sysobjects SO,
       sysindexes SI
 WHERE SO.id=SI.id
   AND SO.type='U'
 ORDER
    BY SO.name,
       SI.indid
```

Create Table vs. Select Into in tempdb

There are two primary ways to create tables in tempdb. One approach is through the use of the CREATE TABLE command and the other by using SELECT INTO. There are many benefits and detriments of both approaches.

One benefit of using the CREATE TABLE command is that the structure of the #table is very easy to decipher when debugging. We can also create all #tables at the beginning of the stored procedure to help reduce lock contention and make the stored procedure more readable. In addition, administration and troubleshooting take less effort. By using this approach we also help reduce lock contention on the system catalog tables (such as syscolumns) in tempdb.

Some detriments of the CREATE TABLE command are that each record inserted into a #table is fully logged in tempdb. If #tables are used excessively in tempdb this can cause queries that access tempdb to run slower because they are waiting on I/O completion for the transaction log.

A benefit of using the SELECT INTO command is that only the extent allocations are logged in the tempdb. This reduced logging results in a single query running much faster. Using SELECT INTO does not require a person to lookup the column properties. This can reduce developer time.

One Detriment of the SELECT INTO command is that in some releases of ASE locks are held on tempdb system catalog tables for the duration of the query. This can cause lock contention issues on the system tables in tempdb and drastically reduce the throughput of the applications.

For applications that have many users executing queries that use tempdb concurrently, it is recommended that CREATE TABLE be used and not SELECT INTO. This will help increase the overall throughput of tempdb. **In addition, after a #table is no longer required it should be truncated before the stored procedure's execution is over by using the TRUNCATE TABLE command**. This is done so that when the stored procedure is finished executing and ASE drops the table by using an internal DROP TABLE, the removal of each record in the #table is not logged. TRUNCATE TABLE is a minimally logged command, and only the extent modifications for an object are recorded.

Tempdb usage recommendations:

- Use CREATE TABLE instead of SELECT INTO.
- Create all tempdb tables first in stored procedures.
- **Prior to a stored procedure's exit, truncate any #table created by using the TRUNCATE TABLE command.**
- Only insert those columns into tempdb that you absolutely require.
- For large #tables created in tempdb that are accessed more than once, **create a viable index on the #table after population, and nest the remaining queries in another stored procedure.** This must be done so that the ASE optimizer is aware that the index exists and knows its statistics.
- **When a #table is created ASE treats this table, regardless of the number of records, as occupying 10 pages and containing 100 rows for the stored procedure execution.** If statistics are necessary for query access to this table, then a second nested stored procedure will have to be created with the code after the #table population. We must do this so that the ASE optimizer is aware of the actual statistics for the table.

Null Values in #tables

By default when you are creating a table in ASE, NULL values are not allowed in the columns. ASE 12.5 enforces this on #tables as well. Once a #table is created, null values are not allowed. If you want to change the null constraint for a column, you will have to alter the column's attribute.

The column constraint for nullability may be specified directly for a column when using the CREATE TABLE command. If the table already exists, you can modify the nullability constraint for a table by using the ALTER TABLE command. When creating a table using the SELECT INTO command, you can specify that a column must be created as allowing NULLS by using the ISNULL function.

Example:
```
SELECT col_01,
       ISNULL(col_02, NULL) AS "col_02"
  INTO tempdb..table
  FROM table
```

Deadlock Avoidance in tempdb Databases

By default, when parallelism is enabled, ASE will use parallelism to create temp tables. For high-throughput OLTP applications that use many tempdb tables, this is very bad news. This can cause a very high number of deadlocks on tempdb..sysobjects and in particular tempdb..syspartitions. This is because tempdb..syspartitions is small and does not currently support anything but allpages locking. As such, many queries will attempt to obtain an exclusive table lock or a single exclusive page lock (which locks the entire table) on tempdb..syspartitions. The reason this occurs is because this table often contains only one page of data. This situation can lead to a very high degree of lock contention on the tempdb system tables. In addition, if adjacent pages in tempdb..syspartitions are locked by different processes and those processes need to lock each other's data pages, a deadlock occurs and the query which had consumed the least amount of cpu time will be rolled back.

As a fix, it is recommended that you enable traceflag 5303 in the RUN_SERVER file and reboot the server so that the traceflag will take effect. Traceflag 5303 is used to disable parallelism for temp table creation.

Server Restart Time

From time to time a developer may wonder when the last time ASE was rebooted. Short of asking your DBA, you can find this out by checking the time when the tempdb database was created.

Example:
```
1> sp_helpdb tempdb
2> go
 name     db_size  owner  dbid created
 -------- -------- ------ ---- --------------
 tempdb   503.0 MB sa        2 Jul 02, 2004
```

The time that tempdb was created is shown as Jul 02, 2004. Hence, that is the time when the ASE server was last rebooted.

Recommended tempdb Configuration for DBAs

The following sections discuss several key configuration areas for the tempdb database.

What is so Important about tempdb

Configuring tempdb is crucial to your server. Applications use it, worktables are created in tempdb, and your server uses it for a variety of other reasons. Thus you need to get optimal performance from your tempdb.

Recommended Configuration Settings

When configuring your tempdb, consider the following:

1. Put your tempdb devices on tmpfs or any other form of RAM disk if possible.
2. Split the data and log in tempdb. This not only yields better performance, but allows you to measure the size of your segments in tempdb with better accuracy.
3. Create a private cache for tempdb with appropriate buffer pools.
4. You may decide to split the tempdb caches into tempdb_data_cache and tempdb_log_cache.
5. Consider using multiple tempdbs and binding certain applications to their own tempdb.
6. Limit user resources in tempdb by using the "sp_add_resource_limit" stored procedure.

We discuss these points below.

Devices on tmpfs

tmpfs is a RAM disk file system type. Files that are written are never put out to disk as long as some RAM is available to keep them in memory. If there is a shortage of RAM, tmpfs pages are stored in swap space. In Solaris, the most common way to use this file system is to mount /tmp, which is associated with tmpfs by default. Linux also provide support for tmpfs. In addition, AIX provides the ability to create a logical volume within RAM. It is recommended that when using AIX to use a raw logical volume and not a file system. This prevents double buffering at the OS layer. Please refer to your OS specific documentation for further information.

Note: Bear in mind that you need free RAM on your host to allocate to tmpfs or a raw logical volume. Consult your UNIX sysadmin if necessary on this topic.

Since tempdb is a temporary database and is rebuilt at ASE reboot, it makes sense to put it on devices created on tmpfs or raw logical volumes created on a RAMDISK. Commonly, systems which use hash tables extensively (large enough ones to cause writes to tempdb), can create contention on system tables. Speeding up writes to tempdb system tables by using tmpfs or a raw logical volume created within RAM, can help prevent most blocking issues on system tables.

For OLTP and analytical type applications, which may create large tempdb tables, many tempdb tables, or many internal worktables which require sorting, tempdb on tmpfs allows ASE to use more OS memory for cache instead of needing to allocate some of the 2.75G of memory in 32-bit versions of ASE. If you are running 32-bit versions of ASE and your queries are hammering tempdb, it will help to put your tempdb devices or parts of it on tmpfs or a raw logical volume within RAM.

How to Create tempdb on tmpfs

In order to use tmpfs, you need to extend your tempdb on tmpfs. The following guidelines will help you.

Assuming that tmpfs is created on /tmp, talk to your UNIX sysadmin to find out the size of devices that you can create on /tmp directory.

You can create ASE devices on /tmp with disk init just as you create any other file system device:

```
disk init name = "tempdb_tmpfs_data",
physname = "/tmp/tempdb_tmpfs_data.dat",
vdevno = 3,
size = 51200,
dsync = 'false'
```

This creates a 100MB device for tempdb on tmpfs. Adaptive Server opens the device file with the dsync setting set to false. This is important because we have no interest in recovering the tempdb database. Once the device is created, extend your tempdb database on this device as usual.

You also need to modify your *RUN_Server* file to issue a UNIX touch command against *tempdb* on the *tmpfs* device before the call to the dataserver. This creates the file if it does not exist, as might happen if the operating system had been rebooted. Upon startup, the server can activate the device and recreate *tempdb*. If the file entry was missing, the server would not be able to activate it and *tempdb* would not be available.

Example:

```
touch /tmp/tempdb_tmpfs_data.dat
touch /tmp/tempdb_tmpfs_log.dat
#
/sybase/ase/sqlserver/1251/ASE-12_5/bin/dataserver \
-slon_gen_sql_tst1 \
-d/sybase/ase/lon_gen_sql_tst1/data/master.dat \
-e/sybase/ase/sqlserver/1251/ASE-12_5/install/lon_gen_sql_tst1.log \
-c/sybase/ase/sqlserver/1251/ASE-12_5/lon_gen_sql_tst1.cfg \
-M/sybase/ase/sqlserver/1251/ASE-12_5 \
```

How to Create tempdb on Raw Logical Volumes

AIX has added the support in version 4.3 and higher to create up to eight logical volumes within RAM. Raw logical volumes are created by using the command / usr/sbin/mkramdisk and specifying the size in 512 KB blocks. The name of the created raw logical volume is created by AIX in order of RAMDISK creation as ramdisk0, ramdisk1, ..., ramdisk8.

Example:

```
## Create A Raw Logical Volume 255 MB
/usr/sbin/mkramdisk 522240

ls /dev/*ramdisk*
/dev/ramdisk0   /dev/rramdisk0
```

You can now use the DISK INIT command to create a device in ASE for 250 MB which can be allocated to the tempdb database.

Example:

```
DISK INIT
NAME='tempdb_data_seg',
PHYSNAME='/dev/rramdisk0',
VDEVNO=99,
SIZE=128000,
VSTART=0,
CNTRLTYPE=0
```

Note: If the AIX server is bounced you will need to recreate this device before starting your ASE server. You can add the logic to your ASE server start script or to the RUN_SERVER file.

Split the Data and Log segments in tempdb

It makes sense to split your data and log devices on tempdb. Some sites have reported contention on extent allocation for large inserts into tempdb. The problem appears to be that as the table is being extended, the log is also extended in the same area! By giving the log its own area, it can be managed separately and ASE can make use of further device structures. All ASE internal worktables for sorts, merges etc. are placed on the system segment of tempdb.

On very high-volume OLTP systems, which have many queries that are small and yet perform sorts, It can be very advantageous to separate the data, system, and log segments. Thus, you may be able to split the data and system segment and put the system segment on tmpfs or a raw logical volume within RAM. For operations which require large sorts (for example, reports), you might be able to place these users into their own tempdb database which has larger allocations for data, system, and log.

Separating the log and the data makes monitoring tempdb usage much easier. In addition, you can create both the data and log devices on tmpfs or a raw logical volume within RAM, if enough resources are available.

Remove tempdb from the Master Device

It is a good idea to remove the first segment of tempdb from the master device. The size of this segment is 2MB. The system tables for tempdb are created there and this can create performance bottlenecks. Once you allocate a second device to tempdb, you can drop the master device from the default and log segments. The safest way to do this is to use the following approach (Make sure you backup your master database prior to all tempdb operations).

Procedure:

```
1>USE master
2>go
1>SELECT *
2>  FROM sysusages
3> WHERE dbid = DB_ID('tempdb')
4>go
 dbid   segmap      lstart      size        vstart      pad
unreservedpgs crdate
 ------ ----------- ----------- ----------- ----------- ------
------------- --------------------------
      2           7           0        1536        4100   NULL
925          Mar  9 2003 10:36AM
      2           3        1536      256000    67108864   NULL
255000          Mar  9 2003  2:51PM
      2           4      257536      256000    50331648   NULL
255000          Mar  9 2003  2:51PM

(3 rows affected)
```

Pay particular attention to the entry where lstart = 0. This is the first entry in sysusages for tempdb. By default its value should be set to 7. This value is a bitmap and is interpreted as system = 1 + default = 2 + logsegment = 4.

```
1> USE tempdb
2> go
1> sp_dropsegment system, tempdb, master
2> go
DBCC execution completed. If DBCC printed error messages, contact a
user with System Administrator (SA) role.
Segment reference to device dropped.
(return status = 0)
```

```
1> sp_dropsegment "default", tempdb, master
2> go
DBCC execution completed. If DBCC printed error messages, contact a
user with System Administrator (SA) role.
Segment reference to device dropped.
(return status = 0)

1> sp_dropsegment logsegment, tempdb, master
2> go
DBCC execution completed. If DBCC printed error messages, contact a
user with System Administrator (SA) role.
DBCC execution completed. If DBCC printed error messages, contact a
user with System Administrator (SA) role.
The last-chance threshold for database tempdb is now 15016 pages.
Segment reference to device dropped.
WARNING: There are no longer any segments referencing device 'master'.
This device will no longer be used for space allocation.
(return status = 0)

1> sp_helpdb tempdb
2> go
 name                      db_size     owner                    dbid
created          status
 ------------------------ ---------- -------------------- ---------
--------------- ------------------------------------------
 tempdb                   1003.0 MB    sa                       2
May 30, 2004     select into/bulkcopy/pllsort, trunc log on chkpt,
abort tran on log full

(1 row affected)

 device_fragments                    size          usage
created                 free kbytes
 ----------------------------- ------------ --------------------
------------------ -----------------------------
 master                              3.0 MB        data only
Mar  9 2003 10:36AM                  1850
 tempdb_data1                        500.0 MB      data only
Mar  9 2003  2:51PM                509940
 tempdb_log1                         500.0 MB      log only
Mar  9 2003  2:51PM not applicable

 ------------------------------------------------------------
 log only free kbytes = 509986
```

```
device                       segment
--------------------- ----------------------------
master                       -- unused by any segments --

tempdb_data1                 default

tempdb_data1                 system

tempdb_log1                  logsegment

(return status = 0)
```

To verify that the default segment no longer includes the master device, issue the following command:

```
1> SELECT dbid,
2>        name,
3>        segmap
4>   FROM sysusages,
5>        sysdevices
6>  WHERE sysdevices.low <= sysusages.size + vstart
7>    AND sysdevices.high >= sysusages.size + vstart -1
8>    AND dbid = DB_ID('tempdb')
9>    AND (status = 2 OR status = 3)
10> go
 dbid   name                           segmap
 ------ ------------------------------ -----------
      2 master                                   0
```

Create a Private Cache for tempdb

We recommend that you create private caches for the both the data and log portions of tempdb. Although this is double-caching (in conjunction with tempdb devices on tmpfs or a raw logical volume within RAM), tests have shown a marked improvement in response times and throughput when private caches are used.

You can start by creating a cache size about 25% the size of the actual device. Create the “tempdb_log_cache” with relaxed LRU and create “tempdb_data cache” with strict LRU. One partition should be sufficient for tempdb_log_ cache. For the tempdb_data_cache, you can find an optimum partition number depending on the number of ASE engines. Bear in mind that this number is required to be even. Setting it to 2 or 4 should be sufficient in most cases.

The tempdb transaction log is normally very active. These log pages are filled with log records and are immediately written to disk. When applications include triggers, deferred updates or transaction rollbacks, some log pages may be read, but usually they are very recently used pages that are still in the cache. Since accessing these pages in cache moves them to the MRU end of a strict-replacement policy cache, log caches may perform better with relaxed LRU replacement. That is why we recommend creating tempdb_log_cache with a relaxed LRU replacement strategy.

How to put tempdb Log on its Own Cache

To create a log cache, one needs to put the databases in single user mode, which is impossible for tempdb. To get around this, you simply need to create the log cache for the model database and tempdb databases will inherit the cache when the server boots. This also means one needs to keep a tight reign on who can create databases, because any user database created in the future will have its log cache bound to the log cache for model. This needs to be removed after the database is created. We believe this is a very small maintenance issue and should be considered for the performance gains.

First you need to create tempdb log cache:

```
1> sp_cacheconfig tempdb_log_cache, '75M','logonly','relaxed',
'cache_partition=1'
2> go
```

Since this is a log cache, it should be mainly made up of 4K buffer pools:

```
1> sp_poolconfig "tempdb_log_cache", "74M", "4K", "2K"
2> go

1> sp_cacheconfig tempdb_log_cache
2> go
 Cache Name                     Status    Type     Config Value Run Value
 ------------------------------ --------- -------- ------------ ------------
 tempdb_log_cache               Active    Log Only     75.00 Mb     75.00 Mb
                                                   ------------ ------------
                                            Total      75.00 Mb     75.00 Mb
=========================================================================
Cache: tempdb_log_cache,   Status: Active,   Type: Log Only
      Config Size: 75.00 Mb,   Run Size: 75.00 Mb
      Config Replacement: relaxed LRU,   Run Replacement: relaxed LRU
```

```
     Config Partition:            1,   Run Partition:            1
 IO Size  Wash Size Config Size  Run Size     APF Percent
 -------- --------- ------------ ------------ -----------
    2 Kb    204 Kb      0.00 Mb      1.00 Mb     10
    4 Kb  15152 Kb     74.00 Mb     74.00 Mb     10
(return status = 0)
```

The next step is to bind the model database transaction log to the tempdb_log_cache:

```
1> USE master
2> go
1> sp_dboption model, single,true
2> go
1> checkpoint model
2> go
1> USE model
2> go
1> sp_bindcache tempdb_log_cache,model,syslogs
2> go
1> USE master
2> go
1> sp_dboption model, single,false
2> go
1> checkpoint model
2> go
```

Now, reboot the server. When the Server starts, tempdb will be built from the model database and the tempdb's transaction log will be bound to the tempdb_log_cache.

```
1> sp_helpcache tempdb_log_cache
2> go
Cache Name           Config Size    Run Size    Overhead
-------------------- ------------- ---------- ----------
tempdb_log_cache          75.00 Mb    75.00 Mb     5.04 Mb

----------------- Cache Binding Information: -----------------

Cache Name       Entity Name          Type   Index Name   Status
---------------- -------------------- ------ ----------   ------
tempdb_log_cache tempdb.dbo.syslogs   table                V
tempdb_log_cache model.dbo.syslogs    table                V
(return status = 0)
```

Create a Data Cache for tempdb

As mentioned earlier, you can create a tempdb data cache around 25% of the tempdb data device size.

Create a mixed cache for tempdb data cache with relaxed LRU:

```
1> sp_cacheconfig "tempdb_data_cache", "200M", "mixed"
2> go
```

Now assign a fair bit to the 16K buffer pool:

```
1> sp_poolconfig "tempdb_data_cache", "40M", "16K", "2K"
2> go
1> USE master
2> go
1> sp_bindcache "tempdb_data_cache", tempdb
2> go

1> sp_helpcache tempdb_data_cache
2> go
Cache Name           Config Size    Run Size      Overhead
-------------------- ------------   ----------    ----------
tempdb_data_cache       200.00 Mb    200.00 Mb       13.11 Mb

------------------ Cache Binding Information: ----------------

Cache Name         Entity Name     Type      Index Name    Status
------------------ ------------    --------  ----------    ------
tempdb_data_cache  tempdb          database                V
(return status = 0)

1> sp_cacheconfig  tempdb_data_cache
2> go
Cache Name                Status   Type    Config Value Run Value
---------------------- -------- ------- ------------ ------------
 tempdb_data_cache     Active   Mixed      200.00 Mb    200.00 Mb
                                        ------------ ------------
                                 Total     200.00 Mb    200.00 Mb
======================================================================
====
Cache: tempdb_data_cache, Status: Active, Type: Mixed
      Config Size: 200.00 Mb, Run Size: 200.00 Mb
      Config Replacement: strict LRU, Run Replacement: strict LRU
```

```
      Config Partition:           1, Run Partition:            1
 IO Size  Wash Size Config Size  Run Size      APF Percent
 -------- --------- ------------ ------------ -----------
     2 Kb  32768 Kb      0.00 Mb    160.00 Mb      10
    16 Kb   8192 Kb     40.00 Mb     40.00 Mb      10
(return status = 0)
```

The New Write Optimization in tempdb

With the advent of write optimization in tempdb one needs to take a fresh look at the sizing of tempdb devices. With the *"tempdb* Write Optimization", Sybase ASE 12.5.1 white paper "Multiple Temporary Database Support in Sybase Adaptive Server Enterprise 12.5.1" states:

*Temporary databases are not recoverable. (During boot time ASE drops and recreates it.) ASE takes advantage of this characteristic and avoids writing data or log buffers to disk, which would have been required for normal databases. For instance, if a user does a select into as select * into tempdb ..temp_table from foo then ASE would have to flush all the data buffers of newly created table temp_table at the end of the transaction. This is because select into is a non-logged operation and to ensure the recoverability we need to make sure that the data hits the disk. This applies to normal databases but not to a temporary database, since a temporary database is not recovered. ASE avoids flushing data buffers to the disk at the end of this operation. For DMLs such as insert/update/delete ASE does not force the write of log at the end of the commit operation. For instance, if a user does the following:*

*insert into tempdb ..temp_table select * from foo*

...then ASE doesn't force the write of the log records to the disk during the commit operation. This means fewer context switches and a lighter load on the log or data devices, resulting in higher throughput. During in-house testing we have seen writes go down as much as 50%.

We need to understand a bit better about what "avoids writing data or log buffers to disk" means. If ASE is going to keep the tempdb database data in memory as much as it can, then a reasonable size tempdb data and tempdb log caches will be required. This is because ASE will have to flush the tempdb buffers to disk as soon as the wash marker in each cache is passed and the smaller the cache, the more often this is going to happen.

It begs the question: How should one size the tempdb devices? and : Do the tempdb devices need to sit on RAMDISK? This is really a cost/benefit issue, and obviously will depend on tempdb usage. Let us take a look at a case study.

ASE 12.5.1, Multiple tempdbs and Settings, a Case Study

My future production hardware is a SunFire V880 hardware with 8x900MHZ CPUs and 16GB of RAM.. The current production server is ASE 11.9.2. This 11.9.2 server has 8GB of tempdb with data and logged mixed. Our studies have shown that unless multiple reports are running, a tempdb of 4GB will do most of the time.

So on my new host, with ASE 12.5.1 64-bit installed, I create the main tempdb database to be 4GB in size. I will also create an additional 4GB user-defined tempdb database for reporting. I will create these user-defined tempdb devices on SAN disks. Going back to the main tempdb devices, I would think it would be wiser to give as much memory to ASE as possible. That is, I would not bother creating tempdb devices on RAMDISK/tmpfs, but rather create them on SAN devices. SAN disks will be fast enough for this purpose. In that way I can allocate that additional 4GB of memory to ASE itself. So finally my setup will look like this:

```
ASE max memory:         14GB

Parameter Name                Run Value
-------------------------- -----------
max memory                    7168000     --> 14GB
total logical memory          6993351
total physical memory         6993352

1> sp_cacheconfig
2> go
Cache Name           Status    Type     Config Value Run Value
-------------------- --------- -------- ------------ ------------
default data cache   Active    Default    7500.00 Mb   7500.00 Mb
log_cache            Active    Log Only   1000.00 Mb   1000.00 Mb
tempdb_data_cache    Active    Mixed       300.00 Mb    300.00 Mb
tempdb_log_cache     Active    Log Only    400.00 Mb    400.00 Mb
dbccdb_cache         Active    Mixed       100.00 Mb    100.00 Mb
```

```
                                  ------------ ------------
                                  Total     9300.00 Mb   9300.00 Mb
=================================================================
Cache: dbcc_cache, Status: Active, Type: Mixed
      Config Size: 100.00 Mb, Run Size: 100.00 Mb
      Config Replacement: strict LRU, Run Replacement: strict LRU
      Config Partition:         1, Run Partition:          1
 IO Size  Wash Size Config Size  Run Size     APF Percent
 -------- --------- ------------ ------------ -----------
    2 Kb   2048 Kb      0.00 Mb     10.00 Mb     10
   16 Kb   8192 Kb     90.00 Mb     90.00 Mb     10
=================================================================
Cache: default data cache, Status: Active, Type: Default
      Config Size: 7500.00 Mb, Run Size: 7500.00 Mb
Config Replacement: strict LRU, Run Replacement: strict LRU
      Config Partition:         4, Run Partition:          4
 IO Size  Wash Size Config Size  Run Size     APF Percent
 -------- --------- ------------ ------------ -----------
    2 Kb 245760 Kb      0.00 Mb   6000.00 Mb     10
    4 Kb  10240 Kb     50.00 Mb     50.00 Mb     10
   16 Kb 245760 Kb   1450.00 Mb   1450.00 Mb     10
=================================================================
Cache: log_cache, Status: Active, Type: Mixed
      Config Size: 1000.00 Mb, Run Size: 1000.00 Mb
      Config Replacement: strict LRU, Run Replacement: relaxed LRU
      Config Partition:         2, Run Partition:          2
 IO Size  Wash Size Config Size  Run Size     APF Percent
 -------- --------- ------------ ------------ -----------
    2 Kb   2048 Kb      0.00 Mb     10.00 Mb     10
    4 Kb  61440 Kb    990.00 Mb    990.00 Mb     10
=================================================================
Cache: tempdb_data_cache,   Status: Active,   Type: Mixed
      Config Size: 300.00 Mb,   Run Size: 300.00 Mb
      Config Replacement: strict LRU,   Run Replacement: strict LRU
      Config Partition:            1,   Run Partition:            1
 IO Size  Wash Size Config Size  Run Size     APF Percent
 -------- --------- ------------ ------------ -----------
    2 Kb  53248 Kb      0.00 Mb    260.00 Mb     10
   16 Kb   8192 Kb     40.00 Mb     40.00 Mb     10
=================================================================
Cache: tempdb_log_cache, Status: Active, Type: Log Only
      Config Size: 400.00 Mb, Run Size: 400.00 Mb
      Config Replacement: strict LRU, Run Replacement: relaxed LRU
      Config Partition:         1, Run Partition:          1
```

```
 IO Size  Wash Size Config Size  Run Size     APF Percent
 -------- --------- ------------ ------------ -----------
     2 Kb    204 Kb      0.00 Mb      1.00 Mb     10
     4 Kb  61232 Kb    299.00 Mb    299.00 Mb     10
    16 Kb  20480 Kb    100.00 Mb    100.00 Mb     10
(return status = 0)
```

Creating Multiple tempdbs

In my test environment for batch reporting purposes, I created a 4 GB user-defined tempdb as follows:

```
CREATE TEMPORARY DATABASE batch_tempdb
ON batch_tempdb_data = 2000
LOG ON batch_tempdb_log = 2000
```

Note that both devices are on UFS file system. I have created the above tempdb for reports. I also have a user called 'batch_user' which will be used for report processing. As such, I bind this user to use the "batch_tempdb" database as its tempdb. However, I also want to ensure that this user does not blow up this tempdb database.

```
EXCE sp_tempdb bind, lg, 'batch_user', DB, batch_tempdb
```

Understanding tables Created in a user-defined tempdb

If an ASE login, in this case batch_user, is bound to a given user-defined tempdb like batch_tempdb above, all batch_user's #tables will be created in batch_tempdb. In addition, worktables created internally by ASE for batch_user's sort/merge operations will also be created in batch_tempdb. However, if batch_user creates a temporary table in the format "CREATE TABLE tempdb..<TABLE_NAME>", this table will be created in the ASE's tempdb database and not in batch_tempdb! To create a table in batch_tempdb, CREATE TABLE statement should say CREATE TABLE batch_tempdb..<TABLE_NAME>. This may require changes to the batch_user's application code, for example, replacing tempdb.. with batch_tempdb.. etc.

Limit Resource Usage in tempdb

Another of my favorites is the use of "sp_add_resource_limit" utility to kill a process if it is messing about with tempdb usage too much. This is really handy!

```
EXEC sp_add_resource_limit batch_user,null,"at all times",
"tempdb_space",50000,2,4,1
go
New resource limit created.
(return status = 0)
```

In the previous example, the user "batch_user" session will be killed if it tries to return more than 50,000 rows.

Use Permanent Tables

Another method of removing contention on tempdb is to use permanent tables instead of #temp tables. In fact, some sites do not allow for users to create their own objects in a tempdb database through change management.

In order to use this method, we must guarantee the same data isolation that #temp tables provide. Another benefit of this approach is that these permanent tables can be queried to determine data contents very easily outside of a session which is using the table. This is great for support purposes, when you need to know what it is in there.

Let's assume that a session needs to create a the following temp table:

```
CREATE TABLE #tmp_tbl(
column01 INT NOT NULL,
column02 INT NOT NULL)
go
```

We could create a permanent table as follows:

```
CREATE TABLE perm_tmp_tbl(
sybs_intrnl_sesn_id INT NULL,
column01 INT NOT NULL,
column02 INT NOT NULL)
LOCK DATAROWS
go
```

```
CREATE CLUSTERED INDEX ix01_perm_tmp_tbl
ON perm_tmp_tbl(sybs_intrnl_sesn_id)
WITH ALLOW_DUP_ROW
go
```

In order to effectively use this as a method, several steps must be taken when accessing the table for a session.

In the location where #tmp_tbl was created, delete all current records which could be in the table from another session's execution.

```
DELETE perm_tmp_tbl
 WHERE sybs_intrnl_sesn_id = @@SPID
go
```

Now use the permanent table just as you would have used the temp table – except when updating, deleting, or selecting, make sure to include the following as part of the WHERE predicate. In addition, when inserting you will need to include @@SPID in the insert and select.

Example:

```
/* INSERTING EXAMPLE */
INSERT
  INTO perm_tmp_tbl(
       sybs_intrnl_sesn_id,
       column01,
       column02)
SELECT @@SPID,
       column01,
       column02
go

/* UPDATING EXAMPLE */
UPDATE perm_tmp_tbl
   SET column02 = 123456
 WHERE sybs_intrnl_sesn_id = @@SPID
go

/* SELECTING EXAMPLE */
SELECT column01,
       column02
  FROM perm_tmp_tbl
 WHERE sybs_intrnl_sesn_id = @@SPID
```

```
go

/* DELETING EXAMPLE */
DELETE perm_tmp_tbl
 WHERE sybs_intrnl_sesn_id = @@SPID
go
```

Defaults and Check Constraints

Do not create defaults or check constraints on any #temp table created in tempdb. When you create defaults or check constraints on tables in tempdb it incurs additional writes to tempdb..syscomments and tempdb..sysprocedures tables. In addition, it requires a higher ***number of open objects*** for the system, causes ***procedure writes to disk*** and increases the number of ***procedure reads from disk*** in sysmon output.

Instead, if you need to have a default or check constraint on a #temp table in tempdb, put the checks in your application code. If for some reason you cannot, create named defaults and named rules in the model database. When you need these properties bind the objects using sp_bindefault and sp_bindrule to the table and columns.

Chapter 6. Tempdb Usage Considerations

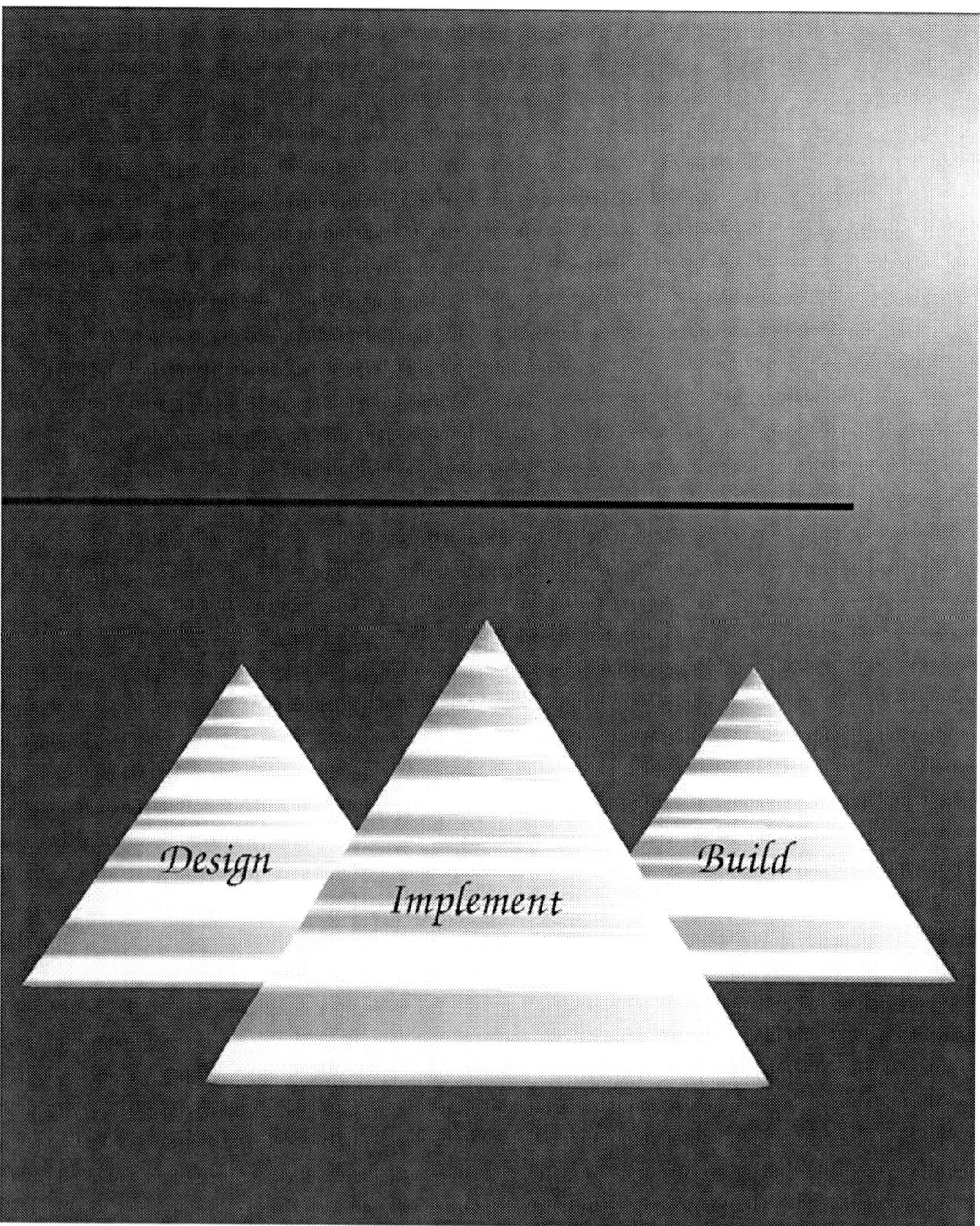
Design
Implement
Build

Chapter 7. Sort Operations

The operations that require some sort of sort include the following:

- CREATE INDEX
- DISTINCT
- GROUP BY
- ORDER BY
- MINUS
- UNION
- UNINDEXED TABLE JOINS

There are many things your DBA can do to improve sorting, such as making sure that there is enough space in tempdb for worktables. The other configuration parameter to consider is the "**number of sort buffers".** This parameter controls the amount of data that can be read and sorted in one batch. Adding more sort buffers increases the batch size, reduces the number of merge runs needed, and makes the sort run faster. Changing **number of sort buffers** is dynamic; as such it is not necessary to restart the server.

Here are some general guidelines for configuring sort buffers:

The sort manager chooses serial sorts when the number of pages in a table is less than 8 times the value of **number of sort buffers**. In most cases, the default value (500) works well for **select** queries and small indexes. At this setting, the sort manager chooses serial sorting for all **create index** and worktable sorts of 4000 pages or less, and parallel sorts for larger result sets, saving worker processes for query processing and larger sorts. It allows multiple sort processes to use up to 500 sort buffers simultaneously.

A temporary worktable would need to be very large before you would need to set the value higher to reduce the number of merge runs for a sort.

If you are creating indexes on large tables while other users are active, configure the number of sort buffers so that you do not disrupt other activity that needs to use the data cache.

If you are re-creating indexes during scheduled maintenance periods when few users are active on the system, you may want to configure a high value for sort buffers. To enhance the speed of your index maintenance, you may want to benchmark the performance of high sort buffer values, large I/O, and cache bindings to optimize your index activity.

The reduction in merge runs is a logarithmic function. Increasing the value of **number of sort buffers** from 500 to 600 has very little effect on the number of merge runs. Increasing the size to a much larger value, such as 5000, can greatly speed up the sort by reducing the number of merge runs and the amount of I/O needed.

If **number of sort buffers** is set to less than the square root of the worktable size, sort performance is degraded. Since worktables include only columns specified in the select list plus columns needed for later joins, worktable size for merge joins is usually considerably smaller than the original table size.

Configure Enough Sort Buffers

The sort buffers determine how many pages of data you can sort in each run. That is the basis for the logarithmic function on calculating the number of runs needed to finish the sort.

For example, if you have 500 buffers, then the number of runs is calculated with "log (number of pages in table) with 500 as the log base".

Also not that the number of sort buffers are shared by the threads in a parallel sort, and if you do not have enough sort buffers, the parallel sort may not work as fast as it should.

When enough sort buffers are configured, fewer intermediate steps and merge runs need to take place during a sort. As such, physical I/O is reduced.

When the number of sort buffers is equal to or greater than the number of pages in the table, the sort can be performed completely in cache, with no physical I/O for the intermediate steps: the only physical I/O required is the physical I/O to read and write the data and index pages.

A Warning about Setting the Number of Sort Buffers

Bear in mind that when you increase the sort buffers to N, you have to ensure that your 'default data cache' can accommodate it. The way sort buffers are reserved (and in ASE 11.9.2 and above this is a dynamic parameter), is that ASE will try to get N sort buffers. If the data cache does not have enough buffers, then ASE will revert to 50 buffers instead of 500 buffers. Perhaps more import is the impact of number of sort buffers on the query plan. Basically, the optimizer may decide that it will be cheaper to do a table scan than using the index.

We found this out the hard way. Basically, there were two identical servers, with identical data cache configuration and identical databases (one loaded a dump from the other). It appeared there was a query using an index on a particular table in a join on one server, but did a table scan on the other. Indexes, statistics, lock scheme, row count and data content were exactly identical...

After a lot of head-scratching, it turned out that the only difference was that the second server (doing the table scan) had 'number of sort buffers' set to 5000, while the first one (using the index) had it set to 500. Putting it back from 5000 to 500 instantly solved the problem and caused the query to use the index again.

We later realized that increasing the sort buffers can have a negative effect on the estimated number of physical I/Os which can impact the final query plan. This is because a larger number of sort buffers mean that there's potentially less data cache available.

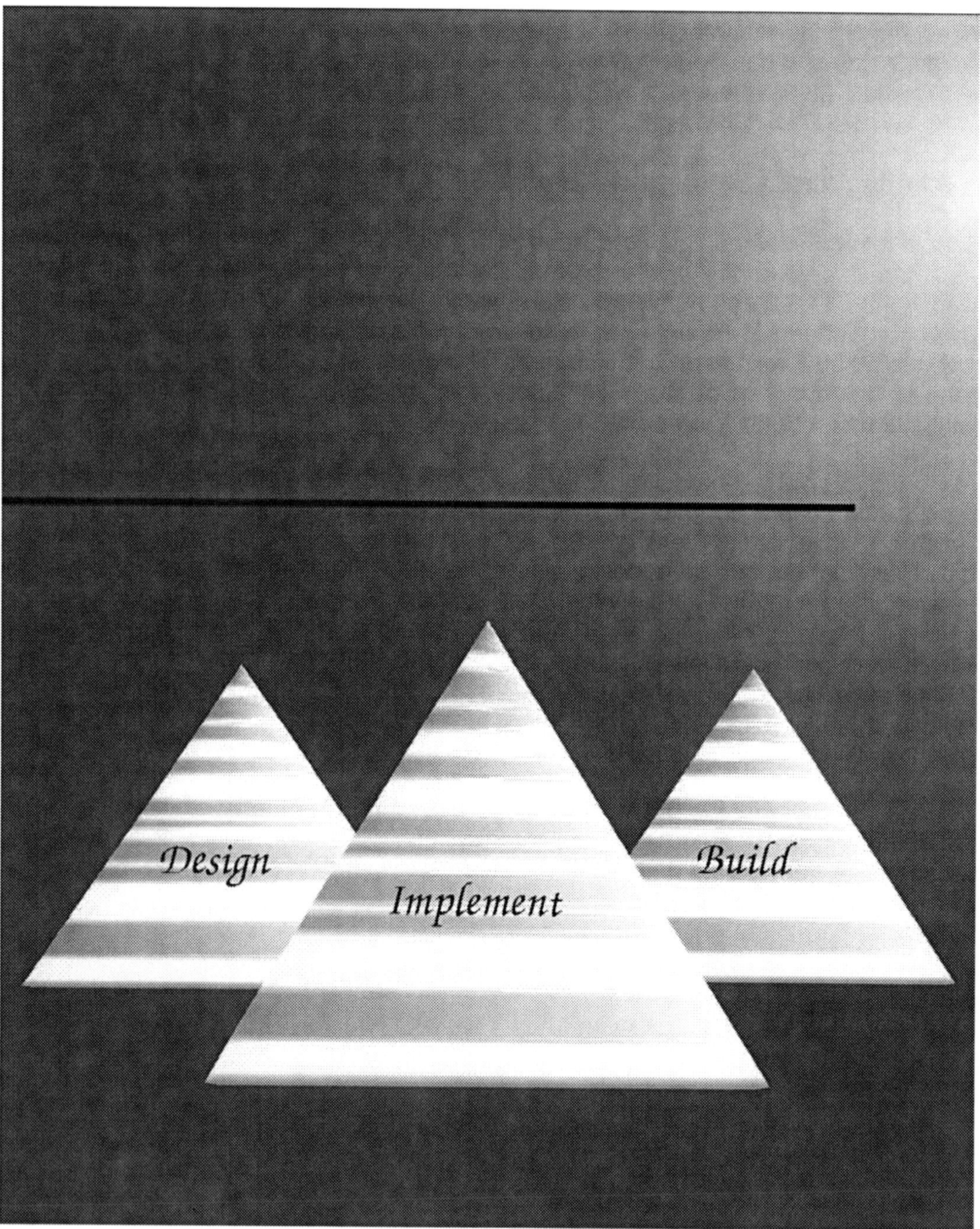
Design
Implement
Build

Chapter 8. Query Tuning

Using SHOWPLAN and NOEXEC

To display the steps that are taken for each query within a batch, optimizer strategies, use of indexes and keys, and join order; ASE incorporates a feature called showplan. In order to enable this facility for a session, you must run the command **set showplan on**.

Some terminology:

1. *Outer table* – The table that ASE will start its scan on, and join to an inner table on the join keys (for any qualifying record).

2. *Inner table* – The table that ASE performs lookups against, using the join keys, while finding rows from the outer table.

When you enable the showplan option, the tables are ordered according to how they will be accessed by ASE. So for table ordering Table_A, Table_B, Table_C arranged vertically, Table_A is an outer table to Table_B, which is an inner table to the outer table Table_A. Table_B is an outer table to Table_C, which is an inner table to the outer table Table_B.

Example (Showplan):

```
set showplan on
go

select *
  from table_1
 where col_1 = '5'
go

Qplan Output:

QUERY PLAN FOR STATEMENT 1 (at line 2).

    STEP 1
```

```
The type of query is SELECT.

FROM TABLE
    table_1
Nested iteration.
Table Scan.
Forward scan.
Positioning at start of table.
Using I/O Size 2 Kbytes for data pages.
With LRU Buffer Replacement Strategy for data pages.
```

The first line of the query plan will tell you which statement in the batch is being executed as well as the line number that the command starts in the batch. With this information, we can typically locate a T-SQL command within a batch that generated a query plan for a command we might want to inspect further.

The Message *STEP N* tells you which step you are looking at in a multi-step query plan, as well as the number of steps necessary to perform the query. Many queries take more than one step to perform. For instance, if a query contains a GROUP BY, then at least one additional step is needed to read the data from the internal worktable created to store the aggregate data for the query.

For most cases you will be concerned with, the message "The type of query is", will be a SELECT, UPDATE, DELETE, or INSERT. This message tells you exactly what command type of T-SQL command was executed.

The message "FROM TABLE", displays what tables are being accessed. The query plan generates the tables in the order in which they will be accessed.

The next message indicates what type of scan is required by the query. In our case "Nested Iteration", indicates that one or more loops through a table are required for the query.

The next message indicates what type of access is required for the table. For the previous query, a table scan was required to access the data. The message "Forward Scan" indicates the direction ASE will traverse the object's pages.

The message "Positioning at start of table", indicates that ASE will perform a forward table scan and start its scan on the first row of the first data page of the object. Some other types of positioning messages include:

1. Positioning at end of table – indicates that ASE will perform a backward table scan and start its scan on the last row of the last page of the object.

2. Positioning by index key – indicates that the index will be used to position the search on the first qualifying row of the object.

3. Positioning by index start – indicates that a non-matching index scan will be used and the scan will begin at the start of the index.

4. Positioning by index end – indicates that a non-matching index scan will be used and the scan will begin at the end of the index.

We are also given information on the I/O size that the optimizer chose for the query. The I/O size indicates how many Kbytes in pages ASE will request while processing the query.

The buffer replacement strategies for a query are LRU and MRU. In the case of the LRU replacement strategy, ASE places the pages that are read from disk onto the LRU end of the cache the object resides. ASE will typically choose the LRU buffer replacement strategy for pages that will be read more than once by a query, most index pages, any Data page modified by a statement, and OAM pages. If the LRU strategy is forced, it will apply to all pages. For pages that will be read frequently, the optimal cache strategy is the LRU strategy. By using this strategy, ASE will be able to cache pages that are frequently read by queries and drastically reduce disk I/O.

MRU replacement is often used for large table scans that do not contain joins and full index scans. This replacement strategy places the pages that are read from disk onto the MRU end of the cache the object resides. MRU replacement helps to maintain the integrity of your caches when large table scans or batch operations have to be performed, as it does not push any other pages out of the cache.

In summary, for each table the I/O cost of each qualifying index is compared with the cost of performing the table scan and the one with the lowest cost is chosen.

What follows is a detailed description of the showplan messages as described by the ASE 12.5 performance and tuning guide.

Basic *showplan* messages

This section describes **showplan** messages that are printed for most **select**, **insert**, **update**, and **delete** operations.

Query plan delimiter message

```
QUERY PLAN FOR STATEMENT N (at line N)
```

Adaptive Server prints this line once for each query in a batch. Its main function is to provide a visual cue that separates one section of **showplan** output from the next section. Line numbers are provided to help you match query output with your input.

Step message

```
STEP N
```

showplan output displays "STEP *N*" for every query, where *N* is an integer, beginning with "STEP 1". For some queries, Adaptive Server cannot retrieve the results in a single step and breaks the query plan into several steps. For example, if a query includes a **group by** clause, Adaptive Server breaks it into at least two steps:

- One step to select the qualifying rows from the table and to group them, placing the results in a worktable
- Another step to return the rows from the worktable

This example demonstrates a single-step query.

```
SELECT au_lname,
       au_fname
  FROM authors
 WHERE city = "Oakland"
```

```
QUERY PLAN FOR STATEMENT 1 (at line 1).

    STEP 1
        The type of query is SELECT.

        FROM TABLE
            authors
        Nested iteration.
        Table Scan.
        Forward scan.
        Positioning at start of table.
        Using I/O Size 2 Kbytes for data pages.
        With LRU Buffer Replacement Strategy for data pages.
```

Query type message

```
The type of query is query
type.
```

This message describes the type of query for each step. For most queries that require tuning, the value for *query type* is SELECT, INSERT, UPDATE, or DELETE. However, the *query type* can include any Transact-SQL command that you issue while **showplan** is enabled. For example, here is output from a **create index** command:

```
STEP 1
        The type of query is CREATE INDEX.
        TO TABLE
            titleauthor
```

FROM TABLE message

```
FROM TABLE
    tablename [ correlation_name ]
```

This message indicates which table the query is reading from. The "FROM TABLE" message is followed on the next line by the table name. If the **from** clause includes correlation names for tables, these are printed after the table names. When queries create and use worktables, the "FROM TABLE" prints the name of the worktable.

When your query joins one or more tables, the order of "FROM TABLE" messages in the output shows you the order in which the query plan chosen by the optimizer joins the tables. This query displays the join order in a three-table join:

```
SELECT a.au_id,
       au_fname,
       au_lname
  FROM titles t,
       titleauthor ta,
       authors a
 WHERE a.au_id = ta.au_id
   AND ta.title_id = t.title_id
   AND au_lname = "Bloom"

QUERY PLAN FOR STATEMENT 1 (at line 1).

    STEP 1
        The type of query is SELECT.

        FROM TABLE
            authors

          a         Nested iteration.
        Index : au_lname_ix
        Forward scan.
        Positioning by key.
        Keys are:
            au_lname  ASC
        Using I/O Size 2 Kbytes for index leaf pages.
        With LRU Buffer Replacement Strategy for index leaf pages.
        Using I/O Size 2 Kbytes for data pages.
        With LRU Buffer Replacement Strategy for data pages.
      FROM TABLE
            titleauthor

       ta         Nested iteration.
        Index : at_ix
        Forward scan.
        Positioning by key.
        Index contains all needed columns. Base table will not be
read.
        Keys are:
            au_id  ASC
```

```
        Using I/O Size 2 Kbytes for index leaf pages.
        With LRU Buffer Replacement Strategy for index leaf pages.

        FROM TABLE
            titles

          t        Nested iteration.
        Using Clustered Index.
        Index : title_id_ix
        Forward scan.
        Positioning by key.
        Index contains all needed columns. Base table will not be
read.
        Keys are:
            title_id  ASC
        Using I/O Size 2 Kbytes for index leaf pages.
        With LRU Buffer Replacement Strategy for index leaf pages.
```

The sequence of tables in this output shows the order chosen by the query optimizer, which is not the order in which they were listed in the **from** clause or **where** clause:

- First, the qualifying rows from the *authors* table are located (using the search clause on *au_lname*).
- Then, those rows are joined with the *titleauthor* table (using the join clause on the *au_id* columns).
- Finally, the *titles* table is joined with the *titleauthor* table to retrieve the desired columns (using the join clause on the *title_id* columns).

FROM TABLE and referential integrity

When you insert or update rows in a table that has a referential integrity constraint, the **showplan** output includes "FROM TABLE" and other messages indicating the method used to access the referenced table. This *salesdetail* table definition includes a referential integrity check on the *title_id* column:

```
CREATE TABLE salesdetail (
        stor_id CHAR(4),
        ord_num VARCHAR(20),
```

```
        title_id tid
    references titles(title_id),
        qty SMALLINT,
        discount FLOAT
)
```

An insert to *salesdetail*, or an update on the *title_id* column, requires a lookup in the *titles* table:

```
INSERT salesdetail
VALUES ("S245", "X23A5", "T10", 15, 40.25)

QUERY PLAN FOR STATEMENT 1 (at line 1).

    STEP 1
        The type of query is INSERT.
        The update mode is direct.

        FROM
TABLE
            titles        Using Clustered Index.
        Index : title_id_ix        Forward scan.
        Positioning by key.
        Keys are:
            title_id
        Using I/O Size 2 Kbytes for index leaf pages.
        With LRU Buffer Replacement Strategy for index leaf pages.
        TO TABLE
            salesdetail
```

The clustered index on *title_id_ix* is used to verify the referenced value.

TO TABLE message

```
TO TABLE
    tablename
```

When a command such as **insert**, **delete**, **update**, or **select into** modifies or attempts to modify one or more rows of a table, the "TO TABLE" message displays the name of the target table. For operations that require an intermediate step to insert rows into a worktable, "TO TABLE" indicates that the results are going to the

"Worktable" table rather than to a user table. This **insert** command shows the use of the "TO TABLE" statement:

```
INSERT sales
VALUES ("8042", "QA973", "12/7/95")

QUERY PLAN FOR STATEMENT 1 (at line 1).

    STEP 1
        The type of query is INSERT.
        The update mode is direct.
        TO TABLE

          sales
```

Here is a command that performs an update:

```
UPDATE publishers
   SET city = "Los Angeles"
 WHERE pub_id = "1389"

 QUERY PLAN FOR STATEMENT 1 (at line 1).

   STEP 1
        The type of query is UPDATE.
        The update mode is direct.

        FROM TABLE

          publishers         Nested iteration.
        Using Clustered Index.
        Index : publ_id_ix
        Forward scan.
        Positioning by key.
        Keys are:
            pub_id  ASC
        Using I/O Size 2 Kbytes for index leaf pages.
        With LRU Buffer Replacement Strategy for index leaf pages.
        Using I/O Size 2 Kbytes for data pages.
        With LRU Buffer Replacement Strategy for data pages.
        TO TABLE
            publishers
```

The update query output indicates that the *publishers* table is used as both the "FROM TABLE" and the "TO TABLE". In the case of **update** operations, the optimizer needs to read the table that contains the row(s) to be updated, resulting in the "FROM TABLE" statement, and then needs to modify the row(s), resulting in the "TO TABLE" statement.

showplan messages for query clauses

Use of certain Transact-SQL clauses, functions, and keywords is reflected in **showplan** output. These include **group by**, aggregates, **distinct**, **order by**, and **select into** clauses.

Use of certain Transact-SQL clauses, functions, and keywords is reflected in **showplan** output. These include **group by**, aggregates, **distinct**, **order by**, and **select into** clauses.

showplan messages for various clauses:

Message	Explanation
GROUP BY	The query contains a **group by** statement.
The type of query is SELECT (into WorktableN).	The step creates a worktable to hold intermediate results.
Evaluate Grouped type AGGREGATE Evaluate Ungrouped type AGGREGATE.	The query contains an aggregate function. "Grouped" indicates that there is a grouping column for the aggregate (vector aggregate). "Ungrouped" indicates that there is no grouping column (scalar aggregate). The variable indicates the type of aggregate.
Evaluate Grouped ASSIGNMENT OPERATOR Evaluate Ungrouped ASSIGNMENT OPERATOR	The query includes **compute** (ungrouped) or **compute by** (grouped).

WorktableN created for DISTINCT.	The query contains the distinct keyword in the select list and requires a sort to eliminate duplicates.
WorktableN created for ORDER BY.	The query contains an **order by** clause that requires ordering rows.
This step involves sorting.	The query includes on **order by** or **distinct** clause, and results must be sorted.
Using GETSORTED	The query created a worktable and sorted it. GETSORTED is a particular technique used to return the rows.
The sort for WorktableN is done in Serial. The sort for WorktableN is done in Parallel.	Indicates how the sort for a worktable is performed.

GROUP BY message

```
GROUP BY
```

This statement appears in the **showplan** output for any query that contains a **group by** clause. Queries that contain a **group by** clause are always executed in at least two steps:

1. One step selects the qualifying rows into a worktable and groups them.

2. Another step returns the rows from the worktable.

Selecting into a worktable

```
The type of query is SELECT (into WorktableN).
```

Queries using a **group by** clause first put qualifying results into a worktable. The data is grouped as the table is generated. A second step returns the grouped rows.

The following example returns a list of all cities and indicates the number of authors that live in each city. The query plan shows the two steps: the first step selects the rows into a worktable, and the second step retrieves the grouped rows from the worktable:

```
SELECT city,
       total_authors = COUNT(*)
  FROM authors
 GROUP
    BY city

QUERY PLAN FOR STATEMENT 1 (at line 1).

    STEP 1
        The type of query is SELECT
(into Worktable1).       GROUP BY       Evaluate Grouped COUNT
AGGREGATE.

        FROM TABLE
            authors
        Nested iteration.
        Table Scan.
        Forward scan.
        Positioning at start of table.
        Using I/O Size 16 Kbytes for data pages.
        With LRU Buffer Replacement Strategy for data pages.
        TO TABLE
            Worktable1.

    STEP 2
        The type of query is SELECT.

        FROM TABLE
            Worktable1.        Nested iteration.
        Table Scan.
        Forward scan.
        Positioning at start of table.
        Using I/O Size 16 Kbytes for data pages.
        With MRU Buffer Replacement Strategy for data pages.
```

Grouped aggregate message

```
Evaluate Grouped type AGGREGATE
```

This message is printed by queries that contain aggregates and **group by** or **compute by**. The variable indicates the type of aggregate--COUNT, SUM OR AVERAGE, MINIMUM, or MAXIMUM. **avg** reports both COUNT and SUM OR AVERAGE; **sum** reports SUM OR AVERAGE. Two additional types of aggregates

(ONCE and ANY) are used internally by Adaptive Server while processing subqueries.

When an aggregate function is combined with **group by**, the result is called a grouped aggregate, or vector aggregate. The query results have one row for each value of the grouping column or columns.

The following example illustrates a grouped aggregate:

```
SELECT type,
       avg(advance)
  FROM titles
 GROUP
    BY type

 QUERY PLAN FOR STATEMENT 1 (at line 1).

   STEP 1
        The type of query is SELECT (into Worktable1).
        GROUP BY
        Evaluate Grouped COUNT
AGGREGATE.
        Evaluate Grouped SUM OR AVERAGE AGGREGATE.
        FROM TABLE
            titles
        Nested iteration.
        Table Scan.
        Forward scan.
        Positioning at start of table.
        Using I/O Size 16 Kbytes for data pages.
        With LRU Buffer Replacement Strategy for data pages.
        TO TABLE
            Worktable1.

    STEP 2
        The type of query is SELECT.

        FROM TABLE
            Worktable1.
        Nested iteration.
        Table Scan.
        Forward scan.
```

```
        Positioning at start of table.
        Using I/O Size 16 Kbytes for data pages.
        With MRU Buffer Replacement Strategy for data pages.
```

In the first step, the worktable is created, and the aggregates are computed. The second step selects the results from the worktable.

Ungrouped aggregate message

```
Evaluate Ungrouped type AGGREGATE.
```

This message is reported by:

1. Queries that use aggregate functions, but do not use **group by**

2. Queries that use **compute**

When an aggregate function is used in a **select** statement that does not include a **group by** clause, it produces a single value. The query can operate on all rows in a table or on a subset of the rows defined by a **where** clause.

When an aggregate function produces a single value, the function is called a scalar aggregate, or an ungrouped aggregate. Here is **showplan** output for an ungrouped aggregate:

```
SELECT AVG(advance)
  FROM titles
 WHERE type = "business"

QUERY PLAN FOR STATEMENT 1 (at line 1).

    STEP 1
        The type of query is SELECT.
        Evaluate Ungrouped COUNT AGGREGATE.
        Evaluate Ungrouped SUM OR AVERAGE AGGREGATE.

        FROM TABLE
            titles
        Nested iteration.
        Index : type_price
```

```
        Forward scan.
        Positioning by key.
        Keys are:
            type  ASC
        Using I/O Size 2 Kbytes for index leaf pages.
        With LRU Buffer Replacement Strategy for index leaf pages.
        Using I/O Size 2 Kbytes for data pages.
        With LRU Buffer Replacement Strategy for data pages.

    STEP 2
        The type of query is SELECT.
```

This is a two-step query, similar to the **showplan** from the **group by** query shown earlier.

Since the scalar aggregate returns a single value, Adaptive Server uses an internal variable to compute the result of the aggregate function, as the qualifying rows from the table are evaluated. After all rows from the table have been evaluated (step 1), the final value from the variable is selected (step 2) to return the scalar aggregate result.

messages for order by and distinct

Some queries that include **distinct** use a sort step to enforce the uniqueness of values in the result set. **distinct** queries and **order by** queries do not require the sorting step when the index used to locate rows supports the **order by** or **distinct** clause.

For those cases where the sort is performed, the **distinct** keyword in a select list and the **order by** clause share some **showplan** messages:

- Each generates a worktable message.
- The message "This step involves sorting.".
- The message "Using GETSORTED".

Worktable message for *distinct*

```
WorktableN created for DISTINCT.
```

A query that includes the **distinct** keyword excludes all duplicate rows from the results so that only unique rows are returned. When there is no useful index, Adaptive Server performs these steps to process queries that include **distinct**:

- It creates a worktable to store all of the results of the query, including duplicates.
- It sorts the rows in the worktable, discards the duplicate rows, and then returns the rows.

Subqueries with existence joins sometimes create a worktable and sort it to remove duplicate rows.

The "Worktable*N* created for DISTINCT" message appears as part of "Step 1" in **showplan** output. "Step 2" for **distinct** queries includes the messages" This step involves sorting" and "Using GETSORTED".

```
SELECT DISTINCT city
  FROM authors

QUERY PLAN FOR STATEMENT 1 (at line 1).

    STEP 1
        The type of query is INSERT.
        The update mode is direct.        Worktable1
created for DISTINCT.
        FROM TABLE
            authors
        Nested iteration.
        Table Scan.
        Forward scan.
        Positioning at start of table.
        Using I/O Size 16 Kbytes for data pages.
        With LRU Buffer Replacement Strategy for data pages.
        TO TABLE
            Worktable1.

    STEP 2
        The type of query is SELECT.
        This
step involves sorting.
```

```
        FROM TABLE
            Worktable1.
        Using
GETSORTED        Table Scan.
        Forward scan.
        Positioning at start of table.
        Using I/O Size 16 Kbytes for data pages.
        With MRU Buffer Replacement Strategy for data pages.
```

Worktable message for *order by*

```
WorktableN created for ORDER BY.
```

Queries that include an **order by** clause often require the use of a temporary worktable. When the optimizer cannot use an index to order the result rows, it creates a worktable to sort the result rows before returning them. This example shows an **order by** clause that creates a worktable because there is no index on the *city* column:

```
SELECT *
  FROM authors
 ORDER
    BY city

QUERY PLAN FOR STATEMENT 1 (at line 1).

    STEP 1
        The type of query is INSERT.
        The update mode is direct.
        Worktable1 created for ORDER
BY.
        FROM TABLE
            authors
        Nested iteration.
        Table Scan.
        Forward scan.
        Positioning at start of table.
        Using I/O Size 16 Kbytes for data pages.
        With LRU Buffer Replacement Strategy for data pages.
        TO TABLE
            Worktable1.
```

```
    STEP 2
        The type of query is SELECT.
        This
step involves sorting.
        FROM TABLE
            Worktable1.
        Using
GETSORTED       Table Scan.
        Forward scan.
        Positioning at start of table.
        Using I/O Size 16 Kbytes for data pages.
        With MRU Buffer Replacement Strategy for data pages.
```

order by queries and indexes

Certain queries using **order by** do not require a sorting step, depending on the type of index used to access the data. Refer to the chapter on Various Best Practices for more information.

Sorting messages

These messages report on sorts.

```
This step involves sorting.
```

This **showplan** message indicates that the query must sort the intermediate results before returning them to the user. Queries that use **distinct** or that have an **order by** clause not supported by an index require an intermediate sort. The results are put into a worktable, and the worktable is then sorted.

GETSORTED message

```
Using GETSORTED
```

This statement indicates one of the ways that Adaptive Server returns result rows from a table.

In the case of "Using GETSORTED," the rows are returned in sorted order. However, not all queries that return rows in sorted order include this step. For example, **order by** queries whose rows are retrieved using an index with a matching sort sequence do not require "GETSORTED."

The "Using GETSORTED" method is used when Adaptive Server must first create a temporary worktable to sort the result rows and then return them in the proper sorted order.

Serial or parallel sort message

```
The sort for WorktableN is done in Serial.

The sort for WorktableN is done in Parallel.
```

These messages indicate whether a serial or parallel sort was performed for a worktable. They are printed after the sort manager determines whether a given sort should be performed in parallel or in serial.

If **set noexec** is in effect, the worktable is not created, so the sort is not performed, and no message is displayed.

Messages describing access methods, caching, and I/O cost
showplan output provides information about access methods and caching strategies.

Auxiliary scan descriptors message

```
Auxiliary scan descriptors required: N
```

When a query involving referential integrity requires a large number of user or system tables, including references to other tables to check referential integrity, this **showplan** message indicates the number of auxiliary scan descriptors needed for the query. If a query does not exceed the number of pre allocated scan descriptors allotted for the session, the "Auxiliary scan descriptors required" message is not printed.

The following example shows partial output for a delete from the *employees* table, which is referenced by 30 foreign tables:

```
DELETE employees
```

```
 WHERE empl_id = "222-09-3482"

QUERY PLAN FOR STATEMENT 1 (at line 1).
Auxiliary
scan descriptors required: 4

    STEP 1
        The type of query is DELETE.
        The update mode is direct.

        FROM TABLE
            employees
        Nested iteration.
        Using Clustered Index.
        Index : employees_empl_i_10080066222
        Forward scan.
        Positioning by key.
        Keys are:
            empl_id  ASC
        Using I/O Size 2 Kbytes for index leaf pages.
        With LRU Buffer Replacement Strategy for index leaf pages.
        Using I/O Size 2 Kbytes for data pages.
        With LRU Buffer Replacement Strategy for data pages.

        FROM TABLE
            benefits
        Index : empl_id_ix
        Forward scan.
        Positioning by key.
        Index contains all needed columns. Base table will not be
read.
        Keys are:
            empl_id  ASC
        Using I/O Size 2 Kbytes for index leaf pages.
        With LRU Buffer Replacement Strategy for index leaf pages.
        .
        .
        .
        FROM TABLE
            dependents
        Index : empl_id_ix
        Forward scan.
        Positioning by key.
```

```
        Index contains all needed columns. Base table will not be
read.
        Keys are:
            empl_id  ASC
        Using I/O Size 2 Kbytes for index leaf pages.
        With LRU Buffer Replacement Strategy for index leaf pages.
        TO TABLE
            employees
```

Nested iteration message

```
Nested Iteration.
```

This message indicates one or more loops through a table to return rows. Even the simplest access to a single table is an iteration, as shown here:

```
SELECT *
  FROM publishers

QUERY PLAN FOR STATEMENT 1 (at line 1).

    STEP 1
        The type of query is SELECT.

        FROM TABLE
            publishers
        Nested iteration.        Table Scan.
        Forward scan.
        Positioning at start of table.
        Using I/O Size 2 Kbytes for data pages.
        With LRU Buffer Replacement Strategy for data pages.
```

For queries that perform nested-loop joins, access to each table is nested within the scan of the outer table.

Merge join messages

```
Merge join (outer table).

Merge join (inner table).
```

Merge join messages indicate the use of a merge join and the table's position (inner or outer) with respect to the other table in the merge join. Merge join messages appear immediately after the table name in the

```
FROM TABLE
```

output. This query performs a mixture of merge and nested-loop joins:

```
SELECT pub_name,
       au_lname,
       price
  FROM titles t,
       authors a,
       titleauthor ta,
       publishers p
 WHERE t.title_id = ta.title_id
   AND a.au_id = ta.au_id
   AND p.pub_id = t.pub_id
   AND type = 'business'
   AND price < $25
```

Messages for merge joins are printed in italicized type in the **showplan** output:

```
QUERY PLAN FOR STATEMENT 1 (at line 1).
Executed in parallel by coordinating process and 3 worker processes.


    STEP 1
        The type of query is INSERT.
        The update mode is direct.
        Executed in parallel by coordinating process and 3 worker
processes.

        FROM TABLE
            titles
            t
        Merge join (outer table).       Parallel data merge using 3
worker processes.
        Using Clustered Index.
        Index : title_id_ix
        Forward scan.
        Positioning by key.
```

```
        Keys are:
            title_id  ASC
        Using I/O Size 16 Kbytes for data pages.
        With LRU Buffer Replacement Strategy for data pages.

        FROM TABLE
            titleauthor
            ta
        Merge join (inner table).        Index : ta_ix
        Forward scan.
        Positioning by key.
        Index contains all needed columns. Base table will not be
read.
        Keys are:
            title_id  ASC
        Using I/O Size 16 Kbytes for index leaf pages.
        With LRU Buffer Replacement Strategy for index leaf pages.

        FROM TABLE
            authors
            a
        Nested iteration.
        Index : au_id_ix
        Forward scan.
        Positioning by key.
        Keys are:
            au_id  ASC
        Using I/O Size 2 Kbytes for index leaf pages.
        With LRU Buffer Replacement Strategy for index leaf pages.
        Using I/O Size 2 Kbytes for data pages.
        With LRU Buffer Replacement Strategy for data pages.
        TO TABLE
            Worktable1.
        Worktable1
created for sort merge join.
    STEP 2
        The type of query is INSERT.
        The update mode is direct.
        Executed by coordinating process.

        FROM TABLE
            publishers
            p
        Nested iteration.
```

```
        Table Scan.
        Forward scan.
        Positioning at start of table.
        Using I/O Size 2 Kbytes for data pages.
        With LRU Buffer Replacement Strategy for data pages.
        TO TABLE
            Worktable2.
        Worktable2 created
for sort merge join.
    STEP 3
        The type of query is SELECT.
        Executed by coordinating process.

        FROM TABLE
            Worktable1.
        Merge join (outer
table).         Serial data merge.        Table Scan.
        Forward scan.
        Positioning at start of table.
        Using I/O Size 2 Kbytes for data pages.
        With LRU Buffer Replacement Strategy for data pages.

        FROM TABLE
            Worktable2.
        Merge join (inner
table).         Table Scan.
        Forward scan.
        Positioning at start of table.
        Using I/O Size 2 Kbytes for data pages.
        With LRU Buffer Replacement Strategy for data pages.

Total estimated I/O cost for statement 1 (at line 1): 4423.
The sort for Worktable1 is done in Serial
The sort for Worktable2 is done in Serial
```

This query performed the following joins:

- A full-merge join on *titles* and *titleauthor*, with *titles* as the outer table.
- A nested-loop join with the *authors* table.

- A sort-merge join with the *publishers* table.

Worktable message

```
WorktableN created for sort merge join.
```

If a merge join requires a sort for a table, a worktable is created and sorted into order by the join key. A later step in the query uses the worktable as either an inner table or outer table.

Table scan message

```
Table Scan.
```

This message indicates that the query performs a table scan. The following query shows a typical table scan:

```
SELECT au_lname,
       au_fname
  FROM authors

QUERY PLAN FOR STATEMENT 1 (at line 1).

    STEP 1
        The type of query is SELECT.

        FROM TABLE
            authors
        Nested iteration.
        Table Scan.          Forward scan.
        Positioning at start of table.
        Using I/O Size 16 Kbytes for data pages.
        With LRU Buffer Replacement Strategy for data pages.
```

Clustered index message

```
Using Clustered Index.
```

This **showplan** message indicates that the query optimizer chose to use the clustered index on a table to retrieve the rows. The following query shows the clustered index being used to retrieve the rows from the table:

```
SELECT title_id,
       title
  FROM titles
 WHERE title_id like "T9%"

QUERY PLAN FOR STATEMENT 1 (at line 1).

    STEP 1
        The type of query is SELECT.

        FROM TABLE
            titles
        Nested iteration.
        Using Clustered Index.         Index : title_id_ix
        Forward scan.
        Positioning by key.
        Keys are:
            title_id  ASC
        Using I/O Size 16 Kbytes for index leaf pages.
        With LRU Buffer Replacement Strategy for index leaf pages.
        Using I/O Size 16 Kbytes for data pages.
        With LRU Buffer Replacement Strategy for data pages.
```

Index name message

```
Index : indexname
```

This message indicates that the query is using an index to retrieve the rows. The message includes the index name.

If the line above this message in the output is "Using Clustered Index," the index is clustered; otherwise, the index is nonclustered.

The keys used to position the search are reported in the "Keys are..." message.

This query illustrates the use of a nonclustered index to find and return rows:

```
SELECT au_id,
       au_fname,
       au_lname
  FROM authors
 WHERE au_fname = "Susan"

QUERY PLAN FOR STATEMENT 1 (at line 1).

    STEP 1
        The type of query is SELECT.

        FROM TABLE
            authors
        Nested iteration.
        Index : au_names_ix        Forward scan.
        Positioning by key.
        Keys are:
            au_fname  ASC
        Using I/O Size 16 Kbytes for index leaf pages.
        With LRU Buffer Replacement Strategy for index leaf pages.
        Using I/O Size 2 Kbytes for data pages.
        With LRU Buffer Replacement Strategy for data pages.
```

Scan direction messages

```
Forward scan.

Backward scan.
```

These messages indicate the direction of a table or index scan.

The scan direction depends on the ordering specified when the indexes were created and the order specified for columns in the **order by** clause.

Backward scans cam be used when the **order by** clause contains the **asc** or **desc** qualifiers on index keys, in the exact opposite of those in the **create index** clause. The configuration parameter **allow backward scans** must be set to 1 to allow backward scans.

The scan-direction messages are followed by positioning messages. Any keys used in the query are followed by "ASC" or "DESC". The forward and backward scan messages and positioning messages describe whether a scan is positioned:

- At the first matching index key, at the start of the table, or at the first page of the leaf-level pages chain, and searching toward end of the index, or
- At the last matching index key, or end of the table, or last page of the leaf-level page chain, and searching toward the beginning.

If **allow backward scans** is set to 0, all accesses use forward scans.

This example uses a backward scan:

```
SELECT *
  FROM sysmessages
 WHERE description LIKE "%Optimized using%"
 ORDER
     BY error DESC

QUERY PLAN FOR STATEMENT 1 (at line 1).

    STEP 1
        The type of query is SELECT.

        FROM TABLE
            sysmessages
        Nested iteration.
        Table Scan.
        Backward scan.        Positioning at end of table.
        Using I/O Size 2 Kbytes for data pages.
        With LRU Buffer Replacement Strategy for data pages.
```

This query using the **max** aggregate also uses a backward scan:

```
SELECT MAX(error)
  FROM sysmessages

QUERY PLAN FOR STATEMENT 1 (at line 1).

    STEP 1
```

```
        The type of query is SELECT.
        Evaluate Ungrouped MAXIMUM AGGREGATE.

        FROM TABLE
            sysmessages
        Nested iteration.
        Index : ncsysmessages
        Backward scan.
        Positioning by key.       Scanning only up to the first
qualifying row.
        Index contains all needed columns. Base table will not be
read.
        Keys are:
            error  ASC        Using I/O Size 2 Kbytes for index leaf
pages.
        With LRU Buffer Replacement Strategy for index leaf pages.

    STEP 2
        The type of query is SELECT.
```

Positioning messages

```
Positioning at start of table.

Positioning at end of table.

Positioning by Row IDentifier (RID).

Positioning by key.

Positioning at index start.

Positioning at index end.
```

These messages describe how access to a table or to the leaf level of an index takes place. The choices are:

- `Positioning at start of table.`

  Indicates a forward table scan, starting at the first row of the table.

- `Positioning at end of table.`

  Indicates a backward table scan, starting at the last row of the table.

- `Positioning by Row IDentifier (RID).`

  It is printed after the OR strategy has created a dynamic index of row IDs.

- `Positioning by key.`

  Indicates that the index is used to position the search at the first qualifying row. It is printed for:

  1. Direct access to an individual row in a point query

  2. Range queries that perform matching scans of the leaf level of an index

  3. Range queries that scan the data pages when there is a clustered index on an allpages-locked table

  4. Indexed accesses to inner tables in joins

- **`Positioning at index start.`**
- **`Positioning at index end.`**

  These messages indicate a nonmatching index scan, used when the index covers the query. Matching scans are positioned by key.

  Forward scans are positioned at the start of the index; backward scans are positioned at the end of the index.

Scanning messages

```
Scanning only the last page of the table.
```

This message indicates that a query containing an ungrouped (scalar) **max** aggregate can access only the last page of the table to return the value.

```
Scanning only up to the first qualifying row.
```

This message appears only for queries that use an ungrouped (scalar) **min** aggregate. The aggregated column needs to be the leading column in the index.

For indexes with the leading key created in descending order, the use of the messages for min and max aggregates is reversed:

min uses "Positioning at index end"

while max prints "Positioning at index start" and "Scanning only up to the first qualifying row."

Index covering message

```
Index contains all needed columns. Base table will not be read.
```

This message indicates that an index covers the query. It is printed both for matching and nonmatching scans. Other messages in **showplan** output help distinguish these access methods:

- A matching scan reports "Positioning by key."
- A nonmatching scan reports "Positioning at index start," or "Positioning at index end" since a nonmatching scan must read the entire leaf level of the index.
- If the optimizer uses a matching scan, the "Keys are..." message reports the keys used to position the search. This message is not included for a nonmatching scan.

The next query shows output for a matching scan, using a composite, nonclustered index on *au_lname*, *au_fname*, *au_id*:

```
SELECT au_fname,
       au_lname,
       au_id
  FROM authors
 WHERE au_lname = "Williams"

QUERY PLAN FOR STATEMENT 1 (at line 1).
```

```
    STEP 1
        The type of query is SELECT.

        FROM TABLE
            authors
        Nested iteration.
        Index : au_names_id
        Forward scan.
        Positioning by key.

    Index contains all needed columns. Base table will not be
read.
        Keys are:
            au_lname
 ASC        Using I/O Size 2 Kbytes for index leaf pages.
        With LRU Buffer Replacement Strategy for index leaf pages.
```

With the same composite index on *au_lname*, *au_fname*, *au_id*, this query performs a nonmatching scan, since the leading column of the index is not included in the **where** clause:

```
SELECT au_fname,
       au_lname,
       au_id
  FROM authors
 WHERE au_id = "A93278"

QUERY PLAN FOR STATEMENT 1 (at line 1).

       STEP 1
        The type of query is SELECT.

        FROM TABLE
            authors
        Nested iteration.
        Index : au_names_id
        Forward scan.
        Positioning at index
start.
        Index contains all needed columns. Base
table will not be read.        Using I/O Size 16 Kbytes for index leaf
pages.
```

```
        With LRU Buffer Replacement Strategy for index leaf pages.
```

Note that the **showplan** output does not contain a "Keys are..." message, and the positioning message is "Positioning at index start." This query scans the entire leaf level of the nonclustered index, since the rows are not ordered by the search argument.

Keys message

```
Keys are:
  key [ ASC | DESC ] ...
```

This message is followed by the index key(s) used when Adaptive Server uses an index scan to locate rows. The index ordering is printed after each index key, showing the order, ASC for ascending or DESC for descending, used when the index was created. For composite indexes, all leading keys in the **where** clauses are listed.

Matching index scans message

```
Using N Matching Index Scans.
```

This **showplan** message indicates that a query using **or** clauses or an **in** (*values list*) clause uses multiple index scans (also called the "special OR strategy") instead of using a dynamic index.

Multiple matching scans can be used only when there is no possibility that the **or** clauses or **in** list items will match duplicate rows - that is, when there is no need to build the worktable and perform the sort to remove the duplicates.

For queries that use multiple matching scans, different indexes may be used for some of the scans, so the messages that describe the type of index, index positioning, and keys used are printed for each scan.

The following example uses multiple matching index scans to return rows:

```
SELECT title
  FROM titles
 WHERE title_id in ("T18168","T55370")
```

```
QUERY PLAN FOR STATEMENT 1 (at line 1).

    STEP 1
        The type of query is SELECT.

        FROM TABLE
            titles
        Nested iteration.
        Using 2 Matching Index Scans        Index : title_id_ix
        Forward scan.
        Positioning by key.
        Keys are:
            title_id
        Index : title_id_ix
        Forward scan.
        Positioning by key.
        Keys are:
            title_id
        Using I/O Size 2 Kbytes for data pages.
        With LRU Buffer Replacement Strategy for data pages.
```

Dynamic index message (OR strategy)

```
Using Dynamic Index.
```

The term *dynamic index* refers to a worktable of row IDs used to process some queries that use **or** clauses or an **in (values list)** clause. When the OR strategy is used, Adaptive Server builds a list of all the row IDs that match the query, sorts the list to remove duplicates, and uses the list to retrieve the rows from the table.

For a query with two SARGs that match the two indexes (one on *au_fname*, one on *au_lname*), the **showplan** output below includes three "FROM TABLE" sections:

- The first two "FROM TABLE" blocks in the output show the two index accesses, one for the first name "William" and one for the last name "Williams".

  These blocks include the output "Index contains all needed columns," since the row IDs can be retrieved from the leaf level of a nonclustered index.

- The final "FROM TABLE" block shows the "Using Dynamic Index" output and "Positioning by Row IDentifier (RID)."

  In this step, the dynamic index is used to access the data pages to locate the rows to be returned.

```
SELECT au_id,
       au_fname,
       au_lname
  FROM authors
 WHERE au_fname = "William"
    OR au_lname = "Williams"

QUERY PLAN FOR STATEMENT 1 (at line 1).

    STEP 1
        The type of query is SELECT.

        FROM TABLE
            authors
        Nested iteration.
        Index : au_fname_ix
        Forward scan.
        Positioning by key.
        Index contains all needed columns. Base table will not be
read.
        Keys are:
            au_fname  ASC
        Using I/O Size 2 Kbytes for index leaf pages.
        With LRU Buffer Replacement Strategy for index leaf pages.

        FROM TABLE
            authors
        Nested iteration.
        Index : au_lname_ix
        Forward scan.
        Positioning by key.
        Index contains all needed columns. Base table will not be
read.
        Keys are:
            au_lname  ASC
        Using I/O Size 2 Kbytes for index leaf pages.
        With LRU Buffer Replacement Strategy for index leaf pages.
```

```
        FROM TABLE
            authors
        Nested iteration.
        Using Dynamic Index.          Forward scan.
        Positioning by Row
IDentifier (RID).          Using I/O Size 2 Kbytes for data pages.
        With LRU Buffer Replacement Strategy for data pages.
```

Reformatting Message

```
WorktableN Created for REFORMATTING.
```

When joining two or more tables, Adaptive Server may choose to use a reformatting strategy to join the tables when the tables are large and the tables in the join do not have a useful index.

The reformatting strategy:

- Inserts the needed columns from qualifying rows of the smaller of the two tables into a worktable.
- Creates a clustered index on the join column(s) of the worktable. The index is built using keys to join the worktable to the other table in the query.
- Uses the clustered index in the join to retrieve the qualifying rows from the table.

The following example illustrates the reformatting strategy. It performs a three-way join on the *titles*, *titleauthor*, and *titles* tables. There are no indexes on the join columns in the tables (*au_id* and *title_id*), so Adaptive Server uses the reformatting strategy on two of the tables:

```
SELECT au_lname,
       title
  FROM authors a,
       titleauthor ta,
       titles t
 WHERE a.au_id = ta.au_id
   AND t.title_id = ta.title_id
```

```
QUERY PLAN FOR STATEMENT 1 (at line 1).


STEP 1
        The type of query is INSERT.
        The update mode is direct.
        Worktable1
created for REFORMATTING.

        FROM TABLE
            titleauthor
            ta
        Nested iteration.
        Table Scan.
        Forward scan.
        Positioning at start of table.
        Using I/O Size 2 Kbytes for data pages.
        With LRU Buffer Replacement Strategy for data pages.
        TO TABLE
            Worktable1.

    STEP 2
        The type of query is INSERT.
        The update mode is direct.
        Worktable2
created for REFORMATTING.
        FROM TABLE
            authors
            a
        Nested iteration.
        Table Scan.
        Forward scan.
        Positioning at start of table.
        Using I/O Size 2 Kbytes for data pages.
        With LRU Buffer Replacement Strategy for data pages.
        TO TABLE
            Worktable2.

    STEP 3
        The type of query is SELECT.

        FROM TABLE
            titles
            t
```

```
        Nested iteration.
        Table Scan.
        Forward scan.
        Positioning at start of table.
        Using I/O Size 2 Kbytes for data pages.
        With LRU Buffer Replacement Strategy for data pages.

        FROM TABLE
            Worktable1.
        Nested iteration.
        Using Clustered
Index.        Forward scan.
        Positioning by key.
        Using I/O Size 2 Kbytes for data pages.
        With LRU Buffer Replacement Strategy for data pages.

        FROM TABLE
            Worktable2.
        Nested iteration.
        Using Clustered Index.        Forward scan.
        Positioning by key.
        Using I/O Size 2 Kbytes for data pages.
        With LRU Buffer Replacement Strategy for data pages.
```

This query was run with **set sort_merge off**. When sort-merge joins are enabled, this query chooses a sort-merge join instead.

Trigger Log Scan Message

```
Log Scan.
```

When an **insert**, **update**, or **delete** statement causes a trigger to fire, and the trigger includes access to the *inserted* or *deleted* tables, these tables are built by scanning the transaction log.

This example shows the output for the update to the *titles* table when this insert fires the *totalsales_trig* trigger on the *salesdetail* table:

```
INSERT salesdetail
VALUES ('7896', '234518', 'TC3218', 75, 40)
```

```
QUERY PLAN FOR STATEMENT 1 (at line 1).

    STEP 1
        The type of query is UPDATE.
        The update mode is direct.

        FROM TABLE
            titles
        Nested iteration.
        Table Scan.
        Forward scan.
        Positioning at start of table.
        Using I/O Size 2 Kbytes for data pages.
        With LRU Buffer Replacement Strategy for data pages.

        FROM TABLE
            salesdetail
        EXISTS TABLE : nested iteration.
        Log
Scan.        Forward scan.
        Positioning at start of table.

        Run subquery 1 (at nesting level 1).
        Using I/O Size 2 Kbytes for data pages.
        With LRU Buffer Replacement Strategy for data pages.
        TO TABLE
            titles

NESTING LEVEL 1 SUBQUERIES FOR STATEMENT 4.

  QUERY PLAN FOR SUBQUERY 1 (at nesting level 1 and at line 23).

    Correlated Subquery.
    Subquery under an EXPRESSION predicate.


    STEP 1
        The type of query is SELECT.
        Evaluate Ungrouped SUM OR AVERAGE AGGREGATE.

        FROM TABLE
            salesdetail
        Nested iteration.
        Log Scan.        Forward scan.
```

```
        Positioning at start of table.
        Using I/O Size 2 Kbytes for data pages.
        With MRU Buffer Replacement Strategy for data pages.
```

I/O Size Messages

```
Using I/O size N Kbtyes for data pages.

Using I/O size N Kbtyes for index leaf pages.
```

The messages report the I/O sizes used in the query. The possible sizes are 2K, 4K, 8K, 16K, 32K, 64K, ...

If the table, index, LOB object, or database used in the query uses a data cache with large I/O pools, the optimizer can choose large I/O. It can choose to use one I/O size for reading index leaf pages, and a different size for data pages. The choice depends on the pool size available in the cache, the number of pages to be read, the cache bindings for the objects, and the cluster ratio for the table or index pages.

Cache strategy messages

```
With <LRU/MRU> Buffer Replacement Strategy for data pages.

With <LRU/MRU> Buffer Replacement Strategy for index leaf pages.
```

These messages indicate the cache strategy used for data pages and for index leaf pages.

Total estimated I/O cost message

```
Total estimated I/O cost for statement N (at line N): X.
```

Adaptive Server prints this message only if a System Administrator has configured Adaptive Server to enable resource limits. Adaptive Server prints this line once for each query in a batch. The message displays the optimizer's estimate of the total cost of logical and physical I/O. If the query runs in parallel, the cost per thread is printed. System Administrators can use this value when setting compile-time resource limits.

If you are using **dbcc traceon(310)**, this value is the sum of the values in the FINAL PLAN output for the query.

The following example demonstrates **showplan** output for an Adaptive Server configured to allow resource limits:

```
SELECT au_lname,
       au_fname
  FROM authors
 WHERE city = "Oakland"

QUERY PLAN FOR STATEMENT 1 (at line 1).

  STEP 1
        The type of query is SELECT.

        FROM TABLE
            authors
        Nested iteration.
        Table Scan.
        Forward scan.
        Positioning at start of table.
        Using I/O Size 16 Kbytes for data pages.
        With LRU Buffer Replacement Strategy for data pages.
Total
estimated I/O cost for statement 1 (at line 1): 1160.
```

showplan messages for parallel queries

showplan reports information about parallel execution, showing which query steps are executed in parallel.

showplan reports information about parallel execution, explicitly stating which query steps are executed in parallel.

showplan messages for parallel queries:

Message	Explanation
Executed in parallel by coordinating process and N worker processes.	Indicates that a query is run in parallel, and shows the number of worker processes used.

Executed in parallel by N worker processes.	Indicates the number of worker processes used for a query step.
Executed in parallel with a N-way hash scan. Executed in parallel with a N-way partition scan.	Indicates the number of worker processes and the type of scan, hash-based of partition-based, for a query step.
Parallel work table merge. Parallel network buffer merge. Parallel result buffer merge.	Indicates the way in which the results of parallel scans were merged.
Parallel data merge using N worker processes.	Indicates that a merge join used a parallel data merge, and the number of worker processes used.
Serial data merge.	Indicates that the merge join used a serial data merge.
AN ADJUSTED QUERY PLAN WILL BE USED FOR STATEMENT N BECAUSE NOT ENOUGH WORKER PROCESSES ARE AVAILABLE AT THIS TIME. ADJUSTED QUERY PLAN:	Indicates that a run-time adjustment to the number of worker processes was required.

Executed in parallel messages

The Adaptive Server optimizer uses parallel query optimization strategies only when a given query is eligible for parallel execution. If the query is processed in parallel, **showplan** uses three separate messages to report:

- The fact that some or all of the query was executed by the coordinating process and worker processes. The number of worker processes is included in this message.
- The number of worker processes for each step of the query that is executed in parallel.
- The degree of parallelism for each scan.

Note that the degree of parallelism used for a query step is not the same as the total number of worker processes used for the query.

Coordinating process message

```
Executed in parallel by coordinating process and N worker processes.
```

For each query that runs in parallel mode, **showplan** reports prints this message, indicating the number of worker processes used.

Worker processes message

```
Executed in parallel by N worker processes.
```

For each step in a query that is executed in parallel, **showplan** reports the number of worker processes for the step following the "Type of query" message.

Scan type message

```
Executed in parallel with a N-way  hash scan.

Executed in parallel with a N-way partition scan.
```

For each step in the query that accesses data in parallel, **showplan** prints the number of worker processes used for the scan, and the type of scan, either "hash" or "partition."

Merge messages

Results from the worker processes that process a query are merged using one of the following types of merge:

- Parallel worktable merge
- Parallel network buffer merge
- Parallel result buffer merge

Merge message for worktables

```
Parallel work table merge.
```

Grouped aggregate results from the worktables created by each worker process are merged into one result set.

In the following example, *titles* has two partitions. The **showplan** information specific to parallel query processing appears in bold.

```
SELECT type,
       SUM(total_sales)
  FROM titles
 GROUP
    BY type

QUERY PLAN FOR STATEMENT 1 (at line 1).

    STEP 1
        The type of query is SELECT (into Worktable1).
        GROUP BY
        Evaluate Grouped SUM OR AVERAGE AGGREGATE.
        Executed in parallel by coordinating
process and 2 worker processes.
        FROM TABLE
```

```
          titles
        Nested iteration.
        Table Scan.
        Forward scan.
        Positioning at start of table.
      Executed in parallel with a 2-way partition scan.        Using
I/O Size 16 Kbytes for data pages.
        With LRU Buffer Replacement Strategy for data pages.
        TO TABLE
            Worktable1.

      Parallel work table merge.

    STEP 2
        The type of query is SELECT.
        Executed by coordinating process.

        FROM TABLE
            Worktable1.
        Nested iteration.
        Table Scan.
        Forward scan.
        Positioning at start of table.
        Using I/O Size 16 Kbytes for data pages.
        With MRU Buffer Replacement Strategy for data pages.
```

Merge message for buffer merges

```
Parallel network buffer merge.
```

Unsorted, non aggregate results returned by the worker processes are merged into a network buffer that is sent to the client. In the following example, *titles* has two partitions.

```
SELECT title_id
  FROM titles

QUERY PLAN FOR STATEMENT 1 (at line 1).
Executed in parallel by coordinating process and 2 worker processes.

    STEP 1
        The type of query is SELECT.
```

```
        Executed in parallel by coordinating process and 2 worker
processes.

        FROM TABLE
            titles
        Nested iteration.
        Table Scan.
        Forward scan.
        Positioning at start of table.
        Executed in parallel with a 2-way partition scan.
        Using I/O Size 16 Kbytes for data pages.
        With LRU Buffer Replacement Strategy for data pages.

        Parallel network buffer merge.
```

Merge message for result buffers

```
Parallel result buffer merge.
```

Ungrouped aggregate results or unsorted, non aggregate variable assignment results from worker processes are merged.

Each worker process stores the aggregate in a result buffer. The result buffer merge produces a single value, ranging from zero-length (when the value is NULL) to the maximum length of a character string.

In the following example, *titles* has two partitions:

```
SELECT SUM(total_sales)
  FROM titles

QUERY PLAN FOR STATEMENT 1 (at line 1).
Executed in parallel by coordinating process and 2 worker processes.

    STEP 1
        The type of query is SELECT.
        Evaluate Ungrouped SUM OR AVERAGE AGGREGATE.
        Executed in parallel by coordinating process and 2 worker
processes.

        FROM TABLE
            titles
        Nested iteration.
        Table Scan.
        Forward scan.
        Positioning at start of table.
        Executed in parallel with a 2-way partition scan.
        Using I/O Size 16 Kbytes for data pages.
        With LRU Buffer Replacement Strategy for data pages.

        Parallel result buffer merge.
    STEP 2
        The type of query is SELECT.
        Executed by coordinating process.
```

Data merge messages

```
Parallel data merge using N worker processes.

Serial data merge.
```

The data merge messages indicate whether a serial or parallel data merge was performed. If the merge is performed in parallel mode, the number of worker processes is also printed.

Runtime adjustment message

```
AN ADJUSTED QUERY PLAN WILL BE USED FOR STATEMENT N BECAUSE NOT ENOUGH
WORKER PROCESSES ARE AVAILABLE AT THIS TIME.
ADJUSTED QUERY PLAN:
```

showplan output displays this message and an adjusted query plan when fewer worker processes are available at runtime than the number specified by the optimized query plan.

showplan messages for subqueries

Since subqueries can contain the same clauses that regular queries contain, their **showplan** output can include many of the messages listed in earlier sections.

The **showplan** messages for subqueries, include delimiters so that you can spot the beginning and the end of a subquery processing block, the messages that identify the type of subquery, the place in the outer query where the subquery is executed, and messages for special types of processing that is performed only in subqueries.

The **showplan** messages for subqueries include special delimiters that allow you to easily spot the beginning and end of a subquery processing block, messages to identify the type of subquery, the place in the outer query where the subquery is executed, or special types of processing performed only in subqueries.

showplan messages for subqueries:

Message	Explanation

Run subquery N (at nesting level N).	This message appears at the point in the query where the subquery actually runs. Subqueries are numbered in order for each side of a union.
NESTING LEVEL N SUBQUERIES FOR STATEMENT N.	Shows the nesting level of the subquery.
QUERY PLAN FOR SUBQUERY N (at nesting level N and at line N). END OF QUERY PLAN FOR SUBQUERY N.	These lines bracket **showplan** output for each subquery in a statement. Variables show the subquery number, the nesting level, and the input line.
Correlated Subquery.	The subquery is correlated.
Non-correlated Subquery.	The subquery is not correlated.
Subquery under an IN predicate.	The subquery is introduced by **in**.
Subquery under an ANY predicate.	The subquery is introduced by **any**.
Subquery under an ALL predicate.	The subquery is introduced by **all**.
Subquery under an EXISTS predicate.	The subquery is introduced by **exists**.
Subquery under an EXPRESSION predicate.	The subquery is introduced by an expression, or the subquery is in the select list.
Evaluate Grouped ANY AGGREGATE. Evaluate Grouped ONCE AGGREGATE. Evaluate Grouped ONCE-UNIQUE AGGREGATE. or Evaluate Ungrouped ANY AGGREGATE. Evaluate Ungrouped ONCE AGGREGATE. Evaluate Ungrouped ONCE-UNIQUE AGGREGATE.	The subquery uses an internal aggregate.
EXISTS TABLE: nested iteration	The query includes an **exists**, **in**, or **any** clause, and the subquery is flattened into a join.

Output for flattened or materialized subqueries

Certain forms of subqueries can be processed more efficiently when:

- The query is flattened into a join query, or
- The subquery result set is materialized as a first step, and the results are used in a second step with the rest of the outer query.

When the optimizer chooses one of these strategies, the query is not processed as a subquery, so you will not see the subquery message delimiters. The following sections describe **showplan** output for flattened and materialized queries.

Adaptive Server can use one of several methods to flatten subqueries into joins.

Subqueries executed as existence joins

When subqueries are flattened into existence joins, the output looks like normal **showplan** output for a join, with the possible exception of the message "EXISTS TABLE: nested iteration."

This message indicates that instead of the normal join processing, which looks for every row in the table that matches the join column, Adaptive Server uses an existence join and returns TRUE as soon as the first qualifying row is located.

Adaptive Server flattens the following subquery into an existence join:

```
SELECT title
  FROM titles
 WHERE title_id IN ( SELECT title_id
                       FROM titleauthor )
   AND title LIKE "A Tutorial%"

QUERY PLAN FOR STATEMENT 1 (at line 1).

    STEP 1
        The type of query is SELECT.

        FROM TABLE
```

```
          titles
        Nested iteration.
        Index : title_ix
        Forward scan.
        Positioning by key.
        Keys are:
            title  ASC
        Using I/O Size 16 Kbytes for index leaf pages.
        With LRU Buffer Replacement Strategy for index leaf pages.
        Using I/O Size 2 Kbytes for data pages.
        With LRU Buffer Replacement Strategy for data pages.

        FROM TABLE
            titleauthor
        EXISTS TABLE : nested iteration.        Index : ta_ix
        Forward scan.
        Positioning by key.
        Index contains all needed columns. Base table will not be
read.
        Keys are:
            title_id  ASC
        Using I/O Size 2 Kbytes for index leaf pages.
        With LRU Buffer Replacement Strategy for index leaf pages.
```

Subqueries using unique reformatting

If there is not a unique index on *publishers.pub_id*, this query is flattened by selecting the rows from *publishers* into a worktable and then creating a unique clustered index. This process is called unique reformatting:

```
SELECT title_id
  FROM titles
 WHERE pub_id IN ( SELECT pub_id
                     FROM publishers
                    WHERE state = "TX")

QUERY PLAN FOR STATEMENT 1 (at line 1).


    STEP 1
        The type of query is INSERT.
        The update mode is direct.
        Worktable1
```

```
created for REFORMATTING.
        FROM TABLE
            publishers
        Nested iteration.
        Table Scan.
        Forward scan.
        Positioning at start of table.
        Using I/O Size 2 Kbytes for data pages.
        With LRU Buffer Replacement Strategy for data pages.
        TO TABLE
            Worktable1.

    STEP 2
        The type of query is SELECT.

        FROM TABLE
            Worktable1.        Nested iteration.
        Using Clustered
Index.        Forward scan.
        Positioning at start of table.
        Using I/O Size 2 Kbytes for data pages.
        With LRU Buffer Replacement Strategy for data pages.

        FROM TABLE
            titles
        Nested iteration.
        Table Scan.
        Forward scan.
        Positioning at start of table.
        Using I/O Size 2 Kbytes for data pages.
        With LRU Buffer Replacement Strategy for data pages.
```

Subqueries using duplicate elimination

This query performs a regular join, selecting all of the rows into a worktable. In the second step, the worktable is sorted to remove duplicates. This process is called duplicate elimination:

```
SELECT title_id,
       au_id,
       au_ord
  FROM titleauthor ta
 WHERE title_id IN ( SELECT ta.title_id
```

```
                        FROM titles t,
                             salesdetail sd
                       WHERE t.title_id = sd.title_id
                         AND ta.title_id = t.title_id
                         AND type = 'travel'
                         AND qty > 10 )

QUERY PLAN FOR STATEMENT 1 (at line 1).

    STEP 1
        The type of query is INSERT.
        The update mode is direct.
        Worktable1
created for DISTINCT.
        FROM TABLE
            salesdetail
            sd
        Nested iteration.
        Table Scan.
        Forward scan.
        Positioning at start of table.
        Using I/O Size 16 Kbytes for data pages.
        With LRU Buffer Replacement Strategy for data pages.

        FROM TABLE
            titles
            t
        Nested iteration.
        Using Clustered Index.
        Index : title_id_ix
        Forward scan.
        Positioning by key.
        Keys are:
            title_id  ASC
        Using I/O Size 2 Kbytes for data pages.
        With LRU Buffer Replacement Strategy for data pages.

        FROM TABLE
            titleauthor
            ta
        Nested iteration.
        Index : ta_ix
        Forward scan.
        Positioning by key.
```

```
        Keys are:
            title_id  ASC
        Using I/O Size 2 Kbytes for index leaf pages.
        With LRU Buffer Replacement Strategy for index leaf pages.
        Using I/O Size 2 Kbytes for data pages.
        With LRU Buffer Replacement Strategy for data pages.
        TO TABLE
            Worktable1.

    STEP 2
        The type of query is SELECT.
        This step involves sorting.
        FROM TABLE
            Worktable1.
        Using GETSORTED
        Table Scan.
        Forward scan.
        Positioning at start of table.
        Using I/O Size 16 Kbytes for data pages.
        With MRU Buffer Replacement Strategy for data pages.
```

Materialized queries

When Adaptive Server materializes subqueries, the query is executed in two steps:

- The first step stores the results of the subquery in an internal variable or worktable.
- The second step uses the internal variable or worktable results in the outer query.

This query materializes the subquery into a worktable:

```
SELECT type,
       title_id
  FROM titles
 WHERE total_sales IN ( SELECT MAX(total_sales)
                          FROM sales_summary
                         GROUP
                            BY type)
```

```
QUERY PLAN FOR STATEMENT 1 (at line 1).

    STEP 1
        The type of query is SELECT (into Worktable1).       GROUP BY
        Evaluate Grouped MAXIMUM AGGREGATE.

        FROM TABLE
            sales_summary
        Nested iteration.
        Table Scan.
        Forward scan.
        Positioning at start of table.
        Using I/O Size 2 Kbytes for data pages.
        With LRU Buffer Replacement Strategy for data pages.
        TO TABLE
            Worktable1.

    STEP 2
        The type of query is SELECT.

        FROM TABLE
            titles
        Nested iteration.
        Table Scan.
        Forward scan.
        Positioning at start of table.
        Using I/O Size 16 Kbytes for data pages.
        With LRU Buffer Replacement Strategy for data pages.

        FROM TABLE
            Worktable1.         EXISTS TABLE : nested iteration.
Table Scan.
        Forward scan.
        Positioning at start of table.
        Using I/O Size 16 Kbytes for data pages.
        With MRU Buffer Replacement Strategy for data pages.
```

The **showplan** message "EXISTS TABLE: nested iteration," near the end of the output, shows that Adaptive Server performs an existence join.

Structure of subquery showplan output

When a query contains subqueries that are not flattened or materialized:

1. The **showplan** output for the outer query appears first. It includes the message "Run subquery *N* (at nesting level *N*)", indicating the point in the query processing where the subquery executes.

2. For each nesting level, the query plans at that nesting level are introduced by the message "NESTING LEVEL *N* SUBQUERIES FOR STATEMENT *N*."

3. The plan for each subquery is introduced by the message "QUERY PLAN FOR SUBQUERY *N* (at nesting level *N* and at line *N*)", and the end of its plan is marked by the message "END OF QUERY PLAN FOR SUBQUERY *N*." This section of the output includes information showing:

4. The type of query (correlated or uncorrelated)

5. The predicate type (IN, ANY, ALL, EXISTS, or EXPRESSION)

Subquery execution message

```
Run subquery N (at nesting level N).
```

This message shows the place where the subquery execution takes place in the execution of the outer query. Adaptive Server executes the subquery at the point in the outer query where it need to be run least often.

The plan for this subquery appears later in the output for the subquery's nesting level. The first variable in this message is the subquery number; the second variable is the subquery nesting level.

Nesting level delimiter message

```
NESTING LEVEL N SUBQUERIES FOR STATEMENT N.
```

This message introduces the **showplan** output for all the subqueries at a given nesting level. The maximum nesting level is 16.

Subquery plan start delimiter

```
QUERY PLAN FOR SUBQUERY N (at nesting level N and at line N).
```

This statement introduces the **showplan** output for a particular subquery at the nesting level indicated by the previous NESTING LEVEL message.

Line numbers to help you match **showplan** output to your input.

Subquery plan end delimiter

```
END OF QUERY PLAN FOR SUBQUERY N.
```

This statement marks the end of the query plan for a particular subquery.

Type of subquery

```
Correlated Subquery.

Non-correlated Subquery.
```

A subquery is either correlated or non-correlated.

- A correlated subquery references a column in a table that is listed in the **from** list of the outer query. If the subquery is correlated, **showplan** includes the message "Correlated Subquery."
- A non-correlated subquery can be evaluated independently of the outer query. Non-correlated subqueries are sometimes materialized, so their **showplan** output does not include the normal subquery **showplan** messages.

Subquery predicates messages

```
Subquery under an IN predicate.
```

```
Subquery under an ANY predicate.

Subquery under an ALL predicate.

Subquery under an EXISTS predicate.

Subquery under an EXPRESSION predicate.
```

Subqueries introduced by **in**, **any**, **all**, or **exists** are quantified predicate subqueries. Subqueries introduced by **>**, **>=**, **<**, **<=**, **=**, **!=** are expression subqueries.

Internal subquery aggregates

Certain types of subqueries require special internal aggregates, as listed in the following table. Adaptive Server generates these aggregates internally - they are not part of Transact-SQL syntax and cannot be included in user queries.

Internal subquery aggregates:

Subquery type	Aggregate	Effect
Quantified predicate	ANY	Returns TRUE or FALSE to the outer query.
Expression	ONCE	Returns the result of the subquery. Raises error 512 if the subquery returns more than one value.
Subquery containing **distinct**	ONCE-UNIQUE	Stores the first subquery result internally and compares each subsequent result to the first. Raises error 512 if a subsequent result differs from the first.

Messages for internal aggregates include "Grouped" when the subquery includes a **group by** clause and computes the aggregate for a group of rows, otherwise the messages include "Ungrouped"; the subquery the aggregate for all rows in the table that satisfy the correlation clause.

Quantified predicate subqueries and the ANY aggregate

```
Evaluate Grouped ANY AGGREGATE.

Evaluate Ungrouped ANY AGGREGATE.
```

All quantified predicate subqueries that are not flattened use the internal ANY aggregate. Do not confuse this with the **any** predicate that is part of SQL syntax.

The subquery returns TRUE when a row from the subquery satisfies the conditions of the subquery predicate. It returns FALSE to indicate that no row from the subquery matches the conditions.

For example:

```
SELECT type,
       title_id
  FROM titles
 WHERE price > ALL ( SELECT price
                       FROM titles
                      WHERE advance < 15000 )

QUERY PLAN FOR STATEMENT 1 (at line 1).

    STEP 1
        The type of query is SELECT.

        FROM TABLE
            titles
        Nested iteration.
        Table Scan.
        Forward scan.
        Positioning at start of table.

        Run subquery 1 (at nesting level 1).
        Using I/O Size 16 Kbytes for data pages.
        With LRU Buffer Replacement Strategy for data pages.

NESTING LEVEL 1 SUBQUERIES FOR STATEMENT 1.

  QUERY PLAN FOR SUBQUERY 1 (at nesting level 1 and at line 4).

    Correlated Subquery.
    Subquery under an
ALL predicate.
    STEP 1
        The type of query is SELECT.
        Evaluate
```

```
Ungrouped ANY AGGREGATE.
        FROM TABLE
            titles
        EXISTS TABLE : nested iteration.
        Table Scan.
        Forward scan.
        Positioning at start of table.
        Using I/O Size 16 Kbytes for data pages.
        With LRU Buffer Replacement Strategy for data pages.

  END OF QUERY PLAN FOR SUBQUERY 1.
```

Expression subqueries and the ONCE aggregate

```
Evaluate Ungrouped ONCE AGGREGATE.

Evaluate Grouped ONCE AGGREGATE.
```

Expression subqueries return only a single value. The internal ONCE aggregate checks for the single result required by an expression subquery.

This query returns one row for each title that matches the **like** condition:

```
SELECT title_id,
       ( SELECT city + " " + state
           FROM publishers
          WHERE pub_id = t.pub_id )
  FROM titles t
 WHERE title LIKE "Computer%"

QUERY PLAN FOR STATEMENT 1 (at line 1).

    STEP 1
        The type of query is SELECT.

        FROM TABLE
            titles
            t
        Nested iteration.
        Index : title_ix
        Forward scan.
        Positioning by key.
```

```
        Keys are:
            title  ASC

        Run subquery 1 (at nesting level 1).
        Using I/O Size 16 Kbytes for index leaf pages.
        With LRU Buffer Replacement Strategy for index leaf pages.
        Using I/O Size 2 Kbytes for data pages.
        With LRU Buffer Replacement Strategy for data pages.

NESTING LEVEL 1 SUBQUERIES FOR STATEMENT 1.

  QUERY PLAN FOR SUBQUERY 1 (at nesting level 1 and at line 1).

    Correlated Subquery.
    Subquery under an EXPRESSION predicate.


    STEP 1
        The type of query is SELECT.
        Evaluate Ungrouped ONCE AGGREGATE.
        FROM TABLE
            publishers
        Nested iteration.
        Table Scan.
        Forward scan.
        Positioning at start of table.
        Using I/O Size 2 Kbytes for data pages.
        With LRU Buffer Replacement Strategy for data pages.

  END OF QUERY PLAN FOR SUBQUERY 1.
```

Subqueries with *distinct* and the ONCE-UNIQUE aggregate

```
Evaluate Grouped ONCE-UNIQUE AGGREGATE.

Evaluate Ungrouped ONCE-UNIQUE AGGREGATE.
```

When the subquery includes **distinct**, the ONCE-UNIQUE aggregate indicates that duplicates are being eliminated:

```
SELECT pub_name
  FROM publishers
```

```
WHERE pub_id = ( SELECT DISTINCT titles.pub_id
                   FROM titles
                  WHERE publishers.pub_id = titles.pub_id
                    AND price > $1000 )

QUERY PLAN FOR STATEMENT 1 (at line 1).

    STEP 1
        The type of query is SELECT.

        FROM TABLE
            publishers
        Nested iteration.
        Table Scan.
        Forward scan.
        Positioning at start of table.

        Run subquery 1 (at nesting level 1).
        Using I/O Size 2 Kbytes for data pages.
        With LRU Buffer Replacement Strategy for data pages.

NESTING LEVEL 1 SUBQUERIES FOR STATEMENT 1.

  QUERY PLAN FOR SUBQUERY 1 (at nesting level 1 and at line 3).

    Correlated Subquery.    Subquery under an
EXPRESSION predicate.

    STEP 1
        The type of query is SELECT.
      Evaluate Ungrouped ONCE-UNIQUE AGGREGATE.
        FROM TABLE
            titles
        Nested iteration.
        Index : pub_id_ix
        Forward scan.
        Positioning by key.
        Keys are:
            pub_id  ASC
        Using I/O Size 16 Kbytes for index leaf pages.
        With LRU Buffer Replacement Strategy for index leaf pages.
        Using I/O Size 2 Kbytes for data pages.
        With LRU Buffer Replacement Strategy for data pages.
```

```
END OF QUERY PLAN FOR SUBQUERY 1.
```

Existence join message

```
EXISTS TABLE: nested iteration
```

This message indicates a special form of nested iteration. In a regular nested iteration, the entire table or its index is searched for qualifying values.

In an existence test, the query can stop the search as soon as it finds the first matching value.

The types of subqueries that can produce this message are:

- Subqueries that are flattened to existence joins
- Subqueries that perform existence tests

There are several ways you can write queries that perform an existence test, for example, using **exists**, **in**, or =**any**. These queries are treated as if they were written with an **exists** clause. The following example shows an existence test. This query cannot be flattened because the outer query contains **or**:

```
SELECT au_lname,
       au_fname
  FROM authors
 WHERE EXISTS ( SELECT *
                  FROM publishers
                 WHERE authors.city = publishers.city )
    OR city = "New York"

QUERY PLAN FOR STATEMENT 1 (at line 1).

    STEP 1
        The type of query is SELECT.

        FROM TABLE
            authors
        Nested iteration.
```

```
        Table Scan.
        Forward scan.
        Positioning at start of table.

        Run subquery 1 (at nesting level 1).
        Using I/O Size 16 Kbytes for data pages.
        With LRU Buffer Replacement Strategy for data pages.

NESTING LEVEL 1 SUBQUERIES FOR STATEMENT 1.

  QUERY PLAN FOR SUBQUERY 1 (at nesting level 1 and at line 4).

    Correlated Subquery.
    Subquery under an
EXISTS predicate.

    STEP 1
        The type of query is SELECT.
        Evaluate Ungrouped ANY AGGREGATE.

        FROM TABLE
            publishers

 EXISTS TABLE : nested iteration.        Table Scan.
        Forward scan.
        Positioning at start of table.
        Using I/O Size 2 Kbytes for data pages.
        With LRU Buffer Replacement Strategy for data pages.

END OF QUERY PLAN FOR SUBQUERY 1.
```

Note: You can find out the query plan that ASE chose for a particular query without actually executing the query. You can enable this feature by running: set showplan, noexec on; and then running the query as normal. To turn this feature off run: set showplan, noexec off.

Join Types

Within ASE there are two type of joins. Nested Iteration joins and Sort Merge joins. Here is the showplan output we listed earlier for a **Nested iteration** join:

```
    STEP 1
        The type of query is SELECT.

        FROM TABLE
            table_1
        Nested iteration.
        Table Scan.
        Forward scan.
        Positioning at start of table.
        Using I/O Size 2 Kbytes for data pages.
        With LRU Buffer Replacement Strategy for data pages.
```

Nested Iteration

A nested iteration join, joins the OUTER TABLE to the INNER TABLE by performing a number of lookups equal to the number of records which qualify to be joined.

Nested Iteration joins can be visualized as follows:

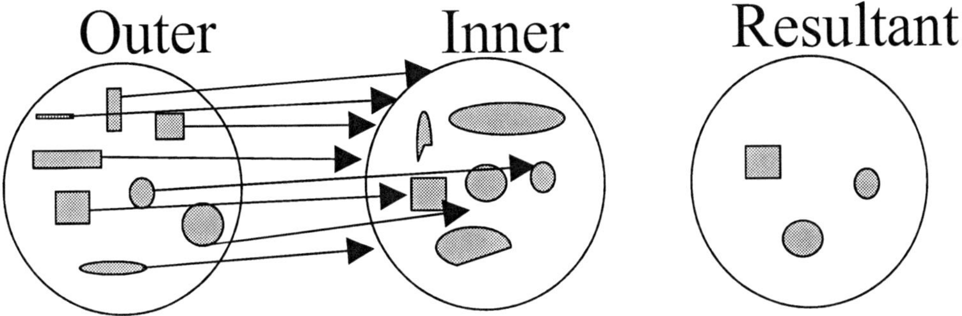

Sort Merge

A sort merge sorts the data in both result sets and scans through *both* result sets comparing values.

We can visualize this as follows:

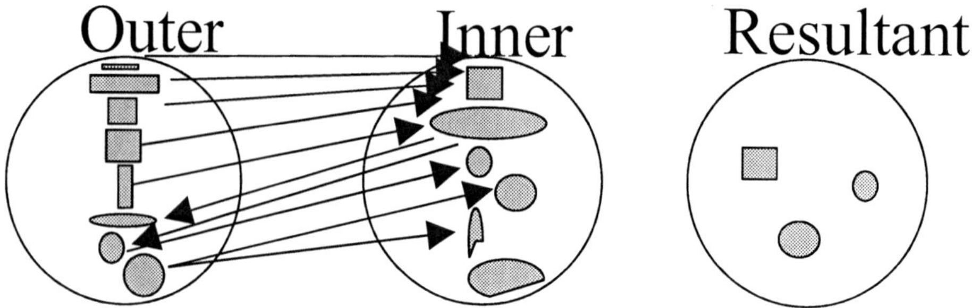

Using FMTONLY

In order to get the query or execution plan for a stored procedure, without actually running the stored procedure, you use the FMTONLY ***SET*** option. If you turn on noexec, you will only receive the showplan of the EXEC statement for the stored procedure call.

Example (NOEXEC ON):

```
/* CREATE A TEST PROCEDURE */
CREATE PROCEDURE test_proc
AS
BEGIN
   PRINT "You made it here"
END
go

/* TURN ON SHOWPLAN AND NOEXEC */
SET SHOWPLAN, NOEXEC ON
go

EXEC test_proc
go
```

```
QUERY PLAN FOR STATEMENT 1 (at line 1).
```

```
    STEP 1
        The type of query is EXECUTE.

/* TURN OFF SHOWPLAN AND NOEXEC */
SET SHOWPLAN, NOEXEC OFF
go
```

As you see *not* really useful for stored procedures.

Example (FMTONLY ON):

```
/* CREATE A TEST PROCEDURE */
CREATE PROCEDURE test_proc
AS
BEGIN
   PRINT "You made it here"
END
go

/* TURN ON SHOWPLAN AND FMTONLY */
SET SHOWPLAN, FMTONLY ON
go

EXEC test_proc
go
```

```
QUERY PLAN FOR STATEMENT 1 (at line 1).


    STEP 1
        The type of query is EXECUTE.


QUERY PLAN FOR STATEMENT 1 (at line 4).


    STEP 1
        The type of query is PRINT.

/* TURN OFF SHOWPLAN AND FMTONLY */
SET SHOWPLAN, FMTONLY OFF
go
```

This displayed the query plan for the PRINT statement. The point here is that when you need the query plan for a stored procedure without executing the procedure, use SHOWPLAN and FMTONLY.

Using STATISTICS IO and TIME

There are many ways to write a query that returns the same result set. Many of those queries will perform differently than their counterparts. To determine which query to execute, one must employ a costing method. You may also need to cost a query when determining the best indexes for a system.

ASE enables you to cost queries by the physical and logical I/O, and the parse and compile time that a query consumes. To enable statistics gathering for I/O and time, execute:

```
SET STATISTICS IO ON
go

SET STATISTICS TIME ON
go
```

Upon enabling these features, any query that is executed will be costed as it is executed. You will be given a summary of the total consumption at the end of the query's execution.

Example:

```
SET STATISTICS IO ON
SET STATISTICS TIME ON
go

SELECT *
  FROM sysobjects
 WHERE 1 = 2
go

Parse and Compile Time 0.
SQL Server cpu time: 0 ms.
Table: sysobjects  scan count 0,  logical reads: (regular=0 apf=0
total=0),
physical reads: (regular=0 apf=0 total=0),  apf IOs used=0
Total writes for this command: 0
```

```
Execution Time 0.
SQL Server cpu time: 0 ms.  SQL Server elapsed time: 6 ms.
 name                             id          uid    type userstat
sysstat
        indexdel schemacnt sysstat2    crdate
        expdate                       deltrig     instrig     updtrig
        seltrig     ckfirst     cache  audflags    objspare
        versionts
 ------------------------------ ----------- ------ ---- --------
-------
       -------- --------- ----------- --------------------------
       -------------------------- ----------- ----------- -----------
       ----------- ----------- ------ ----------- -----------
       --------------------------

(0 rows affected)
```

Evaluating the output:

- The Parse and Compile Time for the query is the total number of CPU ticks used to parse, optimize, and compile the query.
- The SQL Server cpu time shows the CPU time in milliseconds.
- The next fields show how many passes, or scans were performed, and the amount of I/O accumulated during the execution of the query for an object.
- Logical reads show the total amount of 2K pages that were read out of memory for a query. This is broken down into regular reads and asynchronous prefetch reads. You will be mostly concerned with the total number.
- Physical reads show the total number of times that a read off of disk was performed. To determine the number of 2K pages read off of disk multiply the number of reads by the read size. You must enable the showplan output to determine the read size. The physical reads are broken down into regular reads and asynchronous prefetch reads. You will be mostly concerned with the total number.

- The Execution Time is the total number of CPU ticks used to execute the query.
- The Next SQL Server cpu time field shows the total number of CPU ticks used to execute the query converted to milliseconds.
- The SQL Server elapsed time shows the real time taken to execute the query in milliseconds.

Chapter 8. Query Tuning

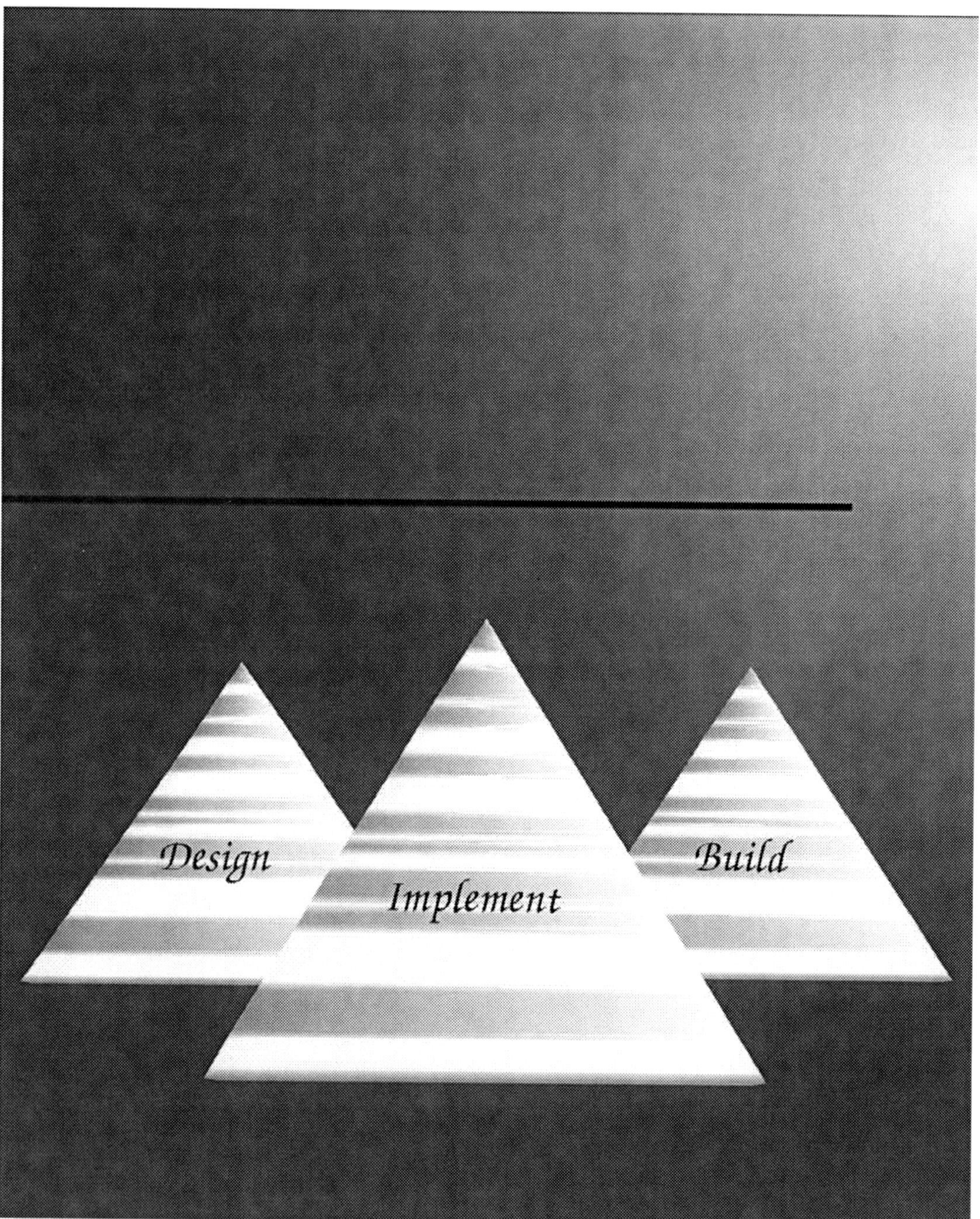
Design
Implement
Build

Chapter 9. Cursors

Declared Cursors

A cursor is symbolic name that is associated with a SELECT statement that enables you to process one row at a time the results returned by the SELECT statement. ASE is very efficient when operating in set-oriented mode and while cursors can have a positive impact on the performance of the server, if used incorrectly cursors can have a negative impact on the system.

What do I need to know before I use a Cursor

You should always declare the cursor's intent: **read only** or **update**. Read-only cursors only display data from a **select** statement and they use shared level locks.

Read-only mode is in effect when:

- You specify **for read only**.
- When the **cursor's** select statement uses **distinct, group by, order by, union,** or aggregate functions.

Update **cursors** can be used to perform positioned updates and deletes. Update mode uses update level locks.

Update mode is in effect when:

1. You specify **for update**.
2. The **select** statement does include **distinct, group by, union,** a subquery, aggregate functions, or the **at isolation read uncommitted** clause.
3. If *column_name_list* is specified, then only those columns are updateable.

NOTE: Always specify the cursor's intent when you declare the cursor since ASE defaults the cursor type to **update** mode if it can.

Where Current of Cursor

When using a cursor specified f**or update** or with a **for update of** list, use the WHERE CURRENT OF ***CURSOR_NAME*** clause of a UPDATE or DELETE command to modify or delete the record which is currently positioned by the CURSOR.

Example:

```
UPDATE table
   SET col01 = "value"
 WHERE CURRENT OF table_cursor
```

Example:

```
DELETE FROM table
 WHERE CURRENT OF table_cursor
```

Optimizer Tips and Index Use

Any index can be used for **read only** cursors. Cursors that are **read only** should produce the same query plan as the **select** statement outside of the cursor. The index requirements for updateable cursors are rather specific, and updateable cursors may produce a different query plan than **read only** cursors.

Update cursors have these indexing requirements:

1. If the cursor is not declared for update, a unique index is preferred over a table scan or a non-unique index. But, a unique index is not required.

2. If the cursor is declared for update **without** a **for update of** list, a unique index is required. An error is raised if no unique index exists.

3. If the cursor is declared for update with a **for update of** list, then only a unique index **without** any columns from the list can be chosen. An error is raised if no unique index qualifies.

When might I use a Cursor

A cursor may be used when it is necessary to manipulate data at the row level for a query that returns multiple rows. If you are performing multiple updates, deletes, and/or inserts to a table by a join to another table(s), and the table is used in the system extensively and requires high throughput, then I would recommend that you declare a **read only** cursor on the join and do your updates, deletes, and/or inserts at the row level from within the cursor. This will cause ASE to free up the locks after every update, delete, and/or insert.

NOTE: Performing updates, deletes, and/or inserts to a table using a set-oriented logic is almost always faster than using a cursor. However, if a large update, insert, and/or delete have to be performed on a production table, the benefit of less lock contention could outweigh the local cost of the cursor.

Phantoms and Cursors

ASE requires a unique index when using a cursor in a update mode. This is to prevent record from getting updated more than one time. A record that gets updated more than once is known as a phantom.

Now, a phantom could occur if a record were updated using a cursor scanning through an index which contained a column to be updated – that is, if the update positioned data in the index at a point further down the scan sequence.

This problem appears most often with All Pages Locked tables (i.e. normal tables). In an APL table, if you update a row and the row moves to another page (either through the change of values in a clustered index, or for a heap table if the new row size is greater than the available space on a page), then the access method (either table scan or index scan) just might encounter that very same row again. This could cause the a row to be viewed and updated twice (or more). This is seen as a very bad condition. Remember, cursors were first introduced in SQL Server 10 in which the only locking scheme was APL, and in fact there was no formal name for it -- it was just the way things were.

In an attempt **not** to have a row updated twice, the optimizer tries to find a scanning order that won't find the row more than once. *If there is no "for update" or "for read only" clause on cursor, then the optimizer assumes the more conservative "for update".* In this case, a unique index is given preference over non-unique indexes or table scans. If there is a "for update" clause, then a unique index is required. If there is a "for update of <column_list>" clause, then a "safe" index is required.

A safe index is unique and is absent of any columns in the <column_list>. Thus, when an update occurs, the row won't move within the scanning order of the index. Hence, the cursor won't have the potential of finding the row more than once.

Many performance problems originate in the fact that programmers writing the DECLARE CURSOR code don't know these rules (nor should they necessarily be required). Now, each table usually has a unique index: its primary key column(s).

Consider a cursor such as:

```
DECLARE c
 CURSOR
    FOR
 SELECT trans_num,
        entry_user,
        entry_date_time,
        trans_date
   FROM syctrans
  WHERE trans_date BETWEEN @low_trans_date and @high_trans_date
```

The optimizer, seeing no "FOR READ ONLY" clause, assumes "FOR UPDATE". The optimizer will use a unique index, probably the one with the least number of columns to minimize (but not necessarily prevent) the chance a row being updated more than once.

Now, there is a non-unique index on trans_date, but that will be given lower preference by the optimizer. Most tables usually just have one unique index, (i.e. the primary key). Thus, the optimizer will probably use the far less efficient unique index on the primary key of (trans_num, sub_num, entry_locale), in order to guarantee the scanning order of the rows (again so that any row that might be updated probably won't be updated more than once).

The unique index on (trans_num, sub_num, entry_locale) will be scanned from its beginning to its end. Since this is a clustered index, this amounts to a table scan (i.e. thirteen million records). If it was a non-clustered index, it would generate *much* more I/O than the table scan.

Now if the query introduces joins, then the optimization path gets even worse as each table that is scanned must be done so in the same manner. Join paths become very suboptimal and I/O increases to the point where cursor performance is perceived as extremely slow.

For various reasons, ASE DOL (datapages or datarows) tables and indexes that were introduced in ASE 11.9.2 do not suffer from the optimizer restrictions on APL tables, so the optimizer won't rule out any indexes during optimization. So with the advent of 64-bit ASE there are fewer reasons *not* to put all the tables in DOL mode.

Using Cursors

In order to use a cursor, you must DECLARE, OPEN, FETCH, LOOP, CLOSE, and DEALLOCATE the cursor.

Declaring a Cursor

In order to use a CURSOR, you must first declare it. This operation consists of giving the cursor a name and result set to browse. Don't forget to specify the intent of a cursor. That is, FOR READ ONLY, FOR UPDATE, or FOR UPDATE OF columns.

```
DECLARE name_of_cursor
 CURSOR
    FOR
 SELECT <column_1>,
        <column_2>,
   FROM <tables>
  WHERE <conditions>
< FOR READ ONLY | FOR UPDATE <OF column_list>>
```

Opening a Cursor

To use a declared cursor you must first open it. This operation actually builds the resultant set "processes the select statement", and prepares the cursors record pointer. Below is the syntax for opening a cursor.

```
OPEN name_of_cursor
```

Fetching Records

Once a CURSOR has been opened, you need to FETCH records. This means that you need to examine the contents of the record set. This is done through the FETCH command, which is used to store the contents of the "NEXT" record into the specified variables. Below is the syntax for fetching from an open cursor.

```
FETCH name_of_cursor
 INTO variable_list
```

Processing a Cursor

The global variable @@SQLSTATUS is used to process the result set of a cursor using a WHILE loop and the FETCH statement. The @@SQLSTATUS variable has the following return states:

- 0, The last FETCH succeeded.
- 1, The last FETCH failed, check @@ERROR for more information.
- 2, There is no more data to process.

Closing a Cursor

When you are finished processing the result set of cursor, you should close the cursor. This involves removing the cursor result set and the record pointer. At this stage, you could reopen the cursor and process the new result set that is built by the open. Below is the syntax for the closing a cursor.

```
CLOSE name_of_cursor
```

Deallocating a Cursor

Deallocating the cursor frees up all resources associated with the cursor. This includes the cursor declaration and the cursor name. Thus, after a cursor is deallocated it must be redeclared to be used again. You should plan to always to deallocate a cursor once you are completely finished with it. This will release system resources sooner and yield better performance of the system as a whole. Below is the syntax for deallocating cursor.

```
DEALLOCATE
    CURSOR name_of_cursor
```

Using a FOR READ ONLY cursor in a stored procedure

Example:

```
DECLARE @table_cursor_state INTEGER
DECLARE @column01 INTEGER
DECLARE @column02 CHAR(100)

DECLARE table_cursor
    FOR
 SELECT column01,
        column02
   FROM table
  WHERE column03 = "value"
FOR READ ONLY

OPEN table_cursor

FETCH table_cursor
 INTO @column01,
      @column02

SELECT @table_cursor_state = @@SQLSTATE

WHILE ( @table_cursor_state = 0 )
BEGIN
   UPDATE table2
      SET column02 = @column02
     FROM table2
    WHERE column01 = @column01

   FETCH table_cursor
    INTO @column01,
         @column02

   SELECT @table_cursor_state = @@SQLSTATE
END

CLOSE table_cursor

DEALLOCATE
    CURSOR table_cursor
```

Using a FOR UPDATE cursor in a stored procedure

Example:

```
DECLARE @table_cursor_state INTEGER
DECLARE @column01 INTEGER
DECLARE @column02 CHAR(100)

DECLARE table_cursor
    FOR
 SELECT column01,
        column02
   FROM table
  WHERE column03 = "value"
FOR UPDATE

OPEN table_cursor

FETCH table_cursor
 INTO @column01,
      @column02

SELECT @table_cursor_state = @@SQLSTATE

WHILE ( @table_cursor_state = 0 )
BEGIN
   UPDATE table
      SET column03 = @column01 * 100
    WHERE CURRENT OF table_cursor

   FETCH table_cursor
    INTO @column01,
         @column02

   SELECT @table_cursor_state = @@SQLSTATE
END

CLOSE table_cursor

DEALLOCATE
    CURSOR table_cursor
```

Using a FOR UPDATE OF cursor in a stored procedure

Example:

```
DECLARE @table_cursor_state INTEGER
DECLARE @column01 INTEGER
DECLARE @column02 CHAR(100)

DECLARE table_cursor
    FOR
 SELECT column01,
        column02
   FROM table
  WHERE column03 = "value"
FOR UPDATE OF column03

OPEN table_cursor

FETCH table_cursor
 INTO @column01,
      @column02

SELECT @table_cursor_state = @@SQLSTATE

WHILE ( @table_cursor_state = 0 )
BEGIN
   UPDATE table
      SET column03 = @column01 * 100
    WHERE CURRENT OF table_cursor

   FETCH table_cursor
    INTO @column01,
         @column02

   SELECT @table_cursor_state = @@SQLSTATE
END

CLOSE table_cursor

DEALLOCATE
    CURSOR table_cursor
```

Using a FOR READ ONLY cursor in a Dynamic SQL batch.

Example:

```
DECLARE table_cursor
    FOR
 SELECT column01,
        column02
   FROM table
  WHERE column03 = "value"
FOR READ ONLY
go
DECLARE @table_cursor_state INTEGER
DECLARE @column01 INTEGER
DECLARE @column02 CHAR(100)

OPEN table_cursor

FETCH table_cursor
 INTO @column01,
      @column02

SELECT @table_cursor_state = @@SQLSTATE

WHILE ( @table_cursor_state = 0 )
BEGIN
   UPDATE table2
      SET column02 = @column02
     FROM table2
    WHERE column01 = @column01

   FETCH table_cursor
    INTO @column01,
         @column02

   SELECT @table_cursor_state = @@SQLSTATE
END

CLOSE table_cursor

DEALLOCATE
    CURSOR table_cursor
go
```

Using a FOR UPDATE cursor in a Dynamic SQL batch.

Example:

```
DECLARE table_cursor
    FOR
 SELECT column01,
        column02
   FROM table
  WHERE column03 = "value"
FOR UPDATE
go
DECLARE @table_cursor_state INTEGER
DECLARE @column01 INTEGER
DECLARE @column02 CHAR(100)

OPEN table_cursor

FETCH table_cursor
 INTO @column01,
      @column02

SELECT @table_cursor_state = @@SQLSTATE

WHILE ( @table_cursor_state = 0 )
BEGIN
   UPDATE table
      SET column03 = @column01 * 100
    WHERE CURRENT OF table_cursor

   FETCH table_cursor
    INTO @column01,
         @column02

   SELECT @table_cursor_state = @@SQLSTATE
END

CLOSE table_cursor

DEALLOCATE
    CURSOR table_cursor
go
```

Using a FOR UPDATE OF cursor in a Dynamic SQL batch.
Example:

```
DECLARE table_cursor
    FOR
 SELECT column01,
        column02
   FROM table
  WHERE column03 = "value"
FOR UPDATE OF column03
go
DECLARE @table_cursor_state INTEGER
DECLARE @column01 INTEGER
DECLARE @column02 CHAR(100)

OPEN table_cursor

FETCH table_cursor
 INTO @column01,
      @column02

SELECT @table_cursor_state = @@SQLSTATE

WHILE ( @table_cursor_state = 0 )
BEGIN
   UPDATE table
      SET column03 = @column01 * 100
    WHERE CURRENT OF table_cursor

   FETCH table_cursor
    INTO @column01,
         @column02

   SELECT @table_cursor_state = @@SQLSTATE
END

CLOSE table_cursor

DEALLOCATE
    CURSOR table_cursor
go
```

Artificial Cursors

An artificial cursor can yield tremendous throughput increases as compared with traditional cursors. This is because artificial cursors operate using set-level logic and thus can be run using many records at once, instead of just a record at a time.

Using a simple while loop Instead of a Cursor

It has been our experience that a cursor is **much slower** than doing an iteration using a while loop. What follows is an example of a while loop which uses a unique index on one column. This can often times replace a cursor.

Example:

```
DECLARE @KEY DATATYPE

DECLARE @MAX_KEY DATATYPE

SELECT @KEY = MIN(KEY)
  FROM table

SELECT @MAX_KEY = MAX(KEY)
  FROM table

WHILE ( @KEY <= @MAX_KEY )
BEGIN
   /* PERFORM MODIFICATIONS IN THIS SECTION */

   /* BREAK IF LAST RECORD TO PREVENT INFINITE LOOP */
   IF ( @KEY = @MAX_KEY )
   BEGIN
      BREAK
   END

  /* GET NEXT KEY */
  SELECT @KEY = MIN(KEY)
    FROM table
   WHERE KEY > @KEY
END
```

Batch Loads, Updates, Deletes, Inserts

Suppose you need to merge a dataset from another system into a system or for that matter, from some source to another source.

Example:

```
/* Create our production table to be loaded in this example */
CREATE
 TABLE test_table(
       column01 INTEGER NOT NULL,
       column02 CHAR(50) NOT NULL,
       CONSTRAINT ix01_test_table
       PRIMARY KEY CLUSTERED ( column01 )
)
LOCK DATAROWS
go


/* Create view to access production table through primary key only */
CREATE
  VIEW vw_ix01_test_table
AS
SELECT column01,
       column02
  FROM test_table (INDEX ix01_test_table)
go


/* Create our batch load table */
CREATE
 TABLE batch_ld(
       column01 INTEGER NOT NULL,
       column02 CHAR(50) NOT NULL,
       column03 CHAR(1) NOT NULL,
       CONSTRAINT ix01_batch_ld
       PRIMARY KEY CLUSTERED (column01)
)
LOCK ALLPAGES
go


/* Create view to access batch load table through primary key only */
CREATE
```

```
  VIEW vw_ix01_batch_ld
AS
SELECT column01,
       column02,
       column03
  FROM batch_ld (INDEX ix01_batch_ld)
go


/* Create our batch load process table */
CREATE
 TABLE batch_ld_prc(
       column01 INTEGER NOT NULL,
       column02 CHAR(50) NOT NULL,
       column03 CHAR(1) NOT NULL
)
LOCK ALLPAGES
go


/* Create view to access batch load process table */
/* through primary key only */
CREATE
  VIEW vw_ix01_batch_ld_prc
AS
SELECT column01,
       column02,
       column03
  FROM batch_ld_prc (INDEX 0)
go


/* Assume batch_ld table has been loaded from bcp */
/* use the script below to the data into the database */
DECLARE @SET_RW_CNT INTEGER
DECLARE @RW_CNT INTEGER

/* PROCESS 100 RECORDS AT A TIME */

/* Note: this value may greatly affect */
/* the throughput of the batch job */
/* as well as the response times of the */
/* applications */
```

```
/* Warning: The higher the value of @@SET_ROW_CNT */
/* the more locks which will be held on tables */
/* and the longer they will be held */
SELECT @SET_RW_CNT =  100

/* ESTABLISH STATEMENT MAXIMUM AFFECTED ROWS */
SET ROWCOUNT @SET_RW_CNT

/* truncate the batch_ld_prc table */
TRUNCATE TABLE vw_ix01_batch_prc

/* Preload the batch_ld_prc table */
INSERT
  INTO vw_ix01_batch_ld_prc(
       column01,
       column02,
       column03
)
SELECT ld.column01,
       ld.column02,
       ld.column03
  FROM vw_ix01_batch_ld ld

SELECT @RW_CNT = @@ROWCOUNT

WHILE ( @RW_CNT > 0 )
BEGIN
   /* UPDATE ROWS FLAGGED TO BE UPDATED OR INSERTED */
   UPDATE vw_ix01_test_table
      SET column02 = prc.column02
     FROM vw_ix01_test_table tt,
          vw_ix01_batch_ld_prc prc
    WHERE tt.column01 = prc.column01
      AND prc.column03 IN ("I", "U")

   /* INSERT ROWS FLAGGED TO BE UPDATED OR INSERTED */
   INSERT
     INTO vw_ix01_test_table(
          column01,
          column02
   )
   SELECT prc.column01,
          prc.column02
     FROM vw_ix01_batch_ld_prc prc
```

```
    WHERE prc.column03 IN ("I", "U")
      AND NOT EXISTS ( SELECT 1
                         FROM vw_ix01_test_table tt
                        WHERE tt.column01 = prc.column01 )

   /* FINALLY DELETE ROWS FLAGGED TO BE DELETED */
   DELETE vw_ix01_test_table
     FROM vw_ix01_test_table tt,
          vw_ix01_batch_ld_prc prc
    WHERE tt.column01 = prc.column01
      AND prc.column03 IN ("D")

   /* DELETE RECORDS WHICH HAVE BEEN PROCESSED */
   DELETE vw_ix01_batch_ld
     FROM vw_ix01_batch_ld ld,
          vw_ix01_batch_ld prc
    WHERE ld.column01 = prc.column01

   TRUNCATE TABLE vw_ix01_batch_ld_prc

   /* Get Next Set of Records to Process */
   INSERT
     INTO vw_ix01_batch_ld_prc(
          column01,
          column02,
          column03
   )
   SELECT ld.column01,
          ld.column02,
          ld.column03
     FROM vw_ix01_batch_ld ld

   SELECT @RW_CNT = @@ROWCOUNT
END
go
```

Performance Benefits

By switching from cursors to artificial cursors, we decreased the run time of several batch jobs from over 6 hours to under 30 minutes. In addition, the overall CPU load on the system was much lighter, because cursors require considerably more processing than do set-level statements.

If you have not considered using artificial cursors, maybe you should after reading this section.

Unnecessary use of #tables and Cursors

In the example that follows, the developer has chosen #tables and cursors for the majority of the work. This is really not necessary as you can rewrite this stored procedure avoiding the #tables and cursors all together!

```
CREATE PROCEDURE bc_proc_carryID_for_muiltileg(
   @leg_id INT,
   @debug_flag INT = 0)
AS
BEGIN
   DECLARE @carry_num INT
   DECLARE @is_spot INT
   DECLARE @leg_num INT
   DECLARE @ver_num INT

-- GET THE CARRY NUM
   SELECT @carry_num = system_deal_num
     FROM bc_trade_leg_header
    WHERE leg_id = @leg_id

-- GRAB LEG DATE & POSITION INFO
   SELECT bc_trade_leg_data.system_ref,
          bc_trade_leg_data.system_deal_num,
          bc_trade_leg_data.version_num,
          bc_trade_leg_data.leg_num,
          bc_trade_leg_data.field_tag,
          bc_trade_leg_data.field_value
     INTO #tmp_details
     FROM bc_trade_leg_data
    WHERE system_deal_num = @carry_num
      AND (field_tag = 'volume'
        OR field_tag = 'valueDate')

-- GET VERSION FOR EACH LEG (MAY BE DIFFERENT FROM ONE LEG TO ANOTHER)
   SELECT DISTINCT
          leg_num,
          MAX(version_num) AS ver_num
     INTO #tmp_legmaxversion
     FROM bc_trade_leg_header
    WHERE system_deal_num = @carry_num
    GROUP
       BY leg_num
```

```
-- GET ONLY RELEVANT VERSION FOR EACH LEG
-- CREATE TEMP TABLE TO HOLD ONLY THE RELEVANT VERSION/LEG
COMBINATIONS
   CREATE TABLE #tmp_dets_rel(
      system_ref      INT NOT NULL,
      system_deal_num INT NOT NULL,
      version_num     INT NOT NULL,
      leg_num         INT NOT NULL,
      field_tag       VARCHAR(25) NOT NULL,
      field_value     VARCHAR(50) NULL)

-- LOOP VERSION/LEG COMBOS AND COPY DATA FROM ONE TABLE TO ANOTHER
   DECLARE leg_version_cursor
    CURSOR
       FOR
    SELECT #tmp_legmaxversion.leg_num,
           #tmp_legmaxversion.ver_num
      FROM #tmp_legmaxversion

   OPEN leg_version_cursor

   FETCH leg_version_cursor
    INTO @leg_num,
         @ver_num

   WHILE ( @@SQLSTATUS = 0 )
   BEGIN
      INSERT
        INTO #tmp_dets_rel
      SELECT #tmp_details.system_ref,
             #tmp_details.system_deal_num,
             #tmp_details.version_num,
             #tmp_details.leg_num,
             #tmp_details.field_tag,
             #tmp_details.field_value
        FROM #tmp_details
       WHERE leg_num = @leg_num
         AND version_num = @ver_num

      FETCH leg_version_cursor
       INTO @leg_num,
            @ver_num
   END
```

```
   CLOSE leg_version_cursor

   DEALLOCATE
       CURSOR leg_version_cursor

-- SELECT JUST THE POSITION INFO
   SELECT #tmp_dets_rel.system_ref,
          #tmp_dets_rel.system_deal_num,
          #tmp_dets_rel.version_num,
          #tmp_dets_rel.leg_num,
          #tmp_dets_rel.field_tag,
          #tmp_dets_rel.field_value
     INTO #tmp_position
     FROM #tmp_dets_rel
    WHERE field_tag = 'volume'

-- CHECK ALL THE LEG DATES AREN'T SAME (I.E. IT'S NOT A SPOT TRADE)
   SELECT @is_spot = COUNT(DISTINCT field_value)
     FROM #tmp_dets_rel
    WHERE field_tag = 'valueDate'

   IF @is_spot <> 1
      SELECT @is_spot = 0

-- GATHER FINAL DATA TO PASS BACK TO THE AVS SCRIPT
   SELECT DISTINCT
          @is_spot as is_spot,
          COUNT(*) AS leg_count,
          system_deal_num AS carry_num,
          SUM(CONVERT(FLOAT, field_value)) AS nett_vol
     FROM #tmp_position
END
go
```

Achieving the same without #tables and CURSOR

Now, the same stored procedure has been revised and revisited, eliminating the use of #tables. More importantly, it avoids using a cursor. Thus, resulting in a much more efficient code.

```
CREATE PROCEDURE bc_proc_carryID_for_muiltileg(
   @leg_id INT,
   @debug_flag INT = 0)
AS
BEGIN
   DECLARE @is_spot INT

-- CHECK ALL THE LEG DATES AREN'T SAME (I.E. IT'S NOT A SPOT TRADE)
   SELECT @is_spot = COUNT(DISTINCT btld.field_value)
     FROM bc_trade_leg_data btld,
          bc_trade_leg_header btlh
    WHERE btld.system_deal_num = btlh.system_deal_num
      AND btld.field_tag = 'valueDate'
      AND btlh.leg_id = @leg_id
      AND btld.version_num = ( SELECT MAX(btld2.version_num)
                                 FROM bc_trade_leg_data btld2
                                WHERE btld2.leg_num = btld.leg_num )

   IF @is_spot <> 1
      SELECT @is_spot = 0

-- GATHER FINAL DATA TO PASS BACK TO THE AVS SCRIPT
   SELECT @is_spot AS is_spot,
          COUNT(*) AS leg_count,
          btld.system_deal_num AS carry_num,
          SUM(CONVERT(FLOAT, btld.field_value)) AS nett_vol
     FROM bc_trade_leg_data btld,
          bc_trade_leg_header btlh
    WHERE btld.system_deal_num = btlh.system_deal_num
      AND btld.field_tag = 'volume'
      AND btlh.leg_id = @leg_id
      AND btld.version_num = ( SELECT MAX(btld2.version_num)
                                 FROM bc_trade_leg_data btld2
                                WHERE btld2.leg_num = btld.leg_num )
    GROUP
       BY btld.system_deal_num
END
```

```
go
```

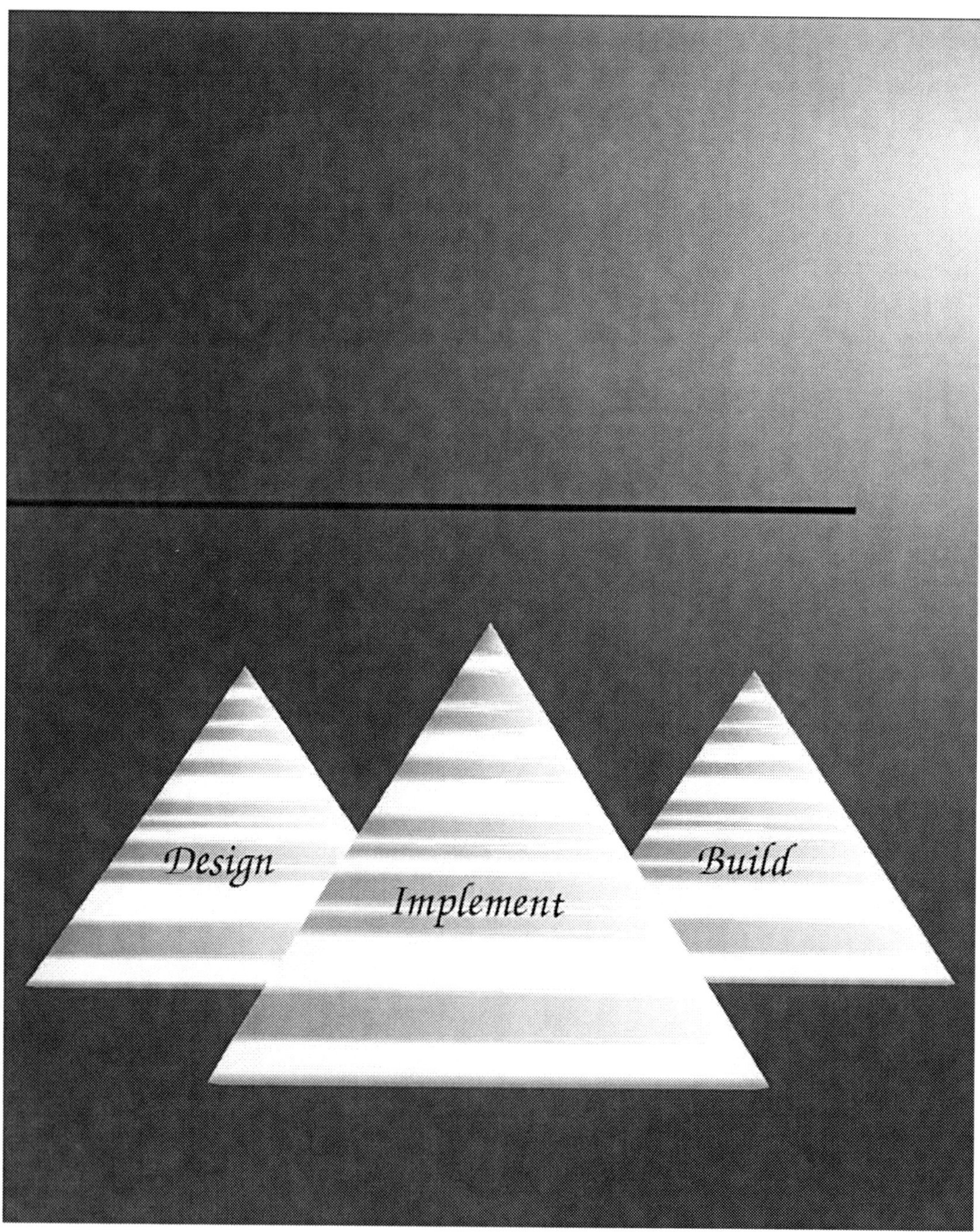
Design
Implement
Build

Chapter 10. Joining Data

Set Theory

Set theory is a branch of mathematics which defines sets (thought of a grouping of things) and operations on them. In a relational database, a ***dataset*** is composed of the data in a table and its columns.

Example:

```
CREATE
 TABLE test_table(
       column01 INT NOT NULL,
       column02 INT NOT NULL,
 CONSTRAINT ix01_test_table
    PRIMARY KEY NONCLUSTERED ( column01 )
)
go

INSERT
  INTO test_table(
       column01,
       column02
)
SELECT 1,
       1
go
```

The test_table ***dataset***:

```
SELECT column01,
       column02
  FROM test_table
go
-----------------------------------------------------------------------
1        1
```

Let's give an overview of some basic set properties. Let's define three sets A, B, and C as follows:

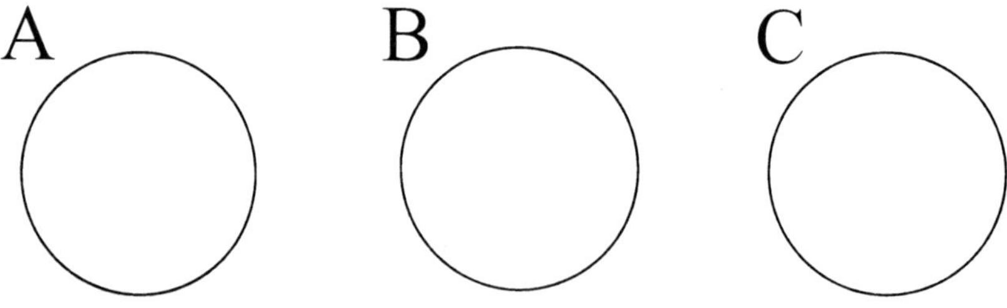

JOINT SETS

Joint sets are sets that share elements. Joint sets can be visualized as follows:

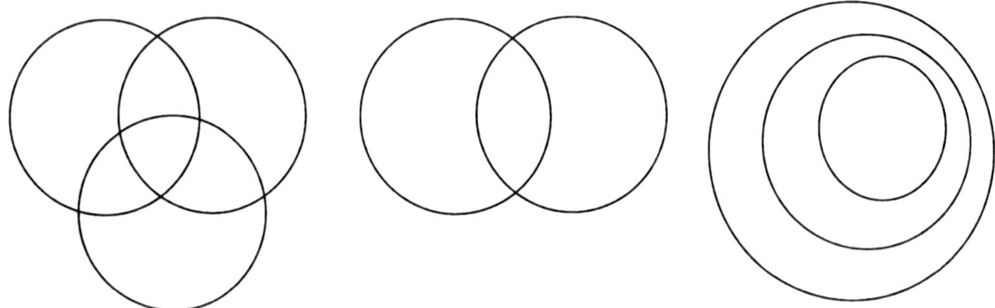

DISJOINT SETS

Disjoint sets are sets that have no shared elements. Disjoint sets can be visualized as follows:

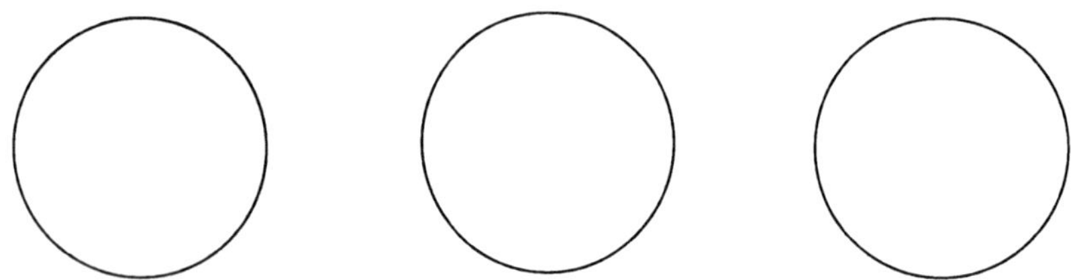

The following SET operations are discussed in more detail in the section on ***Joins***. First, though, we will review how basic set operations are carried out for datasets.

SET Unions

A set union of datasets is the ***dataset*** which arises from the combining of all ***datasets***. In addition, a set union can include the overlaps once or twice from a pair of ***datasets*** which are joint. These type of unions are typically carried out by outer joins, a union, or a union all.

SET Intersections

A set intersection of datasets is their *overlap*: it consists of those elements that exist in all of the datasets. Or simply put, an element which exists in one ***dataset*** must exist in the other ***dataset***. Intersections are typically carried out by equijoins (aka natural joins or even inner joins), an IN, and/or an EXISTS.

SET Subtractions

A set subtraction is the removal of one ***dataset*** from a second dataset. Subtractions are typically carried out by a NOT IN and/or a NOT EXISTS.

SET Multiplications

A notion of set multiplication for datasets is the ***cartesian product***. The cartesian product of a given collection of datasets "explodes" to a dataset consisting of all possible combinations of elements from all datasets. They are typically creating by forming joins with no conditions.

Joins

A join is an operation which combines elements of two or more ***datasets*** by specifying which combinations (within the cartesian product) are valid. In ASE, we do this by specifying conditions on the columns or fields of the ***datasets*** row by row, and linking conditions between ***datasets*** row by row. A join than displays the combined results as a new ***dataset***.

Note: In ASE, the tables or views specified in the join can be in the same database or in different databases.

Example:

```
SET ROWCOUNT 1

SELECT title,
       pub_name,
       advance
  FROM titles,
       publishers
 WHERE titles.pub_id = publishers.pub_id

SET ROWCOUNT 0
go
You Can Combat Computer Stress!      New Age Books        10,125.00
```

A join may be thought of as the product of two or more sets, pivoted about some key or column and a comparison operation. The results that are returned or that are linked are those that match the search criteria specified. The results are those rows or records that are duplicated or joint on the join criteria.

You can embed a join in a select, update, insert, delete, or subquery. Other search conditions and clauses may follow the join conditions.

Joins use the following syntax:

```
start of SELECT, UPDATE, INSERT, DELETE, or subquery
  FROM {table_list | view_list}
 WHERE [NOT]
    [table_name. | view_name.]column_name
                   join_operator
    [table_name. | view_name.]column_name
[{AND | OR} [NOT]
    [table_name.|view_name.]column_name
                  join_operator
    [table_name.|view_name.]column_name]...
End of SELECT, UPDATE, INSERT, DELETE, or subquery
```

Joins and the Relational Model

The join operation is the hallmark of the relational model of database management. More than any other feature, the join distinguishes relational database management systems from other types of database management systems.

In a relational database management system, relationships among data values are left unstated in the definition of a database. They become explicit when the data is manipulated when you query the database, not when you create it. You can ask any question that comes to mind about the data stored in the database, regardless of what was intended when the database was created.

According to the rules of good database design, called normalization rules, each table should describe one kind of entity – a person, place, event, or thing. That is why, when you want to compare information about two or more kinds of entities, you need the join operation. Relationships among data stored in different tables are discovered by joining them.

A corollary of this rule is that the join operation gives you unlimited flexibility in adding new kinds of data to your database. You can always create a new table that contains data about a different kind of entity. If the new table has a field with values similar to those in some field of an existing table or tables, it can be linked to those other tables by joining.

How Joins Are Processed

Conceptually speaking, the first step in processing a join is to form the Cartesian product of the tables with all the possible combinations of the rows from each of the tables. The number of rows in a Cartesian product of two tables is equal to the number of rows in the first table, multiplied by the number of rows in the second table.

To illustrate joins, we'll consider the sample database included with ASE. The Cartesian product of the authors table and the publishers table is 69 (23 authors multiplied by 3 publishers). You can have a look at a Cartesian product with any query that includes columns from more than one table in the SELECT list, more than one table in the FROM clause, and no WHERE clause. For example, if you omit the WHERE clause on a join between the authors and publishers table, ASE combines each of the 23 authors with each of the 3 publishers, and returns all 69 rows.

This Cartesian product does not contain any particularly useful information. In fact, it is downright misleading, because it implies that every author in the database has a relationship with every publisher in the database, which is not true at all.

That is why you must include a WHERE clause in the join, which specifies the columns to be matched and the basis on which to match them. It may also include other restrictions. Once ASE forms the Cartesian product, it eliminates the rows that do not satisfy the join by using the conditions in the WHERE clause.

Equijoins and Natural Joins

Joins based on equality (=) are called equijoins. Equijoins compare the values in the columns being joined for equality and then includes all the columns in the tables being joined in the results.

Example:

```
SELECT *
  FROM authors,
       publishers
WHERE authors.city = publishers.city
```

In the results of that statement, the city column appears twice. By definition, the results of an equijoin contain two identical columns. Because there is usually no point in repeating the same information, one of these columns can be eliminated by restating the query. The result is called a natural join. The query that results in the natural join of publishers and authors on the city column is:

```
SELECT publishers.pub_id,
       publishers.pub_name,
       publishers.state,
       authors.*
  FROM publishers,
       authors
 WHERE publishers.city = authors.city
```

The column publishers.city does not appear in the results.

Another example of a natural join is:

```
SELECT au_fname,
       au_lname,
       pub_name
  FROM authors,
       publishers
 WHERE authors.city = publishers.city
```

You can use more than one join operator to join more than two tables or to join more than two pairs of columns. These "join expressions" are usually connected with "AND", although "OR" is also legal.

The following are two examples of joins connected by "AND". The first lists information about books (type of book, author, and title), ordered by book type. Books with more than one author have multiple listings, one for each author.

```
SELECT type,
       au_lname,
       au_fname,
       title
  FROM authors,
       titles,
       titleauthor
 WHERE authors.au_id = titleauthor.au_id
   AND titles.title_id = titleauthor.title_id
 ORDER
    BY type
```

The second finds the names of authors and publishers that are located in the same city and state:

```
SELECT au_fname,
       au_lname,
       pub_name
  FROM authors,
       publishers
 WHERE authors.city = publishers.city
   AND authors.state = publishers.state
```

Joins with Additional Conditions

The where clause of a join query can include selection criteria as well as the join condition. For example, to retrieve the names and publishers of all the books for which advances of more than $7500 were paid (that is $ as in currency), the statement is:

```
SELECT title,
       pub_name,
       advance
  FROM titles,
       publishers
 WHERE titles.pub_id = publishers.pub_id
   AND advance > $7500
```

```
go
You Can Combat Computer Stress!   New Age Books          10,125.00
The Gourmet Microwave             Binnet & Hardley       15,000.00
Secrets of Silicon Valley         Algodata Infosystems    8,000.00
Sushi, Anyone?                    Binnet & Hardley        8,000.00
```

The columns being joined (pub_id from titles and publishers) do not need to appear in the select list and, therefore, do not show up in the results.

You can include as many selection criteria as you want in a join statement. The order of the selection criteria and the join condition is not important.

Much of the previous material on joins was taken from Chapter 4 of the ASE 12.5 Transact-SQL User's Guide.

Troubleshooting Joins

Joining N tables will result in N-1 Join clauses

- Join columns should have matching data types.
- Join columns should have clustered indexes or non-clustered indexes on them with Index Page Cluster Ratio (IPCR) > 0.9. This value can be obtained through the function DERIVED_STAT('table_name', 'index_name','ipcr')
- Provide a valid SARG on the outer or driving table, otherwise expect a table scan!
- Join queries 8 tables at the time. Use #tables for intermediate results. This makes queries more consistent and your code more readable.

Subqueries

Subqueries, also called inner queries, appear within a WHERE or HAVING clause of another SQL statement or in the SELECT list of a statement. You can use subqueries to handle query requests that are expressed as the results of other queries. A statement that includes a subquery operates on rows from one table, based on its evaluation of the subquery's select list, which can refer to the same table as the outer query, or to a different table. In T-SQL, a subquery can also be used almost anywhere an expression is allowed, if the subquery returns a single value. A case expression can also include a subquery.

SELECT statements that contain one or more subqueries are sometimes called nested queries or nested SELECT statements. The practice of nesting one SELECT statement inside another is one reason for the word "structured" in "Structured Query Language."

Many SQL statements that include a subquery as joins can be formulated as joins. Other statements can be expressed only using subqueries. Some people prefer subqueries to alternative formulations, because they find subqueries easier to understand. Other SQL users avoid subqueries whenever possible. You can choose whichever formulation you prefer. (ASE converts some subqueries into joins before processing them.)

The result of a subquery that returns no values is NULL. If a subquery returns NULL, the query did not retrieve any information.

Subquery Syntax

Always enclose the SELECT statement of a subquery in parentheses. The subquery's SELECT statement has a SELECT syntax that is somewhat restricted, as shown by its syntax:

```
(SELECT [ALL | DISTINCT ] subquery_select_list
  [FROM  [[database.]owner.]{table_name |view_name}
 [({INDEX index_name | PREFETCH SIZE |[LRU|MRU]})]}
        [HOLDLOCK | NOHOLDLOCK] [SHARED]
     [,[[database.]owner.]{table_name |view_name}
 [({INDEX index_name | PREFETCH SIZE |[LRU|MRU]})]}
        [HOLDLOCK | NOHOLDLOCK] [SHARED]]... ]
 [WHERE search_conditions]
 [GROUP
     BY aggregate_free_expression [,
        aggregate_free_expression]... ]
[HAVING search_conditions])
```

Subquery Restrictions

A subquery is subject to the following restrictions:

- The subquery SELECT list must consist of only one column name, except in the exists subquery, in which case the asterisk (*) is usually used in place of the single column name. Do not specify more than one column name. Be sure to qualify column names with table or view names if there is ambiguity about the table or view to which they belong.

- Subqueries can be nested inside the WHERE or HAVING clause of an outer SELECT, INSERT, UPDATE, or DELETE statement, inside another subquery, or in a SELECT list. Alternatively, you can write many statements that contain subqueries as joins; ASE processes such statements as joins.

- In T-SQL, a subquery can appear almost anywhere an expression can be used, if it returns a single value.

- You cannot use subqueries in an ORDER BY, GROUP BY, or COMPUTE list.

- You cannot include a FOR BROWSE clause or a UNION in a subquery.

- The SELECT list of an inner subquery introduced with a comparison operator can include only one expression or column name, and the subquery must return a single value. The column you name in the WHERE clause of the outer statement must be join-compatible with the column you name in the subquery SELECT list.

- text and image datatypes are not allowed in subqueries.

- Subqueries cannot manipulate their results internally, that is, a subquery cannot include the ORDER BY clause, the COMPUTE clause, or the INTO keyword.

- Correlated (repeating) subqueries are not allowed in the SELECT clause of an updateable cursor defined by DECLARE CURSOR.

- There is a limit of 16 nesting levels.
- The maximum number of subqueries on each side of a UNION is 16.
- The WHERE clause of a subquery can only contain an aggregate function if the subquery is in a HAVING clause of an outer query and the aggregate value is a column from a table in the FROM clause of the outer query.
- The sum of the maximum lengths of all the columns specified by a subquery cannot exceed 256 bytes.

Subquery Examples

```
SET ROWCOUNT 1   -- Return only 1 row

SELECT tb1.c1
  FROM table1 tb1
 WHERE EXISTS ( SELECT 1
                  FROM table2 tb2
                 WHERE tb2.c2 = tb1.c2 )

SET ROWCOUNT 0   -- Return all rows
go
---------------------------------------------
31081663
```

```
SET ROWCOUNT 1

SELECT tb1.c1
  FROM table1 tb1,
       table2 tb2
 WHERE tb2.c5 = ( SELECT MAX(c5)
                    FROM table2 )
   AND tb2.c4 = tb1.c4

SET ROWCOUNT 0
go
---------------------------------------------
45298231
```

Most of the previous material on subqueries was taken from Chapter 5 of the ASE 12.5 Transact-SQL User's Guide.

Correlated Subqueries

A correlated subquery is a subquery whose WHERE predicate includes joining conditions on an outer table.

Example:

```
/* In all examples we make reference to the following two tables. */
CREATE
 TABLE test_table1(
       column01 INT NOT NULL,
       column02 INT NOT NULL,
       column03 CHAR(20) NOT NULL,
 CONSTRAINT ix01_test_table1
   PRIMARY KEY CLUSTERED (column01)
)
LOCK DATAROWS
go

CREATE
 TABLE test_table2(
       column01 INT NOT NULL,
       column02 INT NOT NULL,
       column03 CHAR(20) NOT NULL,
 CONSTRAINT ix01_test_table2
   PRIMARY KEY CLUSTERED (column01)
)
LOCK DATAROWS
go

CREATE NONCLUSTERED INDEX ix02_test_table2
ON test_table2 (column02, column03)
go

SELECT t1.column02,
       t1.column03
  FROM test_table t1
 WHERE EXISTS ( SELECT 1
                  FROM test_table2 t2
                 WHERE t1.column01 = t2.column01
                   AND t1.coumn02 != t2.column02 )
go
```

Joint Field Intersections

How can I use a subquery to return results from test_table1 if and only if test_table2 contains a matching record on column02 of test_table1?

```
SELECT t1.column01,
       t1.column02,
       t1.column03
  FROM test_table t1
 WHERE EXISTS ( SELECT 1
                  FROM test_table2
                 WHERE t1.column02 = t2.column02 )
go
```

Joint Field Subtractions

How can I use a subquery to return results from test_table1 if and only if test_table2 does not contain a matching record on column02 of test_table1?

```
SELECT t1.column01,
       t1.column02,
       t1.column03
  FROM test_table t1
 WHERE NOT EXISTS ( SELECT 1
                      FROM test_table2
                     WHERE t1.column02 = t2.column02 )
go
```

Joint Record Intersections

How can I use a subquery to return results from test_table1 if and only if test_table2 contains a match on every field for every record of test_table1?

```
SELECT t1.column01,
       t1.column02,
       t1.column03
  FROM test_table t1
 WHERE EXISTS ( SELECT 1
                  FROM test_table2
                 WHERE t1.column01 = t2.column01
                   AND t1.column02 = t2.column02
                   AND t1.coumn03 = t2.column03 )
go
```

Joint Record Subtractions

How can I use a subquery to return results from test_table1 if and only if test_table2 does not contain a match on every field for every record of test_table1?

```
SELECT t1.column01,
       t1.column02,
       t1.column03
  FROM test_table t1
 WHERE NOT EXISTS ( SELECT 1
                      FROM test_table2
                     WHERE t1.column01 = t2.column01
                       AND t1.column02 = t2.column02
                       AND t1.coumn03 = t2.column03 )
go
```

DisJoint Field Intersections

How can I use a subquery to return results from test_table1 if and only if test_table2 contains a matching record on column02 of test_table1?

```
SELECT t1.column01,
       t1.column02,
       t1.column03
  FROM test_table t1
 WHERE EXISTS ( SELECT 1
                  FROM test_table2
                 WHERE t1.column02 = t2.column02 )
go
```

DisJoint Field Subtractions

How can I use a subquery to return results from test_table1 if and only if test_table2 does not contain a matching record on column02 of test_table1?

```
SELECT t1.column01,
       t1.column02,
       t1.column03
  FROM test_table t1
 WHERE NOT EXISTS ( SELECT 1
                      FROM test_table2
                     WHERE t1.column02 = t2.column02 )
go
```

DisJoint Record Intersections

How can I use a subquery to return results from test_table1 if and only if test_table2 contains a match on every field for every record of test_table1? The answers to these questions are exactly the same whether a set is joint or disjoint.

```
SELECT t1.column01,
       t1.column02,
       t1.column03
  FROM test_table t1
 WHERE EXISTS ( SELECT 1
                  FROM test_table2
                 WHERE t1.column01 = t2.column01
                   AND t1.column02 = t2.column02
                   AND t1.coumn03 = t2.column03 )
go
```

DisJoint Record Subtractions

How can I use a subquery to return results from test_table1 if and only if test_table2 does not contain a match on every field for every record of test_table1?

```
SELECT t1.column01,
       t1.column02,
       t1.column03
  FROM test_table t1
 WHERE NOT EXISTS ( SELECT 1
                      FROM test_table2
                     WHERE t1.column01 = t2.column01
                       AND t1.column02 = t2.column02
                       AND t1.coumn03 = t2.column03 )
go
```

NonCorrelated Subqueries

A Non-Correlated subquery is a subquery whose WHERE predicate does not include joining conditions on any outer table. Non-Correlated subqueries are often used to determine if some aggregate property is true.

Example:

```
/* In all examples we will make reference to the following two tables.
*/
```

```
CREATE
 TABLE test_table1(
       column01 INT NOT NULL,
       column02 INT NOT NULL,
       column03 CHAR(20) NOT NULL,
 CONSTRAINT ix01_test_table1
   PRIMARY KEY CLUSTERED (column01)
)
LOCK DATAROWS
go

CREATE
 TABLE test_table2(
       column01 INT NOT NULL,
       column02 INT NOT NULL,
       column03 CHAR(20) NOT NULL,
 CONSTRAINT ix01_test_table2
   PRIMARY KEY CLUSTERED (column01)
)
LOCK DATAROWS
go

CREATE NONCLUSTERED INDEX ix02_test_table2
ON test_table2 (column02, column03)
go

SELECT t1.column02,
       t1.column03
  FROM test_table t1
 WHERE t1.column03 = ( SELECT MAX(t2.column03)
                         FROM test_table2 )
go
```

How do I display only those records from test_table1 which are equal to the summation of column02 in test_table2?

```
SELECT t1.column02,
       t1.column03
  FROM test_table t1
 WHERE t1.column02 = ( SELECT SUM(t2.column02)
                         FROM test_table t2 )
go
```

Chapter 10. Joining Data

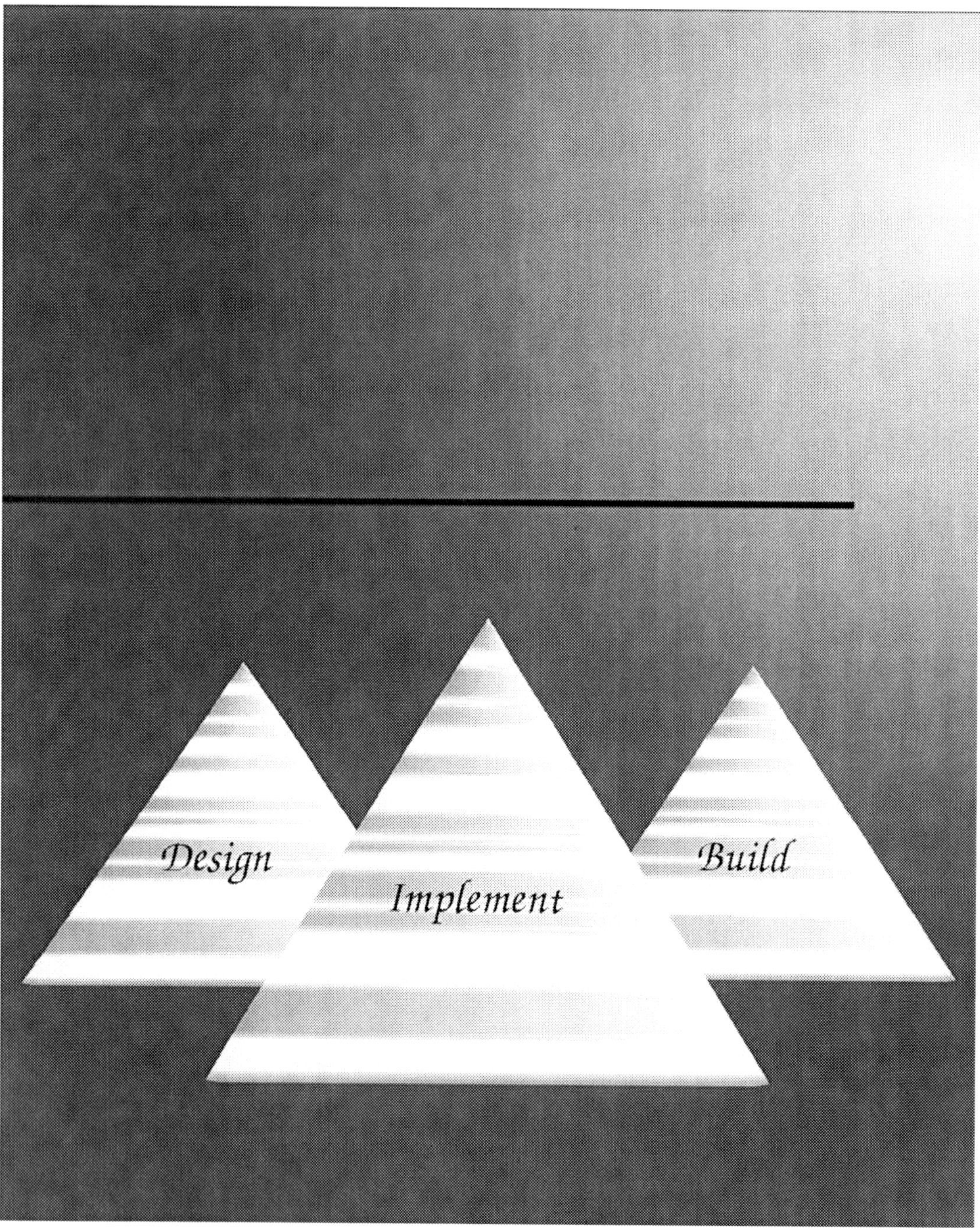
Design
Implement
Build

Chapter 11. Isolation Levels

SQL92 provides four levels of isolation for transactions. Each isolation level specifies the kinds of actions that are **not** permitted while concurrent transactions are executing. Higher levels include the restrictions imposed by the lower levels:

Level 0 - ensures data written by one transaction represents the actual data. It prevents other transactions from changing data that has already been modified (through an INSERT, DELETE, UPDATE, and so on) by an uncommitted transaction. The other transactions are blocked from modifying that data until the transaction commits. However, other transactions can still read the uncommitted data, which results in dirty reads. Transaction Isolation Level 0 is also called "READ UNCOMITTED"

Level 1 - prevents dirty reads. Such reads occur when one transaction modifies a row, and a second transaction reads that row before the first transaction commits the change. If the first transaction rolls back the change, the information read by the second transaction becomes invalid. This is the default isolation level supported by Adaptive Server. Transaction Isolation Level 1 is also called "READ COMITTED"

Level 2 - prevents non repeatable reads. Such reads occur when one transaction reads a row and a second transaction modifies that row. If the second transaction commits its change, subsequent reads by the first transaction yield different results than the original read. (Adaptive Server only supports for DOL tables...) Transaction Isolation Level 2 is also called "REPEATABLE READS".

Level 3 - ensures that data read by one transaction is valid until the end of that transaction, hence preventing phantoms. Adaptive Server supports this level through the HOLDLOCK keyword of the SELECT statement, which applies a read-lock on the specified data. Phantoms occur when one transaction reads a set of rows that satisfy a search condition, and then a second transaction modifies the data (through an INSERT, DELETE, UPDATE, and so on). If the first transaction repeats the read with the same search conditions, it obtains a different set of rows. Transaction Isolation Level 3 is also called "SERIALIZABLE"

Example (HOLDLOCK):

```
BEGIN TRANSACTION

   SELECT action,
          team_id,
          name,
          cty_id,
          cli_id,
          sub_sector_id,
          sub_sector_name
     FROM team_msg_out HOLDLOCK
    WHERE read_flag = "N"

   UPDATE team_msg_out
      SET read_flag = "R"
    WHERE read_flag = "N"

   IF ( @@error !=0 OR @@transtate = 3 )  -- We have a problem!
   BEGIN
      PRINT "procedure get_team_msg_out, cannot update team_msg_out"
      IF ( @@trancount > 0 )  -- rollback the open transaction
         ROLLBACK TRANSACTION
      RETURN -1
   END

COMMIT TRANSACTION  -- All Ok commit and release the locks

RETURN 0
```

You can set the isolation level for your session by using the transaction isolation level option of the set command. You can enforce the isolation level for just a query as opposed to using the at isolation clause of the select statement.

Example:

```
SET TRANSACTION ISOLATION LEVEL 0
go
```

Preventing Dirty Reads, Non-repeatable Reads, and Phantoms

By default, the ASE transaction isolation level is 1. However, the SQL92 standard requires that level 3 be the default isolation for all transactions. This prevents dirty reads, non-repeatable reads, and phantoms. To enforce this default level of isolation, Transact-SQL provides the transaction isolation level 3 option of the SET statement. This option instructs Adaptive Server to apply a HOLDLOCK to all select operations in a transaction.

Example:

```
SET TRANSACTION ISOLATION LEVEL 3
go
```

Applications that use transaction isolation level 3 should set that isolation level at the beginning of each session. However, setting transaction isolation level 3 causes Adaptive Server to hold any read locks for the duration of the transaction. If you also use the chained transaction mode, that isolation level remains in effect for any data retrieval or modification statement that implicitly begins a transaction. In both cases, this can lead to concurrency problems for some applications, since more locks may be held for longer periods of time.

After setting the isolation level for your session, to return your session to the Adaptive Server default isolation level run:

```
SET TRANSACTION ISOLATION LEVEL 1
go
```

Dirty Reads

By default, a unique index is required for a level 0 scan on a table that does not reside in a read-only database.

Applications that are not impacted by dirty reads may have better concurrency and reduced deadlocks when accessing the same data by setting transaction isolation level 0 at the beginning of each session. An example is an application that finds the momentary average balance for all savings accounts stored in a table. Since it requires only a snapshot of the current average balance, which probably changes frequently in an active table, the application should query the table using isolation level 0. Other applications that require data consistency, such as deposits and withdrawals to specific accounts in the table, should avoid using isolation level 0.

Scans at isolation level 0 do not acquire any read locks for their scans, so they do not block other transactions from writing to the same data, and vice versa. However, even if you set your isolation level to 0, utilities (like DBCC) and data modification statements (like UPDATE) still acquire read locks for their scans, because they must maintain the database integrity by ensuring that the correct data has been read before modifying it.

Because scans at isolation level 0 do not acquire any read locks, it is possible that the result set of a level 0 scan may change while the scan is in progress. If the scan position is lost due to changes in the underlying table, a unique index is required to restart the scan. In the absence of a unique index, the scan may be aborted.

Finding the Status of the Current Isolation Level

The global variable @@isolation contains the current isolation level of your Transact-SQL session. Querying @@isolation returns the value of the active level (0, 1, 2, or 3).

Example:

```
SELECT @@isolation
go
-----------
1
```

Changing the Isolation Level for a Query

You can change the isolation level for a query by using the AT ISOLATION LEVEL clause with the SELECT or READTEXT statements. The READ UNCOMMITTED, READ COMMITTED, and SERIALIZABLE options of AT ISOLATION LEVEL represent each isolation level as defined below:

- AT ISOLATION LEVEL 0, READ UNCOMMITED
- AT ISOLATION LEVEL 1, READ COMMITTED
- AT ISOLATION LEVEL 2, REAPETABLE READ
- AT ISOLATION LEVEL 3, SERIALIZABLE

For example, the following two statements query the same table at isolation levels 0 and 3, respectively.

Example:
```
SELECT *
    FROM titles
AT ISOLATION LEVEL 0
go

SELECT *
   FROM titles
AT ISOLATION LEVEL 3
go
```

The AT ISOLATION LEVEL clause is valid only for single SELECT and READTEXT queries or in the DECLARE CURSOR statement. Adaptive Server returns a syntax error if you use AT ISOLATION LEVEL:

- With a query using the INTO clause.
- Within a subquery.
- With a query in the CREATE VIEW statement.
- With a query in the INSERT statement.
- With a query using the FOR BROWSE clause.

Cursors and Isolation Levels

Adaptive Server provides three isolation levels for cursors:

Level 0 - Adaptive Server uses no locks on base table pages that contain a row representing a current cursor position. Cursors acquire no read locks for their scans, so they do not block other applications from accessing the same data. However, cursors operating at this isolation level are not updateable, and they require a unique index on the base table to ensure the accuracy of their scans.

Level 1 - Adaptive Server uses a shared or update lock on base table pages that contain a row representing a current cursor position. The page remains locked until the current cursor position moves off the page (as a result of fetch statements), or the cursor is closed. If an index is used to search the base table rows, it also applies shared or update locks to the corresponding index pages. This is the default locking behavior for Adaptive Server.

Level 2 & 3 - Adaptive Server uses a shared or update lock on any base table pages that have been read in a transaction on behalf of the cursor. In addition, the locks are held until the transaction ends, as opposed to being released when the data page is no longer needed. The HOLDLOCK keyword applies this locking level to the base tables, as specified by the query on the tables or views.

Besides using HOLDLOCK, you can use SET TRANSACTION ISOLATION LEVEL to define one of the isolation levels for your session. After setting this option, any cursor you open uses that isolation level. You can also use the SELECT statement's AT ISOLATION LEVEL clause to change the isolation level for a specific cursor.

Example:

```
DECLARE commit_crsr
 CURSOR cursor
    FOR
 SELECT *
   FROM titles
AT ISOLATION LEVEL 1
```

This statement makes the cursor operate AT ISOLATION LEVEL 1, regardless of the isolation level of the transaction or session. If you declare a cursor at isolation level 0 (read uncommitted), Adaptive Server also defines the cursor as read-only. You cannot specify the FOR UPDATE clause along with AT ISOLATION READ UNCOMMITTED in a DECLARE CURSOR statement.

Adaptive Server determines a cursor's isolation level when you open the cursor (not when you declare it), based on the following:

- If the cursor was declared with the at isolation clause, that isolation level overrides the transaction isolation level in which it is opened.

- If the cursor was not declared with at isolation, the cursor uses the isolation level in which it is opened. If you close the cursor and reopen it later, the cursor acquires the current isolation level of the transaction.

Adaptive Server compiles the cursor's query when you declare it. This compilation process is different for isolation level 0 as compared to isolation levels 1 or 3. If you declare a language or client cursor in a transaction with isolation level 1 or 3, opening it in a transaction at isolation level 0 causes an error.

Example:
```
SET TRANSACTION ISOLATION LEVEL 1
DECLARE publishers_crsr
 CURSOR
    FOR
 SELECT *
   FROM publishers

OPEN publishers_crsr     /* no error */
FETCH publishers_crsr
CLOSE publishers_crsr

SET TRANSACTION ISOLATION LEVEL 0
OPEN publishers_crsr     /* error */
```

Stored Procedures and Isolation Levels

The ASE system procedures always operate at isolation level 1, regardless of the isolation level of the transaction or session. User stored procedures operate at the isolation level of the transaction that executes it. If the isolation level changes within a stored procedure, the new isolation level remains in effect only during the execution of the stored procedure.

Triggers and Isolation Levels

Since triggers are fired by data modification statements (like insert), all triggers execute at either the transaction's isolation level or isolation level 1 whichever is higher. So, if a trigger fires in a transaction at level 0, Adaptive Server sets the trigger's isolation level to 1 before executing its first statement.

Using HOLDLOCK

HOLDLOCK is used on SELECTS to hold shared level locks until a transaction commits. For instance, if you need to hold a lock a on table because you are running at transaction isolation level 1, USE:

```
SELECT columns
  FROM table HOLDLOCK
go
```

Using NOHOLDLOCK

NOHOLDLOCK is used on SELECT to release shared level locks once they are no longer needed by a ***statement***. For instance, if you need to release locks on a table because you are running at transaction isolation 3, USE:

```
SELECT columns
  FROM table NOHOLDLOCK
go
```

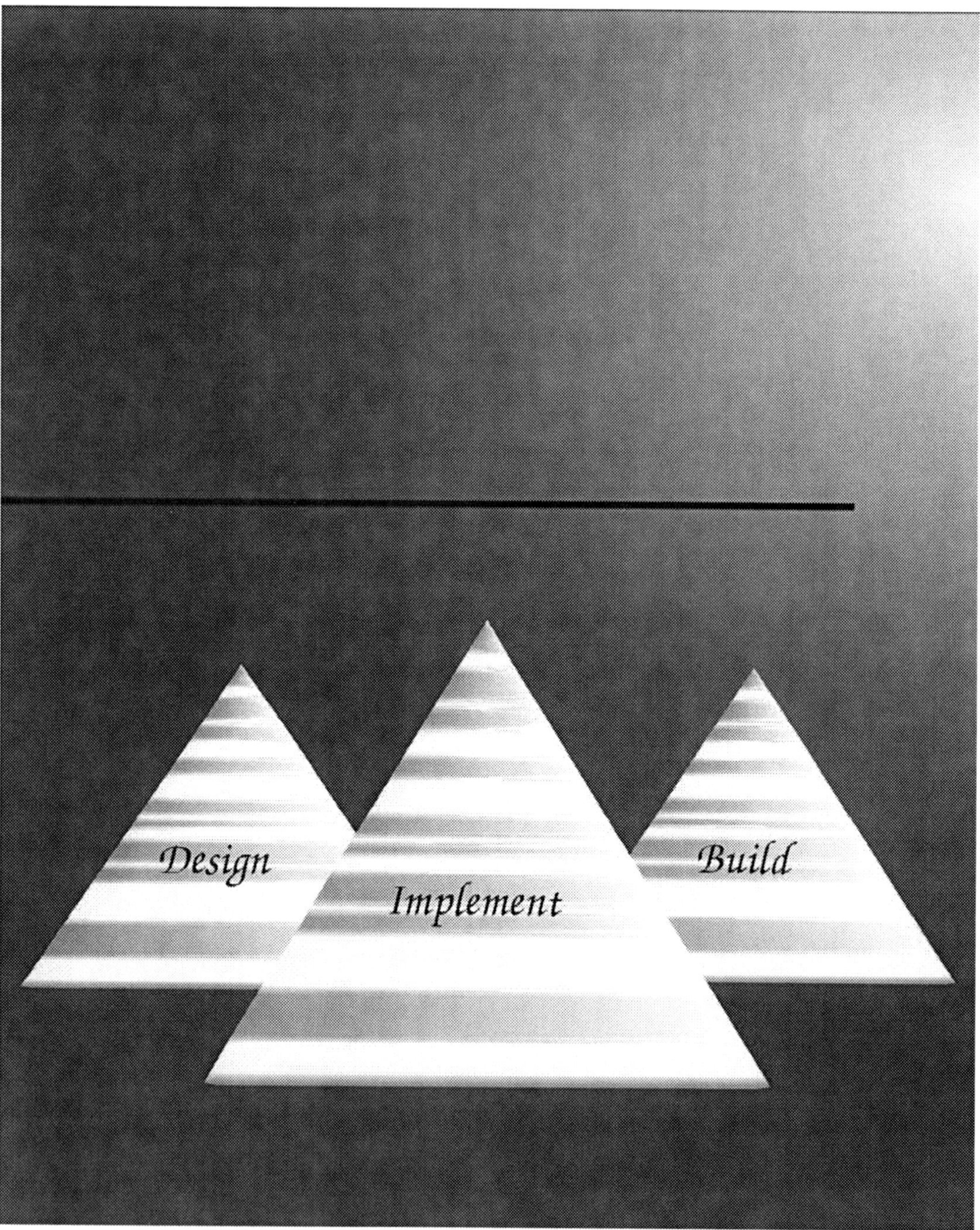
Design
Implement
Build

Chapter 12. sp_who, sp_lock, sp_showplan

Using sp_who [login | spid]

sp_who is an ASE system stored procedure which displays information about current server processes. When executed without any parameters sp_who displays information about all current server processes.

Example:

```
EXEC sp_who
go

fid spid status      loginame  origname hostname blk dbname  cmd
0   13   recv sleep  crowleyd  crowleyd           0  db      AWAITING
COMMAND
0   14   sleeping    [NULL]    [NULL]             0  master NETWORK
HANDLER
0   15   sleeping    [NULL]    [NULL]             0  master NETWORK
HANDLER
0   16   recv sleep  akersjo   akersjo            0  db      AWAITING
COMMAND
0   17   recv sleep  morrisp   morrisp            0  db      AWAITING
COMMAND
```

If only information for all logins with a loginame of morrisp is desired, you should execute sp_who with the login.

Example:

```
EXEC sp_who "morrisp"
go

fid spid status      loginame  origname hostname blk  dbname cmd
0   17   recv sleep  morrisp   morrisp            0   db     AWAITING
COMMAND
```

Alternatively, if only information for a specified spid is desired, you should execute sp_who with the spid.

Example:

```
EXEC sp_who "17"
go

fid spid status     loginame  origname hostname blk dbname cmd
0   17   recv sleep morrisp   morrisp           0   db     AWAITING
COMMAND
```

Various sp_who Status Values

recv sleep - Waiting on a network read.

send sleep - Waiting on a network send.

alarm sleep - Waiting on an alarm, such as waitfor delay "10:00".

lock sleep - Waiting on a lock acquisition.

Sleeping - Waiting on disk I/O or some other resource. Probably indicates a process that is running, but doing extensive disk I/O. Very rarely, a few sleeping processes do not wake up, and require an ASE reboot to clear.

Runnable - In the queue of runnable processes.

Running - Actively running on one of the server engines.

Infected - ASE has detected a serious error condition. Adaptive Server restart probably required to clear process.

Background - A process, such as a threshold procedure, run by Adaptive Server rather than by a user process Immediate. Recommend a careful check of sysprocesses before killing a background process.

log suspend - Processes suspended by reaching the last-chance threshold on the log.

sp_who Columns

Fid – Displays the process id of this worker processes parent. An fid is known as a family id.

Spid – ASE assigned process id. Uniquely identifies a process.

Status - Represents the state of the current process.

Loginame – Displays the client's login name to the server.

Origname – Displays a client's original login name when a client has run set proxy or set session authorization to impersonate a user.

Hostname – Displays the name of the host computer.

Blk – Displays the spid of a login causing lock contention. If 0, then the login is not being blocked.

Dbname – Displays the database the login is currently using.

Cmd – Displays a short description of the client's current executing command.

Using sp_lock [spid1 , spid2]

Displays locks held by one or two processes with the specified spids. When executed without any parameters, sp_lock displays information about all current locks.

Example:

```
EXEC sp_lock
go

fid spid locktype   table_id     page    row dbname   class
context
0   78   Sh_intent  1855710059  0        0   db1      Cursor Id 5111810
Fam dur
0   78   Sh_page    1855710059  30680    0   db1      Cursor Id 5111810
0   117  Sh_intent  23          0        0   db       Non Cursor Lock
0   117  Sh_intent  24          0        0   db       Non Cursor Lock
0   117  Sh_intent  1231447561  0        0   db       Cursor Id 7667715
Fam dur
0   117  Sh_intent  2078630448  0        0   db       Cursor Id 7667713
Fam dur
0   177  Sh_intent  670625432   0        0   db       Cursor Id 11600316
Fam dur
0   177  Sh_page    670625432   2717013 0    db       Cursor Id 11600316
0   204  Sh_intent  287444198   0        0   db       Non Cursor Lock
Fam dur
0   204  Ex_table   80747493    0        0   tempdb Non Cursor Lock
0   221  Sh_intent  1696009073  0        0   master Non Cursor Lock
Fam dur
```

To display all locks for a specified spid run sp_lock by passing one or two spids.

Example:

```
EXEC sp_lock 78
go

fid spid locktype   table_id     page    row dbname   class
context
0   78   Sh_intent  1855710059  0        0   db1      Cursor Id 5111810
Fam dur
0   78   Sh_page    1855710059  30680    0   db1      Cursor Id 5111810
```

sp_lock Columns

Fid – Displays the process id of this worker processes parent. An fid is known as a family id.

Spid – ASE assigned process id. Uniquely identifies a process.

Locktype – Displays the type of lock.

Table id – Displays the id of the table for the lock is being held on in dbname.

Page – Displays the page # being locked.

Row – Displays the row # being locked.

Dbname – Displays the database the lock is in.

Class - Indicates whether a lock is associated with a cursor. It displays one of the following:

- "Non Cursor Lock" indicates that the lock is not associated with a cursor.
- "Cursor Id number" indicates that the lock is associated with the cursor ID number for that Adaptive Server process ID.
- A cursor name indicates that the lock is associated with the cursor cursor_name that is owned by the current user executing sp_lock.

Context - Identifies the context of the lock. Worker processes in the same family have the same context value. Legal values for "context" are as follows:

- "NULL" means that the task holding this lock is either a query executing serially, or is a query executing in parallel in transaction isolation level 1.
- "Sync-pt duration request" means that the task holding the lock will hold the lock until the query is complete.
- "Sync-pt duration request" if the lock is a table lock held as part of a parallel query, if the lock is held by a worker process at transaction isolation level 3, or

if the lock is held by a worker process in a parallel query and must be held for the duration of the transaction.

- "Ind pg" indicates locks on index pages (allpages-locked tables only).
- "Inf key" indicates an infinity key lock (for certain range queries at transaction isolation level 3 on data-only-locked tables).
- "Range" indicates a range lock (for range queries at transaction isolation level 3 on data-only-locked tables).

Using sp_showplan [spid, null, null, null]

The ASE system stored procedure sp_showplan allows you to determine the query plan of a currently executing queries process by process. This is sometimes necessary to use when a query is executing for a long time and you want to determine why and how so that you can make it run faster.

Determine the showplan for the currently executing process id 14.

Example:
```
EXEC sp_showplan 14, null, null, null
go

QUERY PLAN FOR STATEMENT 1 (at line 1).
STEP 1
The type of query is WAITFOR.
```

You should use this output to determine why the query is taking so long. Did ASE choose a sub-optimal plan? Do you know what indexes exist on the objects that are being accessed? Are there are any datatype mismatches? Are you being blocked? Etc.

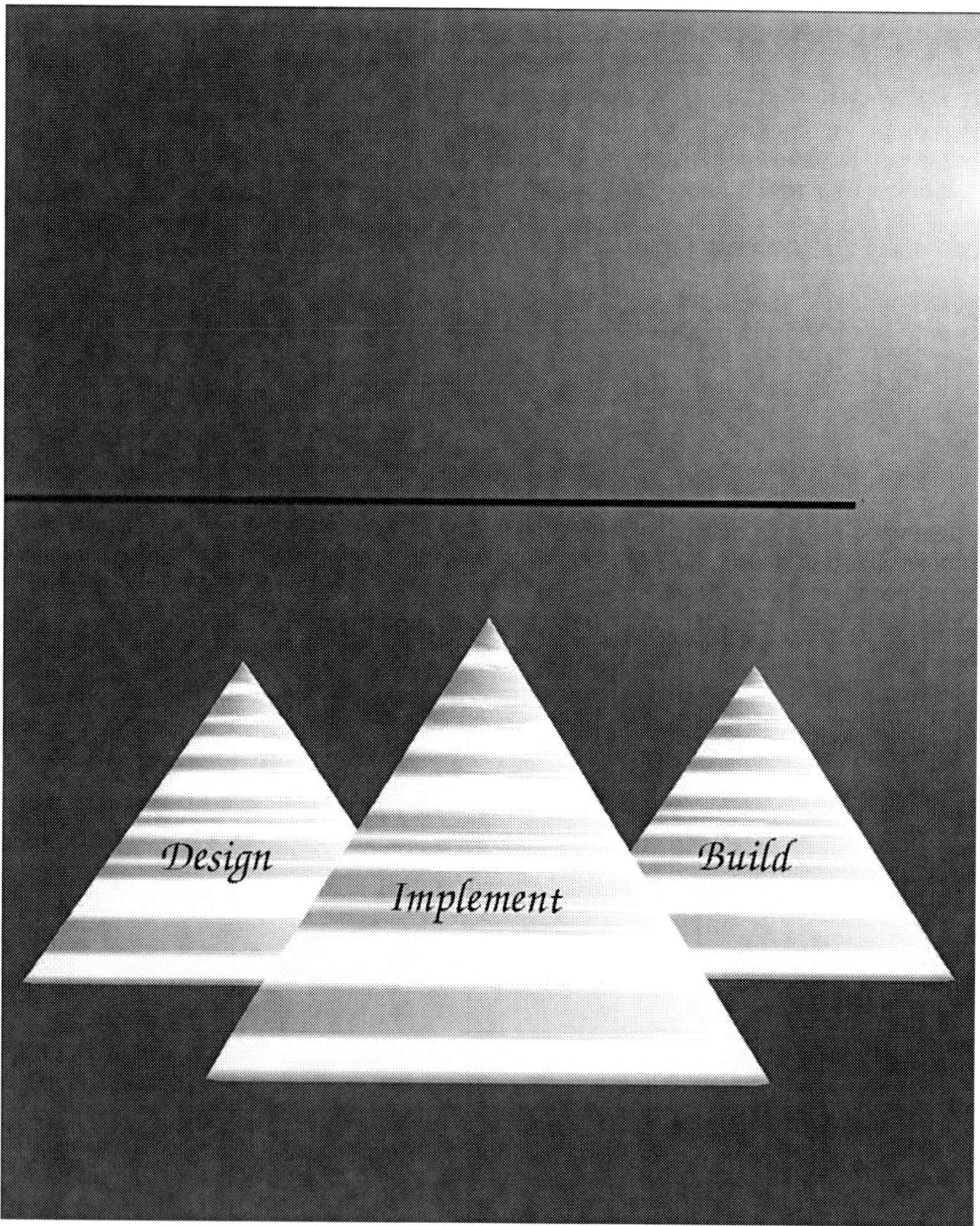
Design
Implement
Build

Chapter 13. Locks

Locks are database components used to guarantee access control. They are necessary to maintain the consistency of records in the database. Were it not for locks, the database could not guarantee that you were the only user making modifications to specific records. Thus, were it not for locks, data integrity would fail very quickly.

Lock contention refers to the requirement that one user wait while another user is making modifications to records which he is requesting. Lock contention can impact ASE's throughput and response time. You need to consider locking during database design, and monitor locking during application design.

Solutions include changing the locking scheme for tables with high contention, or redesigning the application or tables that have the highest lock contention.

For example:

- Add indexes to reduce contention, especially for deletes and updates.
- Keep transactions short to reduce the time that locks are held.
- Check for “hot spots”, especially for inserts on allpages-locked heap tables.

Locking Scheme

When a table is created, by default the locking scheme is the server-wide setting for the configuration parameter ***lock scheme***. The default value for this parameter is “allpages” or APL. In addition, ASE allows you to set the table locking scheme to “datapages” (DPL) or “datarows (DOL).

The most common locking scheme for tables is allpages-locked. The number of locks in ASE is controlled by the configuration parameter “number of locks”. Each lock in ASE takes around 140Bytes. So setting the number of locks to 1,000,000 will only require 140MB of ASE memory. With the advent of 64-bit ASE, you may have less of a worry on how much lock overhead you have in your server. There are no specific rules on what locking scheme you should use, and I do not advocate putting all your tables datapages or datarows under a given locking scheme without appreciating the overhead involved. However, the following guidelines may help:

1. In APL, the data page and the index pages are locked during the operation.

2. In DPL, only the data page is locked, no index page locking.

3. In DOL, only the rows are locked, no index page locking.

4. Identify the most heavily used tables in your database. sp_lock will tell you this easily. Remember the rule of thumb that 80% of the time you are only dealing with 20% of your tables.

5. Turn on 'print deadlock information'.

6. Monitor ASE errorlog for deadlock information. Those tables commonly involved in deadlocks are candidates for DPL or DOL schemes.

7. Tables used for update via cursors are also candidates for DPL or DOL schemes.

8. Large APL tables with non-unique clustered index can create lots of logical and physical I/O with a single row insert. This is normally due to an excessive number of overflow pages. Putting these tables under DPL scheme can often resolve this issue.

Add Indexes to Reduce Contention

An update or delete statement that has no useful index on its search arguments performs a table scan and holds an exclusive table lock for the entire scan time. If the data modification task also updates other tables:

- It can be blocked by select queries or other updates.

- It may be blocked and have to wait while holding a large numbers of locks.

- It can block or deadlock with other tasks.

Creating a useful index for the query allows the data modification statement to use page or row locks, improving concurrent access to the table. If creating an index for a lengthy update or delete transaction is not possible, you can perform the operation in a cursor, with frequent commit transaction statements to reduce the number of page locks.

Keep Transactions Short

Any transaction that acquires locks should be kept as short as possible. In particular, avoid transactions that need to wait for user interaction while holding locks.

Avoid network traffic as much as possible within transactions. The network is slower than Adaptive Server. The following example shows a transaction executed from isql, sent as two packets.

Example:
```
BEGIN TRANSACTION

UPDATE account
   SET balance = balance + 50
 WHERE acct_number = 25
go
```

Warning: isql batch sent to ASE and all locks are held waiting for commit
```
UPDATE account
   SET balance = balance - 50
 WHERE acct_number = 45

COMMIT TRANSACTION
go
```

Note: isql batch sent to ASE and locks are now released because of commit.

Keeping transactions short is especially crucial for data modifications that affect non-clustered index keys on allpages-locked tables.

Non-clustered indexes are dense: the level above the data level contains one row for each row in the table. All inserts and deletes to the table, and any updates to the key value affect at least one non-clustered index page (and adjoining pages in the page chain, if a page split or page deallocation takes place).

While locking a data page may slow access for a small number of rows, locks on frequently-used index pages can block access to a much larger set of rows.

Avoid Hot Spots

Hot spots occur when all updates take place on a certain page, as in an allpages-locked heap table, where all inserts happen on the last page of the page chain.

For example, an un-indexed history table that is updated by everyone always has lock contention on the last page. Some possible ways to alleviate the contention are:

1. Change the lock scheme to datapages or datarows locking.
   - Since these locking schemes do not have chained data pages, they can allocate additional pages when blocking occurs for inserts.

2. Partition the table. Partitioning a heap table creates multiple page chains in the table, and, therefore, multiple last pages for inserts.
   - Concurrent inserts to the table are less likely to block one another, since multiple last pages are available. Partitioning provides a way to improve concurrency for heap tables without creating separate tables for different groups of users.

3. Create a clustered index to distribute the updates across the data pages in the table.
   - Like partitioning, this solution creates multiple insertion points for the table. However, it also introduces overhead for maintaining the physical order of the table's rows.

Additional Locking Guidelines

1. Use the lowest level of locking required by each application. Use isolation level 2 or 3 only when necessary. Updates by other transactions may be delayed until a

transaction using isolation level 3 releases any of its shared locks at the end of the transaction. Use isolation level 3 only when non-repeatable reads or phantoms may interfere with your desired results. If only a few queries require level 3, use the HOLDLOCK keyword or at isolation serializing clause in those queries instead of using set transaction isolation level 3 for the entire transaction. If most queries in the transaction require level 3, use set transaction isolation level 3, but use NOHOLDLOCK or at isolation read committed in the remaining queries that can execute at isolation level 1.

2. If you need to perform mass inserts, updates, or deletes on active tables, you can reduce blocking by performing the operation inside a stored procedure using a cursor, with frequent commits.

3. If your application needs to return a row, provide for user interaction, and then update the row, consider using timestamps and the TSEQUAL function rather than HOLDLOCK.

4. If you are using third-party software, check the locking model in applications carefully for concurrency problems.

There are also other tuning efforts which can help reduce lock contention. For example, if a process holds locks on a page, and must perform a physical I/O to read an additional page, it holds the lock much longer than it would have if the additional page had already been in cache.

Better cache utilization or using large I/O can reduce lock contention in this case. Other tuning efforts that can pay off in reduced lock contention are improved indexing and good distribution of physical I/O across disks.

Lock Types

ASE uses row locks, pages locks, table locks, demand locks, and latches to facilitate and control concurrent access to data.

> **Note:** *Records are stored as rows on the data pages that comprise a table.*

Row Locks

ASE uses three types of row level locks:

- Shared row locks allow concurrent reads of a row, but they block writes. Shared row locks are applied at all transaction isolation levels higher than level 0 (dirty reads.)

- Update row locks are acquired during the read phase of an update. Update row locks allow other shared row locks, but they block other update locks or exclusive locks. If the row needs to be changed, update row locks are promoted to exclusive row locks, once other shared row locks have been released.

- Exclusive row locks allow a single task to modify a row, but they prevent other tasks from accessing the row until the transaction that acquired the lock completes.

Page Locks

ASE uses three types of page level locks:

- Shared page locks allow concurrent reads of a page, but they block writes. Shared page locks are applied at all transaction isolation levels higher than level 0 (dirty reads.)

- Update page locks are acquired during the read phase of an update. Update page locks allow other shared page locks, but they block other update locks or exclusive locks. If the page needs to be changed, update page locks are promoted to exclusive page locks, once other shared page locks have been released.

- Exclusive page locks allow a single task to modify a page, and they prevent other tasks from accessing the page until the transaction that acquired the lock completes.

Table Locks

- Intent table locks indicate the intention to acquire a shared or exclusive lock on a data page. Intent locks are used to prevent other transactions from acquiring shared or exclusive locks on the given page.

- Shared table locks allow concurrent reads of a table, but they block all writes. This type of lock is typically applied during the creation of a non-clustered index.

- Exclusive table locks allow a single task to modify a table, and they prevent other tasks from accessing the table until the transaction that acquired the lock completes. If an update or delete affects the entire table, an exclusive table lock is used. During the creation of a clustered index an exclusive lock is used.

Demand Locks

A demand lock prevents further shared locks from being set. ASE sets a demand lock to indicate that a transaction is next to lock a row, page, or a table.

Latches

To support the data only locking schemes Sybase had to introduce a new type of concurrency mechanism named a latch.

Latches are non-transactional synchronization mechanisms used to guarantee the physical consistency of a page. While rows are being inserted, updated or deleted, only one ASE process can have access to the page at the same time. Otherwise, changes could overwrite each other. Latches are used for both datapages and datarows locking. They are **not** used for changes to tables using the allpages locking scheme.

The most important distinction between a lock and a latch is the duration:

- A lock can persist for a long period of time: while a page is being scanned, for the duration of a statement, or for the duration of a transaction.
- A latch is held only for the time required to insert or move a few bytes on a data page, to copy pointers, columns or rows, or to acquire a latch on another index page.

Optimistic Locking

ASE performs optimistic locking in several ways. It runs by default T-SQL commands and batches in *unchained mode*. That is, unless you declare a transaction, all statements will be wrapped with an implicit *BEGIN TRAN* and *COMMIT TRAN*. This significantly reduces how long locks are held. In addition, ASE runs at *isolation level 1* by default. This prevents *dirty reads*, but it does not prevent the lost update problem.

Lost Update

The lost update occurs when one user reads a record and while modifying the record, another user reads the record and makes a modification before the first user makes their modifications. This can cause the modifications made by the second user to be lost.

Consider:

```
User 1 reads a record to her screen.

User 2 reads a record to his screen.

User 2 changes the record.

User 1 changes the record.
```

Thus, the modifications that were made by user 2 could be lost. There are several ways to help prevent this type of condition from occurring. The first way is by using a special column within ASE known as the timestamp. In order to use this column, it must be part of the table definition.

Using Timestamp

Sybase PowerBuilder uses the timestamp column to determine whether or not a column value has changed. Other applications may need to select the timestamp column and store it along with the record in a temp table or on the client. The timestamp datatype is VARBINARY(8).

Using temp tables, you can insert the primary key and the timestamp of a table into a temporary table. Later, you can join the table to the temporary table on their primary key and the timestamp column to check whether the table was updated.

Example:

```
/* Create temporary table to hold key and timestamp of record */
CREATE TABLE #no_loss(
column01 INT NOT NULL,
column02 VARBINARY(8) NOT NULL)
go

/* Insert the record into the temporary table */
INSERT
  INTO #no_loss(
       column01,
       column02)
SELECT column01,
       timestamp
  FROM table
 WHERE column01 = 123
go

/* Read the record */
SELECT column01
  FROM table
 WHERE column01 = 123
go

/* Modifications are made on the client */
/* Client sends update back to database */
UPDATE table
   SET column03 = "ABC"
  FROM table,
       #no_loss tmp
 WHERE table.column01 = tmp.column01
   AND TSEQUAL(table.timestamp, tmp.column02)
```

```
IF ( @@ROWCOUNT != 0 )
BEGIN
   PRINT "Warning: Update was not Performed"
END
go
```

Note: The TSEQUAL function will generate a 532 error message and abort the command if the timestamp has changed. You may not want this error message. In this case, use an equijoin in place of the TSEQUAL function.

Example:

```
/* Create temporary table to hold key and timestamp of record */
CREATE TABLE #no_loss(
column01 INT NOT NULL,
column02 VARBINARY(8) NOT NULL)
go

/* Insert the record into the temporary table */
INSERT
  INTO #no_loss(
       column01,
       column02)
SELECT column01,
       timestamp
  FROM table
 WHERE column01 = 123
go

/* Read the record */
SELECT column01
  FROM table,
       #no_loss tmp
 WHERE table.column01 = tmp.column01
   AND table.timestamp = tmp.column02

IF ( @@ROWCOUNT != 0 )
BEGIN
   PRINT "Warning: Record has changed since read"
END
go

/* Modifications are made on the client */
```

```
/* Client sends update back to database */
UPDATE table
   SET column03 = "ABC"
  FROM table,
       #no_loss tmp
 WHERE table.column01 = tmp.column01
   AND table.timestamp = tmp.column02

IF ( @@ROWCOUNT != 0 )
BEGIN
   PRINT "Warning: Update was not Performed"
END
go
```

Using Holdlock

Warning: Do not use HOLDLOCK to prevent the lost update problem we have presented. The *HOLDLOCK* keyword is used to hold shared level locks on SELECTS for the duration of the outermost transaction. Shared level locks do prevent other readers from reading, they only prevent modifications from occurring.

Pessimistic Locking

In optimistic locking, shared locks are released by ASE as soon as they are no longer needed by a transaction. In contrast, pessimistic locking mechanisms **hold all locks** until the end of a transaction.

ASE supports pessimistic locking as follows:

- by using the *HOLDLOCK* keyword as part of the *SELECT* command
- or, by using *SET TRANSACTION ISOLATION LEVEL 3*
- or, by using *AT ISOLATION LEVEL 3* with a *SELECT* command.

More About Lost Update

The lost update occurs when one user reads a record and while modifying the record, another user reads the record and makes a modification before the first user makes their modifications. This can cause the modifications made by the second user to be lost.

Consider:

```
User 1 reads a record to her screen.

User 2 reads a record to his screen.

User 1 changes the record.

User 2 changes the record.
```

We have seen how to avoid the lost update problem with timestamps. Note: In order to use the timestamp column, it must be part of the table definition.

The lost update problem can still persist with pessimistic locking.

Question: We have a very high transaction rate table and we need to hold incompatible locks to prevent other readers from making modifications or even seeing the data while another user has it locked.

Solution: You can use an *UPDATE* to hold update locks on the table.

Note: This will block all other commands which need access to the same data.

Example:

```
/* TRANSACTION WHICH NEEDS TO HOLD LOCKS */
/* DECLARE VARIABLES TO HOLD RECORD DATA */
DECLARE @column01 INT

/* START A TRANSACTION */
BEGIN TRANSACTION

/* READ THE RECORD USING UPDATE */
UPDATE table
   SET @column01 = column01
 WHERE column01 = 123
go

/* SELECT THE RECORD */
SELECT @column01 AS "column01"
go
```

```
/* Modifications are made on the client */
/* Client sends update back to database */
UPDATE table
   SET column03 = "ABC"
  FROM table
 WHERE table.column01 = @column01
go

/* Client validates the changes */
SELECT column03
  FROM table
 WHERE column01 = @column01
go

/* Write the records to the database */
/* And release locks */
COMMIT TRANSACTION
go
```

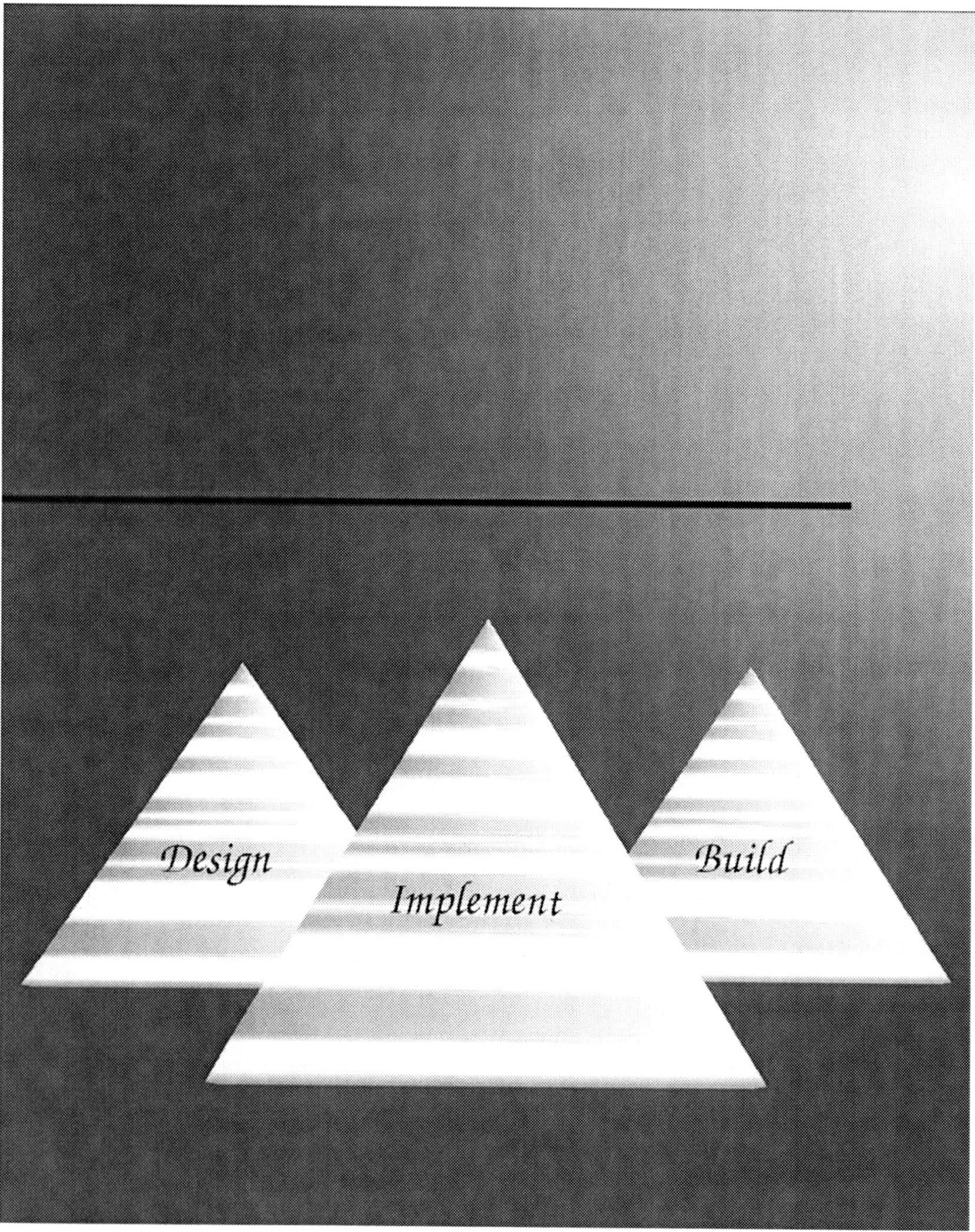
Design
Implement
Build

Chapter 14. Stored Procedures

One of the most important Transact-SQL extensions is the ability to create stored procedures. A stored procedure is a collection of SQL statements and optional control-of-flow statements stored under a name. The creator of a stored procedure can also define parameters to be supplied when the stored procedure is executed.

There are many advantages to using stored procedures including:

- Security - you can revoke access to the base tables and only allow users to access and manipulate the data via the stored procedures. In addition, many times a stored procedure will need to call other stored procedures and it may not be desirable to allow access to the other procedures. That is, we only want the user to be able to execute a stored procedure when it is called from another procedure which the user has execute permissions on. This is easy to perform with stored procedures. Simply revoke or never grant the execute permission on the inner procedures and only grant the execute permission on the outer procedures. Thus, if proc_1 calls proc_2 and the user does not have permissions to execute proc_2, but does have permission to execute proc_1—they will not be able to execute proc_2 outside of proc_1.

- Performance - stored procedures are parsed and a query plan is compiled. This information is stored in the system tables and the parsing only has to be done once.

- Network - if you have users who are on a WAN (slow connection), using stored procedures will improve throughput because fewer bytes need to travel from the client to ASE.

- Tuning - if you have all your SQL code housed in the database, then it's easy to tune the stored procedures without affecting the clients. Dynamic SQL is sometimes hard to monitor and decipher. As a result, performance and tuning on a system that uses dynamic SQL may be very time consuming and expensive.

- Modularity - during application development, the application designer can concentrate on the front-end and the DB designer can concentrate on ASE. In addition, stored procedures may be written that are used in many different applications and/or many different stored procedures.

- Network latency - a client on a LAN may seem slower if it is sending a large number of separate requests to ASE, bundling them into one procedure call may improve responsiveness. Also, servers handling a large number of small requests can spend a surprising amount of CPU time performing network IO.

- Minimize blocks and deadlocks - it is a lot easier to handle a deadlock if the entire transaction is performed in one database request, also locks will be held for a shorter time, improving concurrency and potentially reducing the number of deadlocks. Further, it is easier to ensure that all tables are accessed in a consistent order if code is stored centrally rather than dispersed amongst a number of applications.

Creating and Executing Stored Procedures

You can only create a procedure in the current database and its syntax must match:

```
CREATE PROCEDURE [owner.]procedure_name[;number]
     [[(]@parameter_name
          DATATYPE [(length ) | (precision  [, scale ])]
          [= default][OUTPUT]
     [, @parameter_name
          DATATYPE [(length ) | (precision  [, scale ])]
          [= default][OUTPUT]]...[)]]
     [WITH RECOMPILE]
     AS {SQL_statements | external name dll_name}
```

Parameters

A parameter is an argument to a stored procedure. You can optionally declare one or more parameters in a CREATE PROCEDURE statement. The value of each parameter named in a CREATE PROCEDURE statement must be supplied by the user when the procedure is executed, that is unless a default or NULL has been specified.

Parameter names must be preceded by an @ sign. Parameter names are local to the procedure that creates them; the same parameter names can be used in other procedures. Enclose any parameter value that includes punctuation (such as an object name qualified by a database name or owner name) in single or double quotes. Parameter names, including the @ sign, can be a maximum of 30 bytes long.

Parameters must be given a system datatype (except text or image) or a user-defined datatype, and (if required for the datatype) a length or precision and scale in parentheses.

Optionally, you can assign a default value for the parameter in the CREATE PROCEDURE statement. This value, which can be any constant, is used as the argument to the procedure if the user does not supply one.

Beware that if a parameter is passed to a procedure and is not defined in that procedure, the parameter is ignored. This may cause confusion if the parameter name is just misspelled and the user is thinking the parameter is being passed.

You may create a parameter for output to allow its value to be passed back to the caller or executor.

Example:
```
CREATE PROCEDURE test_proc ( @i_c1 INT )
AS
BEGIN
   SELECT *
     FROM table
    WHERE c1 = @i_c1
END
go
```

To execute the above stored procedure you would run:
```
EXEC test_proc @i_c1 = "value, variable, or parameter"
```

A stored procedure which may pass a parameter back to the caller:
```
CREATE PROCEDURE test_proc ( @o_c1 INT OUTPUT)
AS
BEGIN
   SELECT @o_c1 = 123456
END
go
```

To invoke the stored procedure and accept the output from the parameter, the stored procedure must be executed as follows:

```
DECLARE @output_c1 INT
EXEC test_proc @o_c1 = @output_c1 OUTPUT

SELECT @output_c1
go
```

Nesting Procedure Executions

Nesting occurs when one stored procedure or trigger calls another stored procedure. The nesting level is incremented when the called procedure or trigger begins execution and it is decremented when the called procedure or trigger completes execution. Exceeding the maximum of 16 levels of nesting causes the procedure to fail. The current nesting level is stored in the global variable, @@nestlevel.

Using Temporary Tables

Temporary tables may be created within a stored procedure to help with advanced calculations and to store intermediate results to be passed to other stored procedures.

Temporary tables with names beginning with "# " that are created within stored procedures disappear when the procedure exits. A single procedure can:

- Create a temporary table.
- Insert data into the table.
- Run queries on the table.
- Call other procedures that reference the table.

Temporary tables must exist in order to create procedures that reference it. Therefore, one should:

1. Use CREATE TABLE to create the temporary table.
2. Create the procedures that access the temporary table, but do not create the procedure that creates the table.

3. Drop the temporary table.

4. Create the procedure that creates the table and calls the procedures created in step 2.

Using With Recompile

When using stored procedures which access tables whose data and or statistics can change drastically, and specifically those changes which can affect optimization, it is recommended to execute those procedures with the option "WITH RECOMPILE". This instructs ASE and specifically the optimizer to create a new execution plan for every call to the stored procedure.

***Warning*!**: Use this option only for those procedures which have tables whose and statistics can change drastically. The frequent calculation of execution paths can require a great deal of CPU. It depends upon how many statements are in a procedure and how complicated those statements are which need to be compiled.

Example:

```
CREATE PROCEDURE test_proc(
                 @parm1 INT,
                 @parm2 INT
)
WITH RECOMPILE
AS
BEGIN
   SELECT column02,
          column03
     FROM table
    WHERE column01 = "some value"
END
go
```

Sizing Procedure Cache

The name "procedure cache" is counter-intuitive in that it only mentions procedures. In fact, the procedure cache is used by many commands and processes, including worker processes, update statistics, subqueries, variables, parameters, replication agents, dynamic SQL, triggers, rules, defaults – and, of course, procedures.

Insufficient procedure cache size can greatly reduce application throughput and decrease response time; CPU load may sky rocket. Of course, applications vary and so do their needs. There is no silver bullet. However, we will give a rule to follow when initially sizing procedure cache for an application.

Pick the **smallest** of these three calculations.

Run this select command in all databases and sum the totals. The answer is the number of 2k pages to consider for configuring your procedure cache.

```
SELECT SUM( ( COUNT(*) / 8.0 ) + 1.0 ) * 2
  FROM sysprocedures
go
```

Run this select command in the master database. The answer is the number of 2k pages to consider for configuring your procedure cache.

```
SELECT SUM( size - unreservedpgs ) * .05
  FROM sysusages
go
```

Run this select command in the master database. The answer is the number of 2k pages to consider for configuring your procedure cache.

```
SELECT SUM( scur.value ) * .15
  FROM master.dbo.sysconfigures scon,
       master.dbo.syscurconfigs scur
 WHERE scon.parent = 19
   AND scon.config = 19
   AND scon.config = scur.config
   AND scon.name = scur.comment
go
```

Example:

```
USE my_db1
go
SELECT SUM( ( COUNT(*) / 8.0 ) + 1.0 ) * 2
  FROM sysprocedures
go
103511.000000

USE my_db2
go
SELECT SUM( ( COUNT(*) / 8.0 ) + 1.0 ) * 2
  FROM sysprocedures
go
3909.250000
```

SUM up the two numbers: 107420.25

```
USE master
go
SELECT SUM( size - unreservedpgs ) * .05
  FROM sysusages
go
243547.45
```

```
USE master
go
SELECT SUM( scur.value ) * .15
  FROM master.dbo.sysconfigures scon,
       master.dbo.syscurconfigs scur
 WHERE scon.parent = 19
   AND scon.config = 19
   AND scon.config = scur.config
   AND scon.name = scur.comment
go
115200.00
```

Based on the results from the previous queries I would initially configure my procedure cache for 107421 2k pages. This is only an initial configuration. Periodic monitoring should be performed to validate the procedure cache size and verify that reuse is not occurring heavily.

Cache Reuse

Once you have picked an initial size for procedure cache and have configured it, you should monitor the usage periodically using sp_monitorconfig "procedure cache size".

Example:

```
EXEC sp_monitorconfig "procedure cache size"
go
```

```
Usage information at date and time: May 31 2004 12:45PM.

 Name                  Num_free Num_active Pct_act  Max_Used  Reused
 --------------------- -------- ---------- -------- --------- -------
 procedure cache size     47259     150000    76.04    173142 No
```

You should sample during the peak business hours to determine what the optimal configuration should be. If you are encountering frequent reuse, you may want to consider increasing the size of procedure cache.

Chapter 14. Stored Procedures

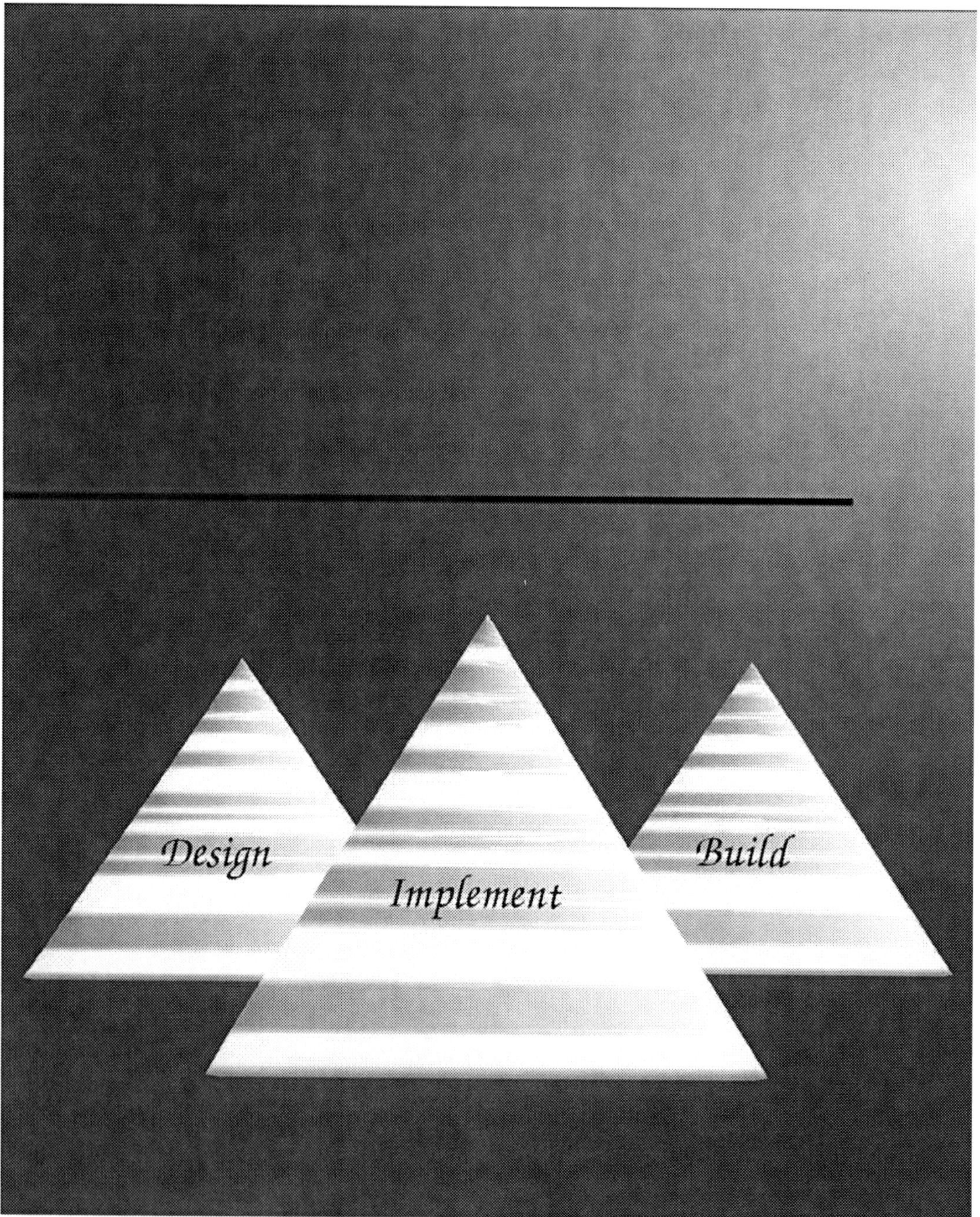
Design
Implement
Build

Chapter 15. Triggers

A trigger is a stored procedure that goes into effect when you INSERT, DELETE, or UPDATE data in a table. You can use triggers to perform a number of automatic actions, such as cascading changes through related tables, enforcing column restrictions, comparing the results of data modifications, and maintaining the referential integrity of data across a database.

Trigger executions are automatic. They work no matter what caused the data modification. A trigger is specific to one or more of the data modification operations, UPDATE, INSERT, and DELETE and is executed once for each SQL statement.

A trigger "fires" only after the data modification statement has completed and Adaptive Server has checked for any datatype, rule, or integrity constraint violation. The trigger and the statement that fires it are treated as a single transaction that can be rolled back from within the trigger. If Adaptive Server detects a severe error, the entire transaction is rolled back.

Triggers are most useful in these situations:

- Triggers can cascade changes through related tables in the database.
- Triggers can disallow, or roll back, changes that would violate referential integrity, canceling the attempted data modification transaction. Such a trigger might go into effect when you try to insert a foreign key that does not match its primary key.
- Triggers can enforce restrictions that are much more complex than those that are defined with rules. Unlike rules, triggers can reference columns or database objects.
- Triggers can perform simple "what if" comparisons.
- Triggers can maintain denormalized data.

Creating Triggers

Syntax:

```
CREATE TRIGGER [owner.]trigger_name
     ON [owner.]table_name
     {FOR {INSERT, UPDATE, DELETE}
     AS SQL_statements
```

The "ON" clause gives the name of the table that activates the trigger. This table is sometimes called the trigger table. A trigger is created in the current database, although it can reference objects in other databases. The owner name for the trigger name must be the same as the owner of the table. Only the table owner can create a trigger on the table. If the table owner is specified with the table name in the create clause, it must be specified in the on clause as well and visa versa.

The FOR clause specifies which data modification commands on the trigger table activate the trigger.

The SQL statements specify trigger conditions and trigger actions. Trigger conditions specify additional criteria that determine whether INSERT, DELETE, or UPDATE causes the trigger actions to be carried out. You can group multiple trigger actions in an "IF" clause with BEGIN and END.

An IF UPDATE clause tests for an INSERT or UPDATE to a specified column. For updates, the IF UPDATE clause evaluates to true when the column name is included in the SET clause of an UPDATE statement, even if the UPDATE does not change the value of the column. Do not use the IF UPDATE clause with DELETE. You can specify more than one column, and you can use more than one IF UPDATE clause in a CREATE TRIGGER statement. Since you specify the table name in the ON clause, do not use the table name in front of the column name with IF UPDATE.

Example:

```
CREATE TRIGGER dbo.tru_table
FOR UPDATE
ON dbo.table
AS
BEGIN
   IF (@@rowcount = 0)
      RETURN

   DECLARE @rw_cnt INT
```

```
    SELECT @rw_cnt = @@rowcount

    IF UPDATE(c1)
    BEGIN
        PRINT "UPDATES TO c1 ARE NOT ALLOWED"
        ROLLBACK TRANSACTION
    END
END
go
```

This trigger will fire upon the invocation of any UPDATE command to the dbo.table table, and will rollback any transactions that attempt to modify the c1 column.

One should almost always check the global variable @@rowcount in a stored procedure and return if no rows were inserted, deleted, or changed from the executing UPDATE, DELETE, or INSERT. Not exiting immediately, could cause a big decrease in performance as many times when an UPDATE, DELETE, or INSERT is executed nothing is performed. This is due, in part, to the remaining code of the trigger needing to be executed.

Triggers fire as part of the transaction, whether an explicit or implicit transaction, and elongate the time a transaction executes. Thus, be careful when creating triggers as they may lead to increased lock contention and decreased application throughput. Triggers are a powerful tool if coded efficiently and used only where necessary.

Inserted Table

In order to provide access to the records that were inserted or updated for a table, ASE provides a fictitious table, really a view into syslogs, called "inserted". This table is read-only and will have the same columns and datatypes as the table the trigger was created on. The inserted table may be used in both triggers created FOR UPDATE and FOR INSERT.

For an INSERT trigger, the inserted table will contain those records that were inserted into the table.

For an UPDATE trigger, the inserted table will contain the new values for all columns for all records modified by the UPDATE.

Since the inserted table is a view into syslogs, it requires reading and rebuilding of log records for the current transaction each and every single time it is read from.

Therefore, try to limit the number of triggers on the system and try to limit the number of queries that read the inserted table.

Deleted Table

In order to provide access to the records that were deleted or updated for a table, ASE provides a fictitious table, really a view into syslogs, called "deleted". This table is read-only and will have the same columns and datatypes as the table the trigger was created on. The deleted table may be used in both triggers created FOR UPDATE and FOR DELETE.

For a DELETE trigger, the deleted table will contain those records that were deleted from the table.

For an UPDATE trigger, the deleted table will contain the old values for all columns for all records modified by the update.

Since the deleted table is a view into syslogs, it requires reading and rebuilding of log records for the current transaction each and every single time it is read from. Therefore, try to limit the number of triggers on the system and try to limit the number of queries that read the deleted table.

SQL Statements Not Allowed in Triggers

Since triggers execute as part of a transaction, the following statements are not allowed in a trigger:

- All create commands, including create database, create table, create index, create procedure, create default, create rule, create trigger, and create view.
- All drop commands.
- alter table and alter database.
- truncate table.
- grant and revoke.
- update statistics.

- reconfigure.
- load database and load transaction.
- disk init, disk mirror, disk refit, disk reinit, disk remirror, disk unmirror.
- select into.

Error Prevention

Triggers can be used to prevent accidental modifications to tables. (Oops!) By accidental, we mean cases in which someone has, for example, forgotten all or part of a *WHERE* clause in a DML statement. Triggers are very efficient for this purpose and can be included on every table for all DML modifications. This is because the necessary checking does not read the syslogs table (transaction log), unless of course unless a statement needs to be rolled back.

Example (DELETE Trigger):

```
CREATE TRIGGER dbo.trd_table
FOR DELETE
ON dbo.table
AS
BEGIN
   IF ( @@rowcount > 500 )
   BEGIN
      DECLARE @trigger_name VARCHAR(30)
      SELECT @trigger_name = OBJECT_NAME(@@PROCID)
      PRINT "too many records: %1!, tran aborted", @trigger_name
      ROLLBACK TRANSACTION
   END
END
go
```

Example (UPDATE Trigger):

```
CREATE TRIGGER dbo.tru_table
FOR UPDATE
ON dbo.table
AS
BEGIN
```

```
    IF ( @@rowcount > 500 )
    BEGIN
       DECLARE @trigger_name VARCHAR(30)
       SELECT @trigger_name = OBJECT_NAME(@@PROCID)
       PRINT "too many records: %1!, tran aborted", @trigger_name
       ROLLBACK TRANSACTION
    END
END
go
```

Example (INSERT Trigger):

```
CREATE TRIGGER dbo.tri_table
FOR INSERT
ON dbo.table
AS
BEGIN

    IF ( @@rowcount > 500 )
    BEGIN
       DECLARE @trigger_name VARCHAR(30)
       SELECT @trigger_name = OBJECT_NAME(@@PROCID)
       PRINT "too many records: %1!, tran aborted", @trigger_name
       ROLLBACK TRANSACTION
    END
END
go
```

Many shops cannot have such logic on their tables, as they are uncertain about how many rows can be modified by an application. However, many of these shops will have support personnel who troubleshoot the application, and who may have rights to modify the data in the database. These users will typically need to modify only a few records that the application may have touched. Such trigger logic can reasonably be granted to the support users. To do this, we will create a role called apl_supt_role. From the triggers, we will check to see if the user has the role or not in addition to the @@rowcount check.

Create a role named apl_supt_role:

```
CREATE ROLE apl_supt_role
go
```

Grant the role to all support accounts:

```
GRANT ROLE apl_supt_role TO <USER NAME>
```

```
go

EXEC sp_modifylogin "USER NAME", "add default role", "apl_supt_role"
go
```

Create your triggers as follows.

Example (DELETE Trigger):

```
CREATE TRIGGER dbo.trd_table
FOR DELETE
ON dbo.table
AS
BEGIN
   IF ( @@rowcount > 500 AND PROC_ROLE('apl_supt_role') > 0 )
   BEGIN
      DECLARE @trigger_name VARCHAR(30)
      SELECT @trigger_name = OBJECT_NAME(@@PROCID)
      PRINT "too many records: %1!, tran aborted", @trigger_name
      ROLLBACK TRANSACTION
   END
END
go
```

Example (UPDATE Trigger):

```
CREATE TRIGGER dbo.tru_table
FOR UPDATE
ON dbo.table
AS
BEGIN
   IF ( @@rowcount > 500 AND PROC_ROLE('apl_supt_role') > 0 )
   BEGIN
      DECLARE @trigger_name VARCHAR(30)
      SELECT @trigger_name = OBJECT_NAME(@@PROCID)
      PRINT "too many records: %1!, tran aborted", @trigger_name
      ROLLBACK TRANSACTION
   END
END
go
```

Example (INSERT Trigger):

```
CREATE TRIGGER dbo.tri_table
FOR INSERT
```

```
ON dbo.table
AS
BEGIN
   IF ( @@rowcount > 500 AND PROC_ROLE('apl_supt_role') > 0 )
   BEGIN
      DECLARE @trigger_name VARCHAR(30)
      SELECT @trigger_name = OBJECT_NAME(@@PROCID)
      PRINT "too many records: %1!, tran aborted", @trigger_name
      ROLLBACK TRANSACTION
   END
END
go
```

Tips

- Avoid reading the inserted and deleted tables many times as these are not true tables and each read of the table requires rebuilding the log records from syslogs. Consider using a cursor to read the syslogs table once only.

- Try to avoid using cursors inside of triggers as this may increase the execution time of the trigger and thus cause locks to be held on the modified table (actually, all locks that are currently being held by an open transaction!!!) longer.

- Never join the inserted and deleted tables from within an update trigger. Instead, join the deleted table to the table which was modified on the primary key or unique key of the table.

- Try to remember to check the @@ROWCOUNT variable in the trigger. Also, if you need to check the variable after running several commands, make sure you declare a variable first in the trigger and store the value of @@ROWCOUNT before running any commands. Failure to do so will result in losing the value.

Chapter 15. Triggers

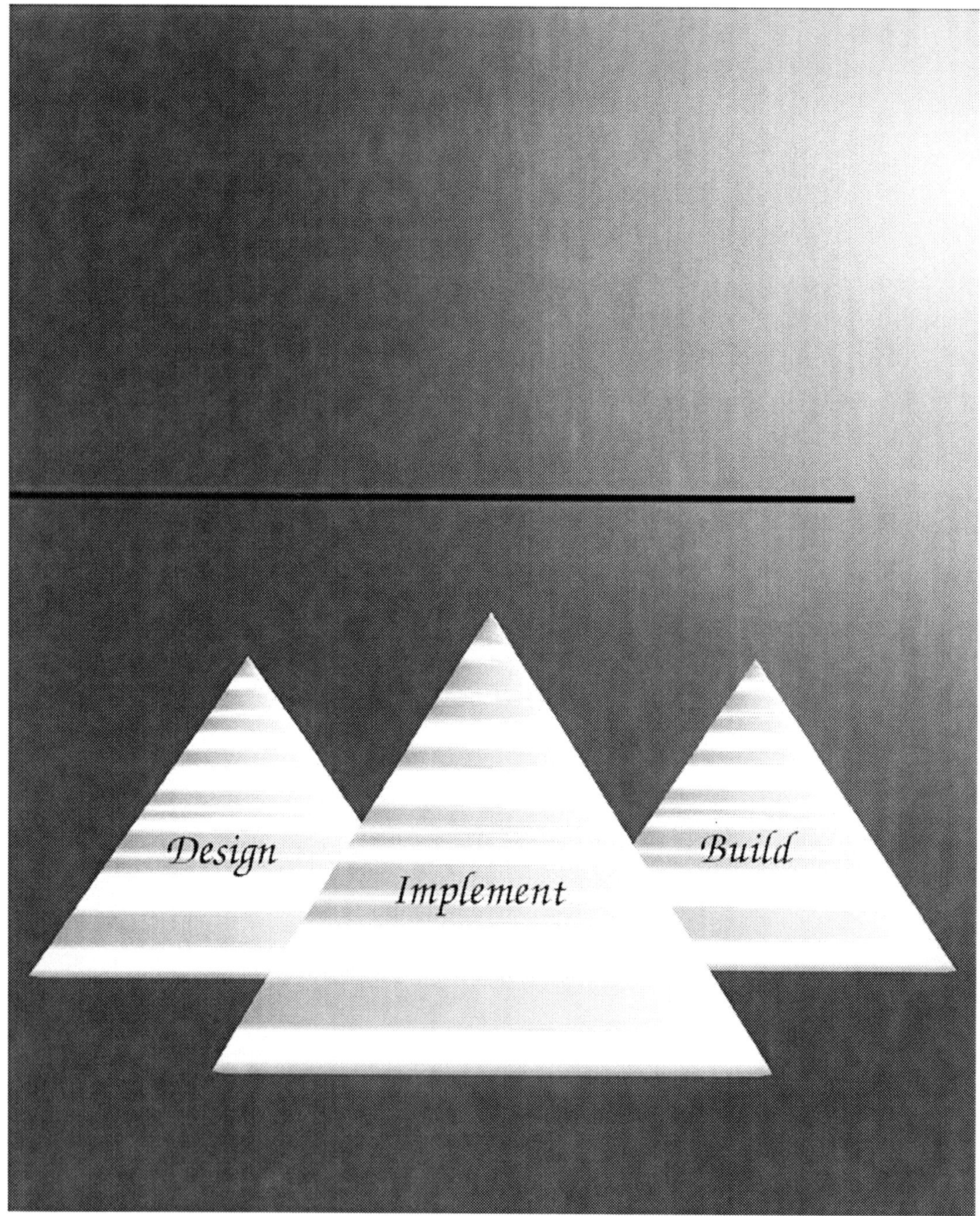
Design
Implement
Build

Chapter 16. Various Showplan Examples

In this chapter we present some examples of good and bad coding techniques.

Using ISNULL

The ASE IsNull() function can cause serious performance problems when used in the WHERE predicate of a selection list. These problems occur because ASE does not know at compilation time whether or not the value used in IsNull() is actually NULL. ASE's cost-based query optimizer estimates the worst-case scenario and traverses that path to the data. However, the value used in the IsNull() function may only rarely be NULL – or it may almost always be NULL. When writing SQL, you should not use the IsNull() function *within* the WHERE predicate. Whenever possible, the test should be performed in an if statement before querying, and the appropriate query (one chosen out of several) then executed.

Example:

```
-- create a database "test" with at least 10mb of space.
CREATE DATABASE test
ON device_name=10
go

-- use the database "test".
USE test
go

CREATE
 TABLE dbo.test_table(
       a int           NOT NULL,
       b numeric(10,0) IDENTITY
)
WITH MAX_ROWS_PER_PAGE=1
go

CREATE UNIQUE CLUSTERED INDEX test_table_ncix
ON dbo.test_table(a)
go
```

```
-- Populate the table with 2000 rows that contain @cnt for field a.
DECLARE @cnt int
SELECT @cnt = 0
WHILE (@cnt < 2000)
BEGIN
   INSERT
     INTO dbo.test_table
   VALUES (@cnt)

   SELECT @cnt = @cnt + 1
end
go

CREATE PROC test_proc_1
AS
BEGIN
   DECLARE @a_id int
   SELECT @a_id = 123

   SELECT *
     FROM test_table
    WHERE a = ISNULL(@a_id, a)

END
go

-- turn on showplan option to show the query plan of the procedure.
SET SHOWPLAN ON
go

-- execute the procedure and look at the showplan output generated.
EXEC test_proc_1
go

STEP 1
        The type of query is SELECT.

        FROM TABLE
            test_table
        Nested iteration.
        Table Scan.
        Forward scan.
        Positioning at start of table.
```

```
        Using I/O Size 2 Kbytes for data pages.
        With LRU Buffer Replacement Strategy for data pages.
```

ASE chose to perform a table scan. Why would **ASE** do this?

- When the query was optimized **ASE** did not know if @a_id was Null or not, so it had to choose the worst case scenario (where @a_id is Null and table scan).

Example:

```
CREATE PROC test_proc_2
AS
BEGIN
   DECLARE @a_id int
   SELECT @a_id = 123

   IF (@a_id IS NULL)
   BEGIN
      SELECT *
        FROM test_table
   END
   ELSE
   BEGIN
      SELECT *
        FROM test_table
       WHERE a = @a_id
   END
END
go

-- turn on showplan option to show the query plan of the procedure.
SET SHOWPLAN ON
go

-- execute the procedure and look at the showplan output generated.
EXEC test_proc_2
go

STEP 1
        The type of query is SELECT.
        FROM TABLE
            test_table
        Nested iteration.
        Using Clustered Index.
```

```
Index : test_table_ncix
Forward scan.
Positioning by key.
Keys are:
    a  ASC
Using I/O Size 2 Kbytes for data pages.
With LRU Buffer Replacement Strategy for data pages.
```

ASE chose to use an index. Why would **ASE** do this?

- When the query was optimized, **ASE** knew that the variable @a_id was not Null that **a** was unique, hence **ASE** knew that the worst case scenario qualified only one row and the optimizer thus chose to use the index.

Datatype Mismatches

In **ASE** versions beyond 11, **ASE** introduced several integer datatype mismatches that were not present in previous versions.

- The comparison of a tinyint field in a table to a smallint or integer datatype is a mismatch. If this comparison is made ASE will scan the table and convert the datatype in the table to that of the datatype being compared. ASE does this to prevent the query from failing. In previous versions of ASE, the query would have failed with an arithmetic overflow message.

- The comparison of a smallint field in a table to an integer datatype is a mismatch. If this comparison is made ASE will scan the table and convert the datatype in the table to that of the datatype being compared. ASE does this to prevent the query from failing. In previous versions of ASE, the query would have failed with an arithmetic overflow message.

Why does ASE convert the values in the table for comparison so that the query doesn't fail?

- In some very critical systems, like medical systems used in a hospital, it is not acceptable for a query to fail even if there is a datatype mismatch.

- By converting the values in the table, the query will not fail with an arithmetic overflow error message.

- Instead the query will run, scan the entire table, and potentially return no results.
- The query may introduce a performance problem, and run for minutes to hours or even days, but the query will not fail.

What are my options?

- Forcing the use of an index can provide some performance benefits, but ASE will scan the entire index converting the values in the index before it does the lookup.
- You might want to force ASE to work the old way. If you set the traceflag 291 on, "DBCC traceon(291)", ASE will handle integer datatypes the way that it used to: "Arithmetic Overflow".
- The best option is to write stored procedures without any datatype dissimilarities or mismatches. If the value that is in the table is of type smallint, your parameter for comparison should be of type smallint.

Example:

```
-- setup the environment.
-- create the database "test" for 5mb.
CREATE DATABASE test
ON device=5
go

USE test
go

-- notice that column "a" is of type tinyint.
CREATE
 TABLE dbo.test_table(
       a tinyint          NOT NULL,
       b numeric(10,0) IDENTITY
)
LOCK ALLPAGES
WITH MAX_ROWS_PER_PAGE=1
go

CREATE UNIQUE NON-CLUSTERED INDEX test_table_ncix
ON dbo.test_table(a)
go
```

```
-- Populate the table with some data.
INSERT INTO test_table VALUES (1)
go
INSERT INTO test_table VALUES (2)
go
INSERT INTO test_table VALUES (3)
go
INSERT INTO test_table VALUES (4)
go
INSERT INTO test_table VALUES (5)
go
INSERT INTO test_table VALUES (6)
go

-- update the statistics for "test_table"
UPDATE STATISTICS test_table
go

-- Force the recompilation of any procedures that use "test_table"
EXEC sp_recompile test_table
go

CREATE PROCEDURE test_proc_1 (@a SMALLINT)
AS
   SELECT *
     FROM test_table
    WHERE a = @a
go

-- set the showplan option to show the query plan of the below
procedure
SET showplan ON
go

EXEC test_proc_1 3
go

    STEP 1
        The type of query is SELECT.

        FROM TABLE
            test_table
        Nested iteration.
```

```
        Table Scan.
        Forward scan.
        Positioning at start of table.
        Using I/O Size 2 Kbytes for data pages.
        With LRU Buffer Replacement Strategy for data pages.
```

Why did ASE scan the table when there appears to a viable index?

- The ASE optimizer chose to do a table scan because there is datatype mismatch between the datatype of column "a", tinyint, and the datatype being compared, smallint.
- ASE does this to prevent the query from failing with an arithmetic overflow message.
- FIX: Declare @a as a tinyint.

Example:

```
CREATE PROCEDURE test_proc_2 (@a INT)
AS
   SELECT *
     FROM test_table
    WHERE a = @a
go

-- set the showplan option to show query plan of the below procedure
SET showplan ON
go

EXEC test_proc_2 3
go

    STEP 1
        The type of query is SELECT.

        FROM TABLE
            test_table
        Nested iteration.
        Table Scan.
        Forward scan.
        Positioning at start of table.
        Using I/O Size 2 Kbytes for data pages.
        With LRU Buffer Replacement Strategy for data pages.
```

Why did ASE scan the table when there appears to a viable index?

- The ASE optimizer chose to do a table scan because there is datatype mismatch between the datatype of column "a", tinyint, and the datatype being compared, int.
- ASE does this to prevent the query from failing with an arithmetic overflow message.
- FIX: Declare @a as a tinyint.

Example:
```
CREATE PROCEDURE test_proc_3 (@a TINYINT)
AS
   SELECT *
     FROM test_table
    WHERE a = @a
go

-- set the showplan option to show query plan of the below procedure
SET showplan ON
go

EXEC test_proc_3 3
go

    STEP 1
        The type of query is SELECT.

        FROM TABLE
            test_table
        Nested iteration.
        Index : test_table_ncix
        Forward scan.
        Positioning by key.
        Keys are:
            a  ASC
        Using I/O Size 2 Kbytes for index leaf pages.
        With LRU Buffer Replacement Strategy for index leaf pages.
        Using I/O Size 2 Kbytes for data pages.
        With LRU Buffer Replacement Strategy for data pages.
```

Why did ASE use the index **test_table_ncix**?

- The ASE optimizer chose to use the index **test_table_ncix**, because there are not any datatype mismatches.
- This is the correct implementation of the procedure.

Example:

```
USE test
go

DROP INDEX test_table.test_table_ncix
go

DROP PROC test_proc_1
DROP PROC test_proc_2
DROP PROC test_proc_3
go

DROP TABLE test_table
go

CREATE
 TABLE dbo.test_table(
       a SMALLINT      NOT NULL,
       b NUMERIC(10,0) IDENTITY
)
LOCK ALLPAGES
WITH MAX_ROWS_PER_PAGE=1
go

CREATE UNIQUE NON-CLUSTERED INDEX test_table_ncix
ON dbo.test_table(a)
go

INSERT INTO test_table VALUES (1)
INSERT INTO test_table VALUES (2)
INSERT INTO test_table VALUES (3)
INSERT INTO test_table VALUES (4)
INSERT INTO test_table VALUES (5)
INSERT INTO test_table VALUES (6)
go

UPDATE STATISTICS test_table
go

EXEC sp_recompile test_table
go

CREATE PROCEDURE test_proc_1 (@a SMALLINT)
AS
```

```
   SELECT *
     FROM test_table
    WHERE a = @a
go

-- set showplan option to show query plan of the below procedure
SET showplan ON
go

EXEC test_proc_1 3
go

    STEP 1
        The type of query is SELECT.

        FROM TABLE
            test_table
        Nested iteration.
        Index : test_table_ncix
        Forward scan.
        Positioning by key.
        Keys are:
            a  ASC
        Using I/O Size 2 Kbytes for index leaf pages.
        With LRU Buffer Replacement Strategy for index leaf pages.
        Using I/O Size 2 Kbytes for data pages.
        With LRU Buffer Replacement Strategy for data pages.
```

Why did ASE use the index **test_table_ncix**?

- The ASE optimizer chose to use the index **test_table_ncix**, because there are not any datatype mismatches.
- This is the correct implementation of the procedure.

Example:

```
CREATE PROCEDURE test_proc_2 (@a INT)
AS
   SELECT *
     FROM test_table
    WHERE a = @a
go
```

```
-- set showplan option to show query plan of the below procedure
SET showplan ON
go

EXEC test_proc_2 3
go

    STEP 1
        The type of query is SELECT.

        FROM TABLE
            test_table
        Nested iteration.
        Table Scan.
        Forward scan.
        Positioning at start of table.
        Using I/O Size 2 Kbytes for data pages.
        With LRU Buffer Replacement Strategy for data pages.
```

Why did ASE scan the table when there appears to a viable index?

- The ASE optimizer chose to do a table scan because there is datatype mismatch between the datatype of column "a", smallint, and the datatype being compared, int.
- ASE does this to prevent the query from failing with an arithmetic overflow message.
- FIX: Declare @a as a smallint.

Example:

```
CREATE PROCEDURE test_proc_3 (@a TINYINT)
AS
   SELECT *
     FROM test_table
    WHERE a = @a
go

-- set showplan option to show query plan of the below procedure
SET showplan ON
go

EXEC test_proc_3 3
```

```
go

    STEP 1
        The type of query is SELECT.

        FROM TABLE
            test_table
        Nested iteration.
        Index : test_table_ncix
        Forward scan.
        Positioning by key.
        Keys are:
            a  ASC
        Using I/O Size 2 Kbytes for index leaf pages.
        With LRU Buffer Replacement Strategy for index leaf pages.
        Using I/O Size 2 Kbytes for data pages.
        With LRU Buffer Replacement Strategy for data pages.
```

Why did ASE use the index **test_table_ncix**?

- The ASE optimizer chose to use the index **test_table_ncix**, despite datatype mismatches, because the parameter being compared is of type tinyint and a tinyint datatype is smaller than that of a smallint. Thus, ASE does not have to convert the values in the table and can use the index.
- This is not a recommended implementation of the procedure, but it works.
- FIX: Declare @a as a smallint.

Example:

```
USE test
go

DROP INDEX test_table.test_table_ncix
go

DROP PROC test_proc_1
DROP PROC test_proc_2
DROP PROC test_proc_3
go

DROP TABLE test_table
```

```
go

CREATE
 TABLE dbo.test_table(
       a INT       NOT NULL,
       b NUMERIC(10,0) IDENTITY
)
LOCK ALLPAGES
WITH MAX_ROWS_PER_PAGE=1
go

CREATE UNIQUE NON-CLUSTERED INDEX test_table_ncix
ON dbo.test_table(a)
go

INSERT INTO test_table VALUES (1)
INSERT INTO test_table VALUES (2)
INSERT INTO test_table VALUES (3)
INSERT INTO test_table VALUES (4)
INSERT INTO test_table VALUES (5)
INSERT INTO test_table VALUES (6)
go

UPDATE STATISTICS test_table
go

EXEC sp_recompile test_table
go

CREATE PROCEDURE test_proc_1 (@a SMALLINT)
AS
   SELECT *
     FROM test_table
    WHERE a = @a
go

-- set showplan option to show query plan of the below procedure
SET showplan ON
go

EXEC test_proc_1 3
go

    STEP 1
```

```
        The type of query is SELECT.

        FROM TABLE
            test_table
        Nested iteration.
        Index : test_table_ncix
        Forward scan.
        Positioning by key.
        Keys are:
            a  ASC
        Using I/O Size 2 Kbytes for index leaf pages.
        With LRU Buffer Replacement Strategy for index leaf pages.
        Using I/O Size 2 Kbytes for data pages.
        With LRU Buffer Replacement Strategy for data pages.
```

Why did ASE use the index **test_table_ncix**?

- The ASE optimizer chose to use the index **test_table_ncix**, despite datatype mismatches, because the parameter being compared is of type smallint and a smallint datatype is smaller than that of a int. Thus, ASE does not have to convert the values in the table and can use the index.

- This is not a recommended implementation of the procedure, but it works.

- FIX: Declare @a as a int.

Example:

```
CREATE PROCEDURE test_proc_2 (@a INT)
AS
   SELECT *
     FROM test_table
    WHERE a = @a
go

-- set the showplan option to show query plan of the below procedure
SET showplan ON
go

EXEC test_proc_2 3
go

    STEP 1
        The type of query is SELECT.
```

```
        FROM TABLE
            test_table
        Nested iteration.
        Index : test_table_ncix
        Forward scan.
        Positioning by key.
        Keys are:
            a  ASC
        Using I/O Size 2 Kbytes for index leaf pages.
        With LRU Buffer Replacement Strategy for index leaf pages.
        Using I/O Size 2 Kbytes for data pages.
        With LRU Buffer Replacement Strategy for data pages.
```

Why did ASE use the index **test_table_ncix**?

- The ASE optimizer chose to use the index **test_table_ncix**, because there are not any datatype mismatches.
- This is the correct implementation of the procedure.

Example:

```
CREATE PROCEDURE test_proc_3 (@a TINYINT)
AS
   SELECT *
     FROM test_table
    WHERE a = @a
go

-- set showplan option to show query plan of the below procedure
SET showplan ON
go

EXEC test_proc_3 3
go

    STEP 1
        The type of query is SELECT.

        FROM TABLE
            test_table
        Nested iteration.
        Index : test_table_ncix
```

```
        Forward scan.
        Positioning by key.
        Keys are:
            a  ASC
        Using I/O Size 2 Kbytes for index leaf pages.
        With LRU Buffer Replacement Strategy for index leaf pages.
        Using I/O Size 2 Kbytes for data pages.
        With LRU Buffer Replacement Strategy for data pages.
```

Why did ASE use the index **test_table_ncix**?

- The ASE optimizer chose to use the index **test_table_ncix**, despite datatype mismatches, because the parameter being compared is of type tinyint and a tinyint datatype is smaller than that of a int. Thus, ASE does not have to convert the values in the table and can use the index.

- This is not a recommended implementation of the procedure, but it works.

- FIX: Declare @a as a int.

Distribution Statistics

When a stored procedure is compiled, ASE reads the distribution page (<11.9.2) or the distribution values (c0 - c79) from the table sysstatistics (>=11.9.2). In order for ASE to optimize the procedure, it has to read these distribution or density values to determine if it is going to use an index on a column, or use a table scan.

ASE will use a table scan or another index on a table, if a SARG qualifies an estimated 20% or more of the table. ASE does this to save on I/O, response time, and the number of locks that it has to manage. What follows are examples of different ways that you can code a procedure for a particular value that has an index on it, and the decision that ASE makes for each.

Example:

```
-- create a database "test" with at least 10mb of space.
CREATE DATABASE test
ON device_name=10
go

-- use the database "test".
USE test
```

```
go

CREATE
 TABLE dbo.test_table(
       a CHAR(255)     NOT NULL,
       b NUMERIC(10,0) IDENTITY
)
WITH MAX_ROWS_PER_PAGE=1
go

CREATE NON-CLUSTERED INDEX test_table_ncix
ON dbo.test_table(a)
go

-- Populate the table with 2000 rows that contain "car" for field a.
DECLARE @cnt int
SELECT @cnt = 0
WHILE (@cnt < 2000)
BEGIN
    INSERT INTO dbo.test_table VALUES ('car')
    SELECT @cnt = @cnt + 1
END
go

-- Populate the table with 1 row that contains "truck" for field a.
INSERT INTO dbo.test_table VALUES ('truck')
go

-- Populate the table with 1 row that contains "suv" for field a.
INSERT INTO dbo.test_table VALUES ('suv')
go

-- Since values were inserted after index creation, run update stats
-- so that we get the most current statistics.
UPDATE STATISTICS test_table
go


-- Run sp_recompile on test_table to force recompilation of procedures
-- after the statistics have been regenerated.
EXEC sp_recompile test_table
go

-- To determine distribution of values in the table, run this query.
```

```
-- Look back to these as needed.
SELECT COUNT(*) AS "count",
       a AS "type"
  FROM test_table
 GROUP
    BY a
HAVING COUNT(*) > 0
go

count        type
2000         car
1            suv
truck

CREATE PROCEDURE test_proc_1
AS
BEGIN
   DECLARE @a CHAR(255)
   SELECT @a = 'car'
   SELECT MAX(b)
     FROM test_table
    WHERE a = @a
END
go

-- turn on showplan option to show query plan of the procedure.
SET showplan ON
go

-- execute the procedure and look at the showplan output generated.
EXEC test_proc_1
go

STEP 1
        The type of query is SELECT.
        Evaluate Ungrouped MAXIMUM AGGREGATE.

        FROM TABLE
            test_table
        Nested iteration.
        Table Scan.
        Forward scan.
        Positioning at start of table.
        Using I/O Size 2 Kbytes for data pages.
```

```
        With MRU Buffer Replacement Strategy for data pages.
```

ASE chose to do a table scan. Why would ASE do this?

- When the query was optimized ASE did not know what the value for "**a**" was, so based on the distribution statistics ASE chose to do a table scan.
- The ASE optimizer does not know what the value of a variable field is, regardless if it is a constant or has true variability, at compilation time.
- Therefore, the ASE optimizer looks at the worst case for the distribution values and creates the query plan based on that value.

Example:

```
CREATE PROCEDURE test_proc_2
AS
BEGIN
   DECLARE @a CHAR(255)
   SELECT @a = 'truck'
   SELECT MAX(b)
     FROM test_table
    WHERE a = @a
END
go

-- turn on showplan option to show query plan of the procedure.
SET showplan ON
go

-- execute the procedure and look at the showplan output generated.
EXEC test_proc_2
go

STEP 1
        The type of query is SELECT.
        Evaluate Ungrouped MAXIMUM AGGREGATE.

        FROM TABLE
            test_table
        Nested iteration.
        Table Scan.
        Forward scan.
```

```
        Positioning at start of table.
        Using I/O Size 2 Kbytes for data pages.
        With MRU Buffer Replacement Strategy for data pages.
```

ASE chose to do a table scan. Why would ASE do this?

- When the query was optimized ASE did not know what the value for "**a**" was, so based on the distribution statistics ASE chose to do a table scan.
- The ASE optimizer does not know what the value of a variable field is, regardless if it is a constant or has true variability, at compilation time.
- Therefore, the ASE optimizer looks at the worst case for the distribution values and creates the query plan based on that value.

Example:

```
CREATE PROCEDURE test_proc_3 (@a CHAR(255) = 'car')
AS
BEGIN
   SELECT MAX(b)
     FROM test_table
    WHERE a = @a
END
go

-- turn on showplan option to show query plan of the procedure.
SET showplan ON
go

-- execute the procedure and look at the showplan output generated.
EXEC test_proc_3
go

STEP 1
        The type of query is SELECT.
        Evaluate Ungrouped MAXIMUM AGGREGATE.

        FROM TABLE
            test_table
        Nested iteration.
        Table Scan.
        Forward scan.
```

```
        Positioning at start of table.
        Using I/O Size 2 Kbytes for data pages.
        With MRU Buffer Replacement Strategy for data pages.
```

ASE chose to do a table scan. Why would ASE do this?

- When the query was optimized ASE knew the value for "**a**", if not passed, would default to "car" and based on the distribution statistics for "car", ASE chose to do a table scan because "car" qualifies over 20% of the table.

- However, once the query plan for this procedure is put into procedure cache and is available for use, even if you pass another value that qualifies less than 20%, ASE will re-use the plan from the cached version which chose to do a table scan. Thus, causing ASE to table scan for a value that may only qualify one row.

- If you create the procedure with recompile then it will generate the plan correctly for all queries, regardless of the value passed. But, there is performance hit taken because ASE has to recompile that procedure every time it is executed.

Example:

```
CREATE PROCEDURE test_proc_4 (@a CHAR(255) = 'truck')
AS
BEGIN
   SELECT MAX(b)
     FROM test_table
    WHERE a = @a
END
go

-- turn on showplan option to show query plan of the procedure.
SET showplan ON
go

-- execute the procedure and look at the showplan output generated.
EXEC test_proc_4
go

STEP 1
        The type of query is SELECT.
        Evaluate Ungrouped MAXIMUM AGGREGATE.

        FROM TABLE
```

```
          test_table
      Nested iteration.
      Index : test_table_ncix
      Forward scan.
      Positioning by key.
      Keys are:
          a  ASC
      Using I/O Size 2 Kbytes for index leaf pages.
      With LRU Buffer Replacement Strategy for index leaf pages.
      Using I/O Size 2 Kbytes for data pages.
      With LRU Buffer Replacement Strategy for data pages.
```

ASE chose to use the index **test_table_ncix**. Why would ASE do this?

- When the query was optimized ASE knew that the value for "**a**", if not passed, would default to "truck" and based on the distribution statistics for "truck", ASE chose to use the qualifying index **test_table_ncix** because "truck" qualifies less than 20% of the table.

- However, once the query plan for this procedure is put into procedure cache and is available for use, even if you pass another value that qualifies more than 20%, ASE will reuse the cached plan that chose to use the index, thus forcing ASE to use the index.

- If you create the procedure with recompile then it will generate the plan correctly for all queries, regardless of the value passed. But, there is performance hit taken because ASE has to recompile the procedure every time it is executed.

Example:

```
CREATE PROCEDURE test_proc_5
AS
BEGIN
   SELECT MAX(b)
     FROM test_table
    WHERE a = 'car'
END
go

-- turn on showplan option to show query plan of the procedure.
SET showplan ON
go
```

```
-- execute the procedure and look at the showplan output generated.
EXEC test_proc_5
go


STEP 1
        The type of query is SELECT.
        Evaluate Ungrouped MAXIMUM AGGREGATE.

        FROM TABLE
            test_table
        Nested iteration.
        Table Scan.
        Forward scan.
        Positioning at start of table.
        Using I/O Size 2 Kbytes for data pages.
        With MRU Buffer Replacement Strategy for data pages.
```

ASE chose to do a table scan. Why would ASE do this?

- When the query was optimized ASE knew the value for "**a**" and based on the distribution statistics for "car", ASE chose to do use a table scan because "car" qualifies over 20% of the table.

- This is how I would recommend all procedures that use known constants be written.

Example:

```
CREATE PROCEDURE test_proc_6
AS
BEGIN
   SELECT MAX(b)
     FROM test_table
    WHERE a = 'truck'
END
go

-- turn on showplan option to show query plan of the procedure.
SET showplan ON
go

-- execute the procedure and look at the showplan output generated.
EXEC test_proc_6
```

```
go

STEP 1
        The type of query is SELECT.
        Evaluate Ungrouped MAXIMUM AGGREGATE.

        FROM TABLE
            test_table
        Nested iteration.
        Index : test_table_ncix
        Forward scan.
        Positioning by key.
        Keys are:
            a  ASC
        Using I/O Size 2 Kbytes for index leaf pages.
        With LRU Buffer Replacement Strategy for index leaf pages.
        Using I/O Size 2 Kbytes for data pages.
        With LRU Buffer Replacement Strategy for data pages.
```

ASE chose to use the index **test_table_ncix**. Why would ASE do this?

- When the query was optimized ASE knew the value for "**a"** and based on the distribution values for "truck", ASE chose to use the index **test_table_ncix** because "truck" qualifies less than 20% of the table.

- This is how I would recommend all procedures that use known constants be written.

Example:

```
CREATE PROCEDURE test_proc_7
AS
BEGIN
   DECLARE @a CHAR(255)
   SELECT @a = 'car'
   SELECT MAX(b)
     FROM test_table (index test_table_ncix)
    WHERE a = @a
END
go

-- turn on showplan option to show query plan of the procedure.
SET showplan ON
go
```

```
-- execute the procedure and look at the showplan output generated.
EXEC test_proc_7
go

STEP 1
        The type of query is SELECT.
        Evaluate Ungrouped MAXIMUM AGGREGATE.

        FROM TABLE
            test_table
        Nested iteration.
        Index : test_table_ncix
        Forward scan.
        Positioning by key.
        Keys are:
            a  ASC
        Using I/O Size 2 Kbytes for index leaf pages.
        With LRU Buffer Replacement Strategy for index leaf pages.
        Using I/O Size 2 Kbytes for data pages.
        With LRU Buffer Replacement Strategy for data pages.
```

ASE was forced to use the index **test_table_ncix**.

- When the query was optimized ASE did not have the choice of whether or not to use an index or a table scan, ASE was forced to use the index **test_table_ncix**.
- Even if a query qualified over 20% over the rows in the table ASE would still use the index.
- Why would you want to force an index in ASE? Sometimes forcing the use of an index or providing an index hint, is the only way to get the ASE optimizer to generate the plan correctly (refer to the chapter on Optimizer Hints).
- Forcing the use of an index is fast and can be done without the risk of changing the data that is returned.
- Forcing an index allows you to compare variable expressions in a query and have ASE generate the plan you believe to be the most efficient.

For instance, if we would have coded **test_proc_2** as follows:

```
    CREATE PROCEDURE test_proc_2
```

```
AS
BEGIN
   DECLARE @a char(255)
   SELECT @a = 'truck'
   SELECT MAX(b)
     FROM test_table (index test_table_ncix)
    WHERE a = @a
END
go
```

Then, ASE would use the index **test_table_ncix,** which is the optimal path to traverse to get to the data.

- Be careful when forcing the use of an index because it breaks a relational theory rule, which states, "the relational database engine should determine the path to traverse to reach the data, not the creator of the **SQL** statement." This relational rule is designed to protect the creator of the **SQL** statement from changes that could cause the forced path to be either inefficient or obsolete.

- If it is decided that an index is to be forced than this should be done by an experienced **DBA** who knows the environment and what changes are going to occur to the database in the future.

- However, if queries whose retrieval arguments have known constants are coded correctly, like **test_proc_5** and **test_proc_6**, little **DBA** intervention will be required.

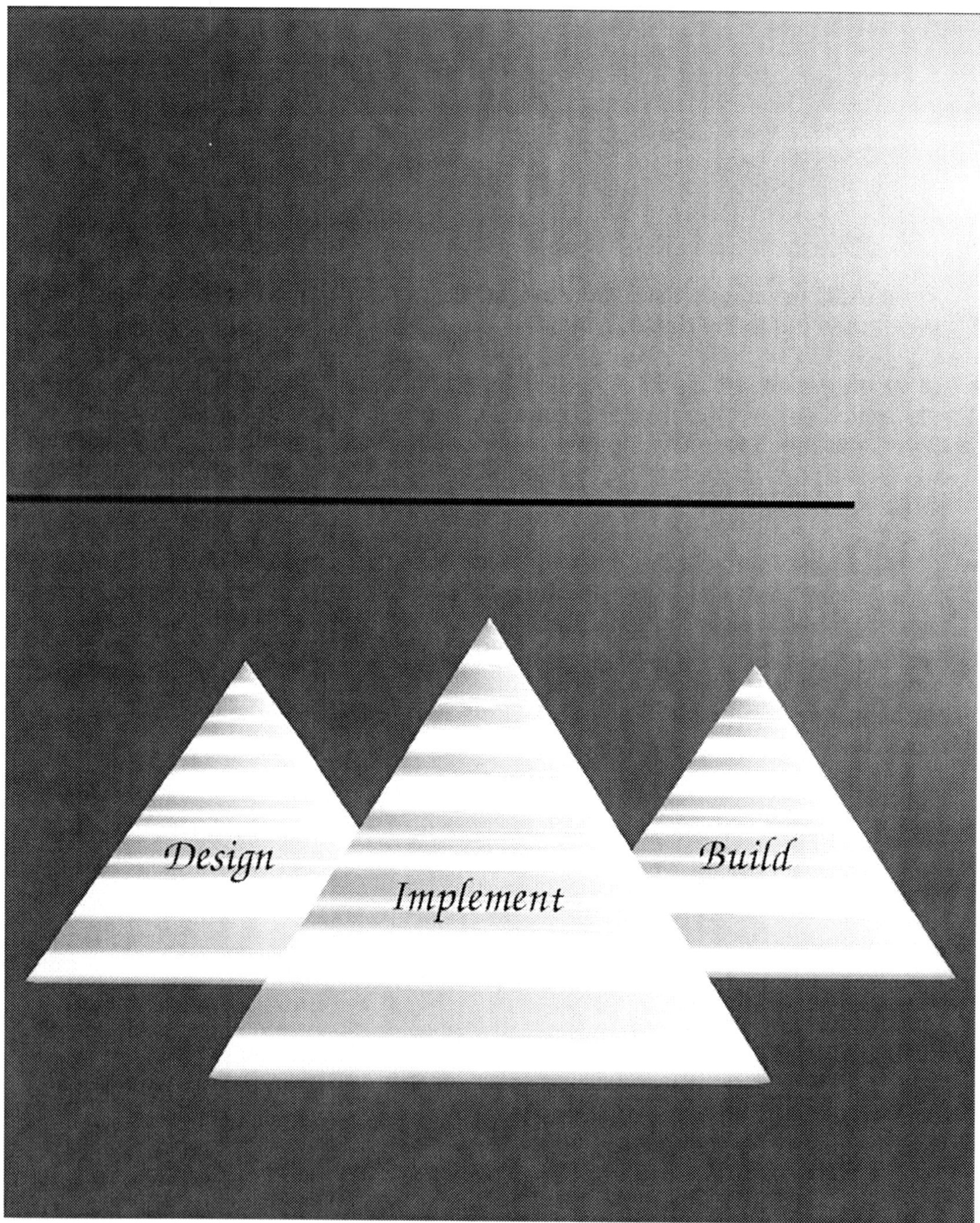
Design
Implement
Build

Chapter 17. Optimizer Hints

Optimizer hints are overrides to the optimizer. They should be used with ***much*** caution. The ASE optimizer does a marvelous job at optimization when data modeling is done correctly, the necessary indexes exist, statistics are up to date, and code is written with thought.

Warning !: Do not use hints unless absolutely necessary. This can cause your code to be harder to maintain and run worse as the system evolves. My suggestion to you is, if you are not highly skilled, just don't do it!

ASE allows you to specify optimizer overrides as follows:

```
[ SET FORCEPLAN ON ]

SELECT columns
  FROM table ( [ INDEX indid or name | PREFETCH size | MRU | LRU ] )
 WHERE columns = something

UPDATE table
   SET columns = something
  FROM table ( [ INDEX indid or name | PREFETCH size | MRU | LRU ] )
 WHERE columns = something

DELETE table
  FROM table ( [ INDEX indid or name | PREFETCH size | MRU | LRU ] )
 WHERE columns = something

[ SET FORCEPLAN OFF ]
```

Specifying Indexes

You can force the use of a particular index using the ***Keyword INDEX*** and specifying either the indid or the index name. If you must force an index to be used you should always use the index name and not the indid. This is because the indid is assigned to many indexes in creation order. Routine database maintenance may cause the indid to change.

You can also specify a table scan by using (INDEX 0). This indicates that ASE should perform a full table scan!

To force an index:

```
SELECT columns
  FROM table ( INDEX index_name )
 WHERE columns = something

UPDATE table
   SET columns = something
  FROM table ( INDEX index_name )
 WHERE columns = something

DELETE table
  FROM table ( INDEX index_name )
 WHERE columns = something
```

To force a Full Table Scan:

```
SELECT columns
  FROM table ( INDEX 0 )
 WHERE columns = something

UPDATE table
   SET columns = something
  FROM table ( INDEX 0 )
 WHERE columns = something

DELETE table
  FROM table ( INDEX 0 )
 WHERE columns = something
```

As we stated earlier using hints can cause application issues for both application maintenance and optimal optimization strategies. However, if you must force an index or table scan, do not do so within your application code. Create a view with the index or table scan forced and use the view as you would the table. This makes maintenance much more easier, and it exposes which objects have indexes or table scans forced.

Example:

```
CREATE
  VIEW vw_[index_name | scan]_test_table
```

```
AS
SELECT columns
  FROM table ( INDEX index_name | 0 )
go
```

The statements needing access to this table, having a forced a method, can now use the view.

Example:

```
SELECT columns
  FROM vw_[index_name | scan]_table
 WHERE columns = something

UPDATE table
   SET columns = something
  FROM vw_[index_name | scan]_table
 WHERE columns = something

DELETE table
  FROM vw_[index_name | scan]_table
 WHERE columns = something
```

Join Orders

To force join order use ***SET FORCEPLAN [ON | OFF]***.

Warning!!! Forcing join orders can increase application maintenance. In addition, system evolution could create a more efficient path.

When you SET FORCEPLAN ON all queries which follow the setting of the option will use the join orders in the order they are specified in a query's FROM clause.

Example:

```
SET FORCEPLAN ON

SELECT t1.columns
  FROM table1 t1,
       table2 t2
 WHERE t1.column01 = t2.column01

SET FORCEPLAN OFF
```

```
go
```

In the previous example, we have forced ASE to start its scan on test_table1 as the *Outer Table*. Depending on the statistics this could be a very, very bad thing. Only a highly skilled DBA should make the call about using such logic.

Prefetch Size

This is a specification of the I/O size that ASE will use for a particular table. This can typically be set without causing too many problems. However, in high volume OLTP systems this value very rarely makes sense to set. When working with large datasets and queries that examine a considerable amount of data, it may make sense to set this value higher if the optimizer is not picking a large size. Very unlikely, though.

In order to determine the impact of this setting, you should run the query with showplan on and statistics io and time on. The size which may be specified for a prefetch size depends upon the server's page size, and if a cache pool of the specified size exists.

Example:
```
SELECT columns
  FROM table (PREFETCH [ 2 | 4 | 8 | 16 | 32 | 64 | 128.....] )
 WHERE columns = something

UPDATE table
   SET columns = something
  FROM table (PREFETCH [ 2 | 4 | 8 | 16 | 32 | 64 | 128.....] )
 WHERE columns = something

DELETE table
  FROM table (PREFETCH [ 2 | 4 | 8 | 16 | 32 | 64 | 128.....] )
 WHERE columns = something
```

MRU and LRU in Data Cache

MRU (most recently used) and LRU (least recently used), are two areas which make up a data cache. When MRU is chosen or forced ASE will fetch-and-discard the read pages. That is, it will not age the pages and will force them out of the cache very quickly. When LRU is chosen or forced, ASE will read the pages and store them such that it will try to hang onto them through aging. The LRU end or bit of cache indicates that the page may be accessed frequently.

Again, ASE does an excellent job at optimization and it very rarely makes sense to change what the optimizer considers optimal.

Below are some examples on how to specify the MRU or LRU data cache strategy.

Note: When MRU is specified, ASE **will not** attempt to keep the pages in cache for access by other commands.

Example (forcing MRU):

```
SELECT columns
  FROM table ( MRU )
 WHERE columns = something
go

UPDATE table
   SET columns = something
  FROM table ( MRU )
 WHERE columns = something
go

DELETE table
  FROM table ( MRU )
 WHERE columns = something
go
```

Note: When LRU is specified, ASE **will** attempt to keep the pages in cache for access by other commands.

Example (forcing LRU):

```
SELECT columns
  FROM table ( LRU )
 WHERE columns = something
go

UPDATE table
   SET columns = something
  FROM table ( LRU )
 WHERE columns = something
```

```
go

DELETE table
  FROM table ( LRU )
 WHERE columns = something
go
```

Chapter 17. Optimizer Hints

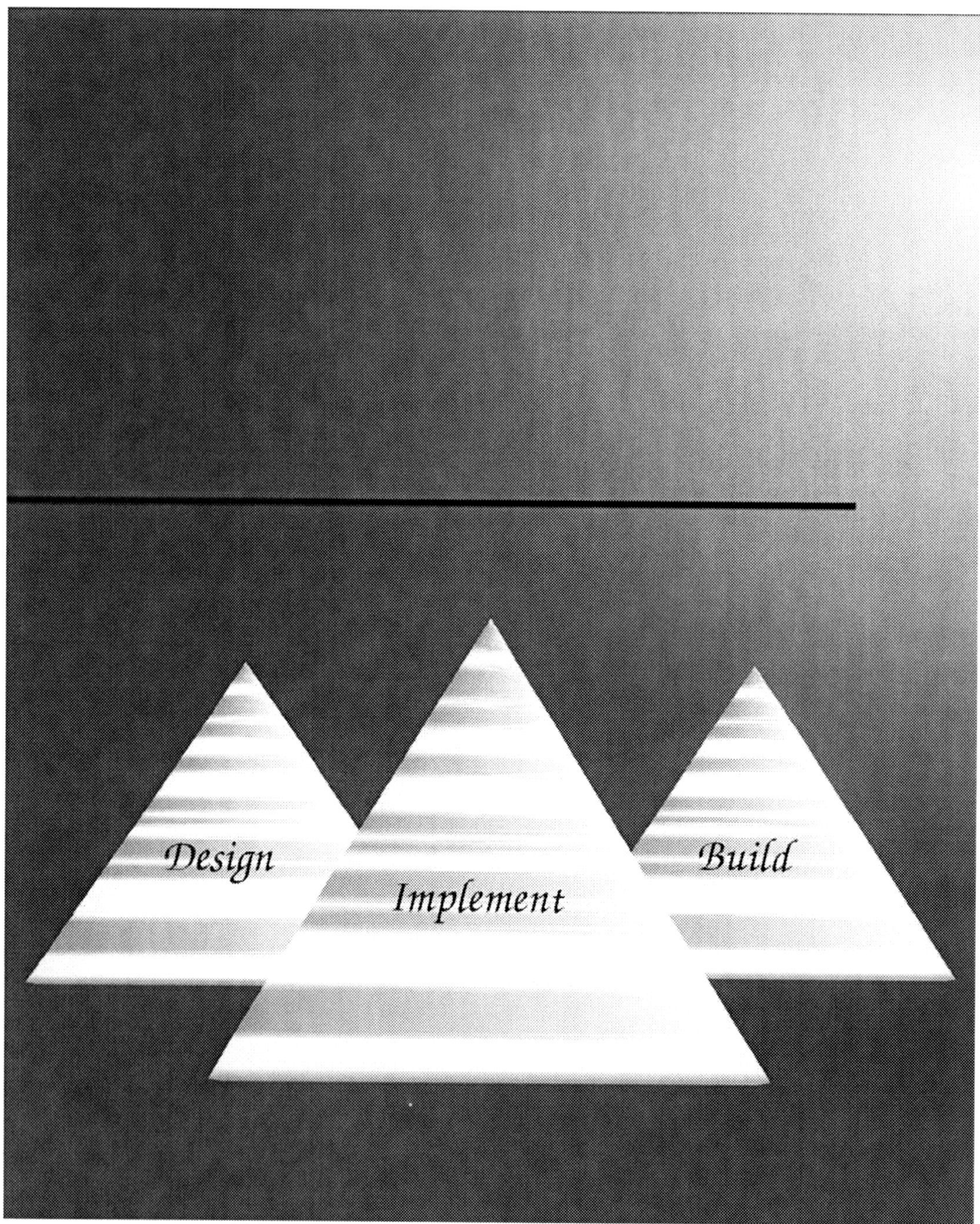
Design
Implement
Build

Chapter 18. System Defined Datatypes

Every variable, parameter, and constant we use in ASE has some associated datatype. This datatype mandates how the variable, parameter, or constant may be used, how many resources are needed, and what can be stored. ASE provides us with a set of system-defined datatypes that we may use in our code.

Below is a table which summarizes the datatypes into several categories: Exact Numeric, Approximate Numeric, Monetary, Date and Time, Character, Binary, Large Objects, and Boolean.

Category	Datatype
Exact Numeric	INT
	INTEGER
	SMALLINT
	TINYINT
	NUMERIC
	DEC
	DECIMAL
Approximate Numeric	FLOAT
	DOUBLE PRECISION
	REAL
Monetary	MONEY
	SMALLMONEY
DATE and TIME	DATE
	TIME
	DATETIME
	SMALLDATETIME
Character	CHAR
	NCHAR
	UNICHAR

	VARCHAR
	NVARCHAR
	UNIVARCHAR
Binary	BINARY
	VARBINARY
Large Objects	TEXT
	IMAGE
Boolean	BIT

Exact Numeric

INT

The INT datatype requires 4 bytes of storage and is used for whole numbers in the range -2,147,483,648 to 2,147,483,647.

INTEGER

The INTEGER datatype requires 4 bytes of storage and used to for whole numbers in the range -2,147,483,648 to 2,147,483,647.

SMALLINT

The SMALLINT datatype requires 2 bytes of storage and is used for whole numbers in the range -32,768 to 32,767.

TINYINT

The TINYINT datatype requires 1 byte of storage and is used for whole numbers in the range 0 to 255.

NUMERIC

The NUMERIC datatype requires CEILING(PRECISION / LOG(256)) + 1 bytes of storage and is used to store numbers with the defined precision and scale. When using a NUMERIC you should specify both the precision and the scale. The precision identifies how many total digits of precision the NUMERIC will have and the scale identifies how many of those digits fall to the right of the decimal point.

For instance, NUMERIC(10, 4) defines an exact NUMERIC with 10 digits of total precision with 4 of those digits to the right of the decimal point and 10 – 4 = 6 digits to the left of the decimal point. To calculate the amount of storage required for the datatype use

```
SELECT CEILING ( 10 / LOG(256) ) + 1
3.0
```

Hence, the NUMERIC(10, 4) requires 3 bytes of storage.

DEC

The DEC datatype requires CEILING(PRECISION / LOG(256)) + 1 bytes of storage and is used to store numbers with the defined precision and scale. When using a DEC you should specify both the precision and the scale. The precision identifies how many total digits of precision the DEC will have and the scale identifies how many of those digits fall to the right of the decimal point.

For instance, DEC(10, 4) defines an exact DEC with 10 digits of total precision with 4 of those digits to the right of the decimal point and 10 – 4 = 6 digits to the left of the decimal point. To calculate the amount of storage required for the datatype use

```
SELECT CEILING ( 10 / LOG(256) ) + 1
3.0
```

Hence, the DEC(10, 4) requires 3 bytes of storage.

DECIMAL

The DECIMAL datatype requires CEILING(PRECISION / LOG(256)) + 1 bytes of storage and is used to store numbers with the defined precision and scale. When using a DECIMAL you should specify both the precision and the scale. The precision identifies how many total digits of precision the DECIMAL will have and the scale identifies how many of those digits fall to the right of the decimal point.

For instance, DECIMAL (10, 4) defines an exact DECIMAL with 10 digits of total precision with 4 of those digits to the right of the decimal point and 10 – 4 = 6 digits to the left of the decimal point. To calculate the amount of storage required for the datatype use

```
SELECT CEILING ( 10 / LOG(256) ) + 1
3.0
```

Hence, the DECIMAL(10, 4) requires 3 bytes of storage.

Approximate Numeric

FLOAT, DOUBLE PRECISION, REAL

The FLOAT, DOUBLE PRECISION, REAL datatypes are used to store approximate numerical values. The FLOAT datatype uses either 4 or 8 bytes of storage depending on the needed precision. The DOUBLE PRECISION datatype uses 8 bytes of storage and the REAL datatype uses 4 bytes of storage.

Warning: These datatypes are approximate numerics and should be used with caution.

Monetary

MONEY

The MONEY datatype requires 8 bytes of storage and may store values in the range -922,337,203,685,477.5808 to 922,337,203,685,477.5807.

SMALLMONEY

The SMALLMONEY datatype requires 4 bytes of storage and may store values in the range -214,748.3648 to 214,748.3647.

Date and Time

DATE

The DATE datatype requires 4 bytes of storage and may store values in the range Jan 1, 0001 to Dec 31, 9999.

TIME

The TIME datatype requires 4 bytes of storage and may store values in the range 12:00:00:000 AM to 11:59:59.999 PM.

DATETIME

The DATETIME datatype requires 8 bytes of storage and may store values in the range Jan 1, 1753 to Dec 31, 9999.

SMALLDATETIME

The SMALLDATETIME datatype requires 4 bytes of storage and may store values in the range Jan 1, 1900 to Jun 6, 2079.

Character

CHAR

The CHAR(n) datatype requires a specified number of n-bytes of storage and is used to store character strings.

UNICHAR

The UNICHAR(n) datatype requires a specified number of n-bytes multiplied by @@UNICHARSIZE of storage and is used to store Unicode character strings.

NCHAR

The NCHAR(n) datatype requires a specified number of n-bytes multiplied by @@NCHARSIZE of storage and is used to store national character strings.

VARCHAR

The VARCHAR(n) datatype accepts up to a number of n-bytes of storage and requires a storage amount equal to that of the string length and is used to store character strings.

UNIVARCHAR

The UNIVARCHAR(n) datatype accepts up to a number of n-bytes of storage and requires a storage amount equal to that of the string length multiplied by @@UNICHARSIZE and is used to store Unicode character strings.

NVARCHAR

The NVARCHAR(n) datatype accepts up to a number of n-bytes of storage and requires a storage amount equal to that of the string length multiplied by @@NCHARSIZE and is used to store national character strings.

Raw Data

BINARY and VARBINARY

The datatypes BINARY(n) and VARBINARY(n) are used to store raw binary data, such as graphics, in hexadecimal notation "0x" in the database. The BINARY(n) datatype requires 1 byte of storage for every two digits of BINARY data. Thus, BINARY(30) requires 30 bytes of storage and can store 60 digits of binary data. The VARBINARY(n) datatype requires a number of bytes of storage equal to the number of digits divided by two and rounded up of storage up to the maximum number "n bytes" to store binary data.

Large Objects

TEXT

The TEXT datatype requires a variable amount of storage dependent upon the amount of bytes to store. The TEXT datatype is used to store printable characters up to 2,147,483,647 bytes in length.

IMAGE

The IMAGE datatype requires a variable amount of storage dependent upon the amount of bytes to store. The IMAGE datatype is used to store raw binary up to 2,147,483,647 bytes in length.

Boolean

BIT

The BIT datatype requires 1 byte of storage and is used to store the values 0 or 1 for true / false decisions.

How ASE Stores Data

ASE stores all data in a storage unit called a page. A page in ASE is somewhat synonymous with a block at the operating system layer. Within a page is an area called the header, which stores information regarding the page's usage. What follows next is the data area and a record offset table for the data area.

How is the data I enter stored?

ASE stores table data as follows:

1. All Not Null Columns first, sorted by creation sequence or Column ID order.

2. All Null Columns last, sorted by creation sequence or Column ID order.

3. When a BIT datatype is encountered, any other bit datatypes (up to seven) are stored along with this BIT. This is because a BIT datatype requires one byte and one byte uses eight binary bits.

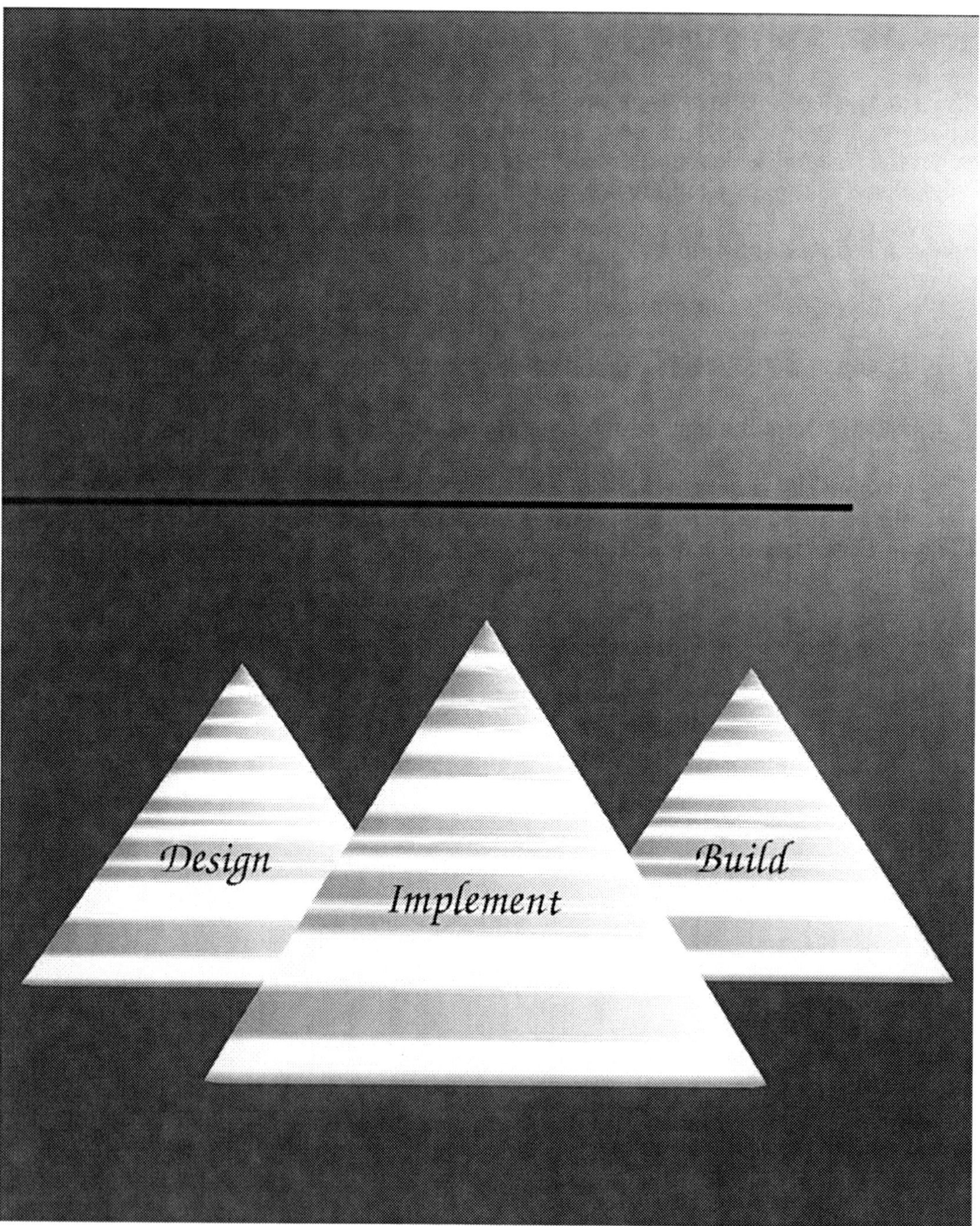
Design
Implement
Build

Chapter 19. Control of Flow Logic

Conditional Logic

IF, ELSE IF, ELSE

ASE supports the if, else if, and else branching logic for conditional statements.

Example 1:

```
IF <conditions>
BEGIN
   <commands>
END
ELSE IF <conditions>
BEGIN
   <commands>
END
ELSE
BEGIN
   <commands>
END
```

In addition, you can nest conditional logic to develop more complex logic.

Example 2:

```
IF <conditions>
BEGIN
   IF < conditions>
   BEGIN
      IF <conditions>
      BEGIN
         <commands>
      END
      <commands>
   END
   <commands>
END
```

Writing your code this way, without any comments, does not do anyone any favors. For the conditional logic, you should indicate the nesting level and in addition, state the purpose of your logic check. We apply this to Examples 1 and 2 to produce more maintainable Examples 3 and 4.

Example 3:

```
/* purpose */
IF <conditions>
BEGIN /* Begin IF Level 1 */
   /* commands purpose */
   <commands>
END /* Begin IF Level 1 */
/* purpose */
ELSE IF <conditions>
BEGIN /* Begin ELSE IF Level 1 */
   /* command purpose */
   <commands>
END /* Begin ELSE IF Level 1 */
/* purpose */
ELSE
BEGIN /* Begin ELSE Level 1 */
    /* commands purpose */
   <commands>
END /* Begin ELSE Level 1 */
```

Example 4:

```
/* purpose */
IF <conditions>
BEGIN /* Begin IF Level 1 */
   /* purpose */
   IF < conditions>
   BEGIN /* Begin IF Level 2 */
      /* purpose */
      IF <conditions>
      BEGIN /* Begin IF Level 3 */
          /* purpose */
         <commands>
      END /* Begin IF Level 3 */
      /* purpose */
      <commands>
   END /* Begin IF Level 2 */
   /* purpose */
   <commands>
```

```
END /* Begin IF Level 1 */
```

CASE, COALESCE, NULLIF

These are three of the most powerful words in T-SQL. They perform conditional checking at a record / row level. COALESCE and NULLIF are just shorthand CASE statements. Were it not for these three words, a significant number of operations would have to be performed using cursors.

Example (CASE):
```
SELECT column_1,
       CASE
         WHEN <condition>
           THEN <expression>
         WHEN <condition>
           THEN <expression>
         ELSE <expression>
       END AS "column_2"
  FROM table
 WHERE column_2 = 5
```

The COALESCE word is used to return the first NOT NULL expression is a series of expressions.

Example (COALESCE):
```
SELECT COALESCE(column_1, column_2, column_3) AS "column_4"
  FROM table
```

The NULLIF word is used to check two expressions for equality. If the two expressions are equal then NULL is returned, else the first expression is returned.

Example (NULLIF):
```
SELECT NULLIF(column_1, column_2) AS "column_3"
  FROM table
```

Control Units

BEGIN, END

The keywords BEGIN and END are used to create a specific control-of-flow unit within T-SQL. We have already seen numerous examples which use the BEGIN and END statement, so little needs to be stated.

Looping Logic

ASE provides us with three methods of looping: WHILE loop, GOTO, and cursors. We will not cover GOTO as a looping method, because it is too dangerous. Instead, we will cover using GOTO and labels as an unconditional branching method apart from the looping logic.

WHILE Loop

The while loop is used to set a condition for the repeated execution of a control unit.

Example 1:

```
WHILE (<conditions>)
BEGIN
   <commands>
END
```

As with the conditional logic, while loops can be nested for further logic handling.

Example 2:

```
WHILE (<conditions>)
BEGIN
   WHILE (<conditions>)
   BEGIN
      <commands>
   END
   <commands>
END
```

To immediately exit out of WHILE loop, you use the BREAK command.

Example 3:
```
WHILE (<conditions>)
BEGIN
   IF (<conditions>)
   BEGIN
      BREAK
   END
   <commands>
END
```

To pass execution back to the innermost WHILE loop without performing any further logic at the remaining base of the WHILE loop, you use the CONTINUE command.

Example 4:
```
WHILE (<conditions>)
BEGIN
   IF (<conditions>)
   BEGIN
      CONTINUE
   END
   <commands>
END
```

As with other T-SQL statements, comments should be used to clarify the programmers intent. We need this is for clarity, support, and maintenance. Let's apply this concept to Example 2.

Example 5:
```
/* purpose */
WHILE (<conditions>)
BEGIN /* Begin WHILE Level 1 */
   /* purpose */
   WHILE (<conditions>)
   BEGIN /* Begin WHILE Level 2 */
      /* purpose */
     <commands>
   END /* Begin WHILE Level 2 */
   /* purpose */
   <commands>
END /* Begin WHILE Level 1 */
```

Cursors

A cursor is a symbolic name associated with a SELECT statement. Thus, a CURSOR has a result set. This result set is accessed via a pointer which points to exactly one record of the result set. A cursor allows manipulation and conditional processing of data at the record or row level of the result set of the SELECT. To use a cursor, you must DECLARE the CURSOR, OPEN the CURSOR, FETCH from the CURSOR, process the record, CLOSE the CURSOR, and DEALLOCATE the CURSOR.

Declaring a Cursor

In order to use a CURSOR, you must first declare it. This operation consists of giving the cursor a name and result set to browse. In addition, you should always declare the cursor's intent (refer to the chapter on cursors for further information). Below is the syntax for declaring a cursor.

```
DECLARE name_of_cursor
 CURSOR
    FOR
 SELECT <column_1>,
        <column_2>,
   FROM <tables>
  WHERE <conditions>
< FOR READ ONLY | FOR UPDATE <OF column_list>>
```

Opening a Cursor

To use a declared cursor you must first open it. This operation actually builds the resultant set "processes the select statement", and prepares the cursors record pointer. Below is the syntax for opening a cursor.

```
OPEN name_of_cursor
```

Fetching Records

Once a CURSOR has been opened, you need to FETCH records. This means that you need to examine the contents of the record set. This is done through the

FETCH command, which is used to store the contents of the "NEXT" record into the specified variables. Below is the syntax for fetching from an open cursor.

```
FETCH name_of_cursor
 INTO variable_list
```

Processing a Cursor

The global variable @@SQLSTATUS is used to process the result set of a cursor using a WHILE loop and the FETCH statement. The @@SQLSTATUS variable has the following return states:

- 0, The last FETCH succeeded.
- 1, The last FETCH failed, check @@ERROR for more information.
- 2, There is no more data to process.

Do not use the @@SQLSTATUS variable directly in the WHILE loop conditions. This always reduces clarity, and it is unsafe if multiple cursors are used. Instead, declare a variable, @name_of_cursor_sqlstatus to hold the status. Let's look at a syntactic example: the process of declaring a cursor, opening cursor, fetching a cursor, and processing the records.

Example:

```
/* purpose */
DECLARE @name_of_cursor_sqlstatus INT

/* purpose */
DECLARE name_of_cursor
 CURSOR
    FOR
 SELECT <column_1>,
        <column_2>,
   FROM <tables>
  WHERE <conditions>
< FOR READ ONLY | FOR UPDATE <OF column_list>>

/* purpose */
OPEN name_of_cursor
```

```
/* purpose */
FETCH name_of_cursor
 INTO variable_list

/* purpose */
SELECT @name_of_cursor_sqlstatus = @@SQLSTATUS

/* purpose */
WHILE (@name_of_cursor_sqlstatus = 0)
BEGIN /* Begin WHILE Level 1 */
   /* purpose */
   <commands>

   /* purpose */
   FETCH name_of_cursor
    INTO variable_list

   /* purpose */
   SELECT @name_of_cursor_sqlstatus = @@SQLSTATUS
END /* Begin WHILE Level 1 */
```

Closing a Cursor

When you are finished processing the result set of cursor, you should close the cursor. This involves removing the cursor result set and the record pointer. At this stage, you could reopen the cursor and process the new result set that is built by the open. Below is the syntax for the closing a cursor.

```
CLOSE name_of_cursor
```

Deallocating a Cursor

Deallocating the cursor frees up all resources associated with the cursor. This includes the cursor declaration and the cursor name. Thus, after a cursor is deallocated it must be redeclared to be used again. You should plan to always to deallocate a cursor once you are completely finished with it. This will release system resources sooner and yield better performance of the system as a whole. Below is the syntax for deallocating cursor.

```
DEALLOCATE
    CURSOR name_of_cursor
```

Unconditional Branching

To perform an unconditional branch or jump, you must declare a label and use the GOTO command to jump to the label's position.

Example 1:

```
/* purpose */
GOTO ENDPROC

/* purpose */
<commands>

/* purpose */
ENDPROC:
```

In the previous example, when the GOTO ENDPROC is encountered, code execution is passed to a point after the label ENDPROC:. Note: We do not use GOTO as looping method. When using labels, processing should never jump backward, always forward.

Unconditional Exiting

To exit out of a stored procedure or SQL batch unconditionally, you use the RETURN command.

Example 1:

```
RETURN <Integer Expression>
```

The specified Integer Expression as part of the RETURN command is passed back to the invoking process for handling. A return value of 0 indicates SUCCESS, while any other value is indicative of some sort of failure.

Displaying Messages

To simply display a message on a client, you use the PRINT command. Below is the syntax of the print command.

```
PRINT <format_string | variable | , <arg_list>>
```

Example 1:
```
To display the value of a local variable
PRINT @variable
```

Example 2:
```
To display the value of a global variable
PRINT @@variable
```

Example 3:
```
To perform string substitution, you use %1!, %2!, …, %n!
PRINT "parm1 is %1!, parm2 is %2!", @var1, @var2
```

Error Raising

The ASE system command RAISERROR is used to generate application error messages. This command sets the variable @@ERROR to the error number in RAISERROR. In addition, RAISERROR displays a warning message to the user about the type of error. Below is the syntax for the command.

RAISERROR *int_error_number > 20000* <@variable | "message text">

To raise the error message "WARNING invalid row count", specifying an error number of 21000 you would execute:

Example 1:
```
RAISERROR 21000 "WARNING invalid row count"
```

Example 2:
```
DECLARE @raised_err_num INT,
        @raised_err_msg VARCHAR(255)

SELECT @raised_err_num = 21000,
       @raised_err_msg = "WARNING invalid row count"
```

```
RAISERROR @raised_err_num @raised_err_msg
```

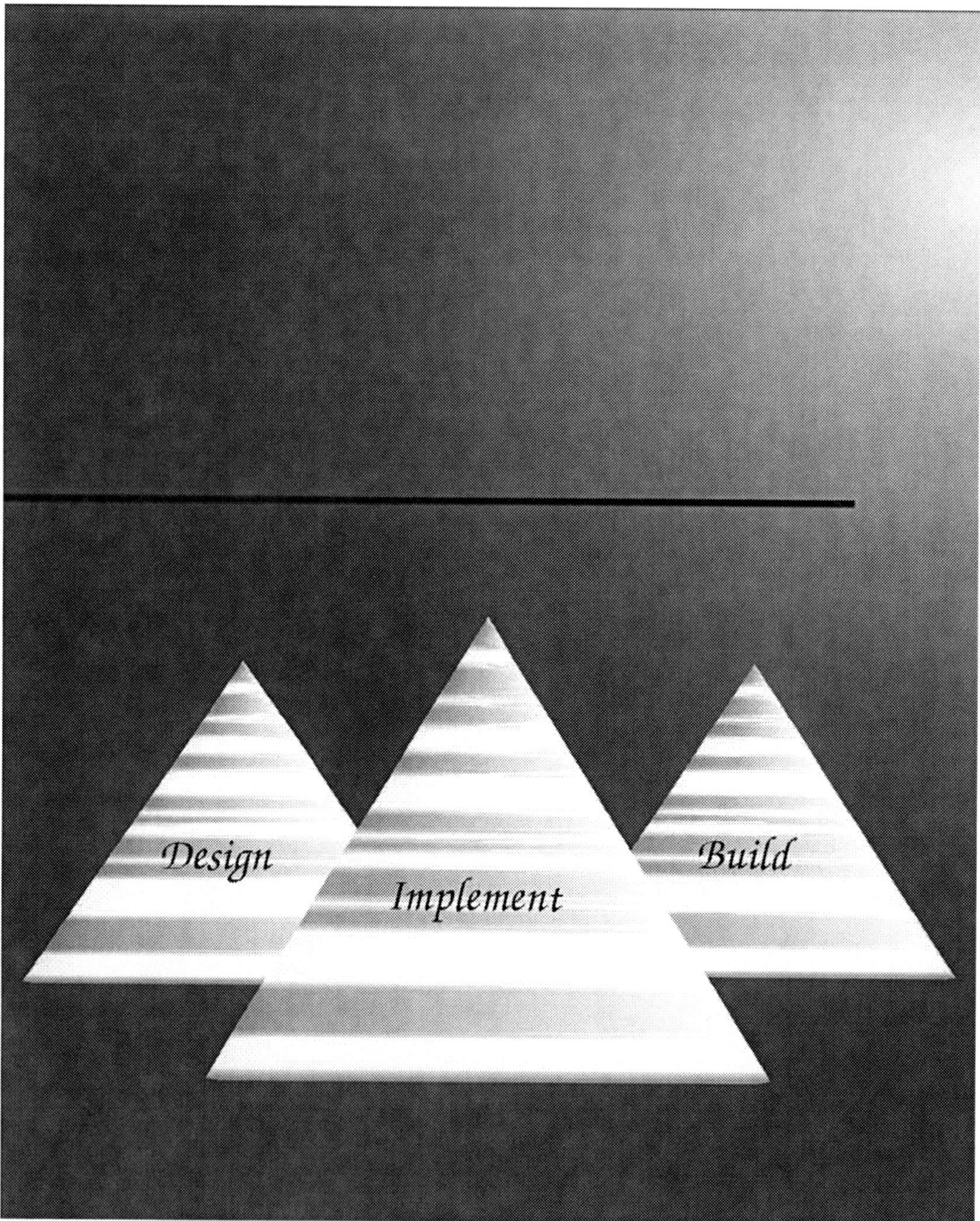
Design
Implement
Build

Chapter 20. EXEC Command

The EXEC command in ASE can be used to execute local stored procedures, remote stored procedures (Referred to as Remote Procedure Calls or RPCs), or SQL as a dynamic SQL statement.

Stored Procedure Calls

Multiple stored procedures within an SQL batch cannot be referenced by their name alone. They must be preceded by the EXEC command.

Example:

```
CREATE PROCEDURE test_proc
AS
BEGIN
   PRINT "You are Here"
END
go
/* EXEC STORED PROCEDURE WITHOUT EXEC */
test_proc
go
```

```
You are Here

/* EXEC STORED PROCEDURE TWO TIMES WITHOUT EXEC */
test_proc
test_proc
go
```

```
You made it Here

/* EXEC STORED PROCEDURE TWO TIMES WITH EXEC USED */
/* FOR THE SECOND PROCEDURE EXECUTION */
test_proc
EXEC test_proc
go
```

```
You made it Here
You made it Here
```

```
/* TO AVOID CONFUSTION WE RECOMMEND THAT YOU ALWAYS USE */
/* EXEC WHEN EXECUTING ANY PROCEDURE */
EXEC test_proc
EXEC test_proc
go
-----------------------------------------------------------
You made it Here
You made it Here
```

Remote Procedure Calls

Remote procedures are stored procedures that exist on another Server. These procedures can be operating system commands through xp_server or stored procedures on another ASE server, Open Server, Oracle instance, MSSQL server instance, or UDB server.

Basically, remote procedure calls allow you to run commands on another server from the ASE server. These procedures while remote to ASE, are local to the other servers. To use RPCs, your DBA must setup the databases to allow them.

To invoke an RPC from ASE, you use the EXEC keyword as you would a normal stored procedure, except that you include the name of the remote server in the execution call.

Example:

```
EXEC ASESRVR2...sp_who
go
```

This would execute the the remote procedure sp_who on ASESRVR2 and return the results to this ASE server. The full syntax of the EXEC RPC is as follows:

```
EXEC server_name.database.owner.remote_procedure parameters
```

Now, if we wanted to run the procedure sp_lock on ASESRVR2, and specify the integer value 30 for @spid1, we would execute:

```
EXEC ASESRVR2...sp_lock @spid1 = 30
go
```

Enterprise Level Sequential Keys

In some shops it necessary to generate an enterprise-level sequential key from a specific site. Using RPCs you can easily make this happen.

Warning!!! In a distributed environment, generating enterprise-level sequential keys in this fashion, can bind the state of your application to the status of the network and the central sequential key server.

In the examples which follow, we will be working with a pair of ASE servers, ASESRVR1 and ASESRVR2. In addition, the DBA has setup the necessary communications for the pair of servers to communicate with one another.

We login into ASESRVR2, and in the test_db database we create the following structures.

```
/* ON ASESRVR2 BUILD THESE OBJECTS */
USE test_db
go

/* create a table used to store and generate sequential keys */
CREATE
 TABLE ent_table_key (
       OBJNAME VARCHAR(30) NOT NULL,
       seq_id INT NOT NULL,
       max_seq_id INT NOT NULL,
       min_seq_id INT NOT NULL,
 CONSTRAINT ix01_table_key
   PRIMARY KEY CLUSTERED ( OBJNAME )
)
LOCK DATAROWS
go

/* create a view with primary key forced to always prevent scans */
CREATE
  VIEW vw_ent_table_key
AS

SELECT OBJNAME,
       seq_id,
       max_seq_id,
       min_seq_id
```

```
  FROM ent_table_key (INDEX ix01_ent_table_key)
go

/* of course lets insert the key values */
INSERT
  INTO vw_table_key(
       OBJNAME,
       seq_id,
       max_seq_id,
       min_seq_id
)
SELECT "test_table",
       1,
       100000000,
       1
go

/* CREATE STORED PROCEDURE TO HAND OUT KEYS */
CREATE PROCEDURE pr_ent_key(
                 @IN_OBJNAME VARCHAR(30),
                 @OUT_seq_id INT OUTPUT
)
AS
BEGIN

   /* GET THE NEXT SEQUENCE KEY FOR SPECIFIED OBJNAME */
   UPDATE vw_ent_table_key
      SET @OUT_seq_id = ( seq_id + 1 ),
          seq_id = CASE
                     WHEN ( seq_id + 1 ) >= max_seq_id
                       THEN min_seq_id
                     ELSE seq_id + 1
                   END
     FROM vw_ent_table_key
    WHERE OBJNAME = @IN_OBJNAME

RETURN 0
END
go
```

Now, many shops need to access servers with different names from servers which share the same code base. In addition, some of these sites have multiple central sites. To reduce the cost of maintaining different code bases for different sites, do not embed the server name of a remote server in your application code.

```
/* ON ASESRVR1 CREATE THESE OBJECTS TO BUILD THE RPC CALL MAP */
USE test_db
go

/* CREATE A TABLE TO STORE REMOTE SERVER TYPES */
CREATE
 TABLE rsrv_typ(
       rsrv_typ_ct VARCHAR(10) NOT NULL,
       rsrv_desc VARCHAR(255) NOT NULL,
 CONSTRAINT ix01_rsrv_typ
   PRIMARY KEY CLUSTERED ( rsrv_typ_ct )
)
LOCK DATAROWS
go

/* CREATE A TABLE TO HOLD ALL POSSIBLE LOCAL SERVER NAMES */
CREATE
  TABLE lsrv(
        LSRVNAME VARCHAR(30) NOT NULL,
        lsrv_desc VARCHAR(255) NOT NULL,
 CONSTRAINT ix01_lsrv
   PRIMARY KEY CLUSTERED ( LSRVNAME )
)
LOCK DATAROWS
go

/* CREATE A TABLE TO STORE SERVER MAPPING INFORMATION */
CREATE
  TABLE rsrv(
        RSRVNAME VARCHAR(30) NOT NULL,
        RDBNAME VARCHAR(30) NOT NULL,
        ROWNER VARCHAR(30) NOT NULL,
        LSRVNAME VARCHAR(30) NOT NULL,
        rsrv_typ_ct VARCHAR(10) NOT NULL,
 CONSTRAINT ix01_rsrv
   PRIMARY KEY CLUSTERED ( LSRVNAME, rsrv_typ_ct ),
 CONSTRAINT lsrv@LSRVNAME
   FOREIGN KEY (LSRVNAME)
     REFERENCES dbo.lsrv (LSRVNAME),
 CONSTRAINT lsrv@RSRVNAME
```

```
   FOREIGN KEY (RSRVNAME)
      REFERENCES dbo.lsrv (LSRVNAME),
 CONSTRAINT rsrv_typ@rsrv_typ_ct
   FOREIGN KEY (rsrv_typ_ct)
      REFERENCES dbo.rsrv_typ (rsrv_typ_ct)
)
LOCK DATAROWS
go

/* POPULATE OUR TABLES WITH SOME INFORMATION */
INSERT
  INTO rsrv_typ(
       rsrv_typ_ct,
       rsrv_desc
)
SELECT "ES",
       "ENTERPRISE SERVER"
go

INSERT
  INTO lsrv(
       LSRVNAME,
       lsrv_desc
)
SELECT "ASESRVR1",
       "TIBET ASE SERVER"
go

INSERT
  INTO lsrv(
       LSRVNAME,
       lsrv_desc
)
SELECT "ASESRVR2",
       "HONG KONG ENTERPRISE CORPORATE SERVER"
go

INSERT
  INTO rsrv(
       RSRVNAME,
       RDBNAME,
       ROWNER,
       LSRVNAME,
       rsrv_typ_ct
```

```
)
SELECT "ASESRVR2",
       "test_db",
       "dbo",
       "ASESRVR1",
       "ES"
go

/* WE ARE NOW READY TO GET A ENTERPRISE SEQUENCE KEY */
DECLARE @OUT_seq_id INTEGER
DECLARE @RSRV_STR VARCHAR(200)

/* GET THE RESERVER EXECUTION INFORMATION */
SELECT @RSRV_STR = RSRVNAME + "."  + RDBNAME + "."
                   + ROWNER + "." + "pr_ent_key"
  FROM rsrv
 WHERE LSRVNAME = @@SERVERNAME
   AND rsrv_typ_ct = "ES"

/* GET THE SEQUENCE KEY */
EXEC @RSRV_STR @IN_OBJNAME = "test_table",
                             @OUT_seq_id = @OUT_seq_id OUTPUT

/* LETS JUST DISPLAY THE SEQUENCE KEY */
SELECT @OUT_seq_id
go
-----------------------------------------------------------------
2
```

Dynamic SQL

The EXEC command can also be used to execute dynamic SQL. However, I have not seen any cases where this was absolutely necessary. In addition, because it is dynamic SQL the optimizer will have to optimize all statements when executed with EXEC. This can cause CPU utilization to increase.

The EXEC command to execute dynamic SQL provides the following features:

1. You can use existence checks for create table, alter table, etc... from within a stored procedure.

2. You can dynamically access objects with variables and potentially in different databases.

3. You may be able to dynamically execute a few SQL statements which may have caused you to use the with recompile option for a stored procedure.

4. You cannot use the create view statement with EXEC in a stored procedure or trigger.

5. You cannot use the EXEC command to execute BEGIN TRAN, COMMIT TRAN, CONNECT TO, DBCC, DISCONNECT FROM, DECLARE CURSOR, DUMP TRAN, ROLBACK TRAN, SET, or USE.

6. You cannot nest EXEC commands.

7. You cannot reference local variables from within the EXEC command.

8. Objects created with EXEC in an SQL batch are not visible to the process until their SQL batch finishes. However, other dynamically executed statements from with their batch can see the objects.

You can use the EXEC command as follows to execute dynamic SQL.

Example:
```
DECLARE @DYNSQL_STR VARCHAR(16384)

SELECT @DYNSQL_STR = "SELECT name" + CHAR(10) +
                     "   FROM master.dbo.sysdatabases" + CHAR(10) +
```

```
                    " WHERE name = 'model'"

EXEC (@DYNSQL_STR)
go
model
```

Notice that you can declare a variable to store the statement to be executed. In addition, when executing dynamic SQL with EXEC, you need to enclose the SQL to be executed within parenthesis ().

If you need to use dynamic SQL, declare a variable as I have done and select your SQL into the variable. In addition, use "+ CHAR(10) +" to format your commands to make them more readable.

Warning!!! The excessive usage of dynamic SQL can cause CPU utilization to increase, and decrease response time and throughput. Therefore, only use when it is absolutely necessary.

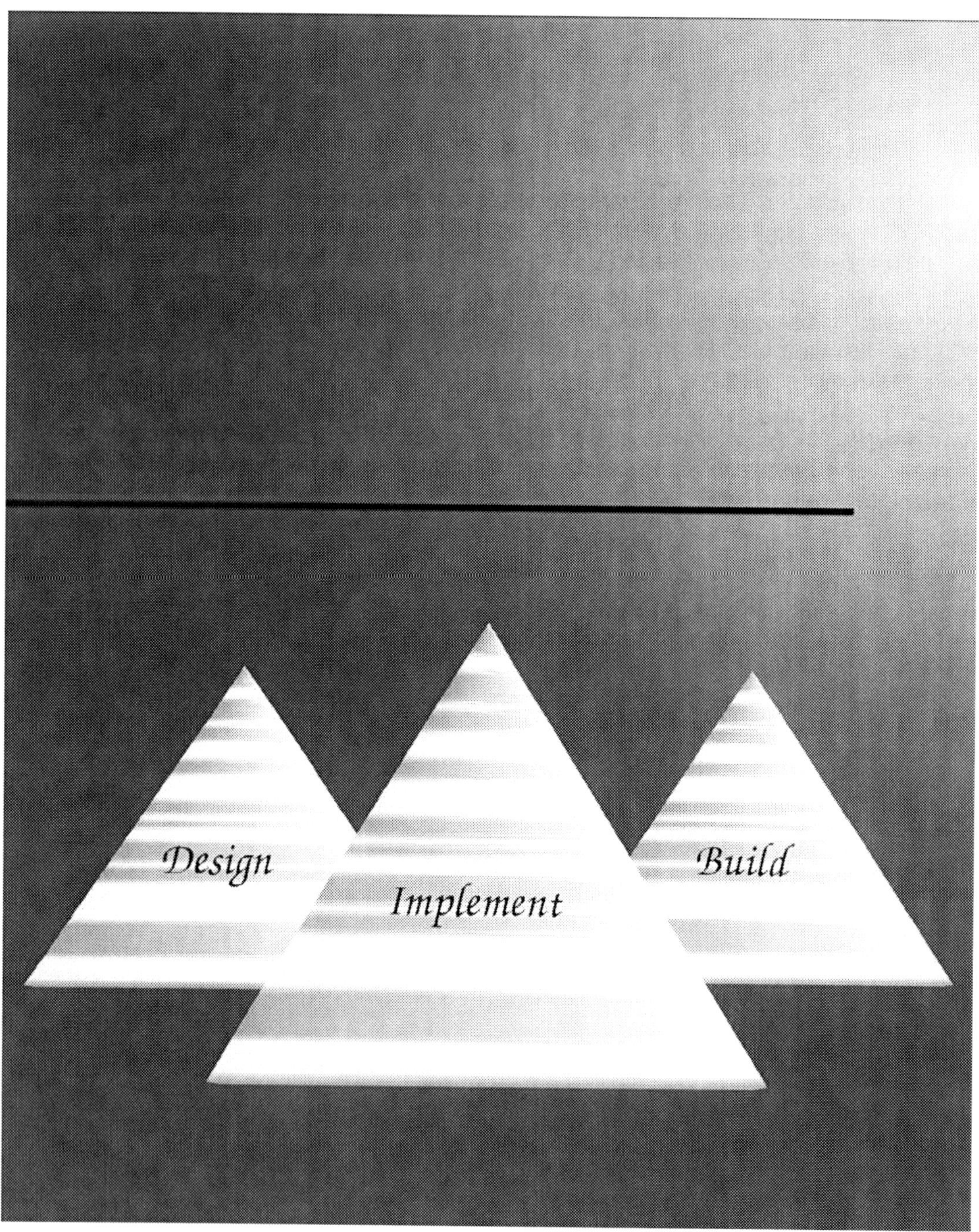
Design
Implement
Build

Chapter 21. Generating Unique Keys

Random Keys

Random keys, when used with clustered indexes to order data for insertion, can be very useful for avoiding "HOT SPOTS" in OLTP systems. Below is an example of a random key generator which generates a random integer number. It uses the ASE system function RAND() and the current system date and time to keep keys random even if someone inadvertently runs a seeded RAND.

```
DECLARE @store_num FLOAT,
        @dt DATETIME,
        @sur_nbr INT


SELECT @dt = GETDATE()
SELECT @store_num = RAND()

SELECT @sur_nbr = ((CONVERT(INT, @store_num * 10) % 2) * 1000000000)
                  + (((@store_num * 10)
                    - CONVERT(INT, @store_num * 10)) * 1000000000)
                  + DATEPART(ms, @dt)*10000
                  + DATEPART(ss, @dt)*1000
                  + DATEPART(mi, @dt)*10
                  + DATEPART(hh, @dt)*10
                  + DATEPART(dw, @dt)
                  + DATEPART(mm, @dt)

SELECT @sur_nbr
go
```

As of ASE 12.5.0.3 you can use the T-SQL function NEWID to generate globally unique random keys. This is a very important feature of random key generation as it allows data transport between systems without the danger of duplicated key values.

Warning: When using the NEWID function make sure that the assignment variable is at least 32 bytes. If it is not, truncation will occur and this could cause duplicate values to be created, not generated.

```
DECLARE @GUID VARCHAR(32)

SELECT @GUID = NEWID()

SELECT @GUID
go
```

Duplicate Values

When using random key generators, it is often necessary to check whether or not a key which has been generated already exists. One can either attempt the insert without checking for a duplicate and @@ERROR, or one can check during the insert and the value of @@ROWCOUNT.

Example (No Insertion Check):

```
DECLARE @store_num FLOAT,
        @dt DATETIME,
        @sur_nbr INT


SELECT @dt = GETDATE()
SELECT @store_num = RAND()

SELECT @sur_nbr = ((CONVERT(INT, @store_num * 10) % 2) * 1000000000)
                    + (((@store_num * 10)
                       - CONVERT(INT, @store_num * 10)) * 1000000000)
                    + DATEPART(ms, @dt)*10000
                    + DATEPART(ss, @dt)*1000
                    + DATEPART(mi, @dt)*10
                    + DATEPART(hh, @dt)*10
                    + DATEPART(dw, @dt)
                    + DATEPART(mm, @dt)

INSERT
  INTO table(
       c1
)
```

```
SELECT @sur_nbr

IF ( @@ERROR = 2601 )
BEGIN
   PRINT "DUPLICATE INSERTION WAS ATTEMPTED"
END
go
```

We do not recommend this approach as it could cause anomalous client errors. Instead, we recommend that you check for a duplicate and perform the insert if a record does not already exist.

Example (With Insertion Check):

```
DECLARE @store_num FLOAT,
        @dt DATETIME,
        @sur_nbr INT


SELECT @dt = GETDATE()
SELECT @store_num = RAND()

SELECT @sur_nbr = ((CONVERT(INT, @store_num * 10) % 2) * 1000000000)
                  + (((@store_num * 10)
                      - CONVERT(INT, @store_num * 10)) * 1000000000)
                  + DATEPART(ms, @dt)*10000
                  + DATEPART(ss, @dt)*1000
                  + DATEPART(mi, @dt)*10
                  + DATEPART(hh, @dt)*10
                  + DATEPART(dw, @dt)
                  + DATEPART(mm, @dt)


INSERT
  INTO table(
       c1
)
SELECT @sur_nbr
 WHERE NOT EXISTS ( SELECT 1
                      FROM table
                     WHERE c1 = @sur_nbr )

IF ( @@ROWCOUNT = 0 )
BEGIN
   PRINT "INSERT NOT PERFORMED, LIKELY DUPLICATE"
```

```
END
go
```

When using random keys for very large tables, duplicates may tend to occur frequently. In such a system, we recommend mixing the insertion check example with a WHILE loop to generate a random key. To avoid any potential infinite loop, you should always establish a race condition.

Example (Insertion Check With Loop):

```
DECLARE @store_num FLOAT,
        @dt DATETIME,
        @sur_nbr INT,
        @loop_cnt TINYINT,
        @rw_cnt INT

SELECT @loop_cnt = 0,
       @rw_cnt = 0

WHILE ( @loop_cnt < 10 AND @rw_cnt = 0 )
BEGIN

   SELECT @dt = GETDATE()
   SELECT @store_num = RAND()

   SELECT @sur_nbr = ((CONVERT(INT, @store_num * 10) % 2)
                      * 1000000000)
                      + (((@store_num * 10)
                       - CONVERT(INT, @store_num * 10)) * 1000000000)
                      + DATEPART(ms, @dt)*10000
                      + DATEPART(ss, @dt)*1000
                      + DATEPART(mi, @dt)*10
                      + DATEPART(hh, @dt)*10
                      + DATEPART(dw, @dt)
                      + DATEPART(mm, @dt)

   INSERT
     INTO table(
          c1
   )
   SELECT @sur_nbr
    WHERE NOT EXISTS ( SELECT 1
                         FROM table
                        WHERE c1 = @sur_nbr )
```

```
   SELECT @rw_cnt = @@ROWCOUNT
   SELECT @loop_cnt = @loop_cnt + 1
END

IF ( @rw_cnt = 0 )
BEGIN
   PRINT "INSERT NOT PERFORMED, LIKELY DUPLICATE"
END
go
```

Sequential Keys

Sequential keys can be very useful for OLTP systems when used along with a non-clustered index and a good clustered index, which orders the data for insertion. On OLTP systems, never create a clustered index on a sequential key on a transaction busy table. This would create a "HOT SPOT" on the last page of the table. In addition, despite row-level locking, this can still cause frequent deadlocks and blocks.

```
/* create a table used to store and generate sequential keys */
CREATE
 TABLE table_key (
       OBJNAME VARCHAR(30) NOT NULL,
       seq_id INT NOT NULL,
       max_seq_id INT NOT NULL,
       min_seq_id INT NOT NULL,
 CONSTRAINT ix01_table_key
   PRIMARY KEY CLUSTERED ( OBJNAME )
)
LOCK DATAROWS
go
/* create a view with primary key forced to always prevent scans */
CREATE
   VIEW vw_table_key
AS
SELECT OBJNAME,
       seq_id,
       max_seq_id,
       min_seq_id
  FROM table_key (INDEX ix01_table_key)
```

```
go
/* of course lets insert the key values */
INSERT
  INTO vw_table_key(
       OBJNAME,
       seq_id,
       max_seq_id,
       min_seq_id
)
SELECT "table",
       1,
       100000000,
       1
go
```

To prevent other applications from acquiring identical keys an update lock should be held against the table, to get the next key. This is done so that duplicate keys are not generated in high volume or high transaction rate environments. This same process can be adopted for many other purposes.

Let's start by giving a bad example of how to get the next key.

Example (Bad Choice):

```
DECLARE @seq_id INT

SELECT @seq_id = ( seq_id + 1 )
  FROM vw_table_key
 WHERE OBJNAME = "table"

INSERT
  INTO table(
       c1
)
SELECT @seq_id
 WHERE NOT EXISTS ( SELECT 1
                      FROM table
                     WHERE c1 = @seq_id )

UPDATE vw_table_key
   SET seq_id = CASE
                 WHEN ( seq_id + 1 ) >= max_seq_id
                   THEN min_seq_id
                 ELSE seq_id + 1
```

```
                END
  FROM vw_table_key
 WHERE OBJNAME = "table"
go
```

The previous example is **not** a good choice because it does not actually prevent any other processes from concurrently accessing the routine and generating the same seq_id.

Example (Another Bad Choice):

```
DECLARE @seq_id INT

BEGIN TRANSACTION

SELECT @seq_id = ( seq_id + 1 )
  FROM vw_table_key
 WHERE OBJNAME = "table"

INSERT
  INTO table(
       c1
)
SELECT @seq_id
 WHERE NOT EXISTS ( SELECT 1
                      FROM table
                     WHERE c1 = @seq_id )

UPDATE vw_table_key
   SET seq_id = CASE
                  WHEN ( seq_id + 1 ) >= max_seq_id
                    THEN min_seq_id
                  ELSE seq_id + 1
                END
  FROM vw_table_key
 WHERE OBJNAME = "table"

COMMIT TRANSACTION
go
```

Although the previous example begins a transaction, it has the exact same pitfalls as the first example. For more information regarding locking, please refer to the chapter about locking.

Example (A Good Choice):

```
DECLARE @seq_id INT

UPDATE vw_table_key
   SET @seq_id = ( seq_id + 1 ),
       seq_id = CASE
                  WHEN ( seq_id + 1 ) >= max_seq_id
                    THEN min_seq_id
                  ELSE seq_id + 1
                END
  FROM vw_table_key
 WHERE OBJNAME = "table"

INSERT
  INTO table(
       c1
)
SELECT @seq_id
 WHERE NOT EXISTS ( SELECT 1
                      FROM table
                     WHERE c1 = @seq_id )
go
```

The best choice involves using a WHILE loop and a race condition as with the random key generation.

Example (Best Choice):

```
DECLARE @seq_id INT,
        @loop_cnt TINYINT,
        @rw_cnt INT,
        @err_val INT,
        @msg_cd INT,
        @msg_str VARCHAR(255)

SELECT @loop_cnt = 0,
       @rw_cnt = 0,
       @msg_str = "OBJECT: "
                  + ISNULL(OBJECT_NAME(@@PROCID), "ADHOC SQL")

WHILE ( @loop_cnt < 10 AND @rw_cnt = 0 )
BEGIN

   UPDATE vw_table_key
```

```
      SET @seq_id = ( seq_id + 1 ),
          seq_id = CASE
                     WHEN ( seq_id + 1 ) >= max_seq_id
                       THEN min_seq_id
                     ELSE seq_id + 1
                   END
     FROM vw_table_key
    WHERE OBJNAME = "table"

   SELECT @err_val = @@ERROR

   IF ( @err_val != 0 )
   BEGIN
      SELECT @msg_cd = 20190
      SELECT @msg_str = @msg_str + SPACE(3)
                        + "error at seq_id generation"
      GOTO EndProc
   END

   INSERT
     INTO table(
          c1
   )
   SELECT @seq_id
    WHERE NOT EXISTS ( SELECT 1
                         FROM table
                        WHERE c1 = @seq_id )

   SELECT @rw_cnt = @@ROWCOUNT,
                    @err_val = @@ERROR,
                    @loop_cnt = @loop_cnt + 1

   IF ( @err_val != 0 )
   BEGIN
      SELECT @msg_cd = 20190
      SELECT @msg_str = @msg_str + SPACE(3)
                        + "error at insertion into table"
      GOTO EndProc
   END
END

EndProc:

IF ( @err_val != 0 )
```

```
BEGIN
   ROLLBACK TRANSACTION
   RAISERROR @msg_cd, @msg_str
END

RETURN @err_val
go
```

Key Ranging

It is sometimes necessary to build key ranges to guarantee uniqueness of data, at an Enterprise level. We call this process key ranging. Ideally, we could simply change the key and add a system identifier. However, because many legacy systems cannot change or are too expensive to change, we do not always have this luxury. Changes have to be cost-justified.

Random Keys

***Warning*!**: System ranges for sequential keys will almost always reduce the lifetime of a key. This will increase the likelihood of generating a duplicate key value.

```
/* Create a table to hold the system identifier */
CREATE
 TABLE sys_opr_id(
       SRVNAME VARCHAR(30) NOT NULL,
       sys_id INTEGER NOT NULL,
 CONSTRAINT ix01_sys_opr_id
   PRIMARY KEY CLUSTERED (SRVNAME)
)
LOCK DATAROWS
go
/* Create a view for table access through index always */
CREATE
  VIEW vw_sys_opr_id
AS
SELECT SRVNAME,
       sys_id
  FROM sys_opr_id (INDEX ix01_sys_opr_id)
go
/* Insert a possible value */
```

```
INSERT
  INTO vw_sys_opr_id(
       SRVNAME,
       sys_id
)
SELECT "ASESRVR",
       100
go
```

Example:

```
DECLARE @store_num FLOAT,
        @dt DATETIME,
        @sur_nbr INT,
        @sys_id INTEGER

SELECT @sys_id = sys_id
  FROM vw_sys_opr_id
 WHERE SRVNAME = @@SERVERNAME

SELECT @dt = GETDATE()
SELECT @store_num = RAND()

SELECT @sur_nbr = (((@store_num * 10)
                      - CONVERT(INT, @store_num * 10)) * 1000000000)
                   + DATEPART(ms, @dt)*100000
                   + DATEPART(ss, @dt)*1000
                   + DATEPART(mi, @dt)*10
                   + DATEPART(hh, @dt)*10
                   + DATEPART(dw, @dt)
                   + DATEPART(mm, @dt)

SELECT @sur_nbr = CONVERT(INT,
                    CONVERT( VARCHAR, @sys_id )
                      + SUBSTRING(
                          CONVERT( VARCHAR, @sur_nbr ), 1, 6 ) )
go
```

Sequential Keys

***Warning*!**: When needing to use sequential keys and system ranges, it will almost always cut into the lifetime of a key and decrease the likelihood of the system key generator to get a unique key. This will increase the likelihood of generating a duplicate key value.

```
/* Create a table to hold the system identifier */
CREATE
 TABLE sys_opr_id(
       SRVNAME VARCHAR(30) NOT NULL,
       sys_id INTEGER NOT NULL,
 CONSTRAINT ix01_sys_opr_id
   PRIMARY KEY CLUSTERED (SRVNAME)
)
LOCK DATAROWS
go

/* Create a view for table access through index always */
CREATE
  VIEW vw_sys_opr_id
AS

SELECT SRVNAME,
       sys_id
  FROM sys_opr_id (INDEX ix01_sys_opr_id)
go

/* Insert possible values */
INSERT
  INTO vw_sys_opr_id(
       SRVNAME,
       sys_id
)
SELECT "ASESRVR1",
       100
go

INSERT
  INTO vw_sys_opr_id(
       SRVNAME,
       sys_id
)
```

```
SELECT "ASESRVR2",
       101
go

/* create a table used to store and generate sequential keys */
CREATE
 TABLE table_key (
       OBJNAME VARCHAR(30) NOT NULL,
       seq_id INT NOT NULL,
       max_seq_id INT NOT NULL,
       min_seq_id INT NOT NULL,
       SRVNAME VARCHAR(30) NOT NULL,
 CONSTRAINT ix01_table_key
   PRIMARY KEY CLUSTERED ( SRVNAME, OBJNAME ),
 CONSTRAINT SRVNAME@sys_opr_id
   FOREIGN KEY ( SRVNAME )
     REFERENCES sys_opr_id ( SRVNAME )
)
LOCK DATAROWS
go

/* create a view with primary key forced to always prevent scans */
CREATE
  VIEW vw_table_key
AS

SELECT OBJNAME,
       seq_id,
       max_seq_id,
       min_seq_id,
       SRVNAME
  FROM table_key (INDEX ix01_table_key)
go

/* of course lets insert the key values */
INSERT
  INTO vw_table_key(
       OBJNAME,
       seq_id,
       max_seq_id,
       min_seq_id,
       SRVNAME
)
SELECT "table",
```

```
        1,
        100000000,
        1,
        "ASESRVR1"
go

/* of course lets insert the key values */
INSERT
  INTO vw_table_key(
        OBJNAME,
        seq_id,
        max_seq_id,
        min_seq_id,
        SRVNAME
)
SELECT "table",
        100000001,
        200000000,
        100000001,
        "ASESRVR2"
go
```

Example:

```
DECLARE @seq_id INT,
         @loop_cnt TINYINT,
         @rw_cnt INT,
         @err_val INT,
         @msg_cd INT,
         @msg_str VARCHAR(255)

SELECT @loop_cnt = 0,
        @rw_cnt = 0,
        @msg_str = "OBJECT: "
                    + ISNULL(OBJECT_NAME(@@PROCID), "ADHOC SQL")

WHILE ( @loop_cnt < 10 AND @rw_cnt = 0 )
BEGIN

   UPDATE vw_table_key
      SET @seq_id = ( seq_id + 1 ),
          seq_id = CASE
                      WHEN ( seq_id + 1 ) >= max_seq_id
                        THEN min_seq_id
                      ELSE seq_id + 1
```

```
                 END
     FROM vw_table_key vtk,
                vw_sys_opr_id vso
    WHERE vtk.OBJNAME = "table"
      AND vso.SRVNAME = @@SERVERNAME
      AND vtk.SRVNAME = vso.SRVNAME

   SELECT @err_val = @@ERROR

   IF ( @err_val != 0 )
   BEGIN
      SELECT @msg_cd = 20190
      SELECT @msg_str = @msg_str + SPACE(3)
                      + "error at seq_id generation"
      GOTO EndProc
   END

   INSERT
     INTO table(
          c1
)
   SELECT @seq_id
    WHERE NOT EXISTS ( SELECT 1
                         FROM table
                        WHERE c1 = @seq_id )

   SELECT @rw_cnt = @@ROWCOUNT,
                    @err_val = @@ERROR,
                    @loop_cnt = @loop_cnt + 1

   IF ( @err_val != 0 )
   BEGIN
      SELECT @msg_cd = 20190
      SELECT @msg_str = @msg_str + SPACE(3)
                      + "error at insertion into table"
      GOTO EndProc
   END
END

EndProc:

IF ( @err_val != 0 )
BEGIN
   ROLLBACK TRANSACTION
```

```
   RAISERROR @msg_cd, @msg_str
END

RETURN @err_val
go
```

New Systems / Tables

The previous examples were designed for use in systems that cannot be modified easily. When creating a new system, we suggest you use the NEWID() function if possible. Otherwise, you might be able to use the following examples of key generators (which are tremendously better than the previous generators), to help guide your development.

The following generator uses a system id, random value, and sequential value. In addition, we define a system id, reversed sequential key for those shops that must have sequential key generation.

System Random Sequential Key

This example generates keys which are unique across systems, has 10000 potential random insertion points about a system id, and uses the Julian seconds as a sequential key. As defined, the system id requires 8 bytes, the random key requires 4 bytes, and the sequential key requires 13 bytes. Thus, the key generator generates a 25 byte character-string key.

Example:

```
/* Create a table to hold the system identifier */
CREATE
 TABLE sys_opr_id(
       SRVNAME VARCHAR(30) NOT NULL,
       sys_id CHAR(8) NOT NULL,
 CONSTRAINT ix01_sys_opr_id
   PRIMARY KEY CLUSTERED (SRVNAME)
)
LOCK DATAROWS
go

/* Create a view for table access through index always */
```

```
CREATE
  VIEW vw_sys_opr_id
AS

SELECT SRVNAME,
       sys_id
  FROM sys_opr_id (INDEX ix01_sys_opr_id)
go

/* Insert possible values */
INSERT
  INTO vw_sys_opr_id(
       SRVNAME,
       sys_id
)
SELECT "ASESRVR1",
       "100"
go

INSERT
  INTO vw_sys_opr_id(
       SRVNAME,
       sys_id
)
SELECT "ASESRVR2",
       "101"
go

DECLARE @JUL_SS CHAR(13)
DECLARE @CDT DATETIME
DECLARE @PCHAR CHAR(1)
DECLARE @RAND_STR CHAR(4)
DECLARE @SYS_STR CHAR(8)
DECLARE @SYS_RAND_SEQ_KEY CHAR(25)

SELECT @CDT = GETDATE()
SELECT @PCHAR = "0"

SELECT @SYS_STR = RIGHT(REPLICATE(@PCHAR, 8)
                        + LTRIM(RTRIM(sys_id)), 8)
  FROM vw_sys_opr_id
 WHERE SRVNAME = @@SERVERNAME

SELECT @RAND_STR = RIGHT(REPLICATE(@PCHAR, 4) +
```

```
                      CONVERT(VARCHAR, RAND() * 1000), 4)

SELECT @JUL_SS = CONVERT(VARCHAR, DATEPART(YY, @CDT))
                 + RIGHT(REPLICATE(@PCHAR, 3)
                     + CONVERT(VARCHAR, DATEPART(DY, @CDT)), 3)
                 + RIGHT(REPLICATE(@PCHAR, 2)
                     + CONVERT(VARCHAR, DATEPART(HH, @CDT)), 2)
                 + RIGHT(REPLICATE(@PCHAR, 2)
                     + CONVERT(VARCHAR, DATEPART(MI, @CDT)), 2)
                 + RIGHT(REPLICATE(@PCHAR, 2)
                     + CONVERT(VARCHAR, DATEPART(SS, @CDT)), 2)

SELECT @SYS_RAND_SEQ_KEY = @SYS_STR + @RAND_STR + @JUL_SS

SELECT @SYS_RAND_SEQ_KEY
go
0000010114572004157015316
```

Duplicates

Let's add a duplicate-handling process to the above code for the system random sequential key generator.

Example:

```
DECLARE @JUL_SS CHAR(13)
DECLARE @CDT DATETIME
DECLARE @PCHAR CHAR(1)
DECLARE @RAND_STR CHAR(4)
DECLARE @SYS_STR CHAR(8)
DECLARE @SYS_RAND_SEQ_KEY CHAR(25)
DECLARE @loop_cnt TINYINT
DECLARE @rw_cnt INT
DECLARE @err_val INT
DECLARE @msg_cd INT
DECLARE @msg_str VARCHAR(255)

SELECT @loop_cnt = 0
SELECT @rw_cnt = 0
SELECT @msg_str = "OBJECT: "
                  + ISNULL(OBJECT_NAME(@@PROCID), "ADHOC SQL")

SELECT @PCHAR = "0"
```

```
SELECT @SYS_STR = RIGHT(REPLICATE(@PCHAR, 8)
                      + LTRIM(RTRIM(sys_id)), 8)
  FROM vw_sys_opr_id
 WHERE SRVNAME = @@SERVERNAME

WHILE ( @loop_cnt < 10 AND @rw_cnt = 0 )
BEGIN
   SELECT @CDT = GETDATE()

   SELECT @RAND_STR = RIGHT(REPLICATE(@PCHAR, 4) +
                       CONVERT(VARCHAR, RAND() * 1000), 4)

   SELECT @JUL_SS = CONVERT(VARCHAR, DATEPART(YY, @CDT))
                  + RIGHT(REPLICATE(@PCHAR, 3)
                      + CONVERT(VARCHAR, DATEPART(DY, @CDT)), 3)
                  + RIGHT(REPLICATE(@PCHAR, 2)
                      + CONVERT(VARCHAR, DATEPART(HH, @CDT)), 2)
                  + RIGHT(REPLICATE(@PCHAR, 2)
                      + CONVERT(VARCHAR, DATEPART(MI, @CDT)), 2)
                  + RIGHT(REPLICATE(@PCHAR, 2)
                      + CONVERT(VARCHAR, DATEPART(SS, @CDT)), 2)

   SELECT @SYS_RAND_SEQ_KEY = @SYS_STR + @RAND_STR + @JUL_SS

   INSERT
     INTO table(
          c1
   )
   SELECT @SYS_RAND_SEQ_KEY
    WHERE NOT EXISTS ( SELECT 1
                         FROM table
                        WHERE c1 = @SYS_RAND_SEQ_KEY )

   SELECT @rw_cnt = @@ROWCOUNT
   SELECT @loop_cnt = @loop_cnt + 1
END

IF ( @rw_cnt = 0 )
BEGIN
   PRINT "INSERT NOT PERFORMED, LIKELY DUPLICATE"
END
go
```

System Reversed Sequential Key

This example generates keys which are unique across systems, and has 10 sequential insertion points about a system id. As defined, the system id requires 8 bytes, and the sequential key requires 17 bytes. Thus, a a 25-byte character string (almost 100,000 trillion !).

Example:
```
/* Create a table to hold the system identifier */
CREATE
 TABLE sys_opr_id(
       SRVNAME VARCHAR(30) NOT NULL,
       sys_id CHAR(8) NOT NULL,
 CONSTRAINT ix01_sys_opr_id
   PRIMARY KEY CLUSTERED (SRVNAME)
)
LOCK DATAROWS
go

/* Create a view for table access through index always */
CREATE
  VIEW vw_sys_opr_id
AS

SELECT SRVNAME,
       sys_id
  FROM sys_opr_id (INDEX ix01_sys_opr_id)
go

/* Insert possible values */
INSERT
  INTO vw_sys_opr_id(
       SRVNAME,
       sys_id
)
SELECT "ASESRVR1",
       "100"
go

INSERT
  INTO vw_sys_opr_id(
       SRVNAME,
```

```
       sys_id
)
SELECT "ASESRVR2",
       "101"
go

/* create a table used to store and generate sequential keys */
CREATE
 TABLE table_key (
       OBJNAME VARCHAR(30) NOT NULL,
       seq_id NUMERIC(17,0) NOT NULL,
       max_seq_id NUMERIC(17,0) NOT NULL,
       min_seq_id NUMERIC(17,0) NOT NULL,
       SRVNAME VARCHAR(30) NOT NULL,
 CONSTRAINT ix01_table_key
   PRIMARY KEY CLUSTERED ( OBJNAME ),
 CONSTRAINT SRVNAME@sys_opr_id
   FOREIGN KEY ( SRVNAME )
     REFERENCES dbo.sys_opr_id ( SRVNAME )
)
LOCK DATAROWS
go

/* create a view with primary key forced to always prevent scans */
CREATE
  VIEW vw_table_key
AS

SELECT OBJNAME,
       seq_id,
       max_seq_id,
       min_seq_id,
       SRVNAME
  FROM table_key (INDEX ix01_table_key)
go

/* of course lets insert the key values */
INSERT
  INTO vw_table_key(
       OBJNAME,
       seq_id,
       max_seq_id,
       min_seq_id,
       SRVNAME
```

```
)
SELECT "table1",
       1,
       99999999999999999,
       1,
       "ASESRVR1"
go

/* of course lets insert the key values */
INSERT
  INTO vw_table_key(
       OBJNAME,
       seq_id,
       max_seq_id,
       min_seq_id,
       SRVNAME
)
SELECT "table2",
       1,
       99999999999999999,
       1,
       "ASESRVR1"
go

DECLARE @PCHAR CHAR(1)
DECLARE @SYS_STR CHAR(8)
DECLARE @SYS_SEQ CHAR(17)
DECLARE @SYS_SEQ_KEY CHAR(25)
DECLARE @seq_id NUMERIC(17, 0)

SELECT @PCHAR = "0"

SELECT @SYS_STR = RIGHT(REPLICATE(@PCHAR, 8)
                        + LTRIM(RTRIM(sys_id)), 8)
  FROM vw_sys_opr_id
 WHERE SRVNAME = @@SERVERNAME

UPDATE vw_table_key
   SET @seq_id = ( seq_id + 1 ),
       seq_id = CASE
                  WHEN ( seq_id + 1 ) >= max_seq_id
                    THEN min_seq_id
                  ELSE seq_id + 1
                END
```

```
  FROM vw_table_key vtk,
       vw_sys_opr_id vso
 WHERE vtk.OBJNAME = "table"
   AND vso.SRVNAME = @@SERVERNAME
   AND vtk.SRVNAME = vso.SRVNAME

SELECT @SYS_SEQ = LEFT(REVERSE(CONVERT(VARCHAR, @seq_id))
                            + REPLICATE(@PCHAR, 17), 17)

SELECT @SYS_SEQ_KEY = @SYS_STR + @SYS_SEQ

SELECT @SYS_SEQ_KEY
go
-------------------------------------------------------------------
0000010120000000000000000
```

Duplicates

Let's add a duplicate-handling process to the above code for the system random sequential key generator.

Example:

```
DECLARE @PCHAR CHAR(1)
DECLARE @SYS_STR CHAR(8)
DECLARE @SYS_SEQ CHAR(17)
DECLARE @SYS_SEQ_KEY CHAR(25)
DECLARE @seq_id NUMERIC(17, 0)
DECLARE @loop_cnt TINYINT
DECLARE @rw_cnt INT
DECLARE @err_val INT
DECLARE @msg_cd INT
DECLARE @msg_str VARCHAR(255)

SELECT @loop_cnt = 0
SELECT @rw_cnt = 0
SELECT @msg_str = "OBJECT: "
                + ISNULL(OBJECT_NAME(@@PROCID), "ADHOC SQL")

SELECT @PCHAR = "0"

SELECT @SYS_STR = RIGHT(REPLICATE(@PCHAR, 8)
                      + LTRIM(RTRIM(sys_id)), 8)
  FROM vw_sys_opr_id
```

```
 WHERE SRVNAME = @@SERVERNAME

WHILE ( @loop_cnt < 10 AND @rw_cnt = 0 )
BEGIN

   UPDATE vw_table_key
      SET @seq_id = ( seq_id + 1 ),
          seq_id = CASE
                     WHEN ( seq_id + 1 ) >= max_seq_id
                       THEN min_seq_id
                     ELSE seq_id + 1
                   END
     FROM vw_table_key vtk,
          vw_sys_opr_id vso
    WHERE vtk.OBJNAME = "table"
      AND vso.SRVNAME = @@SERVERNAME
      AND vtk.SRVNAME = vso.SRVNAME

   SELECT @SYS_SEQ = LEFT(REVERSE(CONVERT(VARCHAR, @seq_id))
                                  + REPLICATE(@PCHAR, 17), 17)

   SELECT @SYS_SEQ_KEY = @SYS_STR + @SYS_SEQ

   INSERT
     INTO table(
          c1
   )
   SELECT @SYS_SEQ_KEY
    WHERE NOT EXISTS ( SELECT 1
                         FROM table
                        WHERE c1 = @SYS_SEQ_KEY )

   SELECT @rw_cnt = @@ROWCOUNT
   SELECT @loop_cnt = @loop_cnt + 1
END

IF ( @rw_cnt = 0 )
BEGIN
   PRINT "INSERT NOT PERFORMED, LIKELY DUPLICATE"
END
go
```

Chapter 21. Generating Unique Keys

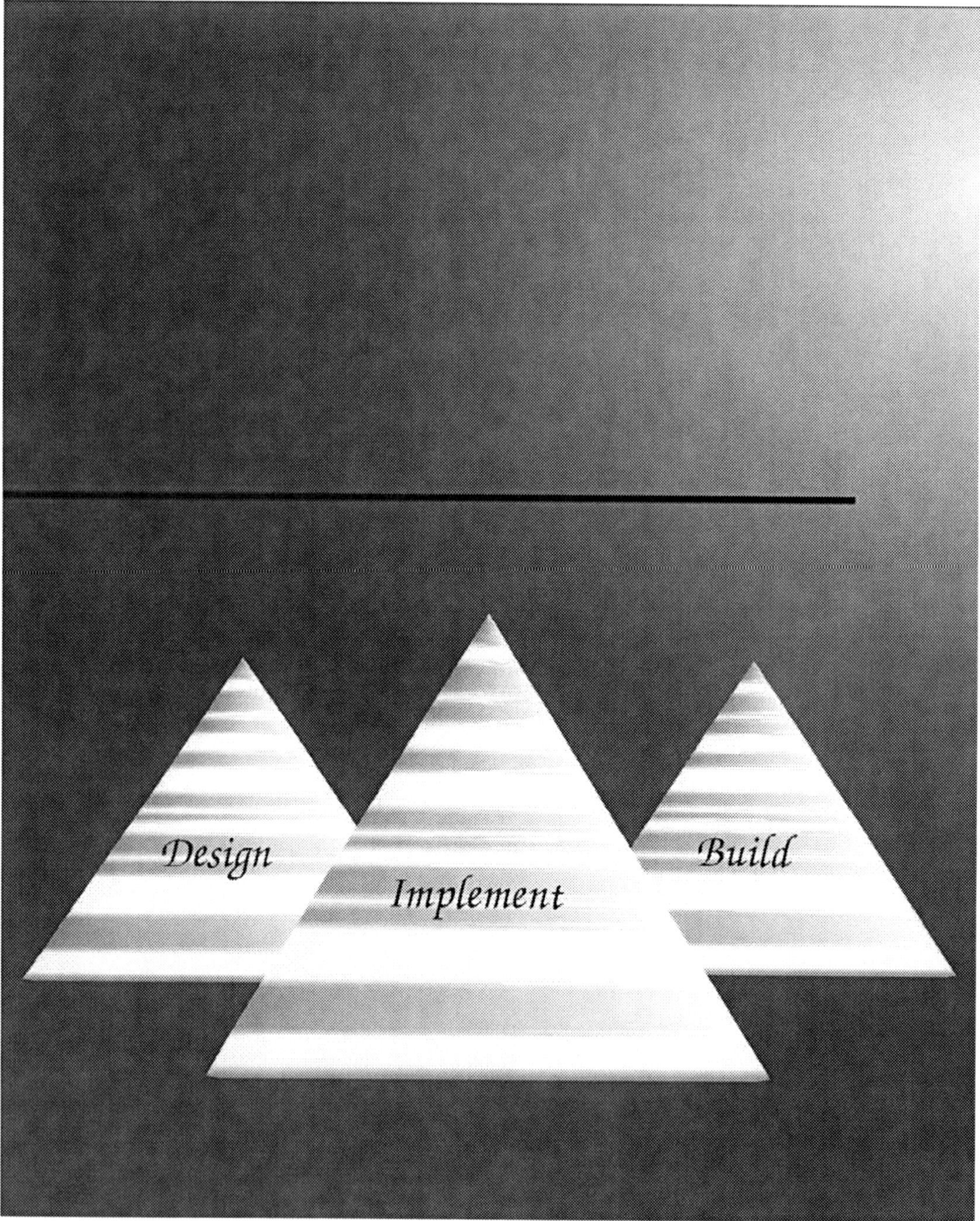
Design
Implement
Build

Chapter 22. Working with Strings

A string is a very interesting concept. It can consist of characters, numbers, punctuation marks and other symbols, and a mixture of the latter. For instance, ABC, 123, .?, and A1?/ are all examples of strings. In ASE, there are two categories of strings: non-varying and varying.

Non-Varying Strings

ASE supports three types of non-varying character strings: CHAR, NCHAR, and UNICHAR. It is very important to note that when a CHAR, NCHAR, or a UNICHAR datatype is used as the datatype for a NULLABLE column of a table, ASE treats these as VARCHAR, NVARCHAR, and UNIVARCHAR respectively – that is, as being of varying length.

Note: NCHAR is required by ANSI to be based upon some character set. The non-varying datatypes CHAR and NCHAR are *both* based upon the server's *default* character set.

CHAR

A CHAR is typically used for both single-byte character sets such as the us_english character set, and for multi-byte character sets such as Japanese.

A CHAR string is always a fixed-length string. When a column, variable, or parameter is defined as being of the datatype CHAR, any and all values that are shorter than the defined storage of the CHAR type are ***right*** padded with blanks. When using CHAR you must specify the number of n-bytes to allocate as CHAR(n).

Example:

```
DECLARE @VAR1 CHAR(10)

SELECT @VAR1 = "ABC"

SELECT @VAR1
go
```

```
ABC
```

Not too stunning. We entered, stored, and retrieved three characters. But did we really?

Try this:

```
DECLARE @VAR1 CHAR(10)

SELECT @VAR1 = "ABC"

SELECT CHAR_LENGTH(@VAR1)
go
----------------------------------------------------------------
10

SELECT CHAR_LENGTH("ABC")
go
----------------------------------------------------------------
3
```

We didn't, we can see now that we entered three characters, stored ten, and retrieved ten characters. Through this illustration, we can visually see that a CHAR type is fixed-length and pads to the right of the string. With what? With spaces .

If you would like to see this for yourself, consider the following.

Example:

```
DECLARE @VAR1 CHAR(10)

SELECT @VAR1 = "ABC"

SELECT ASCII( SUBSTRING(@VAR1, 4, 1) )
----------------------------------------------------------------
32
```

Which happens to be the ASCII character code for a space. Proof positive, *swoosh*. QED.

UNICHAR

The aim of UNICODE is to be able to represent any human written language as a *universal mapping* of bits. As UNICODE has evolved, it set forth a number of standards including UTF-8 (8 bit representation), UTF-16(16 bit representation), and UTF-32 (32 bit representation) as examples. These different encoding standards have come about mainly from not having enough storage to natively store all human written characters as a consistent storage length.

As the world has become smaller and has embraced computers, a growing number of companies, government agencies, universities, etc. need to have a consistent method of communication. In the past and even today, clients needed to convert characters based on some scheme to their language. This has serious performance implications from both the timely delivering and receipt of messages, to frequent errors which can arise.

ASE 12.5.(*n* > 0) uses the UNICODE UTF-16 encoding scheme which requires 16 bits to store a character. In rare cases, a character must be represented as a pair of 16 bits or 32 bits. This is known as surrogate pairs. This is not due to any deficiency within ASE, but with the storage deficiencies (not enough bits!) in the UTF-16 code set to represent all human written language as a consistent number of bits. Out of this arose, UTF-32 which uses 32 bits to represent characters, and a modification of UTF-16 to support more character-to-bit mappings through a process which is known as planeing.

Planeing

Consider Base-2 which consists of only a 0 and a 1. In Base-2 an unsigned integer of 2 bytes has a Base-10 range of 0 to 65535. In Base-2 the range to represent this is 0000000000000000 to 1111111111111111, respectively. So how do we represent negative integers? We split the range of Base-2 numbers to have specific properties based upon two planes. That is, if the integer starts with a 0-Bit it is positive and if it starts with a 1-Bit it is negative. Thus, a plane for positive integers and a plane for negative integers was created.

The range in Base-2 for 2 byte positive integers becomes 0000000000000000 to 0111111111111111 and for 2 byte negative integers becomes 1000000000000000 to 1111111111111111. While although a primitive example of planeing as compared to how it is done with UTF-16, it does give you an idea of what is meant by planeing. Now, UTF-16 is divided into 17 planes. Yuck !!!

In our Base-2 example of understanding planeing, we did not really gain any number of characters. For unsigned integers a Base-10 range of 0 to 32768 or 32769 possible character assignments and signed integers -1 to -32768 or 32768 possible characters assignments. Which happens to yield 65536 possible character assignments. The point is that we need to gain character-to-bit mappings if we expect to be able to map more characters to bits. Thus, the concept of surrogate pairs was adopted in UTF-16.

Surrogate pairs are pairs of 2 bytes. The first 2 bytes are broken into a range which indicates *both* two more bytes to follow and the start of a UTF-16 encoded character. This byte range in the first two bytes of a surrogate pair has become known as the “high surrogate” and has a range of D800 to DBFF. The second set of two bytes which follows the high surrogate is used *both* to signal that this is a surrogate pair and to yield a greater precision of character-to-bit mappings. This second set of two bytes has become known as the “low surrogate” and has a range of DC00 to DFFF. It is only when both of these conditions is true that a surrogate pair exists.

So exactly how does this increase the range of character-to-bit mappings? First off, the ranges of D800 to DBFF and DC00 to DFFF, or simply D800-DFFF are reserved for surrogate pairs. Thus, the number of 2 bytes mappings in plane 0 is defined by the set {0000-FFFF} MINUS the set {D800-DFFF}. Through careful examination of the bytes you can see that this yields (16) * (16) * (16) * (16) - (1) * (8) * (16) * (16) = 65536 - 2048 = 63488 character bit mappings in plane 0. These bit mappings are in the range of 0000-D7FF ***and*** E000-FFFF or CAST as an integer 0-55295 ***and*** 57344-65535.

The other 16 of the 17 planes, planes 1-16, exist within the ***High Surrogate and Low Surrogate***. Remember the blocked off range for the high surrogate was D800-DBFF and the blocked off range for a low surrogate was DC00-DFFF. Also remember, the low surrogate 2 bytes resides immediately after the high surrogate. Which gives us this relationship for a surrogate pair: (D800-DBFF)(DC00-DFFF). This pair of 2 bytes, or single 4 byte, can generate up to (1) * (4) * (16) * (16) * (1) * (4) * (16) * (16) = 1048576 additional character-to-bit mappings as a surrogate pairing. This increases the number of possible representable characters in UTF-16, without surrogate pairs allowed, from 65536 characters to (1048576 + 63488) = 1112064 in UTF-16 with surrogate pairing.

Let's reiterate, as of the writing of this publication, ASE uses the UTF-16 encoding for UNICODE data. This typically requires only 2 bytes or 16 bits of storage. However, in rare cases as discussed previously, 4 bytes or 32 bits of storage may be necessary to store a single character.

Note: When working with UNIICODE data in hexadecimal, it is a common practice to refer to a UNICODE character as U+(Hexadecimal String).

The Global Variable @@UNICHARSIZE is currently equal to 2 for 2 bytes indicating UTF-16 character-to-bit storage. Thus, a single character defined as CHAR requires only 1 byte and a single character as a UNICHAR requires 2 ***OR 4*** bytes. When using UNICHAR, the specified number *n* in UNICHAR(n) is **not** used to indicate how many bytes to allocate, but ***how many characters*** it can store. Thus, the specified number *n* multiplied by @@UNICHARSIZE yields the number of bytes allocated for UNICHAR(n).

Let's illustrate.

Example:

Note: The CHAR_LENGTH function returns the number of characters in a string and the DATALENGTH function returns the number of bytes of storage used by a column, variable, or parameter for its defined datatype.

```
DECLARE @VAR1 CHAR(6)

SELECT @VAR1 = "ABC"

SELECT DATALENGTH(@VAR1)
go
6
```

```
DECLARE @VAR1 UNICHAR(6)

SELECT @VAR1 = "ABC"

SELECT DATALENGTH(@VAR1)
go
12
```

From the preceding example, we can see that the string "ABC" when CAST as a CHAR(6) required 6 bytes of storage and when CAST as a UNICHAR(6) requires12 bytes of storage. This was to be expected.

As with the CHAR datatype, UNICHAR datatypes are right padded to fill all empty space at the right-hand end of the string.

NCHAR

The NCHAR datatype referred to as NATIONAL CHAR, is to used for both single-byte and multi-byte character sets, just as CHAR. Both CHAR and NCHAR operate on the servers ***default character set***. However, whereas space for CHAR is allocated by a specified number of bytes, space for NCHAR is allocated by a specified number of *n* characters multiplied by the storage required for a character @@NCHARSIZE.

Varying Strings

VARCHAR

A VARCHAR string is a variable-length string. When a column, variable, or parameter is defined as being of the datatype VARCHAR, any and all values that are shorter than the defined storage of the VARCHAR are empty, they don't exist. Storage for VARCHAR objects is allocated only as needed, by a specified number of *n*-bytes as VARCHAR(n).

Example:

```
DECLARE @VAR1 VARCHAR(10)

SELECT @VAR1 = "ABC"

SELECT @VAR1
go
------------------------------------------------------------
ABC
```

Not too stunning. We stored and retrieved three characters. But did we really?

Try this:

```
DECLARE @VAR1 VARCHAR(10)

SELECT @VAR1 = "ABC"

SELECT CHAR_LENGTH(@VAR1)
go
---------------------------------------------------
3

SELECT CHAR_LENGTH("ABC")
go
---------------------------------------------------
3
```

Now we can visually see that a VARCHAR type is variable-length and does not pad empty space to the right of the string.

UNIVARCHAR

Please refer to the section on UNICHAR for information regarding UNICODE and UTF-16 encoding.

A UNIVARCHAR string is variable-length string. It is the varying length representation of the UNICHAR datatype. Whereas with the UNICHAR datatype, empty space is padded with spaces, the UNIVARCHAR datatype does not pad. Thus, only allocating storage as necessary up to the specified number *n* in UNIVARCHAR(n) multiplied by @@UNICHARSIZE. As with the UNICHAR datatype, *n* is the number of characters which can be stored in this structure.

NVARCHAR

Please refer to the section on NCHAR for information regarding ***national character set***.

A NVARCHAR string is a variable-length string. It is the varying length representation of the NCHAR datatype. When using the NVARCHAR datatype, the specified number *n* in NVARCHAR(n) indicates how many max characters that this object can hold. To determine the maximum amount of space which could be allocated for a NVARCHAR object multiply *n* by @@NCHARSIZE.

String Operations

Concatenation

String concatenation is the process of inserting one string after another string. In ASE the operand to perform string concatenation is the "+" operand.

Example:

```
DECLARE @STR1 CHAR(10)
DECLARE @STR2 CHAR(10)

SELECT @STR1 = "ABC"
SELECT @STR2 = "DEF"

SELECT @STR1 + @STR2
go
---------------------------------------------------------------
ABC       DEF
```

ASCII

The string function ASCII is used to get the ***integer*** ASCII character code for the first character in a specified string.

Example:

```
DECLARE @STR1 CHAR(10)
DECLARE @CDE1 INTEGER

SELECT @STR1 = "ABC"

SELECT @CD1 = ASCII(@STR1)

SELECT @CD1
go
---------------------------------------------------------------
65
```

CHAR

The string function CHAR is used to get the ***character*** representation of an ASCII character code.

Example:

```
DECLARE @STR1 CHAR(10)
DECLARE @CDE1 INTEGER

SELECT @STR1 = "ABC"

SELECT @CD1 = ASCII(@STR1)

SELECT CHAR(@CD1)
go
----------------------------------------------------------------
A
```

CHARINDEX

The CHARINDEX function is used to get the ***integer*** starting position of a specified string within another string. A position starts with 1 for first character and a 0 is returned if a starting position is not found. That is, if a string is not contained within another string.

Example:

```
DECLARE @STR1 CHAR(10)
DECLARE @STR2 CHAR(10)
DECLARE @PSTN INTEGER

SELECT @STR1 = "DEF"
SELECT @STR2 = "ABCDEFGH"

SELECT @PSTN = CHARINDEX(@STR1, @STR2)

SELECT @PSTN
go
----------------------------------------------------------------
4
```

Example:

```
DECLARE @STR1 CHAR(10)
DECLARE @STR2 CHAR(20)
DECLARE @PSTN INTEGER
```

```
SELECT @STR1 = "IN THERE"
SELECT @STR2 = "IS THE STRING HERE"

SELECT @PSTN = CHARINDEX(@STR1, @STR2)

IF ( @PSTN > 0 )
BEGIN
   PRINT "STRING WAS FOUND"
END
ELSE
BEGIN
   PRINT "STRING NOT FOUND"
END
go
STRING NOT FOUND
```

Example:

```
DECLARE @STR1 CHAR(10)
DECLARE @STR2 CHAR(20)
DECLARE @PSTN INTEGER

SELECT @STR1 = "THE"
SELECT @STR2 = "IS THE STRING HERE"

SELECT @PSTN = CHARINDEX(@STR1, STR2)

SELECT @STR1 + SPACE(1) +
               CASE
                 WHEN @PSTN > 0
                   THEN "STRING WAS FOUND"
                 ELSE "STRING NOT FOUND"
               END AS "IN THERE"
go
THE STRING WAS FOUND
```

CHAR_LENGTH

The CHAR_LENGTH function is used to get the ***integer*** number of ***characters*** that are contained within a string. We cannot stress enough the ***integer*** number of ***characters*** !!!

Example (CHAR):

```
DECLARE @STR1 CHAR(10)
DECLARE @CNT INTEGER

SELECT @STR1 = "ABC"

SELECT @CNT = CHAR_LENGTH(@STR1)

SELECT @CNT
go
10
```

Example (VARCHAR):

```
DECLARE @STR1 VARCHAR(10)
DECLARE @CNT INTEGER

SELECT @STR1 = "ABC"

SELECT @CNT = CHAR_LENGTH(@STR1)

SELECT @CNT
go
3
```

Example (UNICHAR):

```
DECLARE @STR1 UNICHAR(10)
DECLARE @CNT INTEGER

SELECT @STR1 = "ABC"

SELECT @CNT = CHAR_LENGTH(@STR1)

SELECT @CNT
go
10
```

Example (UNIVARCHAR):

```
DECLARE @STR1 UNIVARCHAR(10)
DECLARE @CNT INTEGER

SELECT @STR1 = "ABC"

SELECT @CNT = CHAR_LENGTH(@STR1)

SELECT @CNT
go
---
3
```

Example (NCHAR):

```
DECLARE @STR1 NCHAR(10)
DECLARE @CNT INTEGER

SELECT @STR1 = "ABC"

SELECT @CNT = CHAR_LENGTH(@STR1)

SELECT @CNT
go
---
10
```

Example (NVARCHAR):

```
DECLARE @STR1 NVARCHAR(10)
DECLARE @CNT INTEGER

SELECT @STR1 = "ABC"

SELECT @CNT = CHAR_LENGTH(@STR1)

SELECT @CNT
go
---
3
```

COMPARE

The COMPARE function is used to compare strings based upon the default or specified collation rule. The collation rule can be specified by name or id. The following table lists the collation rules which are applicable.

Description	*Collation ID*	*Collation Name*
Default Unicode multilingual	0	default
Thai dictionary	1	thaidict
CP 850 Alternate no accent	39	altnoacc
CP 850 Alternate lower case first	45	altdict
CP 850 Alternate no case preference	46	altnocsp
CP 850 Scandinavian dictionary	47	scandict
CP 850 Scandinavian no case preference	48	scannocp
Binary sort	50	binary
Latin-1 English, French, German distionary	51	dict
Latin-1 English, French, German no case	52	nocase
Latin-1 English, French, German no case preference	53	nocasep
Latin-1, English, French, German no accent	54	noaccent
Latin-1 Spanish dictionary	55	espdict
Latin-1 Spanish no case	56	espnocs
Latin-1 Spanish no accent	57	espnoac
ISO 8859-5 Russian dictionary	58	rusdict
ISO 8859-5 Cyrillic dictionary	63	cyrdict
ISO 8859-9 Turkish dictionary	72	turdict
Shift-JIS binary order	259	sjisbin

The COMPARE function returns one of the following ***integer*** values:

- 1 to indicate that one string is greater than another
- 0 to indicate that the two strings are equal

- -1 to indicate that one string is less than another
- or, -2 if a specified string IS NULL.

In addition, the string function is used to compare any CHAR, VARCHAR, NCHAR, or NVARCHAR to any CHAR, VARCHAR, NCHAR, or NVARCHAR. Or alternatively, it is used to compare any UNICHAR or UNIVARCHAR to any UNICHAR or UNIVARHCAR.

Note: All examples were created using isql and the -Jutf8 flag. For more information refer to using isql in the Sybase ASE Utility guide.

Example:

```
DECLARE @STR1 CHAR(10)
DECLARE @STR2 NVARCHAR(10)
DECLARE @RETVAL INTEGER

SELECT @STR1 = "ABC"
SELECT @STR2 = "FGH"

SELECT @RETVAL = COMPARE(@STR1, @STR2)
SELECT @RETVAL
go
-1
```

Example:

```
DECLARE @STR1 CHAR(10)
DECLARE @STR2 NVARCHAR(10)
DECLARE @RETVAL INTEGER

SELECT @STR1 = "K"
SELECT @STR2 = "FGH"

SELECT @RETVAL = COMPARE(@STR1, @STR2)
SELECT @RETVAL
go
1
```

Example:

```
DECLARE @STR1 CHAR(10)
DECLARE @STR2 NVARCHAR(10)
DECLARE @RETVAL INTEGER
```

```
SELECT @STR1 = "FGH"
SELECT @STR2 = "FGH"

SELECT @RETVAL = COMPARE(@STR1, @STR2)
SELECT @RETVAL
go
1
```

We tried to sneak one by you, are you stumped? If not, can you explain why we got a return value of 1 before reading on?

We got a return value of 1 because @STR1 is not "ABC". It has been defined as CHAR(10) as thus @STR1 is "ABC   " and @STR2 which has been defined as NVARCHAR(10) is truly "ABC" because it is a varying datatype. Thus, when comparing @STR1 "ABC   " and @STR2 "ABC" we get the correct return value of 1 because @STR1 is greater than @STR2.

Example:

```
DECLARE @STR1 CHAR(10)
DECLARE @STR2 NVARCHAR(10)
DECLARE @RETVAL INTEGER

SELECT @STR1 = "FGH"
SELECT @STR2 = "FGH"

SELECT @RETVAL = COMPARE( RTRIM(@STR1), @STR2 )
SELECT @RETVAL
go
0
```

Example:

```
DECLARE @STR1 CHAR(10)
DECLARE @STR2 NVARCHAR(10)

SELECT @STR2 = "FGH"

SELECT @RETVAL = COMPARE(@STR1, @STR2)
SELECT @RETVAL
go
-2
```

Example:
```
DECLARE @STR1 CHAR(10)
DECLARE @STR2 NVARCHAR(10)

SELECT @STR1 = "ABC"
SELECT @STR2 = "ABC"

SELECT @RETVAL = COMPARE(@STR1, @STR2)

SELECT "COMPARISON OF STRINGS YIELDED: " +
                CASE
                  WHEN ( @RETVAL = -2 )
                    THEN "ONE OF THE STRINGS WAS NULL"
                  WHEN ( @RETVAL = -1 )
                    THEN "FIRST IS LESS THAN SECOND"
                  WHEN ( @RETVAL = 0 )
                    THEN "THE STRINGS ARE EQUAL"
                  WHEN ( @RETVAL = 1 )
                    THEN "FIRST IS GREATER THAN SECOND"
                  ELSE "ERROR WE COULD NOT DETERMINE"
                END
go
COMPARISON OF STRINGS YIELDED: FIRST IS GREATER THAN SECOND
```

COUNT

The COUNT function is used to count all occurrences which are ***not null*** in a column. It can also be used on a string or expression.

Example:
```
DECLARE @STR1 CHAR(10)
DECLARE @CNT INTEGER

SELECT @STR1 = "ABC"

SELECT @CNT = COUNT(@STR1)

SELECT @CNT
go
1
```

Example:
```
DECLARE @STR1 CHAR(10)
DECLARE @CNT INTEGER

SELECT @CNT = COUNT(@STR1)
SELECT @CNT
go
-----------------------------------------------------------
0
```

DATALENGTH

The DATALENGTH function is used to get the ***actual*** byte length of the specified column or expression.

Example (CHAR):
```
DECLARE @STR1 CHAR(10)
DECLARE @CNT INTEGER

SELECT @STR1 = "ABC"

SELECT @CNT = DATALENGTH(@STR1)
SELECT @CNT
go
-----------------------------------------------------------
10
```

Example (VARCHAR):
```
DECLARE @STR1 VARCHAR(10)
DECLARE @CNT INTEGER

SELECT @STR1 = "ABC"

SELECT @CNT = DATALENGTH(@STR1)
SELECT @CNT
go
-----------------------------------------------------------
3
```

Example (UNICHAR):
```
DECLARE @STR1 UNICHAR(10)
DECLARE @CNT INTEGER

SELECT @STR1 = "ABC"
```

```
SELECT @CNT = DATALENGTH(@STR1)
SELECT @CNT
go
20
```

Example (UNIVARCHAR):

```
DECLARE @STR1 UNIVARCHAR(10)
DECLARE @CNT INTEGER

SELECT @STR1 = "ABC"

SELECT @CNT = DATALENGTH(@STR1)
SELECT @CNT
go
6
```

Example (NCHAR):

```
DECLARE @STR1 NCHAR(10)
DECLARE @CNT INTEGER

SELECT @STR1 = "ABC"

SELECT @CNT = DATALENGTH(@STR1)
SELECT @CNT
go
10
```

Example (NVARCHAR):

```
DECLARE @STR1 NVARCHAR(10)
DECLARE @CNT INTEGER

SELECT @STR1 = "ABC"

SELECT @CNT = DATALENGTH(@STR1)
SELECT @CNT
go
3
```

DIFFERENCE

The DIFFERENCE function is used get an ***integer*** value between 0 and 4 representing how similar a pair of strings sound. A return value of 4 indicates that the expressions sound very similar and a return value of 0 indicates that do not sound similar. A return value of NULL indicates that one or both specified strings IS NULL.

Example:
```
DECLARE @STR1 CHAR(10)
DECLARE @STR2 VARCHAR(10)
DECLARE @RETVAL INTEGER

SELECT @STR1 = "dog"
SELECT @STR2 = "fog"

SELECT @RETVAL = DIFFERENCE(@STR1, @STR2)
SELECT @RETVAL
go
---
3
```

Example:
```
DECLARE @STR1 CHAR(10)
DECLARE @STR2 VARCHAR(10)
DECLARE @RETVAL INTEGER

SELECT @STR1 = "dog"
SELECT @STR2 = "clog"

SELECT @RETVAL = DIFFERENCE(@STR1, @STR2)
SELECT @RETVAL
go
---
2
```

Example:
```
DECLARE @STR1 CHAR(10)
DECLARE @STR2 VARCHAR(10)
DECLARE @RETVAL INTEGER

SELECT @STR1 = "stan"
SELECT @STR2 = "pip"
```

```
SELECT @RETVAL = DIFFERENCE(@STR1, @STR2)
SELECT @RETVAL
go
-----------------------------------------------
1
```

Example:

```
DECLARE @STR1 CHAR(10)
DECLARE @STR2 VARCHAR(10)
DECLARE @RETVAL INTEGER

SELECT @STR1 = "Putnam"
SELECT @STR2 = "Talebzadeh"

SELECT @RETVAL = DIFFERENCE(@STR1, @STR2)
SELECT @RETVAL
go
-----------------------------------------------
0
```

Example:

```
DECLARE @STR1 CHAR(10)
DECLARE @STR2 VARCHAR(10)
DECLARE @RETVAL INTEGER

SELECT @STR1 = "dog"

SELECT @RETVAL = DIFFERENCE(@STR1, @STR2)
SELECT @RETVAL
go
-----------------------------------------------
NULL
```

ISNULL

The ISNULL function is specifies an alternate column or expression to use if a specified expression IS NULL.

Example:

```
DECLARE @STR1 CHAR(10)
DECLARE @STR2 CHAR(10)

SELECT @STR2 = "DEF"

SELECT ISNULL(@STR1, @STR2)
```

```
go
DEF
```

LEFT

The LEFT function is used get a specified ***integer*** number of characters from a column or expression from the left side of an expression.

Example:

```
DECLARE @STR1 CHAR(10)

SELECT @STR1 = "ABCDEF"

SELECT LEFT(@STR1, 2)
go
AB
```

Example (Left Padding with a Character):

```
DECLARE @STR1 CHAR(10)
DECLARE @PCHAR CHAR(1)
DECLARE @STRLEN INTEGER

SELECT @STR1 = "ABCDEF"
SELECT @PCHAR = "0"
SELECT @STRLEN = 20

SELECT LEFT(ISNULL(
        REPLICATE( @PCHAR, @STRLEN - CHAR_LENGTH(RTRIM(@STR1))  ),
           SPACE(0) ) + @STR1, @STRLEN )
go
00000000000000ABCDEF
```

Example (Right Padding with a Character):

```
DECLARE @STR1 CHAR(10)
DECLARE @PCHAR CHAR(1)
DECLARE @STRLEN INTEGER

SELECT @STR1 = "ABCDEF"
SELECT @PCHAR = "0"
SELECT @STRLEN = 20

SELECT LEFT( RTRIM(@STR1) + REPLICATE(@PCHAR, @STRLEN), @STRLEN )
```

```
go
ABCDEF00000000000000
```

LEN

The LEN function is used to get the ***integer*** number of characters in a column or expression. The LEN function works exactly like the CHAR_LENGTH function. Please refer to the examples of the CHAR_LENGTH function for more information.

LOWER

The function LOWER is used to convert a character string to lower case.

Example:

```
DECLARE @STR1 CHAR(10)

SELECT @STR1 = "ABC"

SELECT LOWER( @STR1 )
go
abc
```

LTRIM

The function LTRIM is used to remove ***leading*** spaces in a character string.

Example:

```
DECLARE @STR1 CHAR(10)

SELECT @STR1 = SPACE(5) + "ABC"

SELECT LTRIM( @STR1 )
go
ABC
```

MAX

The MAX function is used to get the maximum character string from a column.

Example:
```
CREATE
 TABLE test_table(
       column01 CHAR(10) NOT NULL
)
go

INSERT
  INTO test_table(
       column01
)
SELECT "ABC"
go

INSERT
  INTO test_table(
       column01
)
SELECT "DEF"
go

SELECT MAX(column01)
  FROM test_table
go
DEF
```

MIN

The MIN function is used to get the minimum character string from a column.

Example:
```
CREATE
 TABLE test_table(
       column01 CHAR(10) NOT NULL
)
go

INSERT
```

```
  INTO test_table(
       column01
)
SELECT "ABC"
go

INSERT
  INTO test_table(
       column01
)
SELECT "DEF"
go

SELECT MIN(column01)
  FROM test_table
go
ABC
```

PATINDEX

The PATINDEX function is used to get the first ***integer*** occurrence of a patternized string within another string. It is similar to the function LIKE, except LIKE returns the string if it matches a specified pattern.

Example:

```
DECLARE @STR1 CHAR(10)
DECLARE @PLOC INTEGER

SELECT @STR1 = "FGF"

SELECT @PLOC = PATINDEX( "%G[a-zA-Z]%", @STR1 )

SELECT @PLOC
go
2
```

Example:

```
DECLARE @STR1 CHAR(10)
DECLARE @PLOC INTEGER

SELECT @STR1 = "FGF"
```

```
SELECT @PLOC = PATINDEX( "%G[a-zA-Z]%", @STR1 )

SELECT CASE
        WHEN ( @PLOC > 0 )
          THEN "THE PATTERN WAS FOUND AT LOCATION: "
               + CONVERT(CHAR, @STR1)
        ELSE "THE PATTERN WAS NOT FOUND"
      END
go
THE PATTERN WAS FOUND AT LOCATION: 2
```

REPLICATE

The REPLICATE function is used to generate a specified expression an ***integer*** number of times. That is, to repeat the specified expression a specified integral number of times.

Example:

```
DECLARE @STR1 CHAR(10)

SELECT @STR1 = "ABC"

SELECT REPLICATE( @STR1, 2 )
go
ABC          ABC
```

Maybe not want you wanted. Remember the non-varying string datatypes are all padded with a space to their defined length.

Example:

```
DECLARE @STR1 CHAR(10)

SELECT @STR1 = "ABC"

SELECT REPLICATE( RTRIM(@STR1), 2 )
go
ABCABC
```

REVERSE

The REVERSE function is used to perform a 180 degree or a PI()/2 radians if you will, rotation on a character expression.

Example:
```
DECLARE @STR1 CHAR(10)

SELECT @STR1 = "ABC"

SELECT REVERSE( @STR1 )
go
----------------------------------------------------------------
       CBA
```

Might not be what you wanted. Recall that a non-varying string datatype pads.

Example:
```
DECLARE @STR1 CHAR(10)

SELECT @STR1 = "ABC"

SELECT REVERSE( RTRIM(@STR1) )
go
----------------------------------------------------------------
CBA
```

RIGHT

The RIGHT function is used get a specified ***integer*** number of characters from the right side of a character string or column.

Example:
```
DECLARE @STR1 CHAR(10)

SELECT @STR1 = "ABCDEF"

SELECT RIGHT(@STR1, 6)
go
----------------------------------------------------------------
EF
```

Example (Right Padding with a Character):

```
DECLARE @STR1 CHAR(10)
DECLARE @PCHAR CHAR(1)
DECLARE @STRLEN INTEGER

SELECT @STR1 = "ABCDEF"
SELECT @PCHAR = "0"
SELECT @STRLEN = 20

SELECT RIGHT( ISNULL( RTRIM(@STR1)
                      + REPLICATE( @PCHAR, @STRLEN
                        - CHAR_LENGTH(RTRIM(@STR1))  ),
                        SPACE(0) ), @STRLEN )
go
ABCDEF00000000000000
```

Example (Left Padding with a Character):

```
DECLARE @STR1 CHAR(10)
DECLARE @PCHAR CHAR(1)
DECLARE @STRLEN INTEGER

SELECT @STR1 = "ABCDEF"
SELECT @PCHAR = "0"
SELECT @STRLEN = 20

SELECT RIGHT( REPLICATE(@PCHAR, @STRLEN) + RTRIM(@STR1), @STRLEN )
go
00000000000000ABCDEF
```

RTRIM

The RTRIM function is used to strip trailing blanks from a character string.

Example:

```
DECLARE @STR1 CHAR(10)

SELECT @STR1 = "ABC"

SELECT CHAR_LENGTH( @STR1 ),
       CHAR_LENGTH( RTRIM( @STR1 ) )
go
10          3
```

SORTKEY

The SORTKEY function is used to order query results in an ORDER BY clause. It allows for ASE to perform sorts based upon different collation rules. The SORTKEY function takes a character string as a parameter and the collation name or collation id of the collation rule for ASE to follow when performing the sort. The following table lists the collation rules which are applicable.

Description	***Collation ID***	***Collation Name***
Default Unicode multilingual	0	default
Thai dictionary	1	thaidict
CP 850 Alternate no accent	39	altnoacc
CP 850 Alternate lower case first	45	altdict
CP 850 Alternate no case preference	46	altnocsp
CP 850 Scandinavian dictionary	47	scandict
CP 850 Scandinavian no case preference	48	scannocp
Binary sort	50	binary
Latin-1 English, French, German distionary	51	dict
Latin-1 English, French, German no case	52	nocase
Latin-1 English, French, German no case preference	53	nocasep
Latin-1, English, French, German no accent	54	noaccent
Latin-1 Spanish dictionary	55	espdict
Latin-1 Spanish no case	56	espnocs
Latin-1 Spanish no accent	57	espnoac
ISO 8859-5 Russian dictionary	58	rusdict
ISO 8859-5 Cyrillic dictionary	63	cyrdict
ISO 8859-9 Turkish dictionary	72	turdict
Shift-JIS binary order	259	sjisbin

Note: All examples were created using isql and the -Jutf8 flag. For more information refer to using isql in the Sybase ASE Utility guide.

Example:

```
CREATE
 TABLE test_table(
       column01 UNICHAR(10) NOT NULL
)
go

INSERT
  INTO test_table(
       column01
)
SELECT "aab"
go

INSERT
  INTO test_table(
       column01
)
SELECT "aac"
go

SELECT column01
  FROM test_table
 ORDER
    BY SORTKEY(column01, "dict") ASC
go
```

```
aab
aac
```

```
SELECT column01
  FROM test_table
 ORDER
    BY SORTKEY(column01, "thaidict") ASC
go
```

```
aab
aac
```

SOUNDEX

The SOUNDEX function is used to return a string of four characters representing how a character string sounds.

Example:
```
DECLARE @STR1 CHAR(10)
DECLARE @RETVAL CHAR(4)

SELECT @STR1 = "dog"

SELECT @RETVAL = SOUNDEX( @STR1 )

SELECT @RETVAL
go
D200
```

Example:
```
DECLARE @STR1 CHAR(10)
DECLARE @RETVAL CHAR(4)

SELECT @STR1 = "clog"

SELECT @RETVAL = SOUNDEX( @STR1 )

SELECT @RETVAL
go
C420
```

SPACE

The SPACE function is used to generate a ***n-integer*** number of spaces. A negative integer will result in a NULL return value. A SPACE(0) will generate the empty string.

Example:
```
SELECT "ABC" + SPACE(0) + "DEF"
go
ABCDEF

SELECT "ABC" + SPACE(5) + "DEF"
```

```
go
------------------------------------------------------------
ABC      DEF
```

STR_REPLACE

You should be sure to add this function to your storage. The STR_REPLACE function is used to replace a character string which contains a specified character string with a different specified character string.

Example:

```
DECLARE @STR1 CHAR(10)
DECLARE @STR2 CHAR(10)
DECLARE @STR3 CHAR(10)

SELECT @STR1 = "ABCDEFG"
SELECT @STR2 = "CDE"
SELECT @STR3 = "cde"

SELECT STR_REPLACE( @STR1, @STR2, @STR3 )
go
------------------------------------------------------------
ABCDEFG
```

Now what happened ??? That's right, we are working non-varying data and @STR1 is actually "ABCDEFG   ", @STR2 is "CDE   ", and @STR3 is "cde   ". Hence, ASE did the correct thing here. It did not perform any replacement.

Example:

```
DECLARE @STR1 CHAR(10)
DECLARE @STR2 CHAR(10)
DECLARE @STR3 CHAR(10)

SELECT @STR1 = "ABCDEFG"
SELECT @STR2 = "CDE"
SELECT @STR3 = "cde"

SELECT STR_REPLACE( @STR1, RTRIM(@STR2), RTRIM(@STR3) )
go
------------------------------------------------------------
ABcdeFG
```

That's what we really meant all along.

Example (Remove Carriage Returns and Line Feeds):

```
DECLARE @STR1 CHAR(255)
DECLARE @STR2 CHAR(1)
DECLARE @STR3 CHAR(1)

SELECT @STR2 = CHAR(10)
SELECT @STR3 = CHAR(11)

SELECT @STR1 = "A sometimes annoying issue" + @STR2 + @STR3 +
               "which arises is carriage returns."

SELECT STR_REPLACE( @STR1, @STR2 + @STR3, SPACE(1) )
go
A sometimes annoying issue which arises is carriage returns.
```

Example (Adding the empty string):

```
DECLARE @STR1 CHAR(10)

SELECT @STR1 = "ABCDEFG"

SELECT STR_REPLACE( @STR1, "BCDEF", SPACE(0) )
go
AG
```

STUFF

The STUFF function is used to remove a character string from a specified ***integer*** number of characters from the left of a character string and the number of ***integer*** characters beyond that point to remove and insert a new character string.

Example:

```
DECLARE @STR1 CHAR(10)

SELECT @STR1 = "ABCDEFG"

SELECT STUFF( @STR1, 3, 3, "cde" )
go
ABcdeFG
```

SUBSTRING

The SUBSTRING function is used to get a character string out of another character string. This is performed positionally by specifying an ***integer*** number of characters to start from the left of a string and the number of ***integer*** characters beyond that point to cut.

Example:
```
DECLARE @STR1 CHAR(10)

SELECT @STR1 = "ABCDEFG"

SELECT SUBSTRING(@STR1, 2, 3)
go
BCD
```

TO_UNICHAR

The TO_UNICHAR function is the analogue of the CHAR function. It returns the UNICHAR value of the specified *integer*.

Note: These examples were created using isql and the -Jutf8 flag. For more information refer to using isql in the Sybase ASE Utility guide.

Example:
```
DECLARE @UINT INTEGER

SELECT @UINT = ASCII( CHAR(33) )

SELECT TO_UNICHAR( @UINT )
go
!
```

Example:
```
DECLARE @UINT INTEGER

SELECT @UINT = 257

SELECT TO_UNICHAR( @UINT )
go
ā
```

UHIGHSURR

The UHIGHSURR function is used to determine if a UNICODE character string at a specified ***integer*** position is the ***high surrogate half*** of UTF-16 surrogate pair. The function returns a 1 if it is true that the position specified for the UNICODE character string contains the high surrogate half. Otherwise it returns a 0 for false.

Recall that the range for the ***high surrogate half*** is D800-DBFF.

Note: All examples were created using isql and the -Jutf8 flag. For more information refer to using isql in the Sybase ASE Utility guide.

Example:
```
DECLARE @UNIC BINARY(4)
SELECT @UNIC = 0xfffd
SELECT UHIGHSURR( @UNIC, 1 )
go
0
```

Example:
```
DECLARE @UNIC BINARY(4)
SELECT @UNIC = 0xd800dc00
SELECT UHIGHSURR( @UNIC, 1 )
go
1
```

ULOWSURR

The ULOWSURR function is used to determine if a UNICODE character string at a specified ***integer*** position is the ***low surrogate half*** of UTF-16 surrogate pair. The function returns a 1 if it is true that the position specified for the UNICODE character string contains the low surrogate half. Otherwise it returns a 0 for false.

Recall that the range for the ***low surrogate half*** is DC00-DFFF.

Note: All examples were created using isql and the -Jutf8 flag. For more information refer to using isql in the Sybase ASE Utility guide.

Example:
```
DECLARE @UNIC BINARY(4)
```

```
SELECT @UNIC = 0xd800dc00
SELECT ULOWSURR( @UNIC, 1 )
go
--------------------------------------------------
0
```

Example:

```
DECLARE @UNIC BINARY(4)
SELECT @UNIC = 0xd800dc00
SELECT ULOWSURR( @UNIC, 2 )
go
--------------------------------------------------
1
```

UPPER

The function UPPER is used to convert a character string to upper case.

Example:

```
DECLARE @STR1 CHAR(10)

SELECT @STR1 = "aBc"

SELECT UPPER( @STR1 )
go
--------------------------------------------------
ABC
```

USCALAR

The USCALAR function is the analogue of the ASCII function. It is used to get the ***first*** UNICODE scalar from a UNICODE character string. A UNICODE scalar value in ASE is the integer representation of a UNICODE character.

Note: All examples were created using isql and the -Jutf8 flag. For more information refer to using isql in the Sybase ASE Utility guide.

Example:

```
DECLARE @UCHAR UNICHAR(1)
SELECT @UCHAR = "A"
SELECT USCALAR( @UCHAR )
go
--------------------------------------------------
65
```

Example:
```
DECLARE @UCHAR UNICHAR(3)
SELECT @UCHAR = "ABC"
SELECT USCALAR( @UCHAR )
go
-----------------------------------------------------------------------
65
```

U&

The U& function is used to get a UNICHAR value for the U+***nnnn*** hexadecimal unicode value.

Note: These examples were created using isql and the -Jutf8 flag. For more information refer to using isql in the Sybase ASE Utility guide.

Example:
```
SELECT U&'\0116'
go
-----------------------------------------------------------------------
Ė
```

Chapter 22. Working with Strings

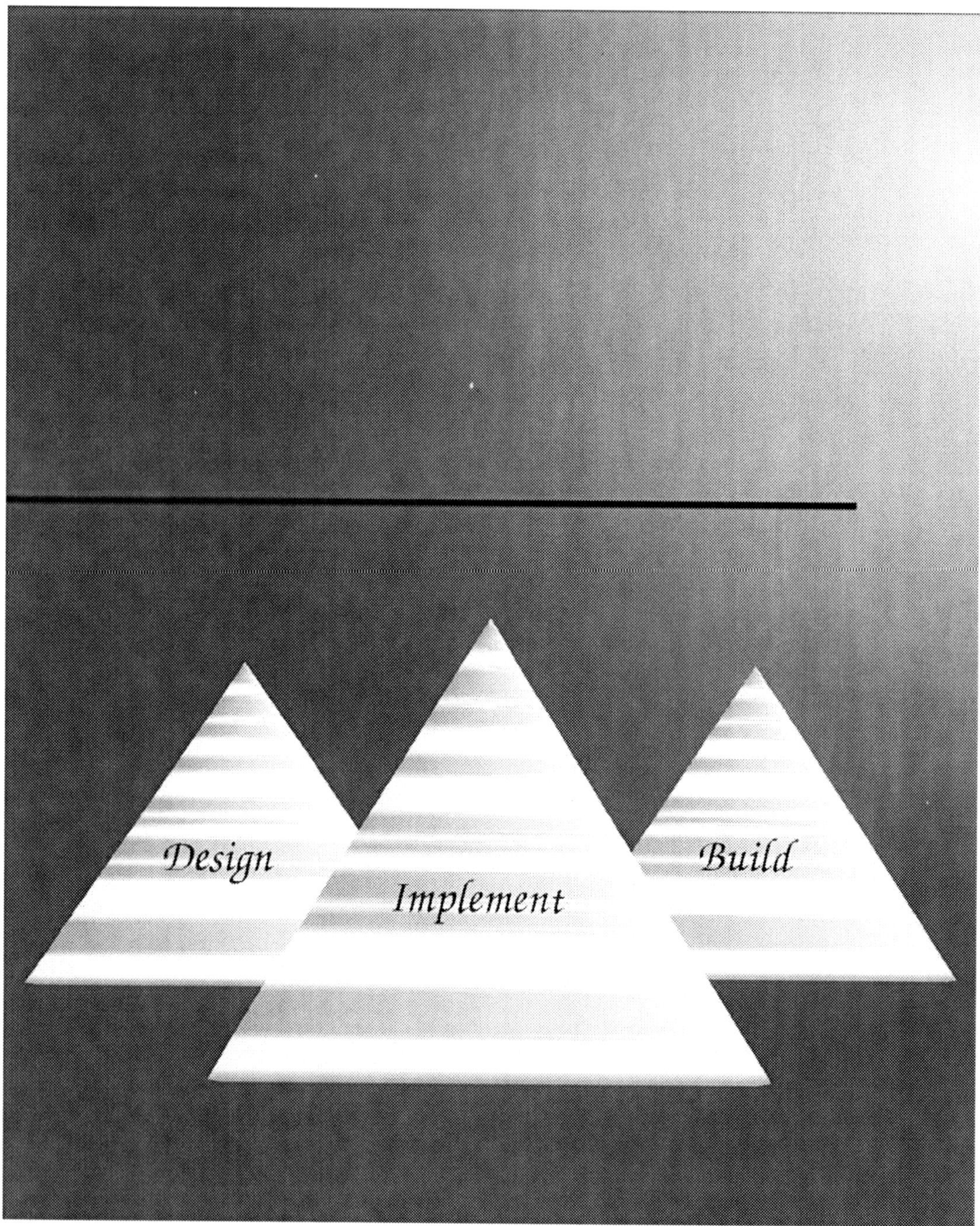
Design
Implement
Build

Chapter 23. Working with Numbers

Almost everything we do in life deals with patterns (including breathing, I hope). And, mathematics can be thought of as realm which deals with pattern recognition and pattern operations.

Numbers too have recognizable patterns and operations. This chapter will discuss how ASE handles numbers and the operations which it performs on them.

Note: The monetary datatypes work the same as the numeric datatypes. Thus, we will not be covering working with monetary.

The table below summarizes many of the ***basic*** operations which ASE performs on numbers. In addition, Operator precedence has been included.

ASSIGNMENT GROUP	*OPERATOR NAME*	*OPERATOR*	*PRECEDENCE*
Arithmetic	Addition	+	3
Arithmetic	Subtraction	-	3
Arithmetic	Multiplication	*	2
Arithmetic	Division	/	2
Arithmetic	Modulo	%	2
Bitwise	AND	&	3
Bitwise	OR	|	3
Bitwise	Exclusive OR	^	1
Bitwise	NOT	~	1
Comparisons	Equals	=	Optimization
Comparison	Greater	>	Optimization
Comparison	Less	<	Optimization

ASSIGNMENT GROUP	OPERATOR NAME	OPERATOR	PRECEDENCE
Comparison	Greater or Equals	>=	Optimization
Comparison	Less or Equals	<=	Optimization
Comparison	Not Equals	<>	Optimization
Comparison	Not Equals	!=	Optimization
Comparison	Not Greater	!>	Optimization
Comparison	Not Less	!<	Optimization
Comparison	Lists	Exists	Optimization
Comparison	Lists	IN	Optimization
Logical Expressions	AND	AND	5
Logical Expressions	OR	OR	6
Logical Expressions	NOT	NOT	4
Aggregates	Maximum	MAX	N/A
Aggregates	Minimum	MIN	N/A
Aggregates	Average	AVG	N/A
Aggregates	Summation	SUM	N/A
Aggregates	Number of Elements	COUNT	N/A

Operand Precedence

When working with numbers, it is very important to understand operand precedence and how ASE treats a numeric expression with multiple operands. Unless overridden with parenthesis, operations are always performed from left to right, with operations of lowest precedence number carried out first. Likewise, operations within parenthesis are performed from left to right, with operations of lowest precedence number carried out first, from the innermost pair of parenthesis outwards.

Example:

```
SELECT 2 + 3 * 5 - 1
go
16
```

Now, the answer to the above question is 16 because ASE starts from left to right examining the operands and their precedence. It performs the multiplication of 3 * 5 first because * has a precedence of 2 which is lower than the precedence of + and – which are 3. Next, ASE adds 2 + 15 to get 17 and than subtracts one from 17 to get 16.

Parenthesis are used to indicate what operations are to be carried out first. Thus, parenthesis can be considered to have the ***highest*** operator precedence. Since operator precedence in ASE is designated by an ***integer*** between 1 and 6, with 1 being the highest and 6 being lowest, we can consider a pair of parenthesis as having an operator precedence of 0.

Example:

```
SELECT ( 2 + 3 ) * 5 - 1
go
24
```

Function Classes

Within ASE many functions can be used on numbers to get aggregates, listings, and single value calculations. While although this is one logical grouping of the functions, we will instead group the functions differently. We will be grouping the functions into the following classifications:

- Basic Algebraic
- Aggregates
- Trigonometric
- Logarithmic

Basically, we will group them in what I call a “natural” grouping. Natural in the sense that the functions are associated with the area in mathematics for which they pertain.

Basic Algebraic

The basic algebraic functions within ASE are the functions which you are most likely to use.

ABS

The ABS function is used get the absolute value of a numeric expression.

Example:
```
DECLARE @NUM1 INTEGER

SELECT @NUM1 = -50

SELECT ABS(@NUM1)
go
----------------------------------------------------------------
50
```

CEILING

The CEILING function is used get the smallest ***integer*** value whose expression is greater than or equal to the numeric expression.

Example:
```
DECLARE @NUM1 NUMERIC(5, 2)

SELECT @NUM1 = 127.23

SELECT CEILING(@NUM1)
go
----------------------------------------------------------------
128
```

EXP

The EXP function is used to generate the ***numeric*** number which is created by raising by raising the transcendental number *e* to the specified power.

Example:
```
DECLARE @NUM1 INTEGER
```

```
SELECT @NUM1 = 3

SELECT EXP(@NUM1)
go
20.085537
```

FLOOR

The FLOOR function is used to get the largest ***integer*** value whose expression is less than or equal to the specified numeric expression.

Example:

```
DECLARE @NUM1 NUMERIC(5, 2)

SELECT @NUM1 = 127.23

SELECT FLOOR(@NUM1)
go
127
```

POWER

The POWER function is used generate a ***numeric*** number which is created by raising one number to the power of another number.

Example:

```
DECLARE @NUM1 INTEGER
DECLARE @NUM2 INTEGER

SELECT @NUM1 = 2
SELECT @NUM2 = 8

SELECT POWER(@NUM1, @NUM2)
go
64
```

RAND

The RAND function is used to generate a random value between 0 and 1 with up to 17 digits of precision. In addition, a seed value may be specified so that random keys are generated following the same sequence after a seed.

Example (No Seed):

```
DECLARE @NUM1 NUMERIC(18, 18)

SELECT @NUM1 = RAND()

SELECT @NUM1
go
-----------------------------------------------------------
0.79359523662999054
```

Example (Seed):

```
DECLARE @NUM1 NUMERIC(17, 17)
DECLARE @SEED INTEGER

SELECT @SEED = 1
SELECT @NUM1 = RAND(1)

SELECT @NUM1

SELECT @NUM1 = RAND()

SELECT @NUM1
go
-----------------------------------------------------------
 0.34595759834440315

-----------------------------------------------------------
 0.79670970225553484

DECLARE @NUM1 NUMERIC(17, 17)
DECLARE @SEED INTEGER

SELECT @SEED = 1
SELECT @NUM1 = RAND(1)

SELECT @NUM1

SELECT @NUM1 = RAND()
```

```
SELECT @NUM1
go
------------------------------------------------------------------------
  0.34595759834440315

------------------------------------------------------------------------
  0.79670970225553484
```

What you should notice is that the RAND function has been seeded, or planted, it grows or branches out in a pre-determined method.

Warning: If your application is using the RAND function to generate random keys for insertions, planting a seed can cause a high number of duplicates to arise. Contact your DBA and determine if it safe to plant a seed on the RAND function. In addition, present this information to them so that you can be more sure that they have rationalized their answer.

ROUND

The ROUND function is used to round a numeric expression a specified number of ***integer*** decimal points of precision. In addition, a 0 indicates no decimal precision and negative ***integers*** moves precision to the left side of the decimal point.

Example:

```
DECLARE @NUM1 NUMERIC(5, 2)
DECLARE @NUM2 TINYINT

SELECT @NUM1 = 127.23
SELECT @NUM2 = 1
SELECT ROUND(@NUM1, @NUM2)
go
------------------------------------------------------------------------
127.20
```

Example:

```
DECLARE @NUM1 NUMERIC(5, 2)
DECLARE @NUM2 TINYINT

SELECT @NUM1 = 127.23
SELECT @NUM2 = 0
SELECT ROUND(@NUM1, @NUM2)
go
------------------------------------------------------------------------
127.00
```

Example:
```
DECLARE @NUM1 NUMERIC(5, 2)
DECLARE @NUM2 TINYINT

SELECT @NUM1 = 127.23
SELECT @NUM2 = -1
SELECT ROUND(@NUM1, @NUM2)
go
130.00
```

SIGN

The SIGN function is used to get the mathematical sign of a numeric value. If the specified numeric value is 0 the function returns a 0. The function returns:

- -1 for negative,
- 0 for zero
- 1 for positive
- and, NULL for a NULL value.

Example:
```
DECLARE @NUM1 NUMERIC(5,2)
SELECT @NUM1 = 0

SELECT SIGN(@NUM1)
go
0
```

Example:
```
DECLARE @NUM1 NUMERIC(5,2)
SELECT @NUM1 = -1.23

SELECT SIGN(@NUM1)
go
-1
```

Example:
```
DECLARE @NUM1 NUMERIC(5,2)
SELECT @NUM1 = 6.52

SELECT SIGN(@NUM1)
```

```
go
---------------
1
```

Example:

```
DECLARE @NUM1 NUMERIC(5,2)

SELECT SIGN(@NUM1)
go
---------------
NULL
```

SQUARE

The SQUARE function raises a numeric value to the power of 2. Since the POWER function exists and SQUARE(n) = POWER(n, 2), SQUARE is really redundant. Still, we have the function available for us to use in our code.

Example:

```
DECLARE @NUM1 INTEGER

SELECT @NUM1 = 12

SELECT SQUARE(@NUM1)
SELECT POWER(@NUM1, 2)
go
---------------
144

---------------
144
```

SQRT

The SQRT function returns the square root of a non-negative numeric value. Since SQRT(n) = POWER(n, .5), like SQUARE, is redundant. Still, it is probably much more intuitive to use SQRT(n) than POWER(n, .5).

Example:

```
DECLARE @NUM1 INTEGER

SELECT @NUM1 = 36

SELECT SQRT(@NUM1)
SELECT POWER(@NUM1, .5)
```

```
go
6

6
```

Aggregates

Aggregates are calculated based upon some grouping of records. They include such things as averages, maximums, and minimums.

The examples which follow on aggregates will all use the following table and records.

```
CREATE
 TABLE test_table(
       column01 INT NOT NULL,
       column02 CHAR(10) NULL,
       column03 INT NULL,
       CONSTRAINT ix01_test_table
       PRIMARY KEY CLUSTERED ( column01 )
)
LOCK DATAROWS
go
INSERT
  INTO test_table(
       column01,
       column02,
       column03
)
SELECT 1,
       "cond_01",
       20
go
INSERT
  INTO test_table(
       column01,
       column02,
       column03
)
SELECT 2,
       "cond_01",
       20
```

```
go
INSERT
  INTO test_table(
       column01,
       column02,
       column03
)
SELECT 3,
       "cond_02",
       30
go
INSERT
  INTO test_table(
       column01,
       column02
)
SELECT 4,
       "cond_01"
go
```

The aggregates which we use will make reference to test_table and this dataset.

```
SELECT column01,
       column02
  FROM test_table
go
--------------------------------------------------
1          cond_01         20
2          cond_01         20
3          cond_02         30
4          cond_01         NULL
```

AVG

The AVG function is used to get the average from a finite set of numeric values. It can either perform the average on all values or only distinct values.

Example:

```
SELECT AVG(column03),
       AVG(DISTINCT column03)
  FROM test_table
go
--------------------------------------------------
23              25
```

Example:
```
SELECT column02,
       AVG(column03),
       AVG(DISTINCT column03)
  FROM test_table
 GROUP
    BY column02
go
-----------------------------------------------
cond01       20          20
cond02       30          30
```

Example:
```
SELECT column02,
       AVG(column03),
       AVG(DISTINCT column03)
  FROM test_table
 GROUP
    BY column02
HAVING AVG(column03) > 25
go
-----------------------------------------------
cond02       30       30
```

COUNT

The COUNT function is used to get the record count from a finite set of numeric values which are NOT NULL. It can either count all values or only distinct values.

Example:
```
SELECT COUNT(column03),
       COUNT(DISTINCT column03)
  FROM test_table
go
-----------------------------------------------
3             2
```

Example:
```
SELECT column02,
       COUNT(column03),
       COUNT(DISTINCT column03)
  FROM test_table
 GROUP
    BY column02
```

```
go
cond_01        2        1
cond_02        1        1
```

MAX

The MAX function is used to get the highest column value.

Example:

```
SELECT MAX(column03)
  FROM test_table
go
30
```

Example:

```
SELECT column02,
       MAX(column03)
  FROM test_table
 GROUP
    BY column02
go
cond_01        20
cond_02        30
```

MIN

The MIN function is used to get the lowest column value.

Example:

```
SELECT MIN(column03)
  FROM test_table
go
20
```

Example:

```
SELECT column02,
       MIN(column03)
  FROM test_table
 GROUP
    BY column02
go
```

```
cond_01        20
cond_02        30
```

***Warning*!:** As we stated earlier, try to avoid mixing MIN and MAX within the same query. If it is absolutely unavoidable, you can use them in separate subqueries.

Example:

```
SELECT ( SELECT MIN(column03) FROM test_table ),
       ( SELECT MAX(column03) FROM test_table)
go
20             30
```

SUM

The SUM function is used to get the summation of numeric values which are NOT NULL. It can either sum all values or only distinct values.

Example:

```
SELECT SUM(column03),
       SUM(DISTINCT column03)
  FROM test_table
go
70               50
```

Example:

```
SELECT column02,
       AVG(column03),
       AVG(DISTINCT column03)
  FROM test_table
 GROUP
    BY column02
go
cond_01           40           20
cond_02           30           30
```

Trigonometric

Trigonometric functions have many applications and are used widely in engineering, the physical sciences, mathematics and statistics.

ACOS

The ACOS function is used to get the inverse cosine in radians.

Example:
```
SELECT ACOS(1)
go
0.000000
```

ASIN

The ASIN function is used to get the inverse sine in radians.

Example:
```
SELECT ASIN( SIN(PI() / 2) )
go
0.000000
```

ATAN

The ATAN function is used to get the inverse tangent in radians.

Example:
```
SELECT ATAN( TAN(PI() / 4) )
go
0.785398
```

ATN2

The ATN2 function is used to get the inverse cotangent in radians.

Example:
```
SELECT ATN2( PI()/4, PI()/4 )
go
```

```
0.785398
```

COS

The COS function is used to get the cosine in radians.

Example:

```
SELECT COS( PI() )
go
-----------------
-1.000000
```

COT

The COT function is used to get the cotangent in radians.

Example:

```
SELECT COT( PI() / 2 )
go
-----------------
1.000000
```

DEGREES

The DEGRESS function is used to convert an angle in radians to degrees. Not really an important function. Because you can easily convert an angle in radians to degrees by multiplying by 180 / PI().

Example:

```
SELECT DEGREES( PI() / 4 ),
       ( 180 / PI() ) * ( PI() / 4 )
go
-----------------
45.000000                45.000000
```

PI

The PI function is used to get the ratio of a circles circumference to its diameter. In fact, all circles have the same ratio !!! This became known as PI.

Example:
```
SELECT PI()
go
3.141593
```

RADIANS

The RADIANS function is used to convert an angle in degrees to radians. Not really an important function. Because you can easily convert an angle in degrees by multiplying by 1 / (180 / PI()) or simply PI() / 180.

Example:
```
SELECT RADIANS(180.0),
       (180.0) * (PI() / 180)
go
3.14159265358979310O          3.141593
```

SIN

The SIN function is used to get the sine in radians.

Example:
```
SELECT SIN( PI() )
go
0.000000
```

TAN

The TAN function is used to get the tangent in radians.

Example:
```
SELECT TAN( 3 * PI() / 4 )
go
-1.000000
```

Logarithmic

Logarithms are used widely in the world today. They are used in seismology, physics, natural sciences, chemistry, and banking. And that is only to mention a few.

Quite simply, a logarithm is the inverse of an exponential function.

For instance, if we let:

$$y=b^x$$

Then the inverse is defined as follows:

$$x=LOGb(y)$$

Where ***b*** is defined as the base of the logarithm.

EXP

The EXP function is used to generate the ***numeric*** number which is created by raising by raising the transcendental number *e* to the specified power.

Example:

```
DECLARE @NUM1 INTEGER

SELECT @NUM1 = 3

SELECT EXP(@NUM1)
go
20.085537
```

LOG

The LOG function is used to get the natural logarithm of a specified numeric.

Example:

```
SELECT LOG(EXP(1))
go
1.000000
```

LOG10

The LOG10 function is used to get the base10 logarithm of a specified numeric.

Example:
```
SELECT LOG10(1000)
go
3.000000
```

OTHER BASES

Many times it may become necessary to work logarithms of different bases. Let's not forget that it is easy to convert a logarithm from one base to another.

For instance:

$$x=LOGb(y)=LOGe(y)/LOGe(y)=LOG10(y)/LOG10(y)$$

Use the above formula in ASE for logarithms with bases other than *e* or *10*.

Example ($x=LOG11(214358881)$) solved with natural logarithm:
```
SELECT LOG(214358881) / LOG(11)
go
8.000000
```

Example ($x=LOG11(214358881)$) solved with base 10 logarithm:
```
SELECT LOG10(214358881) / LOG10(11)
go
8.000000
```

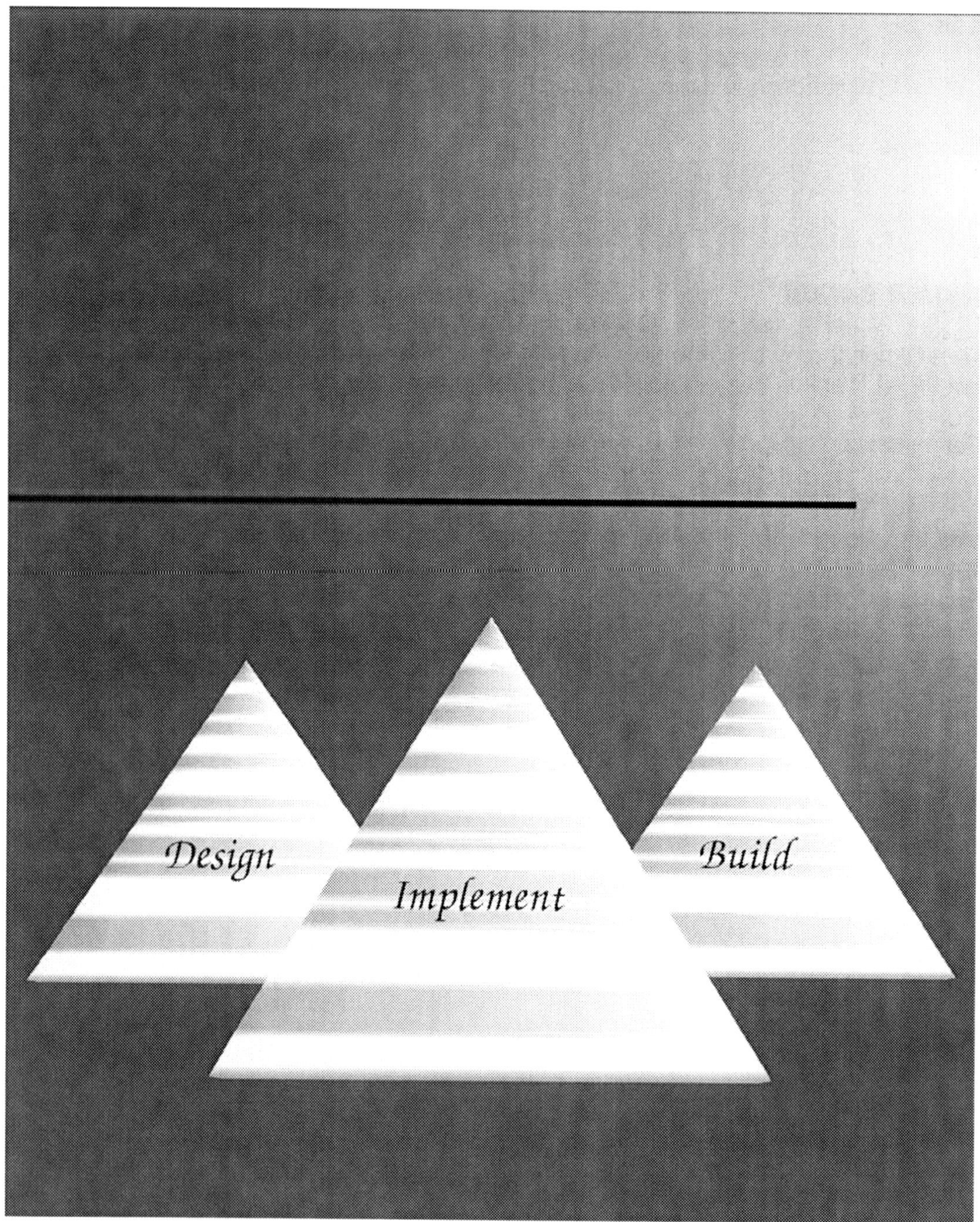
Design
Implement
Build

Chapter 24. Working with Dates and Times

ASE supports four date and time datatypes.

Note: When working dates and times in ASE, you must use as a delimiter either a single (') or double (") quotation mark around the date, date-time, or time.

DATE

The DATE datatype requires 4 bytes of storage and may store values in the range Jan 1, 0001 to Dec 31, 9999.

TIME

The TIME datatype requires 4 bytes of storage and may store values in the range 00:00:00:000 to 23:59:59:999 within 3 milliseconds.

DATETIME

The DATETIME datatype requires 8 bytes of storage and may store values in the range Jan 1, 1753 00:00:00.000 to Dec 31, 9999 23:59:59.999. The first 4 bytes store the date component as the number of days from an internal base date. The second 4 bytes are used to store the time component within 3 milliseconds.

SMALLDATETIME

The SMALLDATETIME datatype requires 4 bytes of storage and may store values in the range Jan 1, 1900 00:00 to Jun 6, 2079 23:59. The first 2 bytes store the date component as the number of days from an internal base date. The second 2 bytes are used to store the time component to the minute.

Date and Time Components

When working with dates and times you will find it necessary or useful many times to dissect the dates and times by their components. ASE recognizes the following dissections. These are used mainly in the functions DATEADD, DATEDIFF, DATENAME, and DATEPART.

Date Component	***Argument***	***Range***
Year	yy	1753 - 9999
Quarter	qq	1 - 4
Month	mm	1 - 12
Week	wk	1 - 54
Day	dd	1 - 31
Day of the Year	dy	1 - 366
Day of the Week	dw	1 - 7
Hour of the Day	hh	0 - 23
Minute of the Hour	mi	0 - 59
Second of the Minute	ss	0 - 59
Millisecond of the Minute	ms	0 - 999

Date and Time Styles

ASE supports a number of date and time styles. These BOTH represent how ASE will display dates and times and how it will treat dates and times when entered. Refer to the table below for the supported styles.

yy Year	*yyyy Year*	*Date and Time Style*	*Date Style*	*Time Style*
	0, 100	mon dd yyyy hh:miAM/PM	mon dd yyyy	hh:miAM/PM
1	101	mm/dd/yyyy	mm/dd/yyyy	
2	102	yyyy.mm.dd	yyyy.mm.dd	
3	103	dd/mm/yyyy	dd/mm/yyyy	
4	104	dd.mm.yyyy	dd.mm.yyyy	
5	105	dd-mm-yyyy	dd-mm-yyyy	
6	106	dd mm yyyy	dd mm yyyy	
7	107	mm dd, yyyy	mm dd, yyyy	
8	108	hh:mi:ss		hh:mi:ss
	9, 109	mon dd yyyy hh:mi:ss:msAM/PM	mon dd yyyy	hh:mi:ss:ms AM/PM
10	110	mm-dd-yyyy	mm-dd-yyyy	
11	111	yyyy/mm/dd	yyyy/mm/dd	
12	112	yyyymmdd	yyyymmdd	
13	113	yyyy/dd/mm	yyyy/dd/mm	
14	114	mm/yyyy/dd	mm/yyyy/dd	
15	115	dd/yyyy/mm	dd/yyyy/mm	
16	116	mon dd yyyy hh:mi:ss	mon dd yyyy	hh:mi:ss
17	117	hh:miAM/PM		hh:miAM/PM
18	118	hh:mi		hh:mi
19	119	hh:mi:ss:msAM/PM		hh:mi:ss:msAM/PM
20	200	hh:mi:ss:ms		hh:mi:ss:ms

Date and Time Functions

ASE has many built-in date and time functions. A firm understanding of these functions is crucial for most applications.

CURRENT_DATE

The CURRENT_DATE function is used to get the current date out of ASE. This function returns the time as well, however the time is not significant.

Example:
```
DECLARE @DTT2 DATE
DECLARE @DTT3 SMALLDATETIME
DECLARE @DTT4 DATETIME

SELECT @DTT2 = CURRENT_DATE()
SELECT @DTT3 = CURRENT_DATE()
SELECT @DTT4 = CURRENT_DATE()

SELECT @DTT2,
       @DTT3,
       @DTT4
go
Jun  6 2004          Jun  6 2004 12:00AM          Jun  6 2004 12:00AM
```

CURRENT_TIME

The CURRENT_DATE function is used to get the current date out of ASE. This function returns the time as well, however the time is not signifcant.

Example:
```
DECLARE @DTT1 TIME
DECLARE @DTT3 SMALLDATETIME
DECLARE @DTT4 DATETIME

SELECT @DTT1 = CURRENT_TIME()
SELECT @DTT3 = CURRENT_TIME()
SELECT @DTT4 = CURRENT_TIME()
```

```
SELECT @DTT1,
       @DTT3,
       @DTT4
go
6:32PM          Jan  1 1900  6:33PM          Jan  1 1900  6:32PM
```

DATEADD

The DATEADD function is used to add an integer component to a specified date. Refer to the table of date components.

Example:

```
DECLARE @DTT4 DATETIME

SELECT @DTT4 = CURRENT_DATE()

SELECT @DTT4,
       DATEADD(yy, 10, @DTT4)
go
Jun  6 2004 12:00AM          Jun  6 2014 12:00AM
```

DATEDIFF

The DATEDIFF function is used to get the specified ***integer*** date component difference between a pair of specified dates. Refer to the table of date components.

Example:

```
DECLARE @DTT2 DATE
DECLARE @DTT4 DATETIME

SELECT @DTT2 = CURRENT_DATE()
SELECT @DTT4 = CURRENT_TIME()

SELECT @DTT2,
       @DTT4,
       DATEDIFF(yy, @DTT2, @DTT4)
go
Jun  6 2004          Jan  1 1900  6:37PM          -104
```

DATENAME

The DATENAME function is used to get the specified ***string*** date component from a specified date. For "dw" and "mm" the return values will be the name of the day and the name of the month. For instance, Monday, Tuesday, etc..., April, May, etc...

Example:

```
SELECT "Ryan Thomas Putnam was born on: "
      + DATENAME(dw, "04/05/1977 17:30")
go
Ryan Thomas Putnam was born on: Tuesday
```

DATEPART

The DATEPART function is used to get the specified ***integer*** date component from a specified date. Refer to the table of date components.

Example:

```
DECLARE @DTT1 TIME
DECLARE @DTT2 DATE
DECLARE @DTT3 SMALLDATETIME
DECLARE @DTT4 DATETIME

SELECT @DTT1 = CURRENT_TIME()
SELECT @DTT2 = CURRENT_DATE()
SELECT @DTT3 = CURRENT_TIME()
SELECT @DTT4 = CURRENT_DATE()

SELECT DATEPART(hh, @DTT1),
       DATEPART(hh, @DTT2),
       DATEPART(hh, @DTT3),
       DATEPART(hh, @DTT4)
go
18          0          18          0
```

DAY

The DAY function is used to get the ***integer*** date component for the day of the month out a specified date.

Example:
```
SELECT DAY("04/05/1977")
go
5
```

GETDATE

The GETDATE function is used to get the current system ***date*** and ***time***.

Example:
```
DECLARE @DTT1 TIME
DECLARE @DTT2 DATE
DECLARE @DTT3 SMALLDATETIME
DECLARE @DTT4 DATETIME

SELECT @DTT1 = GETDATE()
SELECT @DTT2 = GETDATE()
SELECT @DTT3 = GETDATE()
SELECT @DTT4 = GETDATE()

SELECT @DTT1,
       @DTT2,
       @DTT3,
       @DTT4
go
8:31PM  Jun  6 2004      Jun  6 2004  8:31PM      Jun  6 2004  8:31PM
```

YEAR

The YEAR function is used to get the ***integer*** date component for the year from the specified date.

Example:
```
SELECT YEAR("04/05/1977")
go
1977
```

Putting Dates and Times to Work

The examples we gave above for dates and times were very simplistic. As such, we would like to elaborate more on several areas.

Date Arithmetic

What is the date 89 days from now?

```
SELECT DATEADD(dd, 89, GETDATE())
go
Sep  3 2004  9:00PM
```

Are we in a leap year?

```
DECLARE @DT DATETIME
DECLARE @ISLEAPYR VARCHAR(50)
DECLARE @ISNOTLEAPYR VARCHAR(50)

SELECT @DT = GETDATE()
SELECT @ISLEAPYR = "We are in a leap year !!!"
SELECT @ISNOTLEARYR = "We are not in a leap year !!!"

SELECT CASE
         WHEN ( DATEPART(yy, @DT) % 4 = 0
            AND ( DATEPART(yy, @DT) % 100 > 0 ) )
           THEN @ISLEAPYR
         WHEN ( DATEPART(yy, @DT) % 400 = 0 )
           THEN @ISLEAPYR
         ELSE @ISNOTLEAPYR
       END
go
We are in a leap year !!!
```

Was the year 1300 a leap year? I was told Sybase could not answer this...

```
DECLARE @YR SMALLINT
DECLARE @ISLEAPYR VARCHAR(50)
DECLARE @ISNOTLEAPYR VARCHAR(50)

SELECT @YR = 1300
SELECT @ISLEAPYR = "The year "
```

```
                  + CONVERT(VARCHAR, @YR)
                  + " was a leap year"

SELECT @ISNOTLEAPYR = "The year "
                     + CONVERT(VARCHAR, @YR)
                     + " was NOT a leap year"

SELECT CASE
        WHEN ( @YR % 4 = 0
           AND ( @YR % 100 > 0 ) )
          THEN @ISLEAPYR
        WHEN ( @YR % 400 = 0 )
          THEN @ISLEAPYR
        ELSE @ISNOTLEAPYR
      END
go
The year 1300 was NOT a leap year
```

What is a leap year?

Leap years occur every year four years, except four years ending in 00, in which case only if the year is divisible by 400. Leap years are side effect of the small error in our time system.

I need to get the time out of a datetime datatype?

```
DECLARE @DT DATETIME

SELECT @DT = GETDATE()

SELECT CONVERT(VARCHAR, @DT, 108)
go
21:17:35
```

My application needs a date in the format mm&dd&yyyy?

```
DECLARE @DT DATETIME

SELECT @DT = GETDATE()

SELECT STR_REPLACE( CONVERT(VARCHAR, @DT, 101), "/", "&" )
```

```
go
06&06&2004
```

Date Differences

How do I calculate the number of years of difference between two dates?

```
DECLARE @DT1 DATETIME
DECLARE @DT2 DATETIME

SELECT @DT1 = "09/05/2096"
SELECT @DT2 = "06/05/2004"

SELECT ABS( DATEDIFF(yy, @DT1, @DT2) )
go
92
```

Elapsed Times

Well elapsed times are just date and time differences. So this should be no big deal.

How do I calculate the time to run a command?

```
DECLARE @CURRDT DATETIME
DECLARE @CMDTRCDT DATETIME
DECLARE @RUNTRCDT DATETIME
DECLARE @CMDTRCBT BIT
DECLARE @RUNTRCBT BIT
DECLARE @ELAPSEDT INTEGER

SELECT @CMDTRCBT = 1
SELECT @RUNTRCBT = 1

/* CHECK FOR EXECUTION TRACE */
IF @RUNTRCBT = 1
BEGIN
   SELECT @RUNTRCDT = GETDATE()
   SELECT @CURRDT = GETDATE()
   PRINT ">>>>> START EXECUTION TRACE: %1!", @CURRDT
END

/* CHECK FOR COMMAND TRACE */
IF @CMDTRCBT = 1
```

```
BEGIN
   SELECT @CMDTRCDT = GETDATE()
   SELECT @CURRDT = GETDATE()
   PRINT "     +++++ START WAITFOR TRACE: %1!", @CURRDT
END

/* PUT YOUR COMMAND IN PLACE OF THE WAITFOR */
WAITFOR DELAY "00:00:05"

/* CHECK FOR COMMAND TRACE */
IF @CMDTRCBT = 1
BEGIN
   SELECT @CURRDT = GETDATE()
   PRINT "     +++++ END WAITFOR TRACE: %1!", @CURRDT
   SELECT @ELAPSEDT = DATEDIFF(ss, @CMDTRCDT, @CURRDT)
   PRINT "     ##### ELAPSED SECONDS: %1!", @ELAPSEDT
END

/* POTENTIALLY OTHER COMMANDS */

IF @RUNTRCBT = 1
BEGIN
   SELECT @CURRDT = GETDATE()
   PRINT ">>>>> END OF APPLICATION TRACE: %1!", @CURRDT
   SELECT @ELAPSEDT = DATEDIFF(ss, @RUNTRCDT, @CURRDT)
   PRINT "##### ELAPSED SECONDS: %1!", @ELAPSEDT
END
go
```

```
>>>>> START EXECUTION TRACE: Jun  6 2004 10:24PM
     +++++ START WAITFOR TRACE: Jun  6 2004 10:24PM
     +++++ END WAITFOR TRACE: Jun  6 2004 10:24PM
     ##### ELAPSED SECONDS: 5
>>>>> END OF APPLICATION TRACE: Jun  6 2004 10:24PM
##### ELAPSED SECONDS: 5
```

Julian Dates

How do I convert an ASE Gregorian date to a Julian date?

Numerical Method:

```
DECLARE @DTT1 DATETIME

SELECT @DTT1 = GETDATE()

SELECT @DTT1,
       DATEPART(yy, @DTT1) % 100 * 1000 + DATEPART(dy, @DTT1)
go
Jun  6 2004 10:59PM          4158
```

String Method:

```
DECLARE @DTT1 DATETIME

SELECT @DTT1 = GETDATE()

SELECT @DTT1,
       SUBSTRING( (CONVERT(VARCHAR, DATEPART(yy, @DTT1))
                  + ( CONVERT(VARCHAR, DATEPART(dy, @DTT1) ))), 3, 6)
go
Jun  6 2004 11:02PM          04158
```

Gregorian Dates

How do I convert a Julian date to a Gregorian date?

```
DECLARE @DTT1 INTEGER

SELECT @DTT1 = 4158

SELECT @DTT1,
       DATEADD(dd, (@DTT1 % 1000), "12/31/"
       + CONVERT(VARCHAR, DATEPART(yy, GETDATE()) - 1))
go
4158             Jun  6 2004 12:00AM
```

Various Holidays

How do I know if it is Christmas?

```
SELCT CASE
        WHEN ( DATEPART(mm, GETDATE()) = 12
           AND DATEPART(dd, GETDATE()) ) = 25
          THEN "IT IS CHRISTMAS"
        ELSE "IT IS NOT CHRISTMAS"
      END
go
```

```
IT IS NOT CHRISTMAS
```

How do I know if it is Thanksgiving?

```
SELECT CASE
        WHEN ( DATEPART(mm, GETDATE()) = 11
           AND DATEPART(dd, GETDATE()) >= 22
           AND DATEPART(dd, GETDATE()) <= 28
           AND DATEPART(dw, GETDATE()) = 4 )
          THEN "ITS TIME FOR TURKEY"
        ELSE "ITS NOT TURKEY TIME"
      END
go
```

```
ITS NOT TURKEY TIME
```

How do I determine if it is American Independence Day?

```
SELECT CASE
        WHEN ( DATEPART(mm, GETDATE()) = 7
           AND DATEPART(dd, GETDATE()) = 4 )
          THEN "IT IS"
        ELSE "IT IS NOT"
      END
go
```

```
IT IS NOT
```

How do I determine if it is American Memory Day?

```
SELECT CASE
        WHEN ( DATEPART(mm, GETDATE()) = 5
           AND DATEPART(dd, GETDATE()) >= 25
           AND DATEPART(dw, GETDATE()) = 2 )
```

```
            THEN "IT IS"
          ELSE "IT IS NOT"
        END
go
IT IS NOT
```

How do I determine if it is Labor Day?

```
SELECT CASE
          WHEN ( DATEPART(dm, GETDATE()) = 9
             AND DATEPART(dd, GETDATE()) <= 7
             AND DATEPART(dw, GETDATE()) = 2 )
            THEN "IT IS"
          ELSE "IT IS NOT"
        END
go
IT IS NOT
```

How do I determine if it is a New Year?

```
SELECT CASE
          WHEN ( DATEPART(mm, GETDATE()) = 1
             AND DATEPART(dy, GETDATE()) = 1 )
            THEN "IT IS"
          ELSE "IT IS NOT"
        END
go
IT IS NOT
```

Chapter 24. Working with Dates and Times

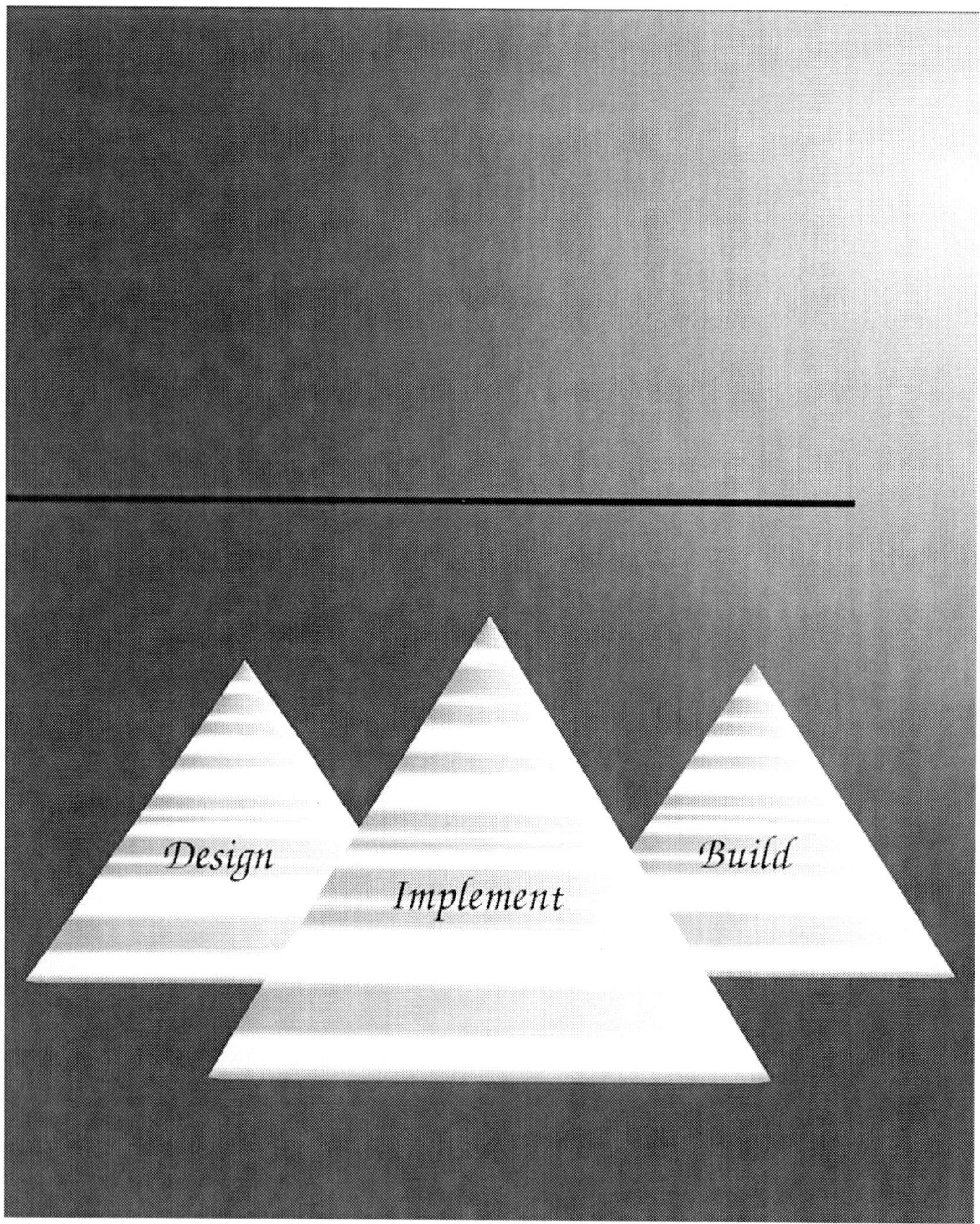
Design
Implement
Build

Chapter 25. Working with Lobs

ASE provides two datatypes for working with LOBS. It provides the TEXT datatype for large strings and IMAGE for large binary data. When creating a table with an image or text datatype ASE creates a separate page chain apart from the tables to store the data.

The text and image datatypes both have the same precision and both store data in raw binary. As such, the datatypes are really synonymous at this point. However, when you need only text you should use text and for binary data for images, video, audio, etc... you should use image. This may seem a bit confusing, however it is not as confusing as another DBMS which dumbfounds us with VARCHAR and VARCHAR2 and recommends not using VARCHAR because they can change it whenever they feel like it. I guess they feel they are a prophet.

Warning: ASE will only create one of these separate page chains. Therefore, if you need a high degree of performance you should create a separate table for each image and text column which you need. Use a driver table to store a central primary key for the 1:1 tables. This is a very easy task to perform during database design.

ASE stores this separate page in sysindexes with a indid of 255 about the tables object id. The name in sysindexes for the object is the table name prefixed with t. Now because this page chain or storage chain is separate from that of the tables, it can be placed onto another segment. As with tables and indexes, you can use ***sp_placeobject*** to move the storage to another segment.

Example:

```
CREATE
 TABLE lobs(
       column01 INT NOT NULL,
       column02 text NULL,
 CONSTRAINT ix01_lobs
   PRIMARY KEY CLUSTERED (column01)
)
LOCK DATAROWS
ON "seg01"
go
```

```
EXEC sp_placeobject "tseg01", "lobs.tlobs"
go
```

Initialize Pointer

In order to use the READTEXT and WRITETEXT functions for text and image data, a valid pointer to the storage of the text or image data must exist. When a table is created this pointer is ***NOT*** initialized. In addition, on tables with text and image columns defined as nullable, the pointer will ***NOT*** be created until actual data has been inserted or updated.

Note: When using text and image datatypes always try to define the columns as nullable. This is to save storage space as the minimum amount of space allocated for a text and image column defined as NOT NULL is a full 2K page.

Pointer Initialization

To initialize the pointer for both text and image data either:

- insert a record which contains data (Non NULL) for the text and/or image column
- or, update a record which contains data for the text and/or image column. This can include updating a text and/or image column with a null value.

Restrictions

You can SELECT, UPDATE, INSERT, and DELETE from tables which contain text and image columns. However, only LIKE and PATINDEX can be used in the WHERE or HAVING predicate. In addition, ASE does not support using text or image columns in an ORDER BY, GROUP BY, or COMPUTE clause. This is to prevent very large sorts. As such, ASE also does not allow for text and image columns to be used in a UNION (UNION ALL may be used as it only merges and does not sort) or SELECT DISTINCT column list. It is also important to mention, image and text datatypes cannot be used for variables or parameters.

When using SELECT to read data for text and image columns you can use the global variable SET TEXTSIZE ***integer*** to define the number of bytes which may be displayed. The default is 32K. If you have modified the TEXTSIZE and just want to change it back to the default 32K you run SET TEXTSIZE 0.

When using isql, the default for the number of characters per line is 80. This can make the output ugly. Consider increasing the width using -w<width>.

READTEXT

The READTEXT function is used to read data from a text or image column.

Syntax:
READTEXT table.column @A_VALID_PTR *offset size* [***USING CHARS* | *BYTES***]

Note: If you do not specify USING CHARS the READTEXT function will default to USING BYTES. This is how ***offset*** and ***size*** are interpreted.

Note: All examples given where generated using an isql width of 2000, -w2000.

Example:

```
CREATE
 TABLE lobs(
       column01 INT NOT NULL,
       column02 text null,
 CONSTRAINT ix01_lobs
   PRIMARY KEY CLUSTERED (column01)
)
LOCK DATAROWS
ON "seg01"
go

EXEC sp_placeobject "tseg01", "lobs.tlobs"
go

INSERT
  INTO lobs(
       column01
)
SELECT 1
go

/* INITIALIZE POINTER */
```

```
UPDATE lobs
   SET column02 = NULL
 WHERE column01 = 1
go

/* LOAD SOME DATA */
UPDATE lobs
   SET column02 = REPLICATE("A", 500)
 WHERE column01 = 1
go

/* READ THE DATA OUT USING WITH USING CHARS */
DECLARE @TEXTPOINTER VARBINARY(16)

SELECT @TEXTPOINTER = TEXTPTR(column02)
  FROM lobs
 WHERE column01 = 1

/* CHECK FOR NOT VALID POINTER */
IF ( TEXTVALID("lobs.column02", @TEXTPOINTER) != 1 )
BEGIN
   RAISERROR 37999 "INVALID TEXT POINTER ENCOUNTERED"
   GOTO ENDPROC
END

/* WE HAVE A VALID TEXTPTR */
READTEXT lobs.column02 @TEXTPOINTER 10 50 USING CHARS

ENDPROC:
go
--------------------------------------------------------------------------------
AAAAAAAAAAAAAAAAAAAAAAAAAAAAAAAAAAAAAAAAAAAAAAAAAA
```

WRITETEXT

The WRITETEXT function is used to write data to a text or image column. WRITETEXT erases all data currently in a text or image column and replaces it with the specified DATA.

Syntax:
WRITETEXT table.column @A_VALID_PTR *[**WITH LOG**]* DATA

Note: If you do not specify the WITH LOG option of WRITETEXT the default is without logging. This requires that the "select into/bulkcopy/pllsort" database option be active. The DATA component specifies the DATA to insert into the specified column. The maximum amount of DATA which may be inserted through WRITETEXT is 120K. When inserting text data, enclose the text within single or double quotes. When inserting binary data, prefix the binary data with 0x.

Note: All examples given where generated using an isql width of 2000, -w2000.

Example:

```
CREATE
 TABLE lobs(
       column01 INT NOT NULL,
       column02 text null,
 CONSTRAINT ix01_lobs
   PRIMARY KEY CLUSTERED (column01)
)
LOCK DATAROWS
ON "seg01"
go

EXEC sp_placeobject "tseg01", "lobs.tlobs"
go

INSERT
  INTO lobs(
       column01
)
SELECT 1
go

/* INITIALIZE POINTER */
UPDATE lobs
   SET column02 = NULL
 WHERE column01 = 1
go

/* READ THE DATA OUT USING WITH USING CHARS */
DECLARE @WRTVAL VARCHAR(16384)
DECLARE @TEXTPOINTER VARBINARY(16)

SELECT @WRTVAL = REPLICATE("A", 500)
```

```
SELECT @TEXTPOINTER = TEXTPTR(column02)
  FROM lobs
 WHERE column01 = 1

/* CHECK FOR NOT VALID POINTER */
IF ( TEXTVALID("lobs.column02", @TEXTPOINTER) != 1 )
BEGIN
   RAISERROR 37999 "INVALID TEXT POINTER ENCOUNTERED"
   GOTO ENDPROC
END

/* WE HAVE A VALID TEXTPTR */
WRITETEXT lobs.column01 @TEXTPOINTER WITH LOG @WRTVAL

READTEXT lobs.column02 @TEXTPOINTER 10 50 USING CHARS

ENDPROC:
go
------------------------------------------------------------------------
AAAAAAAAAAAAAAAAAAAAAAAAAAAAAAAAAAAAAAAAAAAAAAAAAA
```

Chapter 25. Working with Lobs

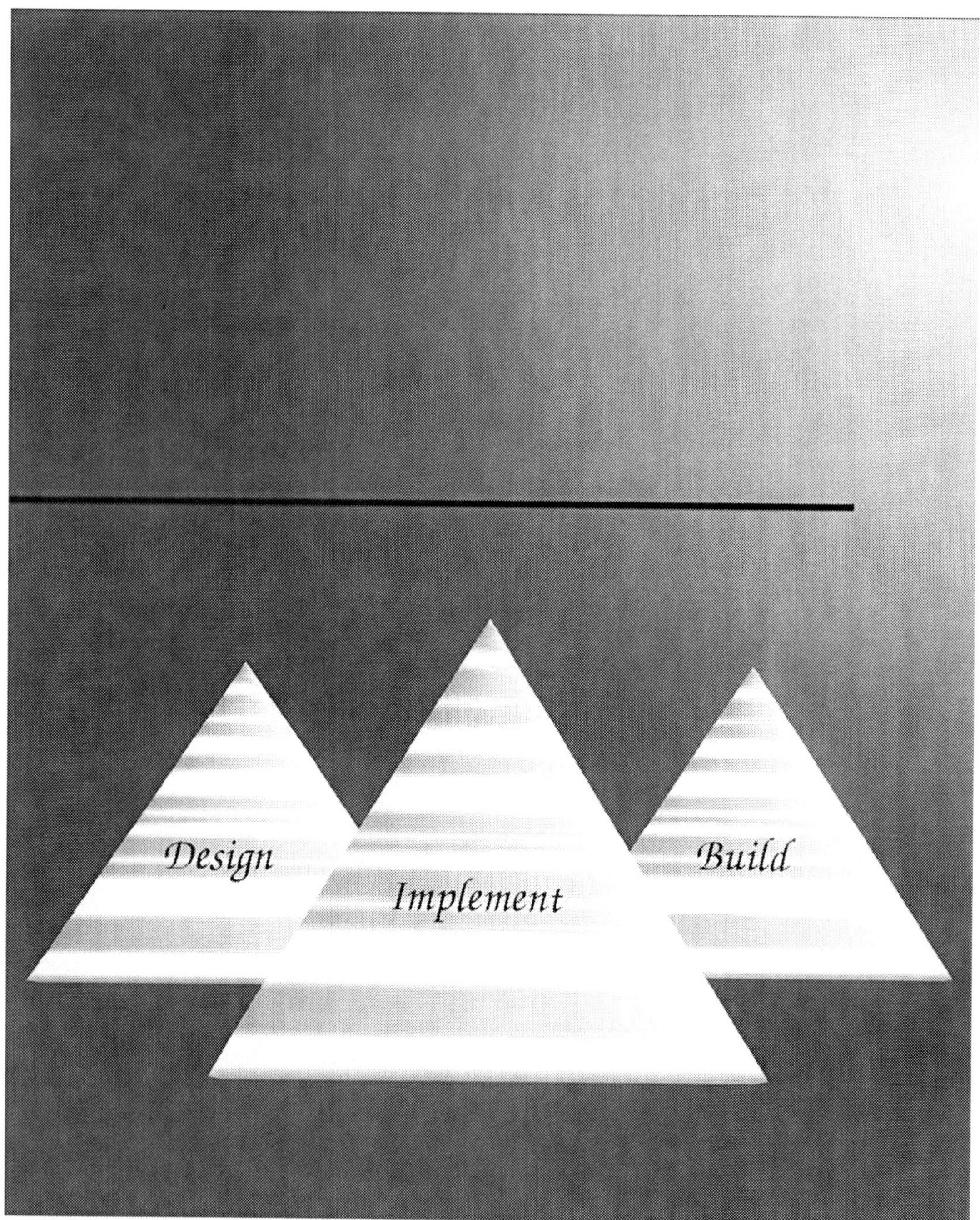
Design
Implement
Build

Chapter 26. Conversions between Datatypes

ASE provides three conversion functions to explicitly convert between datatypes: HEXTOINT, INTOHEX, and CONVERT. The functions HEXTOINT and INTTOHEX are not hardware-dependent.

Warning: Because of hardware emulation and rendering issues, you should not use the CONVERT function to convert between hexadecimal and integer and vice versa.

HEXTOINT

The HEXTOINT function is used to convert a hexadecimal to an integer.

Example:

```
SELECT HEXTOINT("0x1000")
go
4096
```

INTTOHEX

The INTTOHEX function is used to convert an integer to a hexadecimal.

Example:

```
SELECT "0x" + INTTOHEX(4096)
go
0x00001000
```

CONVERT

The remainder of those explicit conversions which can be performed in ASE are done by using the CONVERT function. The CONVERT function can convert integers, dates, and monetary values. Below is a table with syntax for CONVERT.

Conversion	*Syntax*
To Tinyint	CONVERT(TINYINT, VALUE)
To Smallint	CONVERT(SMALLINT, VALUE)
To Integer	CONVERT(INT, VALUE)
To Numeric	CONVERT(NUMERIC, VALUE)
To Numeric	CONVERT(NUMERIC(***p, s***), VALUE)
To Decimal	CONVERT(DECIMAL, VALUE)
To Decimal	CONVERT(DECIMAL(***p, s***), VALUE)
To Money	CONVERT(MONEY, VALUE)
To Smallmoney	CONVERT(SMALLMONEY, VALUE)
To Char	CONVERT(CHAR, VALUE)
To Char	CONVERT(CHAR(***length***), VALUE)
To Varchar	CONVERT(VARCHAR, VALUE)
To Varchar	CONVERT(VARCHAR(***length***), VALUE)
To Unichar	CONVERT(UNICHAR, VALUE)
To Unichar	CONVERT(UNICHAR(***length***), VALUE)
To Univarchar	CONVERT(UNIVARCHAR, VALUE)
To Univarchar	CONVERT(UNIVARCHAR(***length***), VALUE)
To Nchar	CONVERT(NCHAR, VALUE)
To Nchar	CONVERT(NCHAR(***length***), VALUE)
To Nvarchar	CONVERT(NVARCHAR, VALUE)
To Nvarchar	CONVERT(NVARCHAR(***length***, VALUE)
To Date	CONVERT(DATE, VALUE)
To Time	CONVERT(TIME, VALUE)
To Smalldatetime	CONVERT(SMALLDATETIME, VALUE)
To Datetime	CONVERT(DATETIME, VALUE)
To Binary	CONVERT(BINARY, VALUE)
To Binary	CONVERT(BINARY(***length***), VALUE)
To Varbinary	CONVERT(VARBINARY, VALUE)

Conversion	*Syntax*
To Varbinary	CONVERT(VARBINARY(***length***), VALUE)
To Real	CONVERT(REAL, VALUE)
To Float	CONVERT(FLOAT, VALUE)
To Double Precision	CONVERT(DOUBLE PRECISION, VALUE)

Example (INT TO VARCHAR):

```
DECLARE @VAR1 INTEGER,
        @VAR2 VARHCHAR(10)

SELECT @VAR1 = 1025

SELECT @VAR2 = CONVERT(VARCHAR(10), @VAR1)

SELECT @VAR2
go
1025
```

Example (TINYINT TO INT):

```
DECLARE @VAR1 TINYINT,
        @VAR2 INTEGER

SELECT @VAR1 = 45

SELECT @VAR2 = CONVERT(INTEGER, @VAR1)

SELECT @VAR2
go
45
```

Example (VARCHAR TO INT):

```
DECLARE @VAR1 INTEGER,
        @VAR2 VARCHAR(10)

SELECT @VAR2 = "10"

SELECT @VAR1 = CONVERT(INT, @VAR2)

SELECT @VAR1
go
10
```

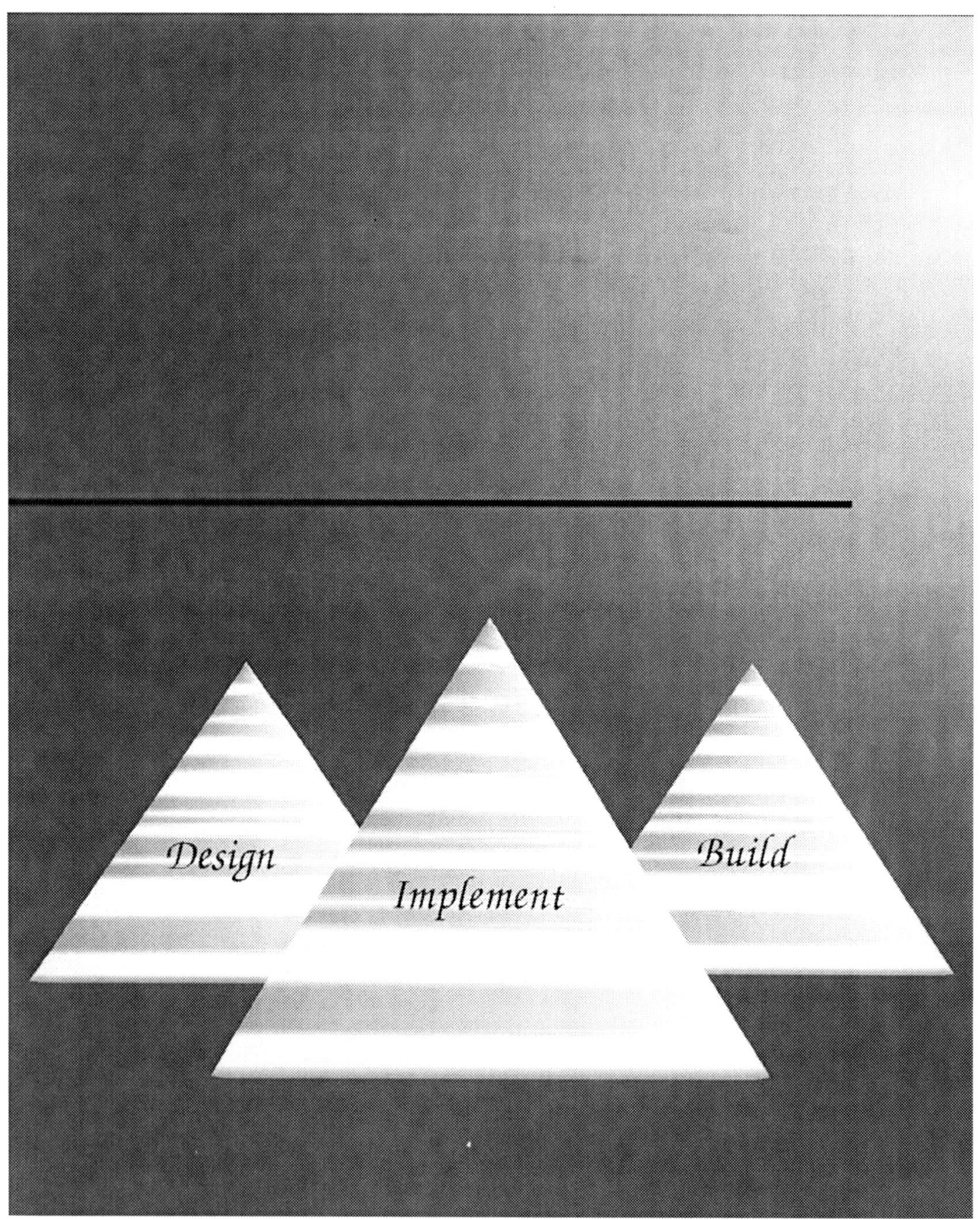
Design
Implement
Build

Chapter 27. Various Statistical Measures

We hope that you are holding tightly onto to the arms of your rocking chair for this section.

Note: You can easily use these methods from a pair of stored procedures: one to build the #stats user worktable and the clustered index, and the second to run against the built table and index.

Medians on Steroids

"I need to calculate the median within ASE. I have heard it is difficult and requires a cursor or multiple self-joins." You have heard wrong. In fact, calculating any nth percentile is very easy within ASE. In addition, very efficient.

Example (50th percentile):

```
SELECT < All primary key columns go here >,
       < The single median column goes here >
  INTO #stats
  FROM table

/* ORDER THE DATA */
CREATE UNIQUE CLUSTERED INDEX ix01_stats
ON #stats (
   < The single median column goes here >,
   < All primary key columns go here >
)
go


DECLARE @RCNT INT
DECLARE @UCNT INT

DECLARE @V50_LOW_CNT INT
DECLARE @V50_HGH_CNT INT
DECLARE @V50_LOW INT
DECLARE @V50_HGH INT
```

```
SELECT @RCNT = COUNT(*)
  FROM #stats

SELECT @UCNT = 0

/* IF ROWCOUNT IS DIVISBLE BY 2 */
IF ( @RCNT % 2 = 0 )
BEGIN
   SELECT @V50_LOW_CNT = ( @RCNT / 2 )
   SELECT @V50_HGH_CNT = @V50_LOW_CNT + 1
END
/* MUST BE AN ODD NUMBER */
ELSE
BEGIN
   SELECT @V50_LOW_CNT = ( @RCNT / 2 ) + 1
   SELECT @V50_HGH_CNT = @V50_LOW_CNT
END

UPDATE #stats
   SET @UCNT = @UCNT + 1,
              @V50_LOW = CASE
                           WHEN ( @UCNT = @V50_LOW_CNT )
                             THEN < median column >
                           ELSE @V50_LOW
                         END,
              @V50_HGH = CASE
                           WHEN ( @UCNT = @V50_HGH_CNT )
                             THEN < median column >
                           ELSE @V50_HGH
                         END
  FROM #stats ( INDEX ix01_stats )

SELECT @UCNT AS "ROW COUNT",
       @V50_LOW AS "LOW MEDIAN",
       @V50_HGH AS "HIGH MEDIAN",
       ( @V50_LOW + @V50_HGH ) / 2 AS "AVG MEDIAN"
go
-----------------------------------------------------------------------
68634         71           71           71
```

Modes on Steroids

Next, we demonstrate that calculating the mode of the 50th percentile within ASE is just as easy and efficient.

Example (Mode of Lower 50th percentile):

Note: This example only gives the last mode of the lower 50th percentile. However, you should be able to modify this example to suit your needs.

```
SELECT < All primary key columns go here >,
       < The single mode column goes here >
  INTO #stats
  FROM table

/* ORDER THE DATA */
CREATE UNIQUE CLUSTERED INDEX ix01_stats
ON #stats (
   < The single mode column goes here >,
   < All primary key columns go here >
)
go

DECLARE @RCNT INT
DECLARE @UCNT INT

DECLARE @V50_LOW_CNT INT
DECLARE @V50_LOW_VAL INT
DECLARE @V50_SAVE_VAL INT
DECLARE @V50_LOW_MOD INT

DECLARE @FREQ_CNT INT
DECLARE @SAVE_FREQ_CNT INT

/* GET ROWCOUNT */
SELECT @RCNT = COUNT(*)
  FROM #stats

/* INITIALIZE UPDATE COUNTER */
SELECT @UCNT = 0

/* INITIALIZE OTHER COUNTERS */
SELECT @FREQ_CNT = 0
SELECT @SAVE_FREQ_CNT = 0
```

```
/* GET LOWER PERCENTILE */
SELECT @V50_LOW_CNT = ( @RCNT / 2 )

UPDATE #stats
   SET @UCNT = @UCNT + 1,
       @V50_LOW_VAL = CASE
                        WHEN ( @UCNT < @V50_LOW_CNT )
                           THEN < mode column >
                        ELSE @V50_LOW_VAL
                      END,
       @FREQ_CNT = CASE
                     WHEN ( @UCNT < @V50_LOW_CNT
                        AND @V50_SAVE_VAL <> @V50_LOW_VAL )
                       THEN 1
                     WHEN ( @UCNT < @V50_LOW_CNT )
                       THEN ( @FREQ_CNT + 1 )
                     ELSE @FREQ_CNT
                   END,
       @V50_LOW_MOD = CASE
                        WHEN ( @UCNT < @V50_LOW_CNT
                           AND @FREQ_CNT > @SAVE_FREQ_CNT )
                          THEN @V50_LOW_VAL
                        ELSE @V50_LOW_MOD
                      END,
       @SAVE_FREQ_CNT = CASE
                          WHEN ( @UCNT < @V50_LOW_CNT
                             AND @FREQ_CNT > @SAVE_FREQ_CNT )
                            THEN @FREQ_CNT
                          ELSE @SAVE_FREQ_CNT
                        END,
       @V50_SAVE_VAL = CASE
                         WHEN ( @UCNT < @V50_LOW_CNT )
                           THEN @V50_LOW_VAL
                         ELSE @V50_SAVE_VAL
                       END
  FROM #stats ( INDEX ix01_stats )

SELECT @UCNT AS "ROW COUNT",
       @V50_LOW_MOD AS "LOW MODE",
       @SAVE_FREQ_CNT AS "FREQUENCY"
go
-----------------------------------------------------
68634          25             1220
```

Means on Steroids

Here is a fast method of calculating the mean of the lower 50th percentile within ASE. Clustered indexes on temporary tables are powerful!

Note: The mean of the 100th percentile is simply AVG(values)... Don't get confused here... If you need the average or mean of all values use AVG(values)...

Example (Mean of Lower 50th percentile):

```
SELECT < All primary key columns go here >,
       < The single mean column goes here >
  INTO #stats
  FROM table

/* ORDER THE DATA */
CREATE UNIQUE CLUSTERED INDEX ix01_stats
ON #stats (
   < The single mean column goes here >,
   < All primary key columns go here >
)
go

DECLARE @RCNT INT
DECLARE @UCNT INT

DECLARE @V50_LOW_CNT INT
DECLARE @V50_MEAN INT

/* GET ROWCOUNT */
SELECT @RCNT = COUNT(*)
  FROM #stats

/* INITIALIZE UPDATE COUNTER */
SELECT @UCNT = 0

/* GET LOWER PERCENTILE */
SELECT @V50_LOW_CNT = ( @RCNT / 2 )
SELECT @V50_MEAN = 0
```

```
UPDATE #stats
   SET @UCNT = @UCNT + 1,
       @V50_MEAN = CASE
                     WHEN ( @UCNT < @V50_LOW_CNT )
                       THEN ( @V50_MEAN + < mean column > )
                     ELSE @V50_MEAN
                   END
  FROM #stats ( INDEX ix01_stats )

SELECT @V50_MEAN = ( @V50_MEAN / @RCNT )

SELECT @UCNT AS "ROW COUNT",
       @V50_MEAN AS "LOW MEAN"
go
----------------------------------------------------------------------
68634          20
```

Variance and Standard Deviation on Steroids

You can use the following to get the population variance.

Example:
```
SET ARITHABORT NUMERIC_TRUNCATION OFF

SELECT (SUM(POWER(CONVERT(NUMERIC(38, 4), <column>), 2.0))
            - POWER(SUM(CONVERT(NUMERIC(38, 4), <column>)), 2.0)
                  / CONVERT(NUMERIC(38, 4), COUNT(*)))
         / CONVERT(NUMERIC(38, 4), COUNT(*))
  FROM table

SET ARITHABORT NUMERIC_TRUNCATION ON
go
4500.681842
```

You can use the following to get the population standard deviation.

Example:
```
SET ARITHABORT NUMERIC_TRUNCATION OFF

SELECT SQRT(
         (SUM(POWER(CONVERT(NUMERIC(38, 4), <column>), 2.0))
            - POWER(SUM(CONVERT(NUMERIC(38, 4), <column>)), 2.0)
                  / CONVERT(NUMERIC(38, 4), COUNT(*)))
           / CONVERT(NUMERIC(38, 4), COUNT(*))
       )
  FROM table

SET ARITHABORT NUMERIC_TRUNCATION ON
go
67.087121
```

You can use the following to get the sample variance.

Example:
```
SET ARITHABORT NUMERIC_TRUNCATION OFF

SELECT (SUM(POWER(CONVERT(NUMERIC(38, 4), <column>), 2.0))
```

```
                - POWER(SUM(CONVERT(NUMERIC(38, 4), <column>)), 2.0)
                            / CONVERT(NUMERIC(38, 4), COUNT(*)))
        / CONVERT(NUMERIC(38, 4), COUNT(*) - 1)
  FROM table

SET ARITHABORT NUMERIC_TRUNCATION ON
go
4500.747418
```

You can use the following to get the sample standard deviation.

Example:

```
SET ARITHABORT NUMERIC_TRUNCATION OFF

SELECT SQRT(
         (SUM(POWER(CONVERT(NUMERIC(38, 4), <column>), 2.0))
               - POWER(SUM(CONVERT(NUMERIC(38, 4), <column>)), 2.0)
                            / CONVERT(NUMERIC(38, 4), COUNT(*)))
             / CONVERT(NUMERIC(38, 4), COUNT(*) - 1)
       )
  FROM table

SET ARITHABORT NUMERIC_TRUNCATION ON
go
67.087610
```

Histograms on Steroids

Histograms can be very useful to determine frequencies as counts within specific ranges. We can use the ***CASE*** statement to efficiently build histograms.

Example:

```
SELECT SUM( CASE
              WHEN ( <column> < 50 )
                THEN 1
              ELSE 0
            END ) AS "CNT_LESS_50",
       SUM( CASE
              WHEN ( <column> BETWEEN 50 AND 100 )
                THEN 1
              ELSE 0
            END ) AS "CNT_BTW_50_N_100",
       SUM( CASE
              WHEN ( <column> > 100 )
                THEN 1
              ELSE 0
            END ) AS "CNT_GRTR_100"
  FROM table
go
```

```
131        50           19
```

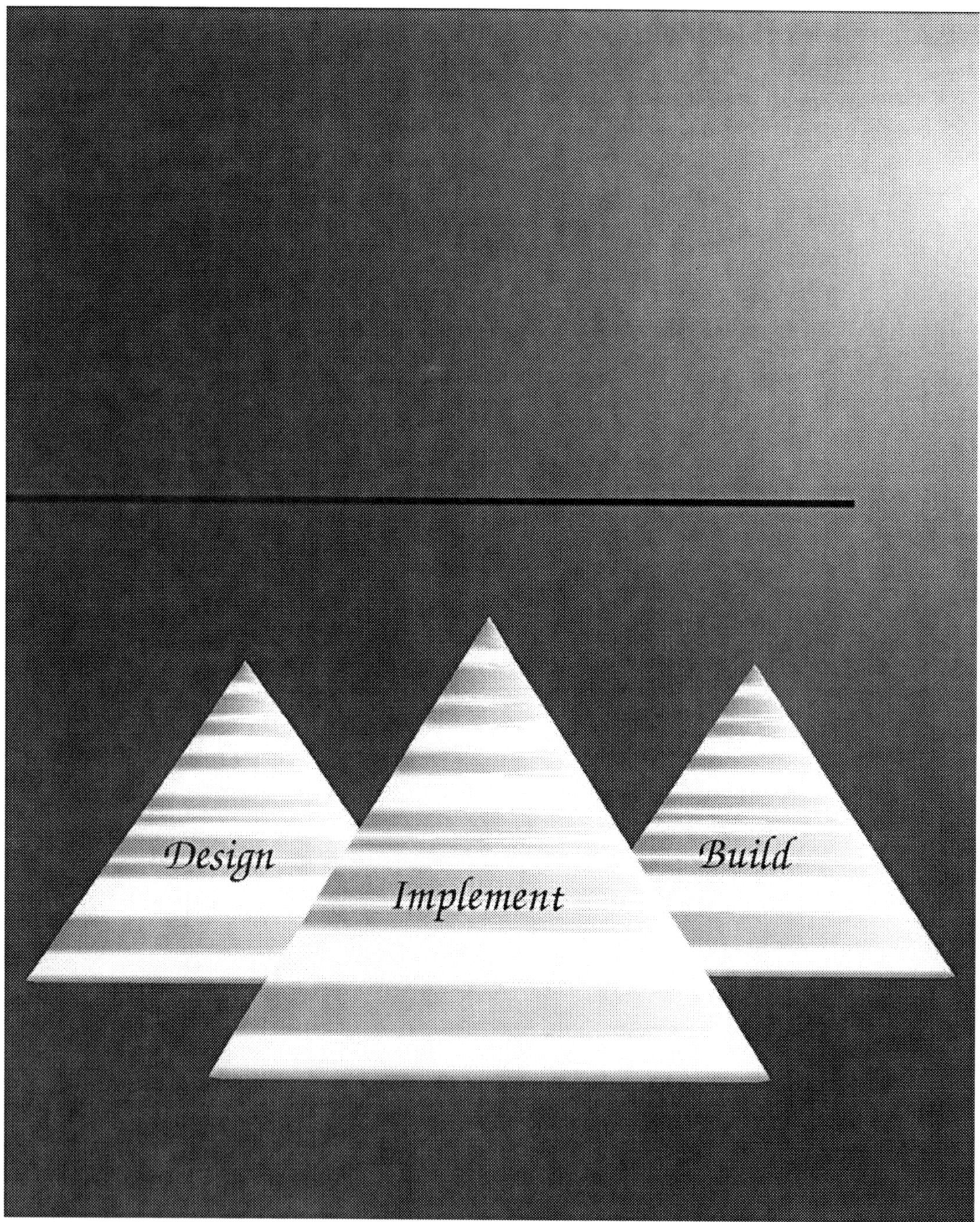
Design
Implement
Build

Chapter 28. Purging and Archiving

The need to purge or archive data is most often business-specific. Businesses that run many transactions often need to purge or archive data on a scheduled basis. A few good reasons to perform these tasks:

1. save on disk disk space
2. increase response time for applications
3. archiving legal data
4. auditing analysis
5. data warehousing

We have put together two different sections on working with purges and archives. The first section discusses purging and archiving in a replicated environment; the second, purging and archiving in a non-replicated environment. Both sections should be read, as they both discuss real-world solutions which the authors have encountered.

Note: As with any process which has the potential to affect large amounts of data, you may need to follow a purge process with a table or index reorganization. We discuss the need to reorg in detail in the chapter on Data Access.

Replicated Environment

Every database requires a form of maintenance to remove the old or unwanted records and prune tables. In addition, many times a regular archiving process does implicit purging by copying the old data to an archive database and deleting the corresponding records from production. Regular archiving is sometimes done on a daily, weekly or monthly basis. The same operation applies to the purging of unwanted data. Support staff including helpdesk, DBA, and Replication Administrator need to coordinate these activities with the customer to ensure the following:

1. The purge and archive processes are run at scheduled times coordinated with the customer.

2. The purge is done in such a way as not to fill up the transaction log. This basically means keeping the batch size reasonable.

3. The purge operation does not coincide with housekeeping tasks. For example, purge and update statistics should not collide.

4. If the database is replicated, then the Replication Server(R) Administrator needs to know the volume of replicated traffic generated via purge and the expected latency. Again, it is essential that the batch size is kept within the acceptable size for the replicated database. ***Note***: This will many times require tuning.

5. Your Replication Administrator needs to make sure that the Replication Server stable devices (stable queues on disk storage) have sufficient capacity to support the purge.

Purge and Batch Size

It is important that both purge processes and archive processes are tested in the development/test environments before sign-off into production. Ultimately, it is the responsibility of the application development staff, DBA, and Replication Administrator to ensure that the production system is not adversely impacted by these processes.

With that, selecting a batch size can be crucial to the operation of a purge and/or archive. Let's say you have an archive table which needs to be cleaned of old records which are more than three months old. The database is also replicated. Hence, you need to keep the following four objectives in mind:

1. Delete audit records on a scheduled basis

2. Do not fill the transaction log

3. Stable devices need to sized to accommodate the volume of replication

4. Any replication latency is business-acceptable.

In the following example, we have shown a shell function which loops over the audit table, audit_table. A weekly purge process deletes records from this table which are more than three months old. The database ${DB} is replicated so care must be taken ***not*** to fill in the transaction log. For this reason, the purge is performed in batches ${BATCH_SIZE} of 50,000 records at a time.

Note: You need to investigate and find an optimum batch size for your deletions.

```
function delete_from_audit_table {
BATCH_SIZE=50000          ## takes into account replication
NO_OF_NONTH_TO_DELETE="-3"

isql -U${USERNAME} -S${SQL_SERVER_NAME} -w1000 << ! >> ${LOG_FILE}
${PASSWORD}
USE ${DB}
go
SET ROWCOUNT ${BATCH_SIZE}
go
DECLARE @cnt int
SELECT @cnt = 1
WHILE EXISTS (SELECT 1
                FROM audit_table
               WHERE audit_date_time <= dateadd(month,$
{NO_OF_NONTH_TO_DELETE},GETDATE()))
BEGIN
   BEGIN TRAN
   SELECT "Start delete of audit_table time limits for batch " +
          CONVERT(CHAR(5),@cnt) +
          "at " +
          CONVERT(CHAR(9),GETDATE(),8)
   DELETE
     FROM audit_table
    WHERE audit_date_time <= DATEADD(month,${NO_OF_NONTH_TO_DELETE},
GETDATE())

   IF ( @@ERROR != 0  OR @@TRANSTATE = 3 )
   BEGIN
      PRINT "ERROR : delete of audit_table failed "
         IF ( @@trancount > 0 )
            ROLLBACK TRAN
      RETURN
   END
```

```
   SELECT "End delete of audit_table time limits for batch " +
          CONVERT(CHAR(5),@cnt) +
          "at " +
          CONVERT(CHAR(9),GETDATE(),8)

   SELECT @cnt = @cnt + 1

   COMMIT TRAN
END
go
SELECT "Finished all for audit_table for time period deletes" +
       "at " +
       CONVERT(CHAR(9),GETDATE(),8)
go
exit
!
}
```

Large Deletes and Replication

Before performing any large deletes, and for that matter, large inserts or updates, contact your DBA or Replication Administrator to see whether the database is replicated.

If the database is replicated (warm or otherwise), you need to consider the following:

1. The timing of the deletion. You need to schedule the task at times of low activity in the database, such as an evening or week-end.

2. The volume of replicated traffic. If you are going to delete say ½ million records and even if you are doing this 50,000 records at a time, you will still be generating a sizable volume of replication traffic. Remember that replication is sequential. In other words, all other replicated data will queue behind your deletes. This may cause any other replicated data not to get through to the replicate databases in a timely manner (large latency). In addition, the replicate tables will be locked by the Replication Maintenance User (by default this user has a name in the form<database_name>_maint in the replicate server). This can cause applications in replicate databases to wait on lock resources.

Customer Impact

For regular purge and archiving, you need to understand the application requirements and you should consider carrying out these types of operations when latency would be the most acceptable to the customer. However, these operations are typically carried out nightly, weekly, or monthly.

Function Replication

You can use function replication to replicate a stored procedure as opposed to underlying tables. By replicating the stored procedure, you avoid the problem of replicated traffic.

For example, suppose you purge records through a stored procedure in the database. Since the stored procedure is replicated, it triggers a replicate stored procedure to be fired at the replicate database and this replicate procedure deletes. The only problem in this case is that you can either replicate the stored procedure, or the underlying table(s) but not both! Let us look at an example of replicating stored procedure:

```
isql -U${USERNAME}  -S${SQL_SERVER} -w1000 << ! >> ${LOG_FILE}
${PASSWORD}
use ${DATABASE}
go
sp_setreptable volatility_detail_arc,false
go
sp_setreptable volatility_list_arc,false
go
--
-- Stored procedure archive_volatility_detail_sp is replicated
--
exec archive_volatility_detail_sp @mnemonic='%',
                                  @trader='NYC',
                                  @from_date=0,
                                  @to_date=20021001,
                                  @debug=0
go
sp_setreptable hts_volatility_detail_arc,true
go
sp_setreptable hts_volatility_list_arc,true
go
exit
```

```
!
```

Note that in the example above, we turn off replication for two tables; "volatility_detail_arc" and "volatility_list_arc" before executing the stored procedure. Once the stored procedure is executed, the replication for the tables are turned on. You need to have a "dbo" role to turn on/off replication for tables. It is important to realize that during the time that replication is turned off for those two tables, any DML operations by any other process on those two tables will not be replicated.

Turning off Replication for a Session

Another option is to run an archive or purge on the production and replicated databases independently. This can be achieved by turning off replication for a session.

Example:

```
isql -U${USERNAME}  -S${SQL_SERVER} -w1000 << ! >> ${LOG_FILE}
${PASSWORD}
USE ${DATABASE}
go
--
-- Turn off replication for this session. Nothing will be replicated
--
SET REPLICATION OFF
go
DELETE FROM …
go
exit
!
```

You then need to run this session for each replicated database.

Running Archive/Purge as Replication Maintenance User

If you prefer the data not to be replicated, you can sometimes run this job as the replication maintenance user -- that is, if you do not send maintenance transactions to the replicate. This is known as replicating the replicate.

Now, the maintenance user normally has "replication_role" on by default. This will prevent any DML by a replication maintenance user from being replicated.

Example:

```
USE ${DATABASE}
go
1> sp_displaylogin RS_maint
2> go
Suid: 425
Loginame: RS_maint
Fullname: RS maint user
Default Database: abc
Default Language:
Auto Login Script:
Configured Authorization:
       replication_role (default ON)
Locked: NO

isql -U${RS_maint} -S${SQL_SERVER} -w1000 << ! >> ${LOG_FILE}
${PASSWORD}
DELETE FROM --
--
go
!
```

However, first check with your DBA to ensure that all is fine and you can actually use this login.

Non-Replicated Environment

When developing purge jobs and archive jobs which need to run against the production database, serious thought needs to go to into the design of these components. There are numerous tools which can aide in Archiving, such as replication server. However, we will be discussing purging and archiving from the point where all you have is one ASE server and must archive and purge the data on this server.

Purges

A purge process should not use a tempdb database to store the records that qualify to be deleted. tempdb is a critical system resource for which we do not have an unlimited amount at our disposal. A database should be created on devices apart from the production database if possible. In addition, this database should have the "trunc log on checkpoint" option and the "select into" options enabled.

Most tables should have a primary key, if not, the table should at a minimum have a unique index. This is necessary so that we do not create duplicate records within a table. A table without a primary key or a unique index would break the laws of relation theory and make our database confusing. In the purge database, use the SELECT INTO operation to create a key table (table of records which qualify to be purged), which only contains the primary key from the production table.

Now, a good purge process in ASE is one that consists of four phases.

1. **Cleanup**: Truncate and drop old tables created with SELECT INTO.

2. **Fetch-n-Store**: Read the data as fast as possible and store the primary key columns for those records (only the key) which qualify to be purged into a key table.

3. **Index-n-Stats**: The index phase should create unique indexes on the tables in the purge database.

4. **Purge**: After Cleanup, Fetch-n-Store, and Index-n-Stats, the Purge process should be invoked to run against the key tables to purge the data.

Cleanup Phase

The Cleanup phase process is responsible for truncating and dropping tables in the purge database once they are no longer needed.

Note: This process should always truncate the tables first as this is a minimally logged operation. You need to be a DBO to perform this operation. Refer the chapter on tempdb usage for more information.

Fetch-n-Store

The Fetch-n-Store process is responsible for running a SELECT INTO command against the production data in order to build the purge key tables.

Note: A SELECT INTO operation should almost always be chosen for this as it is a minimally logged operation. Refer to the chapter on tempdb usage for more information.

Index-n-Stats

The Index-n-Stats process is responsible for creating unique indexes on the columns which comprise a key table. This is a necessity for high throughput in the Purge phase. When an index is created, statistics are automatically stored for the columns which comprise the index. Therefore it is not necessary to run an UPDATE STATISTICS command.

Purge

After Cleanup, Fetch-n-Store, and Index-n-Stats have completed, it is the responsibility of the Purge process to run against the tables created in the purge database to remove the production data. A good purge process will yield when blocking is being caused and will not use cursors because of the CPU overhead and throughput loss. Instead, the Purge process should ***always*** use the artificial cursors method to prune the data from the production database.

Example:
```
/* ASSUME PRODUCTION TABLE NAMED test_table NEEDS PURGED */
/* IT HAS A PRIMARY KEY ON THE COLUMN column01 */
/* CLEANUP RAN SUCCESSFULLY AND DROPPED THE OLD PURGE TABLES */
/* FETCH AND STORE CREATED THE prg_test_table /*
/* IN THE PURGE DATABASE purge_data */
/* IN ADDITION THE INDEX AND STATS PROCESS RAN */
/* AND CREATED A UNIQUE INDEX ON prg_test_table (column01) */

/* OKAY LETS CREATE THE PURGE PROCESSING TABLE */
USE purge_data
go

CREATE
  TABLE dt_test_table(
        column01 INT NOT NULL
)
go

/* DECLARE VARIABLE TO HOLD INFO ABOUT WHETHER OR */
/* NOT THE PURGE PROCESS NEEDS TO GO TO SLEEP */
```

```
DECLARE @NEED_TO_SLEEP BIT
DECLARE @RW_CNT INTEGER
DECLARE @SET_RW_CNT SMALLINT

SELECT @NEED_TO_SLEEP = 0
SELECT @SET_RW_CNT = 100

/* ESTABLISH NUMBEROF RECORDS TO HANDLE IN FETCH */
/* THIS NUMBER CAN GREATLY AFFECT THE THROUGHPUT */
/* OF THE PURGE PROCESSS AT THE EXPENSE OF CAUSING */
/* ISSUES WITHIN THE APPLICATION */
/* I RECOMMEND A VALUE OF 100 TO START AND TUNE */
/* THROUGH MEASUREMENT IF NECESSARY */
SET ROWCOUNT @SET_RW_CNT

INSERT
  INTO dt_test_table(
       column01
)
SELECT column01
  FROM prg_test_table

/* GET THE ROWCOUNT TO DETERMINE IF WE HAVE ROWS TO PROCESS */
SELECT @RW_CNT = @@ROWCOUNT

/* LOOP UNTIL ALL ROWS HAVE BEEN PROCESSED */
WHILE ( @RW_CNT > 0 )
BEGIN
   /* LETS CHECK THE SLEEP BIT TO DETERMINE IF WE NEED TO YIELD */
   /* BECAUSE WE ARE CAUSING CONTENTION ON THE PRODUCTION DATABASE */
   /* IF WE NEED TO SLEEP */
   IF ( @NEED_TO_SLEEP = 1 )
   BEGIN
      /* WE NEED TO SLEEP LETS SLEEP FOR A MINUTE */
      WAITFOR DELAY "00:01:00"
   END

   /* BEGIN A TRAN TO HOLD LOCKS TO DETERMINE IF WE NEED TO YIELD */
   BEGIN TRANSACTION

   /* DELETE QUALIFYING PURGE RECORDS BY PRIMARY KEY */
   /* FROM THE PRODUCTION TABLE */
   DELETE prod_database.dbo.test_table
     FROM dt_test_table dt,
```

```
        prod_database.dbo.test_table prod
   WHERE prod.column01 = dt.column01

   /* LETS DETERMINE IF WE CAUSED ANY BLOCKS TO OCCUR */
   /* IF A BLOCK OCCURRED SET SLEEP BIT TO TRUE */
   /* ELSE SET SLEEP BIT TO FALSE */
   IF ( EXISTS ( SELECT 1
                   FROM master.dbo.sysprocesses
                  WHERE blocked = @@SPID ) )
   BEGIN
      SELECT @NEED_TO_SLEEP = 1
   END
   ELSE
   BEGIN
      SELECT @NEED_TO_SLEEP = 0
   END

   /* COMMIT TRAN TO RELEASE LOCKS ASAP */
   COMMIT TRAN

   /* REMOVE PROCESSED RECORDS FROM THE PURGE TABLE */
   DELETE prg_test_table
     FROM prg_test_table prg,
          dt_test_table dt
    WHERE prg.column01 = dt.column01

   /* REMOVE ALL ROWS FROM dt_test_table TABLE FOR THE NEXT FETCH */
   TRUNCATE TABLE dt_test_table

   /* PERFORM NEXT FETCH */
   INSERT
     INTO dt_test_table(
          column01
   )
   SELECT column01
     FROM prg_test_table

   /* GET THE ROWCOUNT TO DETERMINE IF WE HAVE ROWS TO PROCESS */
   SELECT @RW_CNT = @@ROWCOUNT
END
go
```

Archive without Purge

An archive without purge is the process of archiving data for audits, reporting, and potentially other uses. In addition, the production data is still valid and thus cannot be removed.

As with the purge process, an archive without purge solution should not use a tempdb database to store the records which qualify to be archived. The tempdb databases are a critical system resource for which we do not have an unlimited amount at our disposal. A database should be created on devices apart from the production database if possible. In addition, this database should have the "trunc log on checkpoint" option and the "select into" options enabled.

All tables should have a defined primary key. In the pre-archive database, use the SELECT INTO operation to create a key table (table of records which qualify to be archived), which only contains the primary key from the production table.

Now, a good archive process in ASE is one that consists of four phases.

1. **Cleanup**: Truncate and drop old tables created with SELECT INTO.

2. **Fetch-n-Store**: Read the data as fast as possible and stores the primary key for those records (only the key) which qualify to purged into a key table.

3. **Index-n-Stats**: The index phase should create unique indexes on the tables in the pre-archive database.

4. **Archive**: After Cleanup, Fetch-n-Store, and Index-n-Stats, the Archive process should be invoked to run against the key tables to archive the data.

Cleanup Phase

The Cleanup phase process is responsible for truncating and dropping tables in the pre-archive database once they are no longer needed.

Note: This process should always truncate the tables first as this is a minimally logged operation. Refer to the chapter on tempdb usage for more information.

Fetch-n-Store

The Fetch-n-Store process is responsible for running a SELECT INTO command against the production data in order to build the pre-archive key tables.

Note: A SELECT INTO operation should almost always be chosen for this as it is a minimally logged operation. Refer to the chapter on tempdb usage for more information.

Index-n-Stats

The Index-n-Stats process is responsible for creating unique indexes on the columns which comprise a key table. This is a necessity for high throughput in the pre-archive phase. When an index is created, statistics are automatically stored for the columns which comprise the index. Therefore it is not necessary to run an UPDATE STATISTICS command.

Archive

After Cleanup, Fetch-n-Store, and Index-n-Stats have completed, it is the responsibility of the Archive process to run against the tables created in the pre-archive database to archive the production data. A good archive process will yield when blocking is being caused and will not use cursors because of the CPU overhead and throughput loss. Instead, the Archive process should ***always*** use the artificial cursors method to archive the data from the production database.

Example:

```
/* ASSUME PRODUCTION TABLE NAMED test_table NEEDS ARCHIVED */
/* IT HAS A PRIMARY KEY ON THE COLUMN column01 */
/* THERE IS AN ARCHIVAL TABLE IN THE archival DATABASE */
/* IN ADDITION IT IS NAMED bk_test_table */
/* AND IT NEEDS TO HAVE THE DATA FOR column01 and column02 */
/* CLEANUP RAN SUCCESSFULLY AND DROPPED THE OLD ARCHIVE TABLES */
/* FETCH AND STORE CREATED THE arc_test_table /*
/* IN THE PREARCHIVE DATABASE pre_arch */
/* IN ADDITION THE INDEX AND STATS PROCESS RAN */
/* AND CREATED A UNIQUE INDEX ON arc_test_table (column01) */

/* OKAY LETS CREATE THE ARCHIVE PROCESSING TABLE */
USE pre_arch
go
```

```
CREATE
 TABLE dt_test_table(
      column01 INT NOT NULL
)
go

/* DECLARE VARIABLE TO HOLD INFO ABOUT WHETHER OR */
/* NOT THE PURGE PROCESS NEEDS TO GO TO SLEEP */
DECLARE @NEED_TO_SLEEP BIT
DECLARE @RW_CNT INTEGER
DECLARE @SET_RW_CNT SMALLINT

SELECT @NEED_TO_SLEEP = 0
SELECT @SET_RW_CNT = 100

/* ESTABLISH NUMBEROF RECORDS TO HANDLE IN FETCH */
/* THIS NUMBER CAN GREATLY AFFECT THE THROUGHPUT */
/* OF THE PURGE PROCESSS AT THE EXPENSE OF CAUSING */
/* ISSUES WITHIN THE APPLICATION */
/* I RECOMMEND A VALUE OF 100 TO START AND TUNE */
/* THROUGH MEASUREMENT IF NECESSARY */
SET ROWCOUNT @SET_RW_CNT

INSERT
  INTO dt_test_table(
      column01
)
SELECT column01
  FROM arc_test_table

/* GET THE ROWCOUNT TO DETERMINE IF WE HAVE ROWS TO PROCESS */
SELECT @RW_CNT = @@ROWCOUNT

/* LOOP UNTIL ALL ROWS HAVE BEEN PROCESSED */
WHILE ( @RW_CNT > 0 )
BEGIN
   /* LETS CHECK THE SLEEP BIT TO DETERMINE IF WE NEED TO YIELD */
   /* BECAUSE WE ARE CAUSING CONTENTION ON THE PRODUCTION DATABASE */
   /* IF WE NEED TO SLEEP */
   IF ( @NEED_TO_SLEEP = 1 )
   BEGIN
      /* WE NEED TO SLEEP LETS SLEEP FOR A MINUTE */
      WAITFOR DELAY "00:01:00"
```

```
END

/* BEGIN A TRAN TO HOLD LOCKS TO DETERMINE IF WE NEED TO YIELD */
BEGIN TRANSACTION

/* ARCHIVE QUALIFYING RECORDS BY PRIMARY KEY */
/* FROM THE PRODUCTION TABLE */
INSERT
  INTO archival.dbo.dt_test_table(
       column01,
       column02
)
SELECT prod.column01,
       prod.column02
  FROM dt_test_table dt,
       prod_database.dbo.test_table prod
 WHERE prod.column01 = dt.column01
   AND NOT EXISTS ( SELECT 1
                      FROM archival.dbo.bk_test_table bk
                     WHERE bk.column01 = dt.column01 )

/* LETS DETERMINE IF WE CAUSED ANY BLOCKS TO OCCUR */
/* IF A BLOCK OCCURRED SET SLEEP BIT TO TRUE */
/* ELSE SET SLEEP BIT TO FALSE */
IF ( EXISTS ( SELECT 1
                FROM master.dbo.sysprocesses
               WHERE blocked = @@SPID ) )
BEGIN
   SELECT @NEED_TO_SLEEP = 1
END
ELSE
BEGIN
   SELECT @NEED_TO_SLEEP = 0
END

/* COMMIT TRAN TO RELEASE LOCKS ASAP */
COMMIT TRAN

/* REMOVE PROCESSED RECORDS FROM THE NEEDS ARCHIVE TABLE */
DELETE arc_test_table
  FROM arc_test_table arc,
       dt_test_table dt
 WHERE arc.column01 = dt.column01
```

```
    /* REMOVE ALL ROWS FROM dt_test_table TABLE FOR THE NEXT FETCH */
    TRUNCATE TABLE dt_test_table

    /* PERFORM NEXT FETCH */
    INSERT
      INTO dt_test_table(
           column01
    )
    SELECT column01
      FROM arc_test_table

    /* GET THE ROWCOUNT TO DETERMINE IF WE HAVE ROWS TO PROCESS */
    SELECT @RW_CNT = @@ROWCOUNT
END
go
```

Archive with Purge

An archive with purge is the process of archiving data for audits, reporting, and potentially other uses. In addition, the production data is no longer valid and thus can be removed.

As with the purge process, an archive with purge solution should not use a tempdb database to store the records which qualify to be archived and pruned. The tempdb databases are a critical system resource for which we do not have an unlimited amount at our disposal. A database should be created on devices apart from the production database if possible. In addition, this database should have the "trunc log on checkpoint" option and the "select into" options enabled.

All tables should have a defined primary key. In the purge database, use the SELECT INTO operation to create a key table (table of records which qualify to be archived), which only contains the primary key from the production table.

Now, a good archive process in ASE is one that consists of four phases.

1. **Cleanup**: Truncate and drop old tables created with SELECT INTO.
2. **Fetch-n-Store**: Read the data as fast as possible and stores the primary key for those records (only the key) which qualify to purged into a key table.
3. **Index-n-Stats**: The index phase should create unique indexes on the tables in the purge database.
4. **Archive-n-Purge**: After Cleanup, Fetch-n-Store, and Index-n-Stats, the Archive-n-Purge process should be invoked to run against the key tables to archive and prune the data.

Cleanup Phase

The Cleanup phase process is responsible for truncating and dropping tables in the purge database once they are no longer needed.

Note: This process should always truncate the tables first as this is a minimally logged operation. Refer to the chapter on tempdb usage for more information.

Fetch-n-Store

The Fetch-n-Store process is responsible for running a SELECT INTO command against the production data in order to build the key tables.

Note: A SELECT INTO operation should almost always be chosen for this as it is a minimally logged operation. Refer to the chapter on tempdb usage for more information.

Index-n-Stats

The Index-n-Stats process is responsible for creating unique indexes on the columns which comprise a key table. This is a necessity for high throughput in the Archive-n-Purge phase. When an index is created, statistics are automatically stored for the columns which comprise the index. Therefore it is not necessary to run an UPDATE STATISTICS command.

Archive-n-Purge

After Cleanup, Fetch-n-Store, and Index-n-Stats have completed, it is the responsibility of the Archive-n-Purge process to run against the tables created in the purge database to archive and prune the production data. A good archive process will yield when blocking is being caused and will not use cursors because of the CPU overhead and throughput loss. Instead, the Archive-n-Purge process should ***always*** use the artificial cursors method to archive and prune the data from the production database.

Example:

```
/* ASSUME PRODUCTION TABLE NAMED test_table NEEDS ARCHIVED AND PRUNED
*/
/* IT HAS A PRIMARY KEY ON THE COLUMN column01 */
/* THERE IS AN ARCHIVAL TABLE IN THE archival DATABASE */
/* IN ADDITION IT IS NAMED bk_test_table */
/* AND IT NEEDS TO HAVE THE DATA FOR column01 and column02 */
/* CLEANUP RAN SUCCESSFULLY AND DROPPED THE OLD ARCHIVE TABLES */
/* FETCH AND STORE CREATED THE arc_test_table /*
/* IN THE PREARCHIVE DATABASE pre_arch */
/* IN ADDITION THE INDEX AND STATS PROCESS RAN */
/* AND CREATED A UNIQUE INDEX ON arc_test_table (column01) */

/* OKAY LETS CREATE THE ARCHIVE PROCESSING TABLE */
```

```
USE pre_arch
go
CREATE
 TABLE dt_test_table(
      column01 INT NOT NULL
)
go

/* DECLARE VARIABLE TO HOLD INFO ABOUT WHETHER OR */
/* NOT THE PURGE PROCESS NEEDS TO GO TO SLEEP */
DECLARE @NEED_TO_SLEEP BIT
DECLARE @RW_CNT INTEGER
DECLARE @SET_RW_CNT SMALLINT

SELECT @NEED_TO_SLEEP = 0
SELECT @SET_RW_CNT = 100

/* ESTABLISH NUMBEROF RECORDS TO HANDLE IN FETCH */
/* THIS NUMBER CAN GREATLY AFFECT THE THROUGHPUT */
/* OF THE PURGE PROCESSS AT THE EXPENSE OF CAUSING */
/* ISSUES WITHIN THE APPLICATION */
/* I RECOMMEND A VALUE OF 100 TO START AND TUNE */
/* THROUGH MEASUREMENT IF NECESSARY */
SET ROWCOUNT @SET_RW_CNT

INSERT
   INTO dt_test_table(
        column01
)
SELECT column01
  FROM arc_test_table

/* GET THE ROWCOUNT TO DETERMINE IF WE HAVE ROWS TO PROCESS */
SELECT @RW_CNT = @@ROWCOUNT

/* LOOP UNTIL ALL ROWS HAVE BEEN PROCESSED */
WHILE ( @RW_CNT > 0 )
BEGIN
   /* LETS CHECK THE SLEEP BIT TO DETERMINE IF WE NEED TO YIELD */
   /* BECAUSE WE ARE CAUSING CONTENTION ON THE PRODUCTION DATABASE */
   /* IF WE NEED TO SLEEP */
   IF ( @NEED_TO_SLEEP = 1 )
   BEGIN
      /* WE NEED TO SLEEP LETS SLEEP FOR A MINUTE */
```

```
    WAITFOR DELAY "00:01:00"
END

/* BEGIN A TRAN TO HOLD LOCKS TO DETERMINE IF WE NEED TO YIELD */
/* AND TO GUARANTEE DATA INTEGRITY.  THAT IS GUARANTEE THAT WE */
/* BOTH BACKUP AND PRUNE THE PRODUCTION DATA */
BEGIN TRANSACTION

/* ARCHIVE QUALIFYING RECORDS BY PRIMARY KEY */
/* FROM THE PRODUCTION TABLE */
INSERT
  INTO archival.dbo.dt_test_table(
       column01,
       column02
)
SELECT prod.column01,
       prod.column02
  FROM dt_test_table dt,
       prod_database.dbo.test_table prod
 WHERE prod.column01 = dt.column01
   AND NOT EXISTS ( SELECT 1
                      FROM archival.dbo.bk_test_table bk
                     WHERE bk.column01 = dt.column01 )

/* DELETE QUALIFYING PURGE RECORDS BY PRIMARY KEY */
/* FROM THE PRODUCTION TABLE */
DELETE prod_database.dbo.test_table
  FROM dt_test_table dt,
       prod_database.dbo.test_table prod
 WHERE prod.column01 = dt.column01

/* LETS DETERMINE IF WE CAUSED ANY BLOCKS TO OCCUR */
/* IF A BLOCK OCCURRED SET SLEEP BIT TO TRUE */
/* ELSE SET SLEEP BIT TO FALSE */
IF ( EXISTS ( SELECT 1
                FROM master.dbo.sysprocesses
               WHERE blocked = @@SPID ) )
BEGIN
   SELECT @NEED_TO_SLEEP = 1
END
ELSE
BEGIN
   SELECT @NEED_TO_SLEEP = 0
END
```

```
    /* COMMIT TRAN TO RELEASE LOCKS ASAP */
    COMMIT TRAN

    /* REMOVE PROCESSED RECORDS FROM THE NEEDS ARCHIVE TABLE */
    DELETE arc_test_table
      FROM arc_test_table arc,
           dt_test_table dt
     WHERE arc.column01 = dt.column01

    /* REMOVE ALL ROWS FROM dt_test_table TABLE FOR THE NEXT FETCH */
    TRUNCATE TABLE dt_test_table

    /* PERFORM NEXT FETCH */
    INSERT
      INTO dt_test_table(
           column01
    )
    SELECT column01
      FROM arc_test_table

    /* GET THE ROWCOUNT TO DETERMINE IF WE HAVE ROWS TO PROCESS */
    SELECT @RW_CNT = @@ROWCOUNT
END
go
```

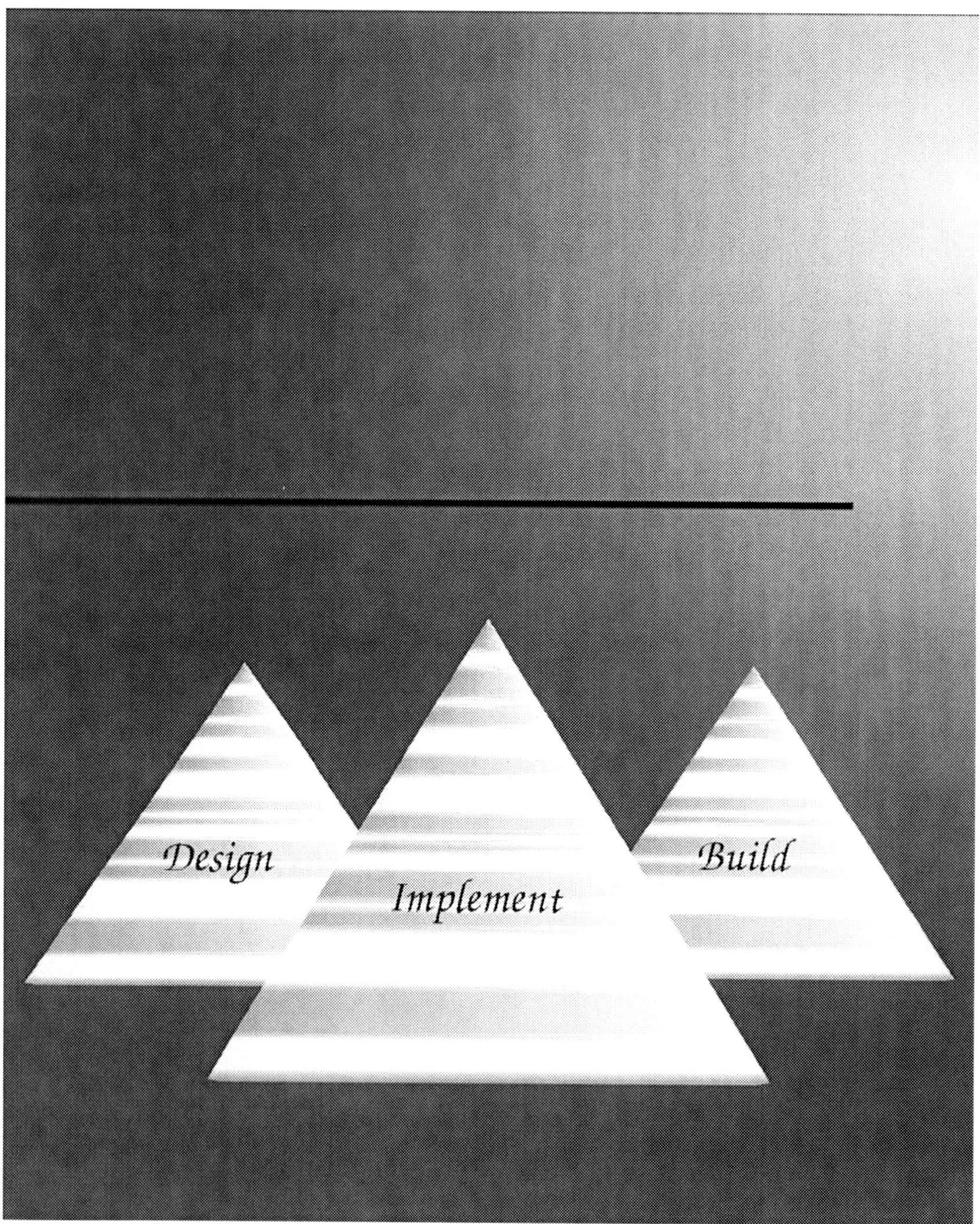
Design
Implement
Build

Chapter 29. Application Contexts

Application contexts allow for session level global variables to be created. These global variables can be used by the applications for properties which need to be constant across the application. They can be setup through the session or application and/or through the use of login triggers.

Now, the application contexts built-in functions require permissions in the default database in order to SELECT them, however, you should create a role and grant SELECT on each of the application context functions in all databases to the role. After which, grant all logins which require the usage of application contexts to the role. This reduces the number of records needed to be maintained in the database catalog and it does away with permissions explicitly for users.

Note: Once an application context and attribute has been created it cannot be modified without removing either the attribute from the context or the entire context. For more information, refer to using SET_APPCONTEXT and RM_APPCONTEXT in the following sections on application contexts.

Example:

```
CREATE ROLE apl_apctx_role
go
GRANT ROLE apl_apctx_role TO <USER NAME>
go
EXEC sp_modifylogin "USER NAME", "add default role", "apl_apctx_role"
go

USE DB
go
GRANT SELECT ON GET_APPCONTEXT TO apl_apctx_role
go
GRANT SELECT ON LIST_APPCONTEXT TO apl_apctx_role
go
GRANT SELECT ON RM_APPCONTEXT TO apl_apctx_role
go
GRANT SELECT ON SET_APPCONTEXT TO apl_apctx_role
go
```

Application contexts require a *context_name*, *attribute_name*, and a *context_attribute_value*. The *context_name* identifies to what specific application context an *attribute_name* belongs. The *context_attribute_value* is the data to be used by a session. Thus, an application context or global variable can be referenced by the *context_name* and *attribute_name*.

The *context_name* and *attribute_name* both have the system defined datatype of CHAR(30). The *context_attribute_value* has a system defined datatype of CHAR (2048).

Sybase provides four functions which are used when working with application contexts. GET_APPCONTEXT, LIST_APPCONTEXT, RM_APPCONTEXT, and SET_APPCONTEXT.

SET_APPCONTEXT

To create application contexts you use the function SET_APPCONTEXT. The SET_APPCONTEXT function returns a 0 for success and a -1 for failure.

Usage: SET_APPCONTEXT("*context_name*", "*attribute_name*", "*VALUE*")

Example:

```
SELECT SET_APPCONTEXT("CTX01", "ATR01", "An Example")
go
0
```

Example:

```
DECLARE @CTX_ERR INTEGER

SELECT @CTX_ERR = SET_APPCONTEXT("CTX01", "ATR01", "An Example")

IF ( @CTX_ERR != 0 )
BEGIN
   PRINT "ERROR OCCURRED"
END
ELSE
BEGIN
   PRINT "NO ERRORS SETTING CONTEXT"
END
```

```
go
NO ERRORS SETTING CONTEXT
```

LIST_APPCONTEXT

The LIST_APPCONTEXT is used to display to the **screen** either all contexts and attributes and their values, all attributes and values for a specified context, or the value of a specified context and attribute. The function LIST_APPCONTEXT returns a 0 for success and a -1 for failure.

Usage: LIST_APPCONTEXT("*context_name*", "*attribute_name*")

Example:

```
DECLARE @CTX_ERR INTEGER

SELECT @CTX_ERR = SET_APPCONTEXT("CTX01", "ATR01", "An Example")

IF ( @CTX_ERR != 0 )
BEGIN
   PRINT "ERROR OCCURRED"
END

/* USE AN * TO DISPLAY ALL CONTEXTS.ATTRIBUTES and THEIR VALUES */
SELECT @CTX_ERR = LIST_APPCONTEXT("*")

IF ( @CTX_ERR != 0 )
BEGIN
   PRINT "ERROR OCCURRED"
END
go
Context Name is (CTX01)
Attribute Name (ATR01) Value (An Example)
```

Example:

```
DECLARE @CTX_ERR INTEGER

SELECT @CTX_ERR = SET_APPCONTEXT("CTX01", "ATR01", "An Example")

IF ( @CTX_ERR != 0 )
BEGIN
   PRINT "ERROR OCCURRED"
END
```

```
/* SPECIFY THE CONTEXT TO DISPLAY ALL ATTRIBUTES and VALUES */
SELECT @CTX_ERR = LIST_APPCONTEXT("CTX01")

IF ( @CTX_ERR != 0 )
BEGIN
   PRINT "ERROR OCCURRED"
END
go
--------------------------------------------------------------
Context Name is (CTX01)
Attribute Name (ATR01) Value (An Example)
```

Example:

```
DECLARE @CTX_ERR INTEGER

SELECT @CTX_ERR = SET_APPCONTEXT("CTX01", "ATR01", "An Example")

IF ( @CTX_ERR != 0 )
BEGIN
   PRINT "ERROR OCCURRED"
END

/* SPECIFY THE CONTEXT AND ATTRIBUTE TO DISPLAY ALL VALUES */
SELECT @CTX_ERR = LIST_APPCONTEXT("CTX01", "ATR01")

IF ( @CTX_ERR != 0 )
BEGIN
   PRINT "ERROR OCCURRED"
END
go
--------------------------------------------------------------
Context Name is (CTX01)
Attribute Name (ATR01) Value (An Example)
```

GET_APPCONTEXT

To retrieve the value for an application context and attribute, use the GET_APPCONTEXT function. The GET_APPCONTEXT function returns the CHAR (2048) value for the specified application context and attribute. The built-in Global Variable @@ERROR is set to 0 to indicate success and a -1 indicates a failure.

Usage: GET_APPCONTEXT("*context_name*", "*attribute_name*")

Example:

```
DECLARE @CTX_ERR INTEGER
DECLARE @CTX01_ATR01 CHAR(2048)

SELECT @CTX_ERR = SET_APPCONTEXT("CTX01", "ATR01", "An Example")

IF ( @CTX_ERR != 0 )
BEGIN
   PRINT "ERROR OCCURRED"
END

SELECT @CTX01_ATR01 = GET_APPCONTEXT("CTX01", "ATR01")

SELECT @CTX_ERR = @@ERROR

IF ( @CTX_ERR != 0 )
BEGIN
   PRINT "ERROR OCCURRED"
END

SELECT @CTX01_ATR01
go
---------------------------------------------------------------
An Example
```

RM_APPCONTEXT

In order to change the value of an application context you must first delete the attribute for a context. The function RM_APPCONTEXT is used for this purpose. In addition, the function returns a 0 for success and a -1 for failure.

Usage: RM_APPCONTEXT("*context_name*", "*attribute_name*")

Example:

```
DECLARE @CTX_ERR INTEGER
DECLARE @CTX01_ATR01 CHAR(2048)

SELECT @CTX_ERR = SET_APPCONTEXT("CTX01", "ATR01", "An Example")
IF ( @CTX_ERR != 0 )
BEGIN
   PRINT "ERROR OCCURRED"
END

SELECT @CTX01_ATR01 = GET_APPCONTEXT("CTX01", "ATR01")
SELECT @CTX_ERR = @@ERROR
IF ( @CTX_ERR != 0 )
BEGIN
   PRINT "ERROR OCCURRED"
END

SELECT @CTX01_ATR01

SELECT @CTX_ERR = RM_APPCONTEXT("CTX01", "ATR01")
IF ( @CTX_ERR != 0 )
BEGIN
   PRINT "ERROR OCCURRED"
END

SELECT @CTX01_ATR01 = GET_APPCONTEXT("CTX01", "ATR01")
SELECT @CTX_ERR = @@ERROR
IF ( @CTX_ERR != 0 )
BEGIN
   PRINT "ERROR OCCURRED"
END

SELECT @CTX01_ATR01
go
```

```
An Example
NULL
```

You can also use the RM_APPCONTEXT function to remove all attributes associated with a context by specifying "*" for the *attribute_name*.

Example:

```
DECLARE @CTX_ERR INTEGER
DECLARE @CTX01_ATR01 CHAR(2048)

SELECT @CTX_ERR = SET_APPCONTEXT("CTX01", "ATR01", "An Example")
IF ( @CTX_ERR != 0 )
BEGIN
   PRINT "ERROR OCCURRED"
END

SELECT @CTX01_ATR01 = GET_APPCONTEXT("CTX01", "ATR01")
SELECT @CTX_ERR = @@ERROR
IF ( @CTX_ERR != 0 )
BEGIN
   PRINT "ERROR OCCURRED"
END

SELECT @CTX01_ATR01

SELECT @CTX_ERR = RM_APPCONTEXT("CTX01", "*")
IF ( @CTX_ERR != 0 )
BEGIN
   PRINT "ERROR OCCURRED"
END

SELECT @CTX01_ATR01 = GET_APPCONTEXT("CTX01", "ATR01")
SELECT @CTX_ERR = @@ERROR
IF ( @CTX_ERR != 0 )
BEGIN
   PRINT "ERROR OCCURRED"
END

SELECT @CTX01_ATR01
go
```

```
An Example
NULL
```

You can also use the RM_APPCONTEXT function to remove all contexts for a session. This can be performed by specifying "*" for the *context_name* and a "*" for the *attribute_name*.

Example:

```
DECLARE @CTX_ERR INTEGER
DECLARE @CTX01_ATR01 CHAR(2048)

SELECT @CTX_ERR = SET_APPCONTEXT("CTX01", "ATR01", "An Example")
IF ( @CTX_ERR != 0 )
BEGIN
   PRINT "ERROR OCCURRED"
END

SELECT @CTX01_ATR01 = GET_APPCONTEXT("CTX01", "ATR01")
SELECT @CTX_ERR = @@ERROR
IF ( @CTX_ERR != 0 )
BEGIN
   PRINT "ERROR OCCURRED"
END

SELECT @CTX01_ATR01

SELECT @CTX_ERR = RM_APPCONTEXT("*", "*")
IF ( @CTX_ERR != 0 )
BEGIN
   PRINT "ERROR OCCURRED"
END

SELECT @CTX01_ATR01 = GET_APPCONTEXT("CTX01", "ATR01")
SELECT @CTX_ERR = @@ERROR
IF ( @CTX_ERR != 0 )
BEGIN
   PRINT "ERROR OCCURRED"
END

SELECT @CTX01_ATR01
go
```

```
An Example
NULL
```

Chapter 29. Application Contexts

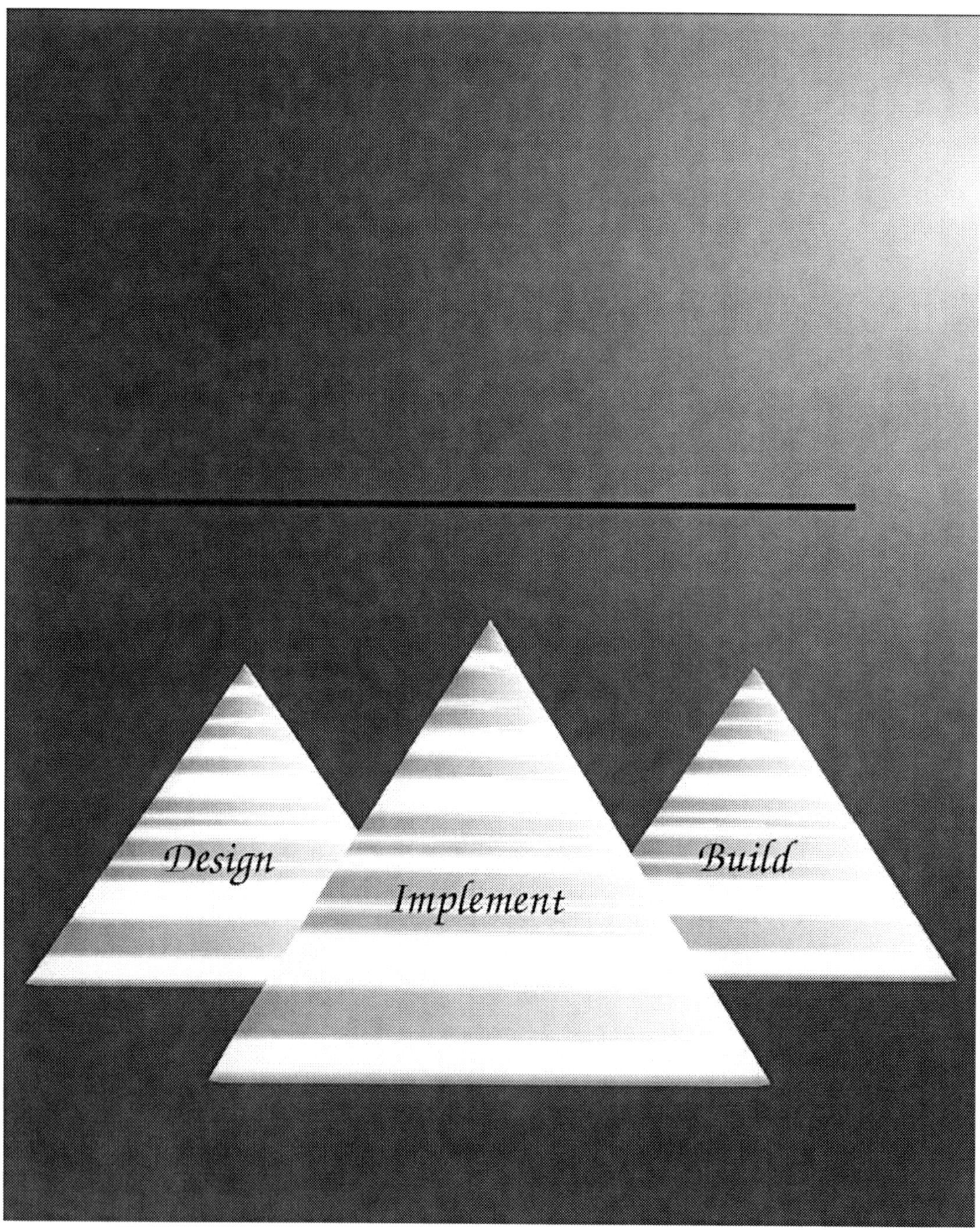
Design
Implement
Build

Chapter 30. Login Triggers

A login trigger is nothing more than a stored procedure which is bound to a user account. When a user initializes a connection request, as part of a successful connection, Sybase executes the stored procedure bound to their account (The Login Trigger). If the stored procedure returns a negative integer ASE will abort the connection.

Login Triggers or stored procedures bound to user accounts, whichever you prefer, are useful for many reasons.

Including:

1. Prevent a connection to the database for an account.

2. Setup Application Contexts.

3. Setup Access Rules.

However, Login Triggers have the following limitations:

1. The time to establish a connection is increased by the time it takes the stored procedure to execute.

2. As with all stored procedures, temporary tables which are created in a stored procedure are dropped by ASE when the execution of the procedure is complete.

3. Any SET options which are used in the procedure are returned to the state before the procedure was executed.

4. Errors from a Login Trigger are typically logged into the ASE server log. Thus, your SA should grant the ability to read the log to most everyone.

5. The login to which a stored procedure is bound should be able to execute the stored procedure. If not, the connection will fail.

6. The stored procedure which is bound to a user account must exist in the user's default database. This is where ASE will attempt to execute the login trigger. Currently it is not possible to bind a stored procedure to a user account in a database other than the user's default database.

7. Only a user a system administrator or security officer can modify user accounts.

8. Many applications will need to use SET_APPCONTEXT, thus security should be administered through knowledge between groups and not by revoking SELECT permission on SET_APPCONTEXT or RM_APPCONTEXT.

9. Stored procedures which are bound to a user account must accept default values for all parameters or not have a parameter list.

Creating a Login Trigger

First, we need to determine the default database for a user or a set of users. And, unless we change the default database for a user, we must create the stored procedure in the current default database for the user.

Determine Default Database:

```
SELECT NAME,
       DBNAME
  FROM SINF_LOGINS
go
```

```
junk12      master
junk13      master
probe       sybsystemdb
sa          master
```

Determine Default Database for the user junk12:

```
SELECT NAME,
       DBNAME
  FROM SINF_LOGINS
 WHERE NAME = "junk12"
go
```

```
junk12        master
```

Let's create a Login Trigger for the user junk12 to prevent them from establishing more than 20 connections to the database.

Example:

```
CREATE PROCEDURE lpr_not_more_than_20
AS
BEGIN

   DECLARE @LOGIN VARCHAR(30)

   SELECT @LOGIN = SUSER_NAME()

   IF ( ( SELECT COUNT(*)
            FROM SINF_PROCESSES
           WHERE LOGIN = @LOGIN ) > 20 )
   BEGIN
      PRINT "LOGIN: %1! FAILED, TOO MANY CONNECTIONS", @LOGIN
      RETURN -1
   END

   RETURN 0
END
go
```

```
GRANT EXECUTE ON lpr_not_more_than_20 TO PUBLIC
go
```

```
EXEC sp_modifylogin "junk12", "login script", "lpr_not_more_than_20"
go
```

Now when the user attempts his 21 connection the stored procedure will return a -1 to ASE and ASE will abort the connection. The message which we are printing will display in the ASE errorlog.

To remove the login trigger for login junk12 execute:

```
EXEC sp_modifylogin "junk12", "login script", NULL
go
```

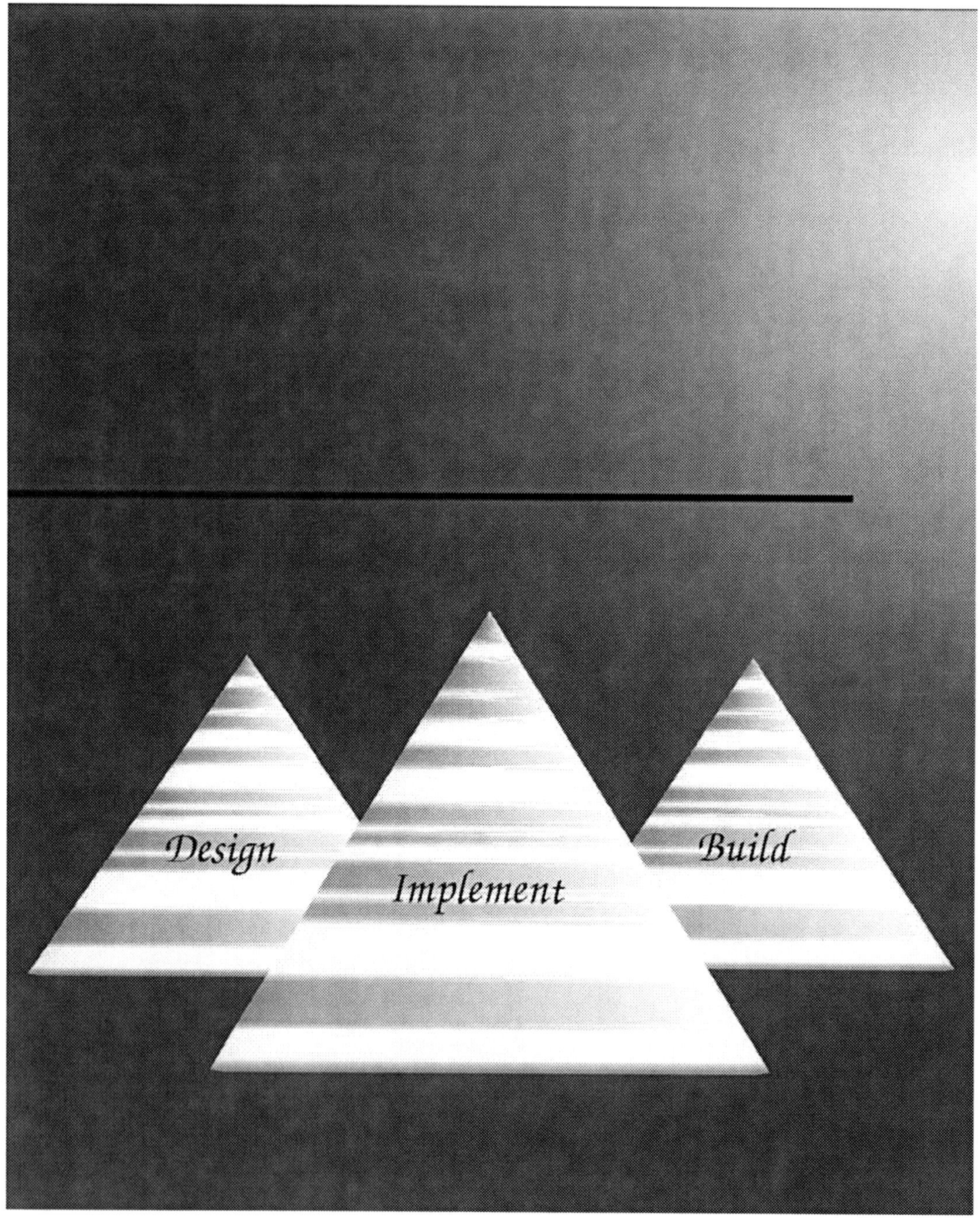
Design
Implement
Build

Chapter 31. Application Functions

In ASE we can create application defined functions by using stored procedures, dynamic SQL, or by storing the results at login time for each procedure run using a login trigger and subsequent procedure executions.

Using Stored Procedures

We can use stored procedures to get a return parameter to pass back. Let's create a procedure to return the original login of a session which is using proxy or session level authentication measures.

Example:

```
CREATE PROCEDURE pr_orig_login(
                 @ORIG_LOGIN VARCHAR(30) OUTPUT
)
AS
BEGIN
   SELECT @ORIG_LOGIN = ORIG_LOGIN
     FROM SINF_PROCESSES
    WHERE SPID = @@SPID
END
go
```

```
DECLARE @ORIG_LOGIN VARCHAR(30)

EXEC @pr_orig_login @ORIG_LOGIN = @ORIG_LOGIN OUTPUT

SELECT SUSER_NAME() AS "CURR_LOGIN",
       @ORIG_LOGIN AS "ORIG_LOGIN"
go
```

```
junk12       junk13
```

Dynamic SQL

Using dynamic SQL calls we can run SQL which is cataloged. This allows us to create the same function from the stored procedure above using dynamic SQL. Notice how ugly it is, and that it will not perform as well as the stored procedure.

Example:

```
/* First let's create a set of tables
** to store our dynamic SQL statements. */
CREATE
 TABLE APL_FNC_DSQL_ID(
       DSQL_ID INTEGER NOT NULL,
       DSQL_DSC VARCHAR(255) NOT NULL,
  CONSTRAINT IX01_APL_FNC_DSQL_ID
     PRIMARY KEY CLUSTERED ( DSQL_ID )
)
LOCK ALLPAGES
go

CREATE
 TABLE APL_FNC_DSQL(
       DSQL_ID INTEGER NOT NULL,
       DSQL_SEQ_ID INTEGER NOT NULL,
       DSQL_TEXT VARCHAR(255) NOT NULL,
  CONSTRAINT IX01_APL_FNC_DSQL
    PRIMARY KEY CLUSTERED ( DSQL_ID, DSQL_SEQ_ID ),
  CONSTRAINT APL_FNC_DSQL_ID@APL_FNC_DSQL
    FOREIGN KEY ( DSQL_ID )
      REFERENCES APL_FNC_DSQL_ID ( DSQL_ID )
)
LOCK ALLPAGES
go

CREATE
 TABLE APL_FNC_DSQL_RSLTS(
       sybs_intrnl_sesn_id INTEGER NOT NULL,
       DSQL_OUTPUT VARCHAR(255) NOT NULL,
  CONSTRAINT IX01_APL_FNC_DSQL_RSLTS
    PRIMARY KEY CLUSTERED ( sybs_intrnl_sesn_id )
)
LOCK DATAROWS
go
```

```
/* Let's populate the function information */
INSERT
  INTO APL_FNC_DSQL_ID(
       DSQL_ID,
       DSQL_DSC
)
SELECT 1,
       "An Example"
go

INSERT
  INTO APL_FNC_DSQL(
       DSQL_ID,
       DSQL_SEQ_ID,
       DSQL_TEXT
)
SELECT 1,
       1,
       "INSERT INTO APL_FNC_DSQL_RSLTS(DSQL_OUT)"
go

INSERT
  INTO APL_FNC_DSQL(
       DSQL_ID,
       DSQL_SEQ_ID,
       DSQL_TEXT
)
SELECT 1,
       2,
       "SELECT ORIG_LOGIN"
go

INSERT
  INTO APL_FNC_DSQL(
       DSQL_ID,
       DSQL_SEQ_ID,
       DSQL_TEXT
)
SELECT 1,
       3,
       "  FROM SINF_PROCESSES"
go

INSERT
```

```
  INTO APL_FNC_DSQL(
       DSQL_ID,
       DSQL_SEQ_ID,
       DSQL_TEXT
)
SELECT 1,
       4,
       " WHERE SPID = @@SPID"
go

/* Let's create a procedure to use function */
CREATE PROCEDURE pr_test_function
AS
BEGIN

DECLARE DSQL_CURSOR
 CURSOR
    FOR
 SELECT DSQL_TEXT
   FROM APL_FNC_DSQL
  WHERE DSQL_ID = 1
  ORDER
     BY DSQL_SEQ_ID ASC
FOR READ ONLY

DELETE APL_FNC_DSQL_RSLTS
 WHERE sybs_intrnl_sesn_id = @@SPID

DECLARE @DSQL_TEXT VARCHAR(255)
DECLARE @DSQL_CMD VARCHAR(16384)
DECLARE @DSQL_OUT VARCHAR(30)

OPEN DSQL_CURSOR

FETCH DSQL_CURSOR
 INTO @DSQL_TEXT

WHILE ( @@SQLSTATUS = 0 )
BEGIN
   SELECT @DSQL_CMD = @DSQL_CMD + @DSQL_TEXT + CHAR(10)

   FETCH DSQL_CURSOR
    INTO @DSQL_TEXT
END
```

```
CLOSE DSQL_CURSOR

DEALLOCATE
    CURSOR DSQL_CURSOR

EXEC (@DSQL_CMD)

SELECT @DSQL_OUT = DSQL_OUT
  FROM DSQL_OUTPUT
 WHERE sybs_intrnl_sesn_id = @@SPID

SELECT SUSER_NAME(),
       @DSQL_OUT
END
go

/* Let's call the procedure */
EXEC pr_test_function
go
```

```
junk12      junk13
```

Login Triggers

Using a login trigger we can store the results from dynamic SQL statements either into a table for later reference by an application or by using application contexts.

Using Tables

This process is similar to using a stored procedure except that only results are available and they are only available after each run of the stored procedure. This stored procedure can be called through the login trigger or directly to update the results. However, the application context method should perform better because it does not require any tables !!!

Example:

```
CREATE
 TABLE FNC_RSLTS(
       sybs_intrnl_sesn_id INTEGER NOT NULL,
       FNC_RSLTS_ID INTEGER NOT NULL,
       FNS_RSLTS_OUTPUT VARCHAR(255) NOT NULL,
  CONSTRAINT IX01_FNC_RSLTS
    PRIMARY KEY CLUSTERED ( sybs_intrnl_sesn_id, FNC_RSLTS_ID )
)
LOCK DATAROWS
go

CREATE PROCEDURE lpr_functions
AS
BEGIN
   DELETE FNC_RSLTS
    WHERE sybs_intrnl_sesn_id = @@SPID

    INSERT
      INTO FNC_RSLTS(
           sybs_intrnl_sesn_id,
           FNC_RSLTS_ID,
           FNC_RSLTS_OUTPUT
)
   SELECT @@SPID,
          1,
          ORIG_LOGIN
     FROM SINF_PROCESSES
    WHERE SPID = @@SPID
```

```
END
go
```

```
/* Get latest results by calling stored procedure directly */
EXEC lpr_functions
go
```

```
/* See what we have */
SELECT SUSER_NAME() AS "CURR_LOGIN",
       FNC_RSLTS_OUTPUT AS "ORIG_LOGIN"
  FROM FNC_RSLTS
 WHERE sybs_intrnl_sesn_id = @@SPID
   AND FNC_RSLTS_ID = 1
go
```

```
junk12      junk13
```

```
/* Bind stored procedure to login */
EXEC sp_modifylogin "junk12", "login script", "lpr_functions"
go
```

```
/* When we run the select we do not have valid results even though
we /*
/* have changed to a different session */
SELECT SUSER_NAME() AS "CURR_LOGIN",
        FNC_RSLTS_OUTPUT AS "ORIG_LOGIN"
  FROM FNC_RSLTS
 WHERE sybs_intrnl_sesn_id = @@SPID
   AND FNC_RSLTS_ID = 1
go
```

```
junk12      NULL
```

Using Application Contexts

Using application contexts is much more straightforward. In addition, should perform much better because it does not need tables to store its results.

Example:

```
CREATE PROCEDURE lpr_functions
AS
BEGIN
   DECLARE @CTX_ERR INTEGER
   DECLARE @CTX_VALUE CHAR(2048)

   SELECT @CTX_ERR = RM_APPCONTEXT("CTX01", "ATR01")

   SELECT @CTX_VALUE = ORIG_LOGIN
     FROM SINF_PROCESSES
    WHERE SPID = @@SPID

   SELECT @CTX_ERR = SET_APPCONTEXT("CTX01", "ATR01", @CTX_VALUE)
END
go
```

```
/* Get latest results by calling stored procedure directly */
EXEC lpr_functions
go
```

```
/* See what we have */
SELECT SUSER_NAME(),
       CONVERT(VARCHAR(30), GET_APPCONTEXT("CTX01", "ATR01") )
go
```

```
junk12       junk13

/* Bind stored procedure to login */
EXEC sp_modifylogin "junk12", "login script", "lpr_functions"
go
```

```
/* When we run the select we do not have valid results even though
we /*
/* have changed to a different session */
SELECT SUSER_NAME(),
       CONVERT(VARCHAR(30), GET_APPCONTEXT("CTX01", "ATR01") )
go
```

```
junk12        NULL

/* We execute the procedure to get latest results */
EXEC lpr_functions
go

/* See what we have */
SELECT SUSER_NAME(),
       CONVERT(VARCHAR(30), GET_APPCONTEXT("CTX01", "ATR01") )
go
junk12        junk13
```

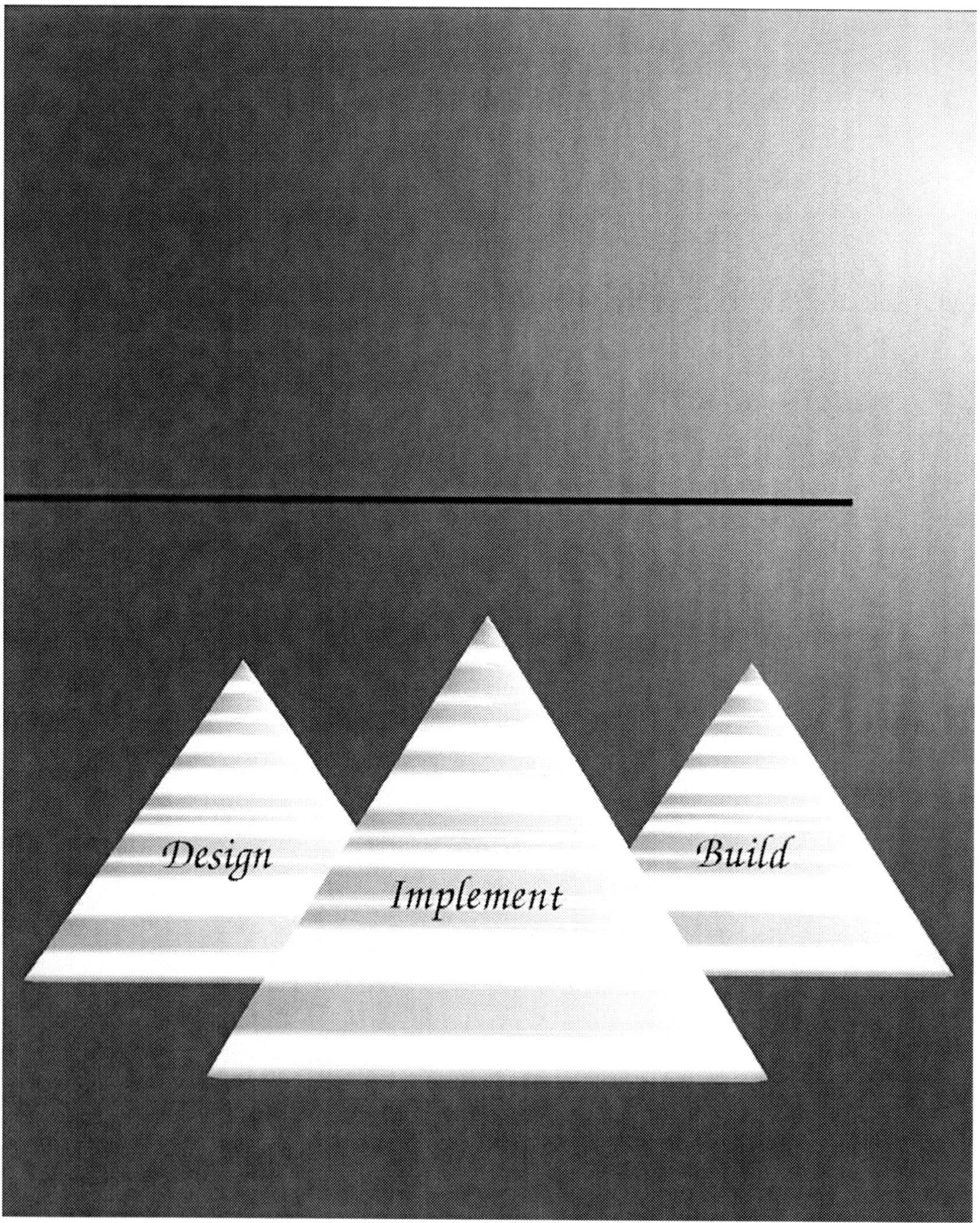
Design
Implement
Build

Chapter 32. Error Handling and Exception Reporting

An application program must anticipate runtime errors and should attempt to recover from them. Thus a significant part of every application program must be devoted to error handling. The main benefit of error handling is that it enables your program to continue operating in the presence of errors. Errors arise from design faults, coding mistakes, hardware failures, invalid user input, and many other sources.

Hence, you cannot anticipate all possible errors, but you can plan to handle certain kinds of errors meaningful to your program. For Sybase TSQL, error handling means detecting and recovering from SQL statement execution errors.

When writing applications for ASE one needs to understand the type of errors that need to be handled. There are two formal types or classifications of errors within ASE. These are the Application Generated Errors and the ASE System Generated Errors respectively.

ASE System Generated Errors

The ASE system generated errors should almost always be raised by the application upon encountering such an error. In fact, in most cases ASE will do this for you. In addition, all modification should be immediately rolled back. Again, in most cases ASE will automatically do this for you.

If you have encountered an ASE system generated error, it is because you have not defined an appropriate error handler, something is wrong with the command syntax, an object is missing, you do not have permissions, something is wrong with the server resources, or some sort of datatype issue.

ASE generated errors consist of the following parts:

1. The message "**Msg**" number which is used to uniquely identify an error message for a language.

2. The severity level "**Level**" number which is used to indicate both the type and severity of the error. The severity level will fall between 10 and 26.

3. The error state "**State**" number which indicates the line of ASE internal code the error was encountered. In most cases this is useless for us.

4. The server "**Server**" name identifies what ASE server encountered the error.

5. The line "**Line**" number indicates what line number in the SQL batch encountered the error.

6. Last, the error message indicates what the problem was that was encountered and may even offer suggestions to remedy the situation.

Let's give an example of an ASE generated error which occurs when you query a table that does not exist.

Example:

```
USE master
go
SELECT COUNT(*)
  FROM sysmessages

SELECT COUNT(*)
  FROM sysmessages2
go

Msg 208, Level 16, State 1:
Server 'ASESRVR1', Line 4:
sysmessages2 not found. Specify owner.objectname or use sp_help to
check whether the object exists (sp_help may produce lots of output).
```

Decrypting the output we see that the error message number which was encountered was 208, the severity level was 16, the error state was 1, the ASE server which encountered the error was ASESRVR1, the error was encountered on line number 4 of the SQL batch, and the message was that the table sysmessages2 does not exist. In addition, ASE has given us a suggestion on how to proceed.

Most often the action you take will be based upon the severity level "**Level**" of the error message which was encountered. Again, ASE defines severity levels as being between 10 and 26. In addition, each severity level has a rather specific meaning which is as follows:

1. Level 10 – Does not indicate an error has occurred, it is mainly used for status information. Not an Error !!!
2. Level 11 – ASE cannot find a specified object.
3. Level 12 – A datatype issue was encountered.
4. Level 13 – Invalid syntax for a user defined transaction.
5. Level 14 – A permission issue was encountered.
6. Level 15 – Something is wrong with command syntax.
7. Level 16 – A potpourri error has occurred which does not explicitly fall into any category but this one.
8. Level 17 – An ASE resources issue was encountered.
9. Level 18 – An ASE internal error was encountered.
10. Level 19 through 26 – Indicates an ASE fatal error was encountered.

All errors should be reported immediately to your SA except 11, 12, 13, or 15 severity level errors. However, if you cannot fix the error which is occurring for a 11, 12, 13, or 15 severity level error, you may need to contact your SA for assistance.

Let us look at another example below. Here we have a stored procedure which inserts a single record into a table. If there is an error, the procedure rolls back the transaction and raises a user defined error number 50011.

Example:

```
CREATE PROCEDURE InsertManRoleType(
                 @manRoleTypeKey KeyType = NULL OUTPUT,
                 @roleTypeCode RoleTypeCodeType,
                 @description RoleTypeDescriptionType
)
AS
BEGIN
```

```
   BEGIN TRANSACTION

   INSERT ManRoleType(
          roleTypeCode,
          description
   )
   SELECT @roleTypeCode,
          @description

   IF ( @@rowcount != 1 OR @@error != 0 OR @@transtate = 3 )
   BEGIN
      IF ( @@trancount > 0 )
      BEGIN
         ROLLBACK TRAN
      END
      RAISERROR 50011 "'Cannot Insert ManRoleType'
                      :@roleTypeCode=%1!", @roleTypeCode
      RETURN
   END

   SELECT @manRoleTypeKey = @@IDENTITY

   COMMIT TRANSACTION
END
go
```

Another example of a routine which handles errors for an application.

Example:

```
IF EXISTS ( SELECT 1
              FROM sysobjects
             WHERE name = "cf_error_check_sp"
               AND type = "P")
BEGIN
   PRINT "dropping Stored Procedure cf_error_check_sp"
   DROP PROC cf_error_check_sp
END
ELSE IF ( OBJECT_ID("cf_error_check_sp") IS NOT NULL )
BEGIN
   PRINT "OBJECT: cf_error_check_sp EXISTS AND IS NOT A PROCEDURE"
END
go
```

```
CREATE PROCEDURE cf_error_check_sp(
                 @err_no INT = @@ERROR,
                 @raise_error BIT = 1,
                 @log_error BIT = 1,
                 @rollback_transaction BIT = 1,
                 @error_type CHAR(1) = "S",
                 @message VARCHAR(255) = NULL,
                 @arg1 VARCHAR(32) = NULL,
                 @arg2 VARCHAR(32) = NULL,
                 @arg3 VARCHAR(32) = NULL,
                 @arg4 VARCHAR(32) = NULL,
                 @proc_name VARCHAR(255) = NULL,
                 @proc_id INTEGER = NULL,
                 @category CHAR(5) = NULL,
                 @continuation TINYINT = 0
)
AS
BEGIN
   DECLARE @rest VARCHAR(255),
           @firstbit VARCHAR(255),
           @secondbit VARCHAR(255),
           @thirdbit VARCHAR(255),
           @fourthbit VARCHAR(255),
           @validmes VARCHAR(255),
           @nextarg INTEGER,
           @siteid CurrentSite_type,
           @sitetype SiteType_type

   /* Exit immediately if there are no errors */
   IF ( @err_no = 0 )
   BEGIN
      RETURN
   END

   /* If category null, default according to error number */
   SELECT @category = CASE
                        WHEN ( @err_no < 20000 )
                          THEN "SysEr"
                        Else "SprEr"
                      END
    WHERE @category IS NULL

    /* Get user or system error message */
    SELECT @message = CASE
```

```
                    WHEN ( @err_no < 20000 AND @category = "SysEr"
)
                      THEN ( SELECT DISTINCT description
                              FROM master.dbo.sysmessages
                             WHERE error = @err_no )
                    WHEN ( @message IS NOT NULL )
                      THEN ( @message )
                    ELSE ( SELECT DISTINCT description
                             FROM sysusermessages
                            WHERE error = @err_no )

/* Replace all occurrences of %N! with @argN */
SELECT @message = STR_REPLACE(
                    STR_REPLACE(
                       STR_REPLACE(
                          STR_REPLACE(@message, "%1!", @arg1),
                       "%2!", @arg2),
                    "%3!", @arg3),
                 "%4!", @arg4)

/* Get calling process name if one is not supplied */
SELECT @proc_name = OBJECT_NAME(@procid)
 WHERE @proc_name IS NULL
   AND @proc_id IS NOT NULL

/* Get current site details from system parameter table */
SELECT @siteid = Value
  FROM SystemParameter
 WHERE Parameter = "SiteId"

SELECT @sitetype = Value
  FROM SystemParameter
WHERE Parameter = "SiteType"

/* Insert a row in the ErrorLog table for logging */
INSERT
  INTO ErrorLog(
       UserId,
       LogNumber,
       LogDateTime,
       ProgramName,
       RaiseError,
       ErrorType,
       LogError,
```

```
        RollbackTransaction,
        LogText,
        Arg1,
        Arg2,
        Arg3,
        Arg4,
        Category,
        Continuation,
        SiteId,
        SiteType
    )
    SELECT SUSER_NAME(),
        @err_no,
        GETDATE(),
        @proc_name,
        @raise_error,
        @error_type,
        @log_error,
        @rollback_transaction,
        @message,
        @arg1,
        @arg2,
        @arg3,
        @arg4,
        @category,
        @continuation,
        @siteid,
        @sitetype

END
go
```

Application Generated Errors

The Application generated errors are those errors which need to be handled by the application. These should include trying to insert duplicates, foreign key violations, write invalid application data, or read invalid application data.

We need to define the two modes of handling application errors. Namely, silent and non-silent.

Silent Mode

In silent mode, application errors should *ALWAYS* be logged to an ASE table. In addition, the error which was encountered should either be skipped or corrected. We define the method "NONE" for this purpose.

Non-Silent Mode

In non-silent mode, the Application generated errors should *ALWAYS* be logged to an ASE table and raised by the application. In addition, the transaction in progress should be rolled back. We define the method "PASS" for this purpose.

We also need to define notification methods for when an error occurs. We will be using the notification methods of "MAIL" for email, "PAGE" for pager, "BOTH" for both email and pager, and "NONE" for no notification.

Working with the Application Errors

In order to handle errors in our application we need to define several structures to store the error messages and a table to store logged messages.

First, let's create the tables we will need to store a relationship between an SQL component name and an assigned error name. An assigned SQL component name is a procedure name, a trigger name, a dynamic SQL batch name, or an embedded SQL batch name.

***Definitions for the objects which we will create and use*:**

1. Table sql_cmpnt_err – Used to store an error number map to a named SQL batch or component in TSQL.
   - Column sql_cmpnt_err_nm – Used to store the SQL component associated with an error number.
   - Column sql_cmpnt_err_num – Used to store the error number associated with a SQL component.

2. Table apl_err – Used to store high level application errors.
   - Column apl_err_num – Used to store the error number for a description of an error.
   - Column apl_err_dsc – Used to store the error description for an error number.

3. Table apl_err_log – Used to store logged error messages by an application for later analysis.
    - Column apl_err_seq_id – Used to store a sequential identity column for guaranteed uniqueness.
    - Column sybs_intrnl_sesn_id – Used to store the ASE process ID logging an error message.
    - Column sybs_usr_id – Used to store the login name of the ASE process ID.
    - Column sql_cmpnt_err_num – Used to store associated sql_cmpnt_err.sql_cmpnt_err_num.
    - Column sql_cmpnt_seq_id – Used to store location in SQL batch of error.
    - Column sql_cmpnt_msg – Used to store the message text for the error.
    - Column apl_err_num – Used to store associated apl_err.apl_err_num.
    - Column apl_err_log_ts – Used to store ASE system time the error was created.
    - Column resv_flg – Used to indicate if this error has been resolved or not "N" = NO, "Y" = YES.
    - Column resv_dsc – Used to indicate the resolution process or description.
    - Column resv_usr_id – Used to indicate who is working on this error and/or who resolved the error.
    - Column resv_ts – Used to indicate when this message was resolved or updated to a working progress if resv_usr_id is set and resv_flg = "N".

4. Table notify_grp – Used to store groups of users for notification.
    - Column grp_nm – Name of group.

5. Table notify_usr – Used to store user information for notification.
    - Column grp_usr – Name of User.
    - Column mail_add – Email Address of User.
    - Column page_add – Pager Address of User.

6. Table notify_grp_usr – Used to store groups of users for notification.
    - Column grp_nm – Name of group.
    - Column grp_usr – Name of user in a group.

7. Procedure pr_errhandle – Used to invoke an error.
    - Column @METHOD – Used to specify method of silence. "NONE" = silent, "PASS" = return.

- Column @NOTIFY – Used to specify notification method. “NONE” = no notification, “BOTH” = notification via both pagers and email, “MAIL” = email notification, and “PAGE” = pager notification.
- Column @GRP_NM – Used to specify notification group.
- Column @DBNAME – Used to log database name.
- Column @SQL_CMPNT_NM – Used to log SQL component name.
- Column @SQL_CMPNT_SEQ_ID – Used to log sequence ID within and SQL component.
- Column @APL_ERR_NUM – Used to log type of application error.
- Column @SPCL_MSG – Used to log specified message.

8. Procedure pr_errcheck – Used to select all unresolved error messages.

9. Procedure pr_errresv – Used to change resv_flg, resv_usr_id, resv_dsc, and resv_ts by a specified apl_err_seq_id.
   - Column @apl_err_seq_id – Unique numeric identity in apl_err_log, can be determined by executing pr_errcheck.
   - Column @resv_flg – Used to specify flag for this record.
   - Column @resv_usr_id – Used to specify user modifying this record.
   - Column @resv_dsc – Used to specify why.
   - Column @resv_ts – Used to specify when.

Unix Mail and Page Utility ***/sybase/tools/notify.sh***

```
#!/bin/sh

##########################################################################
##
## Author: Ryan Putnam
##
## Intent: Send Emails and Alphanumeric Pages
##
## Return: Nothing
##
## Revise: Created July 16, 2001
##
##########################################################################

####################################
## TRAP AND REMOVE JUNK UPON EXIT ##
####################################
```

```
trap '$RM -f /tmp/*.$$' EXIT INT QUIT KILL TERM

######################
## GLOBAL CONSTANTS ##
######################
STRING="${*}"
HOST="`hostname -s`"

SERVER="${1}"
METHOD="${2}"
GROUP="${3}"

SYBUSR="login"
SYBPASS="password"
SYBDB="apl_err_db"

print "${STRING}" >/tmp/page.$$

#########################
## LETS GO GET ADDRESS ##
#########################
isql -U${SYBUSR} -P${SYBPASS} -D${SYBDB} -S${SERVER} -w2000 << EOF \
  | sed "1,2d" \
  >/tmp/addresses.$$
SET NOCOUNT ON
go
SELECT nu.mail_add
  FROM notify_usr nu,
       notify_grp_usr ngu
 WHERE ngu.grp_nm = "${GROUP}"
   AND nu.usr_nm = ngu.usr_nm
   AND nu.mail_add IS NOT NULL
   AND "${METHOD}" IN ("MAIL", "BOTH")

UNION ALL

SELECT nu.page_add
  FROM notify_usr nu,
       notify_grp_usr ngu
 WHERE ngu.grp_nm = "${GROUP}"
   AND nu.usr_nm = ngu.usr_nm
   AND nu.page_add IS NOT NULL
   AND "${METHOD}" IN ("PAGE", "BOTH")
go
```

```
EOF

########################
## LETS LOOP AND MAIL ##
## BEEP BEEP         ##
########################
while read ADDRESS filler
do
   mail -s"${SERVER}@${HOST}" "${ADDRESS}" </tmp/page.$$
done </tmp/addresses.$$

exit 0


/* Create the apl_err_db Database to Store Error Messages as Catalog
*/
USE master
go

CREATE DATABASE apl_err_db
ON SYBDEV001 = 500
LOG ON SYBDEV002 = 100
go

/* Turn on trunc log on chkpt database option */
EXEC sp_dboption "apl_err_db", "trunc log on chkpt", "true"
go

USE apl_err_db
go

CHECKPOINT
go

USE apl_err_db
go

/* check for object existence and drop if any exist */
IF ( OBJECT_ID("apl_err_log") IS NOT NULL )
   DROP TABLE apl_err_log
go

IF ( OBJECT_ID("apl_err") IS NOT NULL )
   DROP TABLE apl_err
```

```
go

IF ( OBJECT_ID("sql_cmpnt_err") IS NOT NULL )
   DROP TABLE sql_cmpnt_err
go

IF ( OBJECT_ID("notify_grp_usr") IS NOT NULL )
   DROP TABLE notify_grp_usr
go

IF ( OBJECT_ID("notify_grp") IS NOT NULL )
   DROP TABLE notify_grp
go

IF ( OBJECT_ID("notify_usr") IS NOT NULL )
   DROP TABLE notify_usr
go

/* Create table to store notification groups */
CREATE
 TABLE notify_grp(
       grp_nm VARCHAR(30) NOT NULL,
 CONSTRAINT ix01_notify_grp
   PRIMARY KEY CLUSTERED ( grp_nm )
)
LOCK ALLPAGES
go

INSERT
  INTO notify_grp(
       grp_nm
)
SELECT "test_grp01"
go

/* Create table to store notification users */
CREATE
 TABLE notify_usr(
       usr_nm VARCHAR(30) NOT NULL,
       mail_add VARCHAR(255) NULL,
       page_add VARCHAR(255) NULL,
 CONSTRAINT ix01_notify_usr
   PRIMARY KEY CLUSTERED ( usr_nm )
)
```

```
LOCK ALLPAGES
go

INSERT
  INTO notify_usr(
       usr_nm,
       mail_add
)
SELECT "test_usr01",
       "email@domain",
       "pager@domain@through_domain"
go

/* Create table to store notification mapping */
CREATE
 TABLE notify_grp_usr(
       grp_nm VARCHAR(30) NOT NULL,
       usr_nm VARCHAR(30) NOT NULL,
 CONSTRAINT ix01_notify_grp_usr
   PRIMARY KEY CLUSTERED ( grp_nm, usr_nm ),
 CONSTRAINT notify_grp@notify_grp_usr
   FOREIGN KEY ( grp_nm )
     REFERENCES notify_grp ( grp_nm ),
 CONSTRAINT notify_usr@notify_grp_usr
   FOREIGN KEY ( usr_nm )
     REFERENCES notify_usr ( usr_nm )
)
LOCK ALLPAGES
go
CREATE UNIQUE NONCLUSTERED INDEX ix02_notify_grp_usr
ON notify_grp_usr ( usr_nm, grp_nm )
go

INSERT
  INTO notify_grp_usr(
       grp_nm,
       usr_nm
)
SELECT "test_grp01",
       "test_usr01"
go

/* Create table to store sql batch to print or raised error number */
CREATE
```

```
 TABLE sql_cmpnt_err(
       sql_cmpnt_nm VARCHAR(30) NOT NULL,
       sql_cmpnt_err_num INT NOT NULL,
 CONSTRAINT ix01_sql_cmpnt_err
   PRIMARY KEY NONCLUSTERED ( sql_cmpnt_err_num )
)
LOCK ALLPAGES
go
CREATE UNIQUE CLUSTERED INDEX ix02_sql_cmpnt_err
ON sql_cmpnt_err ( sql_cmpnt_nm )
go

/* Lets insert some records */
INSERT
  INTO sql_cmpnt_err(
       sql_cmpnt_nm,
       sql_cmpnt_err_num
)
SELECT "NA",
       25000
go

INSERT
  INTO sql_cmpnt_err(
       sql_cmpnt_nm,
       sql_cmpnt_err_num
)
SELECT "test_proc01",
       25001
go

INSERT
  INTO sql_cmpnt_err(
       sql_cmpnt_nm,
       sql_cmpnt_err_num
)
SELECT "test_proc02",
       25002
go

INSERT
  INTO sql_cmpnt_err(
       sql_cmpnt_nm,
       sql_cmpnt_err_num
```

```
)
SELECT "dyn_sql01",
       25003
go

INSERT
  iNTO sql_cmpnt_err(
       sql_cmpnt_nm,
       sql_cmpnt_err_num
)
SELECT "emb_sql01",
       25004
go

/* Create table to store defined application errors */
CREATE
 TABLE apl_err(
       apl_err_num INT NOT NULL,
       apl_err_dsc VARCHAR(255) NOT NULL,
 CONSTRAINT ix01_apl_err
   PRIMARY KEY CLUSTERED ( apl_err_num )
)
go

/* Lets insert some records */
INSERT
  INTO apl_err(
       apl_err_num,
       apl_err_dsc
)
SELECT 1,
       "Duplicate Data Encountered"
go

INSERT
  INTO apl_err(
       apl_err_num,
       apl_err_dsc
)
SELECT 2,
       "Foreign Key Violation"
go

INSERT
```

```
  INTO apl_err(
       apl_err_num,
       apl_err_dsc
)
SELECT 3,
       "Attempt to Write Invalid Data"
go

INSERT
  INTO apl_err(
       apl_err_num,
       apl_err_dsc
)
SELECT 4,
       "Attempt to Read Invalid Data"
go

/* Create table to store logged error messages */
CREATE
 TABLE apl_err_log(
       apl_err_seq_id NUMERIC(15, 0) IDENTITY,
       sybs_intrnl_sesn_id INT NOT NULL,
       sybs_usr_id VARCHAR(30) NOT NULL,
       sql_cmpnt_err_num INT NOT NULL,
       sql_cmpnt_seq_id INT NOT NULL,
       sql_cmpnt_msg VARCHAR(255) NOT NULL,
       DBNAME VARCHAR(30) NOT NULL,
       apl_err_num INT NOT NULL,
       apl_err_log_ts DATETIME NOT NULL,
       resv_flg CHAR(1) DEFAULT "N" NOT NULL,
       resv_dsc VARCHAR(255) NULL,
       resv_usr_id VARCHAR(30) NULL,
       resv_ts DATETIME NULL,
 CONSTRAINT ix01_apl_err_log
   PRIMARY KEY CLUSTERED ( resv_flg,
                  sybs_usr_id,
                       sybs_intrnl_sesn_id,
                       sql_cmpnt_err_num,
                       sql_cmpnt_seq_id,
                       apl_err_num,
                       apl_err_log_ts,
                       apl_err_seq_id ),
 CONSTRAINT sql_cmpnt_err@apl_err_log
   FOREIGN KEY ( sql_cmpnt_err_num )
```

```
      REFERENCES sql_cmpnt_err ( sql_cmpnt_err_num ),
 CONSTRAINT apl_err@apl_err_log
   FOREIGN KEY ( apl_err_num )
     REFERENCES apl_err ( apl_err_num )
)
LOCK DATAROWS
go

CREATE NONCLUSTERED INDEX ix02_apl_err_log
ON apl_err_log ( sql_cmpnt_err_num,
                 sql_cmpnt_seq_id,
                 sybs_usr_id,
                 sybs_intrnl_sesn_id )
go

CREATE NONCLUSTERED INDEX ix03_apl_err_log
ON apl_err_log ( apl_err_num,
                 sybs_usr_id,
                 sybs_intrnl_sesn_id )
go

CREATE UNIQUE NONCLUSTERED INDEX ix04_apl_err_log
ON apl_err_log ( apl_err_seq_id )
go

IF ( OBJECT_ID("pr_errhandle") IS NOT NULL )
BEGIN
   DROP PROC pr_errhandle
END
go
/* CREATE PROCEDURE TO HANLDE ERRORS */
CREATE PROCEDURE pr_errhandle(
                 @METHOD CHAR(4) = "NONE",
                 @NOTIFY CHAR(4) = "NONE",
                 @GRP_NM VARCHAR(30) = NULL,
                 @DBNAME VARCHAR(30),
                 @SQL_CMPNT_NM VARCHAR(30),
                 @SQL_CMPNT_SEQ_ID INTEGER,
                 @APL_ERR_NUM INTEGER,
                 @SPCL_MSG VARCHAR(120) = NULL
)
AS
BEGIN
   /* Declare variable to store error message */
```

```
DECLARE @ERR_MSG VARCHAR(255)

/* Declare variable to store sql_cmpnt_err_num */
DECLARE @SQL_CMPNT_ERR_NUM INTEGER

/* Declare variable to store xp_cmdshell commands */
DECLARE @CMDS VARCHAR(1024)

/* Get error number for SQL component */
SELECT @SQL_CMPNT_ERR_NUM = sql_cmpnt_err_num
  FROM sql_cmpnt_err
 WHERE sql_cmpnt_nm = @SQL_CMPNT_NM

/* If for some reason we did not find a map use NA component */
IF ( @SQL_CMPNT_ERR_NUM IS NULL )
BEGIN
   SELECT @SQL_CMPNT_ERR_NUM = sql_cmpnt_err_num
     FROM sql_cmpnt_err
    WHERE sql_cmpnt_nm = "NA"
END

/* lets build the error message */
SELECT @ERR_MSG = "APL_ERR: "
                + CONVERT(VARCHAR, @SQL_CMPNT_ERR_NUM)
                + " SEQUENCE: "
                + CONVERT(VARCHAR, @SQL_CMPNT_SEQ_ID)
                + " ERR_TYP: "
                + CONVERT(VARCHAR, @APL_ERR_NUM)
                + " DBNAME: " + @DBNAME
                + " SQL_CMPNT: " + @SQL_CMPNT_NM
                + CASE
                    WHEN ( @SPCL_MSG IS NOT NULL )
                      THEN " MSG: " + @SPCL_MSG
                    ELSE SPACE(0)
                  END

/* Determine Notification Strategy */
IF ( UPPER(@NOTIFY) IN ("PAGE", "MAIL", "BOTH") )
BEGIN
   SELECT @CMDS = "/sybase/tools/notify.sh " + @@SERVERNAME + " "
            + UPPER(@NOTIFY) + " "
            + @GRP_NM + " "
            + @ERR_MSG
```

```
        EXEC xp_cmdshell @CMDS
    END

    /* Log Message */
    INSERT
      INTO apl_err_log(
           sybs_intrnl_sesn_id,
           sybs_usr_id,
           sql_cmpnt_err_num,
           sql_cmpnt_seq_id,
           sql_cmpnt_msg,
           DBNAME,
           apl_err_num,
           apl_err_log_ts
    )
    SELECT @@SPID,
           SUSER_NAME(),
           @SQL_CMPNT_ERR_NUM,
           @SQL_CMPNT_SEQ_ID,
           @ERR_MSG,
           @DBNAME,
           @APL_ERR_NUM,
           GETDATE()

    /* if return is specified */
    IF ( UPPER(@METHOD) = "PASS" )
    BEGIN
       /* add rollback alert */
       SELECT @ERR_MSG = @ERR_MSG + REPLICATE(".", 5) + "ROLLING BACK"

       /* raise the error */
       RAISERROR @SQL_CMPNT_ERR_NUM @ERR_MSG

       /* issue rollback */
       ROLLBACK TRANSACTION

       /* return error number */
       RETURN @SQL_CMPNT_ERR_NUM
    END

    /* if we made it here we default to none */
    RETURN 0
END
go
```

```
IF ( OBJECT_ID("pr_errcheck") IS NOT NULL )
BEGIN
   DROP PROC pr_errcheck
END
go
/* CHECK FOR NOT RESOLVED ERRORS */
CREATE PROCEDURE pr_errcheck
AS
BEGIN
   SELECT *
     FROM apl_err_log
    WHERE resv_flg = "N"
END
go

IF ( OBJECT_ID("pr_errresv") IS NOT NULL )
BEGIN
   DROP PROC pr_errresv
END
go
/* RESOLVE AND/OR UPDATE WORK INDICATOR */
CREATE PROCEDURE pr_errresv(
                 @apl_err_seq_id NUMERIC (15, 0),
                 @resv_flg CHAR(1) = "N",
                 @resv_usr_id VARCHAR(30) = NULL,
                 @resv_ts DATETIME = NULL,
                 @resv_dsc VARCHAR(255) = NULL
)
AS
BEGIN
   IF ( @resv_usr_id IS NULL )
      SELECT @resv_usr_id = SUSER_NAME()

   IF ( @resv_ts IS NULL )
      SELECT @resv_ts = GETDATE()

   IF ( @resv_dsc IS NULL )
      PRINT "***** YOU SHOULD REALLY ENTER A DESCRIPTION TEXT"

   PRINT ">>>>> STATUS INFORMATION BEFORE UPDATE: "

   SELECT *
     FROM apl_err_log
```

```
    WHERE apl_err_seq_id = @apl_err_seq_id

   UPDATE apl_err_log
      SET resv_flg = @resv_flg,
          resv_usr_id = @resv_usr_id,
          resv_dsc = @resv_dsc,
          resv_ts = @resv_ts
     FROM apl_err_log
    WHERE apl_err_seq_id = @apl_err_seq_id

   PRINT ">>>>> STATUS INFORMATION AFTER UPDATE: "

   SELECT *
     FROM apl_err_log
    WHERE apl_err_seq_id = @apl_err_seq_id
END
go

USE db1
go
DROP PROC test_proc01
go
CREATE PROCEDURE test_proc01(
                 @IS_ERROR CHAR(1),
                 @METHOD CHAR(4) = "NONE",
                 @SEQ_ID INTEGER = 0
)
AS
BEGIN
   /* Declare variable to store database name */
   DECLARE @DBNAME VARCHAR(30)

   /* Declare variable to store procedure name */
   DECLARE @SQL_CMPNT_NM VARCHAR(30)

   /* Declare pr_errhandle return variable */
   DECLARE @PR_ERR_RET INTEGER

   /* Get database name */
   SELECT @DBNAME = DB_NAME()

   /* Get stored procedure name */
   SELECT @SQL_CMPNT_NM = OBJECT_NAME(@@PROCID)
```

```
   /* we will use a sequence which is increased by 100 */
   /* to indicate the location within the SQL component */

   /* Error at Sequence 100, if we have error and none */
   IF ( @IS_ERROR = "Y" AND @METHOD = "NONE" AND @SEQ_ID = 100 )
   BEGIN
      /* call error handler */
      EXEC @PR_ERR_RET = apl_err_db..pr_errhandle "NONE", "NONE",
                         "NONE", @DBNAME,
                         @SQL_CMPNT_NM, 100, 1, "COULD NOT HANDLE"
      IF ( @PR_ERR_RET != 0 )
       GOTO ERRHANDLE
   END
   /* Error at sequence 100 and return is specified */
   ELSE IF ( @IS_ERROR = "Y" AND @METHOD = "PASS" AND @SEQ_ID = 100 )
   BEGIN
      /* call error handler */
      EXEC @PR_ERR_RET = apl_err_db..pr_errhandle "PASS", "BOTH",
                         "test_grp01", @DBNAME,
                         @SQL_CMPNT_NM, 100, 1, "COULD NOT HANDLE"
      IF ( @PR_ERR_RET != 0 )
       GOTO ERRHANDLE
   END
   /* we are at sequence 100 and no error occurred */
   ELSE IF ( @SEQ_ID = 100 )
   BEGIN
      PRINT "YOU ARE AT SEQUENCE: %1!", @SEQ_ID
   END

   PRINT "ALL IS WELL"
   RETURN 0

   /* set label for error jump */
   ERRHANDLE:
      RETURN @PR_ERR_RET
END
go
```

Let's execute test_proc01 now and indicate an error has occurred at sequence 100. In addition, we will indicate that the silent method should be pass back the error.

Example:

```
EXEC text_proc01 @IS_ERROR = "Y",
                 @METHOD = "PASS",
                 @SEQ_ID = 100
go
```

```
Msg 25001, Level 16, State 1:
Server 'SL0982LW', Procedure 'pr_errhandle', Line 90:
APL_ERR: 25001 SEQUENCE: 100 ERR_TYP: 1 DBNAME: db1
SQL_CMPNT: test_proc01
MSG: COULD NOT HANDLE.....ROLLING BACK
(return status = 25001)
```

Let's execute test_proc01 now and indicate an error has occurred at sequence 100. In addition, we will indicate that the silent method is none for silent.

Example:

```
EXEC text_proc01 @IS_ERROR = "Y",
                 @METHOD = "NONE",
                 @SEQ_ID = 100
go
```

```
(return status = 0)

/* Lets look at the error that was logged */

SELECT *
  FROM apl_err_log
go
```

Checking and resolving errors

Execute apl_err_db.dbo.pr_errcheck to check for unresolved errors.

Example:

```
EXEC apl_err_db.dbo.pr_errcheck
go
apl_err_seq_id   sybs_intrnl_sesn_id  sybs_usr_id   sql_cmpnt_err_num
   sql_cmpnt_seq_id   sql_cmpnt_msg

DBNAME   apl_err_num   apl_err_log_ts
   resv_flg resv_dsc
resv_usr_id   resv_ts
1                 48                   sa            25001
   100                    APL_ERR: 25001 SEQUENCE: 100 ERR_TYP: 1
DBNAME: db1 SQL_CMPNT: test_proc01 MSG: COULD NOT HANDLE
db1       1               Jun 26 2004 12:02PM
   N         NULL
NULL          NULL
```

Execute apl_err_db.dbo.pr_errresv to resolve errors.

Example:

```
EXEC apl_err_db.dbo.pr_errresv 1, "N", NULL, NULL, "Just A Test"
go
>>>>> STATUS INFORMATION BEFORE UPDATE:
apl_err_seq_id   sybs_intrnl_sesn_id  sybs_usr_id   sql_cmpnt_err_num
   sql_cmpnt_seq_id   sql_cmpnt_msg

DBNAME   apl_err_num   apl_err_log_ts
   resv_flg resv_dsc
resv_usr_id   resv_ts
1              48                    sa            25001
   100                 APL_ERR: 25001 SEQUENCE: 100 ERR_TYP: 1
DBNAME: db1 SQL_CMPNT: test_proc01 MSG: COULD NOT HANDLE
db1        1            Jun 26 2004 12:02PM
   N        NULL
NULL           NULL

>>>>> STATUS INFORMATION AFTER UPDATE:
apl_err_seq_id   sybs_intrnl_sesn_id  sybs_usr_id   sql_cmpnt_err_num
   sql_cmpnt_seq_id   sql_cmpnt_msg

DBNAME   apl_err_num   apl_err_log_ts
   resv_flg resv_dsc
resv_usr_id   resv_ts
1              48                    sa            25001
   100                 APL_ERR: 25001 SEQUENCE: 100 ERR_TYP: 1
DBNAME: db1 SQL_CMPNT: test_proc01 MSG: COULD NOT HANDLE
db1        1            Jun 26 2004 12:02PM
   N        Just A Test
               sa              Jun 26 2004 12:12PM
```

Chapter 32. Error Handling and Exception Reporting

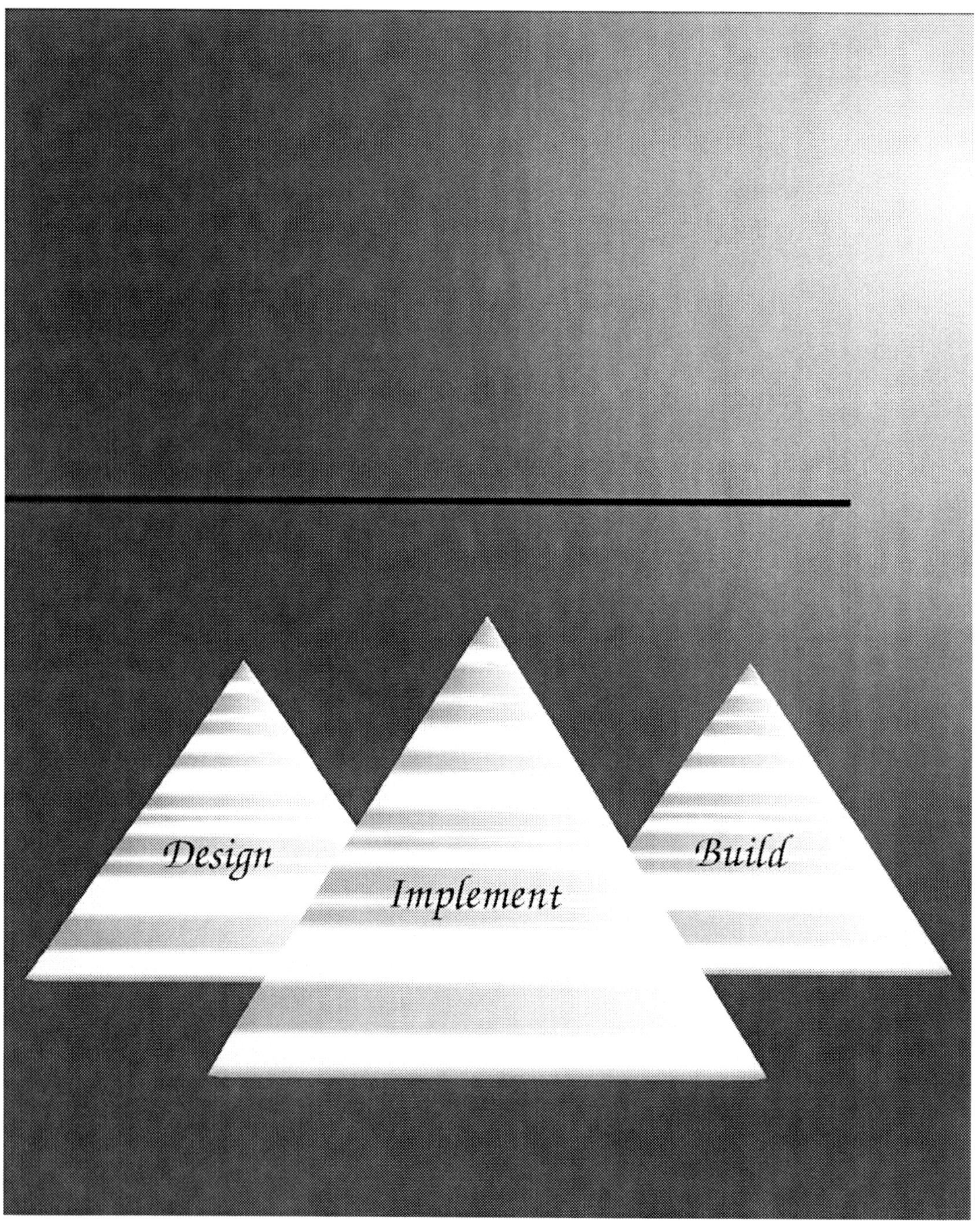
Design
Implement
Build

Appendix A. Language Fundamentals

Language Fundamentals

Every language has rules which much be followed in order to carry out conversation. *T-SQL* is no different. It consists of a character set, special symbols, and lexical units.

Character Set

The spoken or written language of *T-SQL* consists of the characters which comprise its language or vocabulary. Below is a list of the *ASCII* characters which comprise the language.

<table>
<tr><th>TYPE</th><th>CHARACTERS</th></tr>
<tr><td>Letter</td><td>A-Z a-z</td></tr>
<tr><td>Numeric</td><td>0-9</td></tr>
<tr><td>Separator</td><td>spaces, tabs, carriage returns</td></tr>
<tr><td>Symbol</td><td>!@#$%^&*()_-+=`~\|;:'"<>,.[]{}?/</td></tr>
</table>

Special Symbols

Special characters and words within ASE are those characters and words which are used to perform operations like multiplication, addition, and subtraction. Below is list of the most common special characters and words by group and including operator precedence.

ASSIGNMENT GROUP	*OPERATOR NAME*	*OPERATOR*	*PRECEDENCE*
Arithmetic	Addition	+	3
Arithmetic	Subtraction	-	3
Arithmetic	Multiplication	*	2

ASSIGNMENT GROUP	*OPERATOR NAME*	*OPERATOR*	*PRECEDENCE*
Arithmetic	Division	/	2
Arithmetic	Modulo	%	2
Bitwise	AND	&	3
Bitwise	OR	|	3
Bitwise	Exclusive OR	^	1
Bitwise	NOT	~	1
Comparisons	Equals	=	Optimization
Comparison	Greater	>	Optimization
Comparison	Less	<	Optimization
Comparison	Greater or Equals	>=	Optimization
Comparison	Less or Equals	<=	Optimization
Comparison	Not Equals	<>	Optimization
Comparison	Not Equals	!=	Optimization
Comparison	Not Greater	!>	Optimization
Comparison	Not Less	!<	Optimization
Comparison	Lists	Exists	Optimization
Comparison	Lists	IN	Optimization
Comparison	Likeness	LIKE	Optimization
Joins	Left Outer Join	*=	Optimization
Joins	Left Outer Join	LEFT JOIN	Optimization
Joins	Right Outer Join	=*	Optimization
Joins	Right Outer Join	RIGHT JOIN	Optimization
Joins	Inner Join	=	Optimization

ASSIGNMENT GROUP	OPERATOR NAME	OPERATOR	PRECEDENCE
Joins	Inner Join	INNER JOIN	Optimization
Logical Expressions	AND	AND	5
Logical Expressions	OR	OR	6
Logical Expressions	NOT	NOT	4
Characters	Concatenation	+	N/A
Characters	Continuation	\	N/A
Aggregates	Maximum	MAX	N/A
Aggregates	Minimum	MIN	N/A
Aggregates	Average	AVG	N/A
Aggregates	Summation	SUM	N/A
Aggregates	Number of Elements	COUNT	N/A
Comments	Line comment	--	N/A
Comments	Begin a Block comment	/*	N/A
Comments	End a Block Comment	*/	N/A
Terminators	Statement Terminators	Carriage Return	N/A
Terminators	Execution Terminators	go	N/A

ASSIGNMENT GROUP	OPERATOR NAME	OPERATOR	PRECEDENCE
Wildcards	Anything After	%	N/A
Wildcards	Any single character	_	N/A
Wildcards	Any single character within range	[A-Z]	N/A
Wildcards	Range Separator	-	N/A
Wildcards	Any single character not within range	[^A-Z]	N/A

Lexical Units

In *T-SQL* lexical units consist of literals, identifiers, reserved words, and comments.

Literals

Literals are simply values. The following table lists several types of literals.

TYPE	EXAMPLE
Numeric	123
Numeric	99.01
Numeric	-45.13
Numeric	NULL
Date and Time	"01/01/2004"
Date and Time	NULL
Character	"ABC"
Character	NULL

TYPE	*EXAMPLE*
Boolean	0
Boolean	1
Boolean	NULL
Bit	0
Bit	1
Bit	NULL
Binary	0x00010AE
Binary	NULL

Identifiers

Identifiers are names of specific *T-SQL* objects. They can include tables, columns, views, procedures, variables, parameters, reserved words, cursors, datatypes, and more. Identifiers may be up 30 characters long (30 bytes), and except in the cases of @ and _ must start with a letter. After which, any letter, numeric, or $, @, #, and _ are allowed.

The following table summarizes some valid and invalid identifiers.

IDENTIFIER NAME	*VALID OR INVALID*
column_1	valid
1_column	invalid
@var1	valid
@@var1	invalid

Reserved Words

Reserved words are ASE system defined words that cannot be used to name your objects. The following is list of current ASE reserved words, as well as ANSI current and potential reserved words. For simplicity and error prevention, these words should not be used to name anything in a database. These words should only be used as part of a SQL command syntax.

A

absolute, action, allocate, are, assertion, add, all, alter, and, any, arith_overflow, as, asc, at,, authorization, avg, after, alias, async

B

before, boolean, breadth, begin, between, break, browse, bulk, by, bit, bit_length, both

C

call, completion, cycle, cascade, case, char_convert, check, checkpoint, close, clustered, coalesce, commit, compute, confirm, connect, constraint, continue, controlrow, convert, count, create, current, cursor, cascaded, case, cast, catalog, char, char_length, character, character_length, coalesce, collate, collation, column, connection, constraints, corresponding, cross, current_date, current_time, current_timestamp, current_user

D

data, depth, dictionary, database, dbcc, deallocate, declare, default, delete, desc, deterministic, disk distinct, double, drop, dummy, dump, date, day, dec, decimal, deferrable, deferred, describe, descriptor, diagnostics, disconnect, domain

E

each, elseif, equals, else, end, endtran, errlvl, errordata, errorexit, escape, except, exclusive, exec, execute, exists, exit, exp_row_size, external, end-exec, exception, extract

F

false, first, float, found, full, fetch, fillfactor, for, foreign, from, func

G

general, get, global, go, goto, grant, group

H
having, holdlock, hour

I
identity, identity_gap, identity_insert, identity_start, if, in, index, inout, insert, install, intersect, into, is, isolation, ignore, immediate, indicator, initially, inner, input, insensitive, int, integer, interval

J
jar, join, join

K
key, kill

L
language, last, leading, left, local, lower, leave, less, limit, loop, level, like, lineno, load, lock

M
match, minute, module, month, max, max_rows_per_page, min, mirror, mirrorexit, modify

N
names, natural, nchar, next, no, nullif, numeric, national, new, noholdlock, nonclustered, not, null, nullif, numeric_truncation, new, none

O
object, oid, old, operation, operators, others, octet_length, outer, output, overlaps, of, off, offsets, on, once, online, only, open, option, or, order, out, output, over

P
pad, partial, position, preserve, prior, parameters, pendant, preorder, private, protected, partition, perm, permanent, plan, precision, prepare, primary, print, privileges, proc, procedure, processexit, proxy_table, public

Q
quiesce

R
raiserror, read, readpast, readtext, reconfigure, references remove, reorg, replace, replication, reservepagegap, return, returns, revoke, role, rollback, rowcount, rows, rule, real, relative, restrict, right, recursive, ref, referencing, resignal, return, returns, routine, row

S
save, schema, select, set, setuser, shared, shutdown, some, statistics, stringsize, stripe, sum, syb_identity, syb_restree, syb_terminate, savepoint, search, sensitive, sequence, signal, similar, sqlexception, structure, scroll, second, section, session_user , size , smallint, space, sql, sqlcode, sqlerror, sqlstate, substring, system_user

T
table, temp, temporary, textsize, to, tran, transaction, trigger, truncate, tsequal, test, there, type, then, time, timestamp, timezone_hour, timezone_minute, trailing, translate, translation, trim, true

U
under, union, unique, unpartition, update, use, user, user_option, using, unknown, upper, usage

V
value, varchar, values, varying, view, variable, virtual, visible

W
wait, without, waitfor, when, where, while, with, work, writetext, when, whenever, write, year

Z
zone

Utility Procedure To Read Source Code

Below is a procedure which you can install into the sybsystemprocs database to help read *T-SQL* code stored in the database. The procedure takes two parameters: <"OWNER">, <"OBJECT NAME">

Example:

```
USE sybsystemprocs
go

EXEC sp_get_txt "dbo", "sp_get_txt"
go

CREATE PROCEDURE sp_get_txt(
                 @OWNER VARCHAR(32),
                 @OBJNAME VARCHAR(32)
)
AS
BEGIN

/*******************************************************************
** AUTHOR: Ryan Putnam
**
** INTENT: Generate Text FROM SYSCOMMENTS
**
** REVISE: Jun 02, 2002
**
** VERSION: 1.0001
*******************************************************************/

SET NOCOUNT ON

/* DECLARATION SECTION */
DECLARE @ONECHAR CHAR(1)
DECLARE @TEXTVAL VARCHAR(16384)
DECLARE @TEXTSTRING VARCHAR(1024)
DECLARE @LOOPCNT INT
DECLARE @COLID INT
DECLARE @MAXCOLID INT
DECLARE @OBJID INT
DECLARE @COLID2 INT
```

```
/* INITIALIZATION SECTION */
SELECT @COLID = 0
SELECT @ONECHAR = NULL
SELECT @TEXTVAL = NULL
SELECT @TEXTSTRING = NULL
SELECT @OBJID = NULL
SELECT @MAXCOLID = 0

/* read and store object id of specified object */
SELECT @OBJID = C.id
  FROM syscomments C,
       sysobjects O
WHERE C.id=O.id
  AND O.name = @OBJNAME
  AND O.uid = USER_ID(@OWNER)

/* declare cursor to read get columns from syscomments */
DECLARE process_colid2_cursor
 CURSOR
    FOR
 SELECT C.colid2,
        MAX(C.colid)
   FROM syscomments C
  WHERE C.id = @OBJID
  GROUP
     BY C.colid2
  ORDER
     BY C.colid2 ASC
FOR READ ONLY

/* open cursor */
OPEN process_colid2_cursor

/* fetch from cursor */
FETCH process_colid2_cursor
 INTO @COLID2,
      @MAXCOLID

/* while cursor just fetched a row */
WHILE ( @@SQLSTATUS = 0 )
BEGIN

   /* establish label ROUTINE for GOTO */
   ROUTINE:
```

```
SELECT @ONECHAR =  NULL
SELECT @TEXTVAL =  NULL
SELECT @LOOPCNT = 1

/* read text from current columns */
SELECT @TEXTVAL = C.text
  FROM syscomments C
WHERE C.id=@OBJID
  AND C.colid = @COLID
  AND C.colid2 = @COLID2

IF ( @COLID = 0 AND @COLID2 = 1
 AND SUBSTRING(@TEXTVAL, 1, 1) = CHAR(10) )
BEGIN
   SELECT @TEXTVAL=SUBSTRING(@TEXTVAL,2,
                                  CHAR_LENGTH(@TEXTVAL) - 1)
END

WHILE @LOOPCNT < 256 AND @COLID <= @MAXCOLID
BEGIN
  SELECT @ONECHAR = SUBSTRING(@TEXTVAL, @LOOPCNT, 1)

  SELECT @TEXTSTRING = @TEXTSTRING
                         + SUBSTRING(@TEXTVAL,@LOOPCNT,1)

   IF ( @ONECHAR = CHAR(10) AND ASCII(@TEXTSTRING) > 0 )
   BEGIN
      PRINT "%1!", @TEXTSTRING
      SELECT @TEXTSTRING = NULL
   END

   IF ( (@ONECHAR != CHAR(10))
    AND @LOOPCNT >= 255
    AND @COLID < @MAXCOLID )
   BEGIN
      SELECT @LOOPCNT = @LOOPCNT + 1
      SELECT @ONECHAR = SUBSTRING(@TEXTVAL, @LOOPCNT, 1)
      SELECT @TEXTSTRING = @TEXTSTRING
                         + SUBSTRING(@TEXTVAL, @LOOPCNT, 1)
      SELECT @COLID = @COLID + 1
      GOTO ROUTINE
   END
   ELSE IF @LOOPCNT >= 255 AND @COLID < @MAXCOLID
   BEGIN
```

```
            SELECT @COLID = @COLID + 1
            GOTO ROUTINE
         END
         ELSE IF CHAR_LENGTH(@TEXTSTRING) >= 500 AND @ONECHAR = ","
         BEGIN
            PRINT "%1!", @TEXTSTRING
            SELECT @TEXTSTRING = NULL
         END

         SELECT @LOOPCNT = @LOOPCNT + 1
      END

      SELECT @COLID = 0

      FETCH process_colid2_cursor
       INTO @COLID2,
            @MAXCOLID
END

IF CHAR_LENGTH(@TEXTSTRING) > 0 AND ASCII(@TEXTSTRING) > 0
BEGIN
   PRINT "%1!", @TEXTSTRING
END

CLOSE process_colid2_cursor

DEALLOCATE
    CURSOR process_colid2_cursor

END
```

Unix Shell Script To Invoke sp_get_txt

```
#!/bin/sh

## Author: Ryan Putnam
## Intent: GET syscomments Text Objects

###############
## FUNCTIONS ##
###############

## FUNCTION TO BUILD TSQL CODE
generate_create_statement()
{
```

```
isql -U${1} -P${2} -S${3} -D${4} -w20000 -o./temp.sql<<EOF
SET NOCOUNT ON
go
EXEC sp_get_txt "${5}", "${6}"
go
EOF

## LOOK FOR CODE BEFORE AND CODE AFTER STATEMENTS
typeset -i CODESTART=`grep -n "*CODE BEFORE:" ./temp.sql \
  | cut -f1 -d":" | head -1`

typeset -i CODEEND=`grep -n "*CODE AFTER:" ./temp.sql \
  | cut -f1 -d":" | head -1`

## FILENAME FOR RESULTS
FF="${5}.${6}"

if (( $CODEEND > $CODESTART ));then
   head -`expr $CODEEND - 1` ./temp.sql \
     | tail -`expr $CODEEND - $CODESTART - 1` >./${FF}.presql
   print "go" >>./${FF}.presql
fi

## APPEND CREATION TEXT AFTER PRESQL
cat ./temp.sql >>./${FF}.presql

typeset -i REMEND
REMEND=`cat ./${FF}.presql | wc -l`
REMEND=`expr $REMEND - 1`
head -$REMEND ./${FF}.presql >./${FF}.sql
print "go" >>./${FF}.sql

## ADD EXISTENCE CHECK TO SQL FILE
print "IF OBJECT_ID('${5}.${6}') IS NOT NULL" >>./${FF}.sql
print "BEGIN" >>./${FF}.sql
print "   print 'OBJECT ${5}.${6} EXISTS'" >>./${FF}.sql
print "END" >>./${FF}.sql
print "ELSE" >>./${FF}.sql
print "BEGIN" >>./${FF}.sql
print "   print 'OBJECT ${5}.${6} DOES NOT EXIST'" >>./${FF}.sql
print "END" >>./${FF}.sql
print "go" >>./${FF}.sql

cat ./${FF}.sql
```

```
## FILE CLEANUP
rm ./${FF}.presql
rm ./temp.sql
rm ./${FF}.sql
}

##############
## MAINLINE ##
##############
## CALL FUNCTION WITH LOGIN, PASSWD, SRVNAME, DBNAME, OWNER, OBJNAME
generate_create_statement "${1}" "${2}" "${3}" "${4}" "${5}" "${6}"

exit 0
```

The above shell script will parse the object for *CODE BEFORE: and *CODE AFTER: statements and place the *CODE BEFORE: statements before the creation text. This is necessary for stored procedures which use temporary tables that are created outside of the procedure.

The shell script takes the following parameters:
Server Login, Server Password, Server Name, Database Name, Object Owner, Object Name

Appendix A. Language Fundamentals

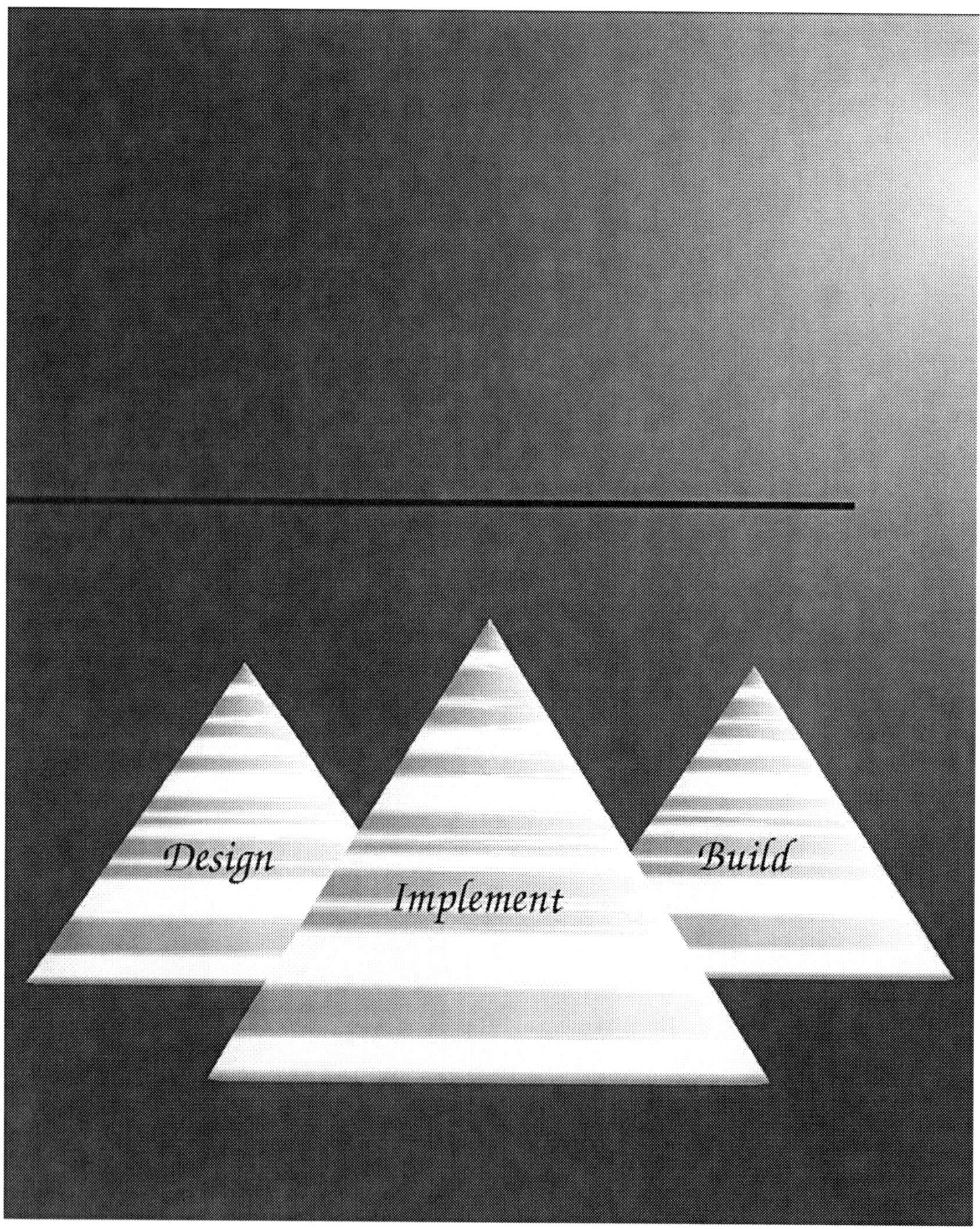
Design
Implement
Build

Appendix B. Feedback System

T-SQL is structured as a feedback system. It takes input to produce output. You can consider input a question and output as the answer. When asking a question the following stages are traversed to yield the answer: Parse, Normalize, Optimize, and Execute. The entire process is known as compilation. The below diagram illustrates compilation.

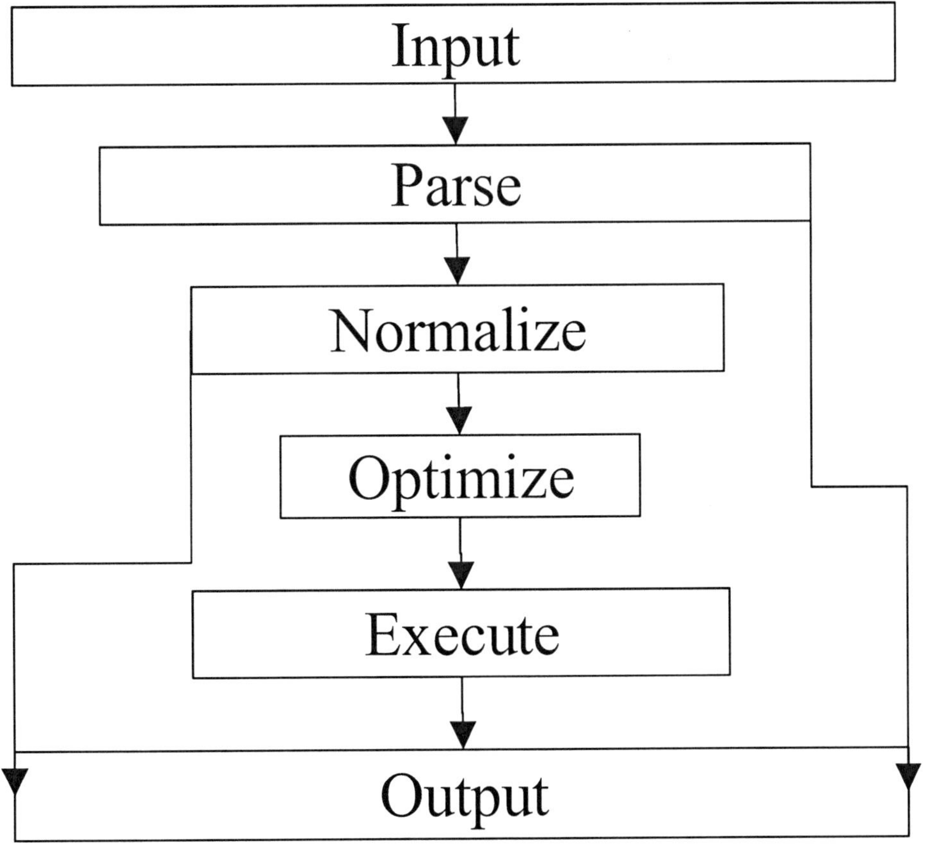

Parse

The input to the parse module is the question or input. Parsing involves determining whether or not the vocabulary is understood. If the vocabulary is not understood the parse module will call the output module to give an error as the answer to your question. Otherwise, the vocabulary is understood and the parse module will call the normalize module.

Normalize

The input to the normalize module is vocabulary which is understood. The normalization module locates objects within the database and determines whether or not you have the appropriate permissions to perform your question. If the you do not have the appropriate permissions the normalize module will call the output to give an error as the answer to your question. Otherwise, you have valid permissions in the database to carry out your question and the normalize module will call the optimize module.

Optimize

The input to the optimize module is a question which has valid vocabulary, by a user who has the appropriate permissions to ask the question. The optimization module then determines the optimal paths, through rules and statistics, to go after the answer to the question. Once the optimize module determines the optimal strategy, it calls the execution module.

Execute

The input to the execute module is a question which has valid vocabulary, by a user who has the appropriate permissions to ask the question. In addition, the question has been optimized for the most efficient access methods by the optimize module. The execute module then takes the output from the optimize module and executes it within ASE. The execution module calls the output module. When execution is complete the answer to your question will be presented.

Appendix B. Feedback System

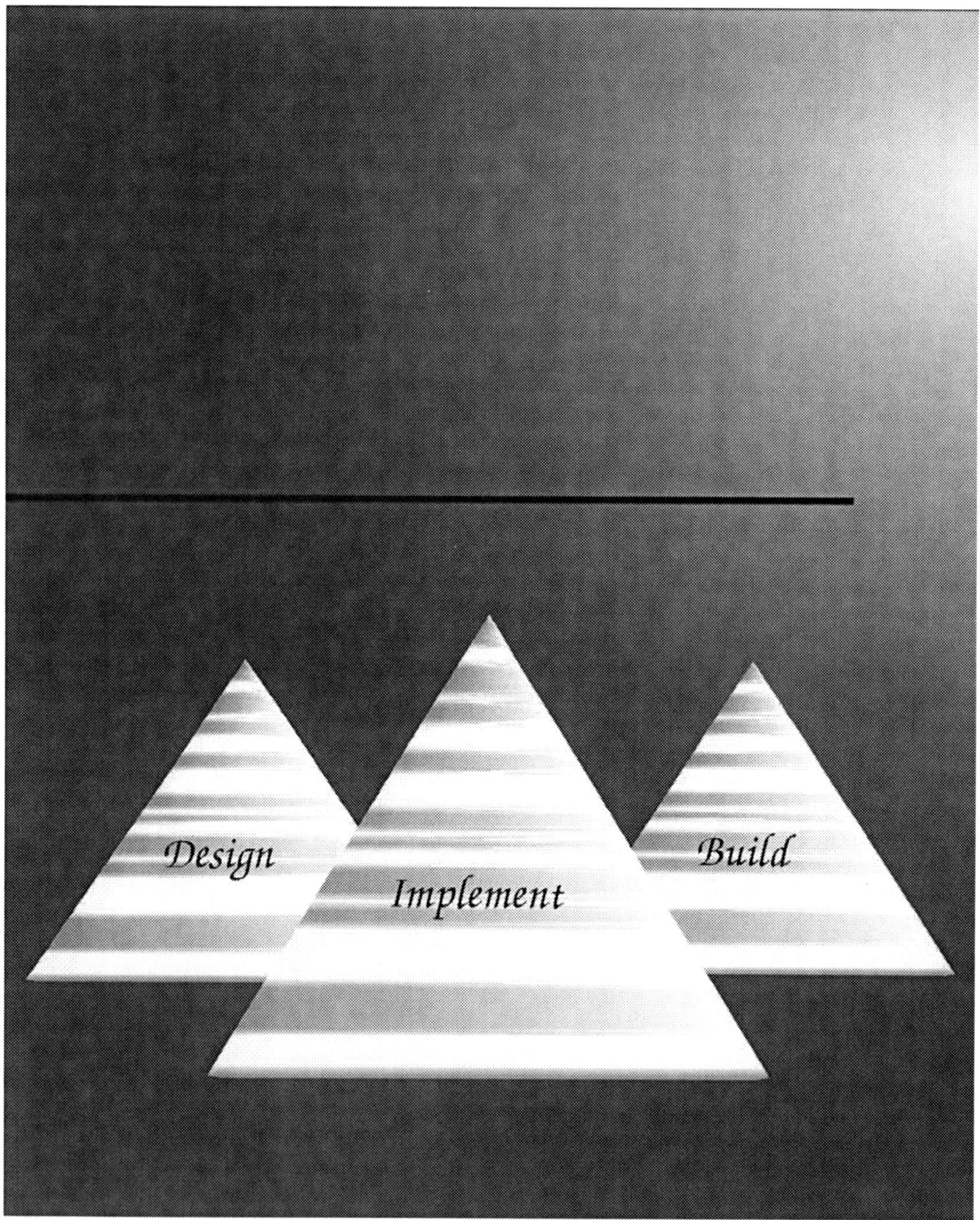
Design
Implement
Build

Appendix C. Data Access Basics

Variables

A variable is a symbol used to temporarily store a data value. The operations which may be performed on a variable are determined by the datatype of the variable. To use a variable you must first *DECLARE* it. In other words, give it a name for reference and a datatype for storage and retrieval.

Format:
DECLARE @<VARIABLE NAME> <DATATYPE>

Example:
Declare a variable named var1 for *INTEGER* storage

```
DECLARE @var1 INTEGER
```

Variables can be used to store and retrieve information about anything specific to its datatype. They are often used in *SELECTS, UPDATES, DELETES, INSERTS,* and *CONTROL-OF-FLOW* statements.

There are primarily four ways to assign a variable. You may assign a variable using *SELECT, SET, UPDATE, or FETCH.*

USING SELECT
Example:

```
DECLARE @var1 INTEGER
SELECT @var1 = 123456
go
```

USING SET
Example:

```
DECLARE @var1 INTEGER
SET @var1 = 123456
go
```

USING UPDATE

Example:

```
DECLARE @var1 INTEGER
UPDATE <table>
   SET @var1 = 123456
  FROM <table list>
 WHERE <conditions>
go
```

Note: For more regarding *UPDATE* refer to the section on modifying data.

USING FETCH

For information regarding the usage of *FETCH* refer to the section on using cursors.

Reading Data

To read data out of table or view you use the ANSI standard ***SELECT*** Keyword. The *SELECT* command has the following syntax:

```
SELECT <columns>
  FROM <tables>
 WHERE <conditions>
 ORDER
    BY <columns>
 GROUP
    BY <columns>
HAVING <conditions>
COMPUTE <aggregates>
```

SELECT *<columns>* specifies what is to be returned or retrieved from data. *<columns>* may include columns, variables, expressions, parameters, aggregates, and/or a mix of all five.

Example:

```
SELECT column1 * @var1
  FROM table
go
```

Modifying Data

To modify data within ASE you use the ANSI standard ***UPDATE*** Keyword. The *UPDATE* command the following syntax:

```
UPDATE <table>
   SET <columns> = <values>
  FROM <tables>
 WHERE <conditions>
```

UPDATE *<table>* specifies what table is to be modified by the SET *<columns>* = *<values>*. In addition, *<columns>* may include columns, variables, and parameters, and/or a mix of all three.

Example:

```
UPDATE table
   SET column1 = @var1,
       @var1 = column2
 WHERE column3 = "some value"
go
```

Creating Data

To create or insert data within ASE, use the ANSI standard ***INSERT*** Keyword. The *INSERT* command the following syntax:

```
INSERT
  INTO <ins_table>(
       <ins_columns>
)
SELECT <columns>
  FROM <tables>
 WHERE <conditions>
 ORDER
    BY <columns>
 GROUP
    BY <columns>
HAVING <conditions>
COMPUTE <aggregates>
```

Or alternatively,

```
 INSERT
   INTO <ins_table>(
        <ins_columns>
)
VALUES ( <columns> )
```

INSERT *<ins_table>* specifies what table is to be inserted into. In addition, the SELECT command can be formatted just as a normal SELECT. The alternative method can only be used to insert one record at a time.

Example (multi-record method):

```
INSERT
  INTO test_table(
       column1,
       column2,
       column3
)
SELECT column1 * @var1,
       @var2,
       @parm1
  FROM table
 WHERE column1 = "some value"
```

```
go
```

Example (single record method):

```
INSERT
  INTO test_table(
       column1,
       column2,
       column3
)
VALUES(@var1,
       @var2,
       @parm1
)
go
```

Removing Data

To remove data within ASE, use the ANSI standard ***DELETE*** Keyword. The *UPDATE* command the following syntax:

```
DELETE <table>
  FROM <tables>
 WHERE <conditions>
```

DELETE <*table*> specifies what table is to have data removed or deleted.

Example:

```
DELETE table1
  FROM table1 t1,
       table2 t2
 WHERE t1.column1 = t2.column1
   AND t2.column2 = "some value"
go
```

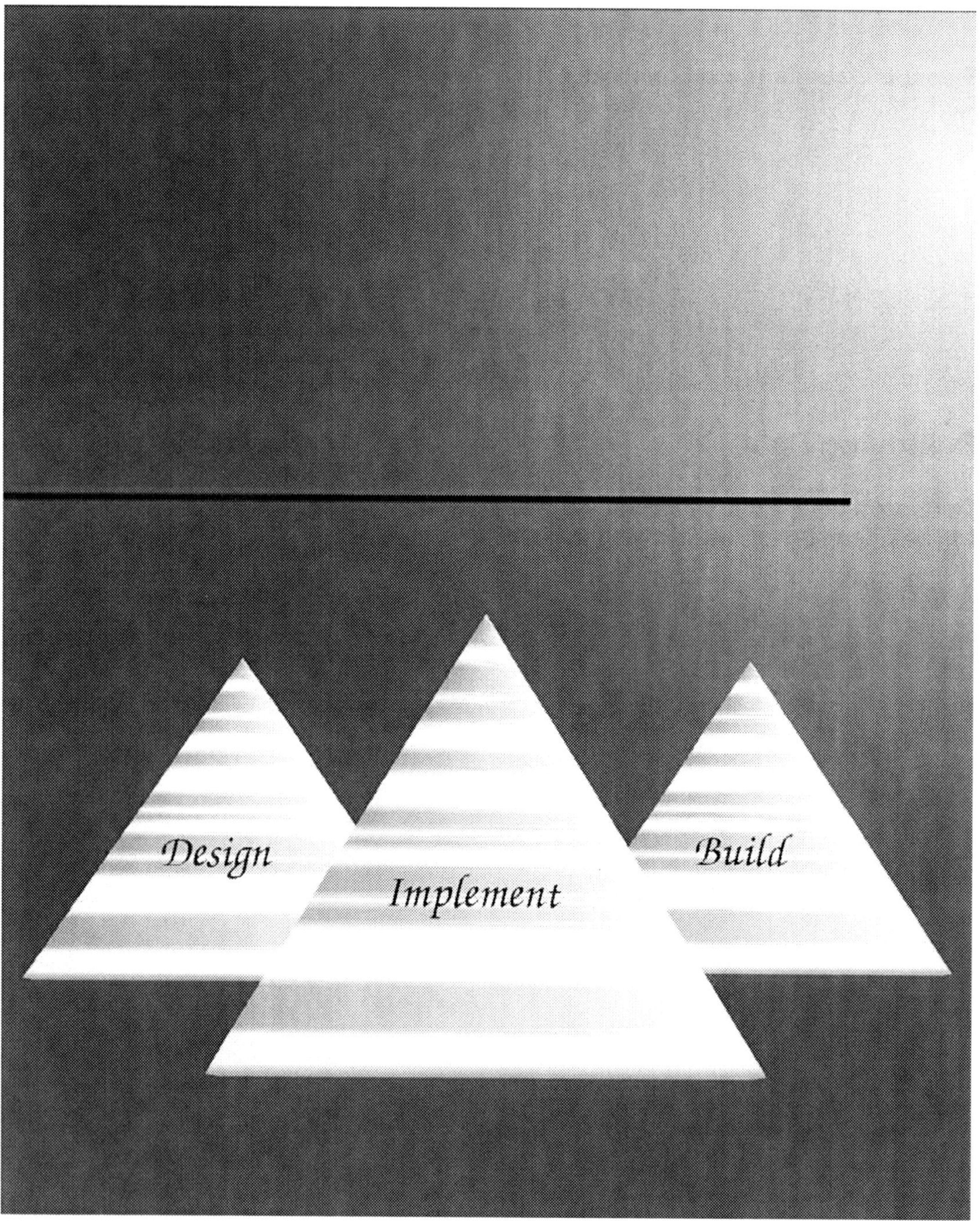
Design
Implement
Build

Appendix D. Functions

T-SQL Functions

ASE supports the following T-SQL functions and when used should always be in UPPER CASE so that they are easy to identify and make code more readable.

ABS

Usage: The ABS function is used to generate the absolute value of a numeric expression.

Syntax: ABS(Numeric Expression)

Example:

```
SELECT ABS(-5)
go
5
```

ACOS

Usage: The ACOS function is used to generate the angle in radians from the cosine expression.

Syntax: ACOS(Cosine Expression)

Example:

```
SELECT ACOS(0)
go
1.5707963
```

ASCII

Usage: The ASCII function is used to generate the ascii character code for the first character in an expression.

Syntax: ASCII(Character Expression)

Example:

```
SELECT ASCII("aBc")
go
----------------------------------------------------------------
97
```

ASIN

Usage: The ASIN function is used to generate the angle in radians from the sine expression.

Syntax: ASIN(Sine Expression)

Example:

```
SELECT ASIN(0)
go
----------------------------------------------------------------
0.0
```

ATAN

Usage: The ATAN function is used to generate the angle in radians from the tangent expression.

Syntax: ATAN(Tangent Expression)

Example:

```
SELECT ATAN(1)
go
----------------------------------------------------------------
0
```

ATN2

Usage: The ATN2 function is used to generate the angle in radians from the sine and cosine expression.

Syntax: ATN2(Sine Expression, Cosine Expression)

Example:

```
SELECT ATN2(0, 1)
go
0.0
```

AVG

Usage: The AVG function is used to generate the mean from a finite set of numeric values.

Syntax: AVG(<ALL | DISTINCT> Numerical Expression)

Considerations: The parameter ALL is the default for the AVG function. It specifies that the average should be calculated for all values returned to the AVG function. The parameter DISTINCT is used to return only those values which are DISTINCT to the AVG function. Thus only computing the average for the unique values of those returned to the AVG function.

Example:

```
SELECT AVG(column_1)
  FROM table
go
Average of all numeric values in column_1


SELECT AVG(ALL column_1)
  FROM table
go
Average of all numeric values in column_1

SELECT AVG(DISTINCT column_1)
  FROM table
go
Average of all DISTINCT values in column_1
```

CEILING

Usage: The CEILING function is used to generate the smallest integer value whose expression is greater than or equal to the numeric expression.

Syntax: CEILING(Numeric Expression)

Example:
```
SELECT CEILING(123.431332)
go
------------------------------------------------------------
123
```

CHAR

Usage: The CHAR function is used to generate the character value of a specified ascii integer character code.

Syntax: CHAR(Integer Expression)

Example:
```
SELECT CHAR(97)
go
------------------------------------------------------------
a
```

CHARINDEX

Usage: The CHARINDEX function is used to generate the integer starting position of a character expression within a character expression from one. Zero is returned if there is no match.

Syntax: CHARINDEX(Character Expression, Character Expression)

Example:
```
SELECT CHARINDEX("DEF", "ABCDEFG")
go
------------------------------------------------------------
4
```

CHAR_LENGTH

Usage: The CHAR_LENGTH function is used to generate the integer number of characters that are in a character expression.

Syntax: CHAR_LENGTH(Character Expression)

Example:
```
SELECT CHAR_LENGTH("ABC")
go
------------------------------------------------------------------
3
```

COMPARE

Usage: The COMPARE function is used to compare strings based upon the default or specified collation rule. The collation rule can be specified as either the name or id of the collation rule.

Syntax:
COMPARE(Character Expression, Character Expression, [Collation Id | Name])

The following table lists the collation rules which are applicable.

Description	*Collation ID*	*Collation Name*
Default Unicode multilingual	0	default
Thai dictionary	1	thaidict
CP 850 Alternate no accent	39	altnoacc
CP 850 Alternate lower case first	45	altdict
CP 850 Alternate no case preference	46	altnocsp
CP 850 Scandinavian dictionary	47	scandict
CP 850 Scandinavian no case preference	48	scannocp
Binary sort	50	binary
Latin-1 English, French, German distionary	51	dict
Latin-1 English, French, German no case	52	nocase

Description	Collation ID	Collation Name
Latin-1 English, French, German no case preference	53	nocasep
Latin-1, English, French, German no accent	54	noaccent
Latin-1 Spanish dictionary	55	espdict
Latin-1 Spanish no case	56	espnocs
Latin-1 Spanish no accent	57	espnoac
ISO 8859-5 Russian dictionary	58	rusdict
ISO 8859-5 Cyrillic dictionary	63	cyrdict
ISO 8859-9 Turkish dictionary	72	turdict
Shift-JIS binary order	259	sjisbin

The COMPARE function returns one of the following ***integer*** values:

- 1 to indicate that one string is greater than another
- 0 to indicate that the two strings are equal
- -1 to indicate that one string is less than another
- or, -2 if a specified string IS NULL.

In addition, the string function is used to compare any CHAR, VARCHAR, NCHAR, or NVARCHAR to any CHAR, VARCHAR, NCHAR, or NVARCHAR. Or alternatively, it is used to compare any UNICHAR or UNIVARCHAR to any UNICHAR or UNIVARHCAR.

Note: These examples were created using isql and the -Jutf8 flag. For more information on isql, refer to the Sybase Utilities Guide.

Example:
```
DECLARE @STR1 CHAR(10)
DECLARE @STR2 NVARCHAR(10)
DECLARE @RETVAL INTEGER

SELECT @STR1 = "ABC"
SELECT @STR2 = "FGH"
```

```
SELECT @RETVAL = COMPARE(@STR1, @STR2)

SELECT @RETVAL
go
-1
```

CONVERT

Usage: The CONVERT function is to used for conversion to another datatype. It is also used to modify datetime display format.

Syntax: CONVERT(DATATYPE<(LENGTH) | (PRECISION<, SCALE>)> <NULL | NOT NULL>, EXPRESSION<, STYLE>)

Example:

```
-- CAST the character string “10” as an integer.
SELECT CONVERT(INT, “10”)
go
10

/* CAST the integer 10 as a varying length
** character string of length 10. */
SELECT CONVERT(VARCHAR(10), 10)
go
10
```

COS

Usage: The COS function is used to generate the cosine of an angle in radians.

Syntax: COS(Angle In Radians)

Example:

```
SELECT COS(PI()/2)
go
0.0
```

COT

Usage: The COT function is used to generate the cotangent of an angle in radians.

Syntax: COT(Angle In Radians)

Example:
```
SELECT COT(PI()/4)
go
1.0
```

COUNT

Usage: The COUNT function is used to generate the integer number of NOT NULL values in a finite set of values or a resultant row size.

Syntax: COUNT(<ALL | DISTINCT> Expression)

Considerations: The parameter ALL is the default for the COUNT function. It specifies that the count should be calculated for all NOT NULL values returned to the COUNT function. The parameter DISTINCT is used to return only those values which are DISTINCT to the COUNT function. Thus only computing the count for the unique values of those returned to the COUNT function.

Example:
```
SELECT COUNT(column_1)
  FROM table
go
Count of all NOT NULL values in column_1

SELECT COUNT(ALL column_1)
  FROM table
go
Count of all NOT NULL values in column_1

SELECT COUNT(DISTINCT column_1)
  FROM table
go
Count of all DISTINCT NOT NULL values in column_1
```

CURRENT_DATE

Usage: The function CURRENT_DATE() is used to return the current date.

Syntax: CURRENT_DATE()

Example:
```
SELECT CURRENT_DATE()
go
Jul 4 2004
```

CURRENT_TIME

Usage: The function CURRENT_TIME() is used to return the current time.

Syntax: CURRENT_TIME()

Example:
```
SELECT CURRENT_TIME()
go
     8:18 PM
```

DATALENGTH

Usage: The function DATALENGTH is used to get the actual byte length of the specified column or expression.

Syntax: DATALENGTH(<COLNAME | Expression>)

Example:
```
SELECT DATALENGTH("ABC")
go
3
```

DATEADD

Usage: The function DATEADD is used to add a date or time component to that of the expression or column passed to the function.

Syntax: DATEADD(Date Component, Integer Amount to add to Date, Date Expression)

Date Components: year(yy), quarter(qq), month(mm), week(wk), day(dd), dayofyear (dy), weekday(dw), hour(hh), minute(mi), second(ss), millisecond(ms)

Example:

```
SELECT DATEADD(hh, 1, GETDATE())
go
4/9/2004 9:18:22.896 AM
```

DATEDIFF

Usage: The function DATEDIFF is used to generate the difference between two date expressions for the component specified.

Syntax: DATEDIFF(Date Component, Date Expression, Date Expression)

Date Components: year(yy), quarter(qq), month(mm), week(wk), day(dd), dayofyear (dy), weekday(dw), hour(hh), minute(mi), second(ss), millisecond(ms)

Example:

```
SELECT DATEDIFF(hh, "04/04/2004", "04/05/2004")
go
24
```

DATEPART

Usage: The function DATEPART is used to get the integer value of a specified date component for given date expression.

Syntax: DATEPART(Date Component, Date Expression)

Date Components: year(yy), quarter(qq), month(mm), week(wk), day(dd), dayofyear (dy), weekday(dw), hour(hh), minute(mi), second(ss), millisecond(ms)

Example:

```
SELECT DATEPART(hh, "04/04/2004")
go
------------------------------------------------------------
0
```

DAY

Usage: The function DAY is used to get the integer value for the day of the month out of a date expression.

Syntax: DAY(Date Expression)

Example:

```
SELECT DAY("04/05/2004")
go
------------------------------------------------------------
5
```

DB_ID

Usage: The function DB_ID is used to get the current database id or the id of the database whose name is specified.

Syntax: DB_ID(<DBNAME>)

Example:

```
SELECT DB_ID()
go
------------------------------------------------------------
1
```

DB_NAME

Usage: The function DB_NAME is used to get the current database name or the name of database whose id is specified.

Syntax: DB_NAME(<DBID>)

Example:
```
SELECT DB_NAME()
go
master
```

DEGREES

Usage: The function DEGREES is used to convert angle in radians to degrees.

Syntax: DEGREES(Radians Expression)

Example:
```
SELECT DEGREES(PI()/2)
go
90
```

DIFFERENCE

Usage: The function DIFFERENCE is used to get an integer between 0 and 4 representing the how similar sounding two character expressions are, with 4 being the best.

Syntax: DIFFERENCE(Character Expression 1, Character Expression 2)

Example:
```
SELECT DIFFERENCE("RYAN", "RYAN")
go
4
```

EXP

Usage: The function EXP is used to generate the numeric number which is created by raising the transcendental number e to the power which is specified.

Syntax: EXP(Power Expression)

Example:

```
SELECT EXP(2)
go
7.38905609893065
```

FLOOR

Usage: The FLOOR function is used to generate the largest integer value whose expression is less than or equal to the numeric expression.

Syntax: FLOOR(Numeric Expression)

Example:

```
SELECT FLOOR(123.431332)
go
123
```

GET_APPCONTEXT

Usage: The function GET_APPCONTEXT is used to get the value of an attribute in a specified context. This value is set using SET_APPCONTEXT function.

Syntax: GET_APPCONTEXT("Context Name", "Attribute Name")

Example:

```
SELECT GET_APPCONTEXT('LOGIN_PROPS', 'USER_NAME')
go
putnamr_app
```

GETDATE

Usage: The function GETDATE is used to retrieve the current system date and time.

Syntax: GETDATE()

Example:
```
SELECT GETDATE()
go
4/9/2004 11:29:28.183 AM
```

HEXTOINT

Usage: The function HEXTOINT is used to convert a hexadecimal string to an integer.

Syntax: HEXTOINT("Hexadecimal String")

Example:
```
SELECT HEXTOINT("0x1001")
go
4097
```

HOST_ID

Usage: The function HOST_ID is used to get the OS process id for your Sybase process.

Syntax: HOST_ID()

Example:
```
SELECT HOST_ID()
go
1864
```

HOST_NAME

Usage: The function HOST_NAME is used to get the OS process name for your Sybase process.

Syntax: HOST_NAME()

Example:

```
SELECT HOST_NAME()
go
hostname
```

INTTOHEX

Usage: The function INTTOHEX is used to convert an integer into a hexadecimal.

Syntax: INTTOHEX(Integer Expression)

Example:

```
SELECT INTTOHEX(4097)
go
00001001
```

ISNULL

Usage: The function ISNULL is used for expression substitution when another expression is NULL {}.

Syntax: ISNULL(Expression, Expression)

Example:

```
SELECT ISNULL(NULL, "ABC")
go
ABC
```

LEFT

Usage: The function LEFT is used to get a specified integer number of characters out of character expression from the left end of the expression.

Syntax: LEFT(Character Expression, Integer Expression)

Example:
```
SELECT LEFT("ABC", 2)
go
AB
```

LEN

Usage: The function LEN is used to get the integer number of characters that at are in a character string.

Syntax: LEN(Character Expression)

Example:
```
SELECT LEN("ABC")
go
3
```

LOG

Usage: The function LOG is used to generate the natural logarithm of a number.

Syntax: LOG(Numeric Expression)

Example:
```
SELECT LOG(1)
go
0
```

LOG10

Usage: The function LOG10 is used to generate the logarithm of a number to the base 10.

Syntax: LOG10(Numeric Expression)

Example:

```
SELECT LOG10(10)
go
----------------------------------------
1
```

LOWER

Usage: The function LOWER is used to convert a character expression to lower case.

Syntax: LOWER(Character Expression)

Example:

```
SELECT LOWER("ABC")
go
----------------------------------------
abc
```

MAX

Usage: The function MAX is used to return the highest column value.

Syntax: MAX(Expression)

Example:

```
SELECT MAX(column_1)
  FROM table
go
----------------------------------------
99.999
```

MIN

Usage: The function MIN is used to return the lowest column value.

Syntax: MIN(Expression)

Example:
```
SELECT MIN(column_1)
  FROM table
go
1.119
```

PATINDEX

Usage: The PATINDEX function is used to get the first ***integer*** occurrence of a patternized string within another string. It is similar to the function LIKE, except LIKE returns the string if it matches a specified pattern.

Syntax: PATINDEX(Search Expression, Character Expression)

Example:
```
DECLARE @STR1 CHAR(10)
DECLARE @PLOC INTEGER

SELECT @STR1 = "FGF"

SELECT @PLOC = PATINDEX( "%G[a-zA-Z]%", @STR1 )

SELECT @PLOC
go
2
```

PI

Usage: The function PI is used to get the constant value 3.1415926535897936.

Syntax: PI()

Example:
```
SELECT PI()
go
-----------------------------------------------
3.1415926535897936
```

POWER

Usage: The function POWER is used to raise a numeric number to a numeric power.

Syntax: POWER(Numeric Expression to Raise, Numeric Expression of Power)

Example:
```
SELECT POWER(3.1, 2.1)
go
-----------------------------------------------
10.8
```

PROC_ROLE

Usage: The function PROC_ROLE is used to determine to determine whether a specified role is active or not. If the function returns 0 the user does not have role. Any other value indicates that the role is active.

Syntax: PROC_ROLE(Role Name)

Example:
```
SELECT PROC_ROLE("sa_role")
go
-----------------------------------------------
1
```

RADIANS

Usage: The function RADIANS is used to convert an angle in degrees to angle in radians.

Syntax: RADIANS(Numeric Expression)

Example:

```
SELECT RADIANS(90.0)
go
1.57
```

RAND

Usage: The function RAND is used to generate a random value between 0 and 1.

Syntax: RAND()

Example:

```
SELECT RAND()
go
0.403345091921904
```

REPLICATE

Usage: The function REPLICATE is used to repeat a string an integer specified number of times.

Syntax: REPLICATE(Character Expression, Integer Expression)

Example:

```
SELECT REPLICATE("A", 5)
go
AAAAA
```

REVERSE

Usage: The function REVERSE is used perform a 180 on a character expression.

Syntax: REVERSE(Character Expression)

Example:
```
SELECT REVERSE("ABC")
go
CBA
```

RM_APPCONTEXT

Usage: The function RM_APPCONTEXT is used to remove a value for a context name and attribute name combination.

Syntax: RM_APPCONTEXT(Context Name, Attribute Name)

Example:
```
SELECT RM_APPCONTEXT("LOGIN_PROPS", "USER_NAME")
go
0
```

RIGHT

Usage: The function RIGHT is used to get a specified integer number of characters out of character expression from the right end of the expression.

Syntax: RIGHT(Character Expression, Integer Expression)

Example:
```
SELECT RIGHT("ABC", 2)
go
BC
```

ROLE_CONTAIN

Usage: The function ROLE_CONTAIN is used to see if a role is contained within another role. The function will return 0 if false and any other value for true.

Syntax: ROLE_CONTAIN(Role Expression, Role Contained in Expression)

Example:
```
SELECT ROLE_CONTAIN("ROLE001", "ROLE002")
go
0
```

ROUND

Usage: The function ROUND is used to mathematically round a numeric to a specific number of integer decimal places.

Syntax: ROUND(Numeric Expression, Integer Precision Expression)

Example:
```
SELECT ROUND(123.123, 2)
go
123.12
```

RTRIM

Usage: The RTRIM function is used trim off trailing blanks from a character expression.

Syntax: RTRIM(Character Expression)

Example:
```
SELECT RTRIM("ABC   ")
go
ABC
```

SET_APPCONTEXT

Usage: The function SET_APPCONTEXT is used to set a value for a context name and attribute name combination.

Syntax: SET_APPCONTEXT(Context Name, Attribute Name, Context.Attribute Value)

Example:
```
SELECT SET_APPCONTEXT("LOGIN_PROPS", "USER_NAME", "putnamr")
go
0
```

SHOW_ROLE

Usage: The function SHOW_ROLE is used to show a login's active roles.

Syntax: SHOW_ROLE()

Example:
```
SELECT SHOW_ROLE()
go
sa_role replication_role
```

SIGN

Usage: The function SIGN is used to get the mathematical factor for numeric value such that numeric + sign*numeric = 0. Returns –1, 0, and +1.

Syntax: SIGN(Numeric Expression)

Example:
```
SELECT SIGN(-123)
go
-1
```

SIN

Usage: The SIN function is used to generate the sine of an angle in radians.

Syntax: SIN(Angle In Radians)

Example:
```
SELECT SIN(PI()/2)
go
1.0
```

SORTKEY

Usage: The SORTKEY function is used to order query results in an ORDER BY clause. It allows for ASE to perform sorts based upon different collation rules. The SORTKEY function takes a character string as a parameter and the collation name or collation id of the collation rule for ASE to follow when performing the sort.

Syntax: ORDER
BY SORTKEY(column, [collation id | name])

The following table lists the collation rules which are applicable.

Description	***Collation ID***	***Collation Name***
Default Unicode multilingual	0	default
Thai dictionary	1	thaidict
CP 850 Alternate no accent	39	altnoacc
CP 850 Alternate lower case first	45	altdict
CP 850 Alternate no case preference	46	altnocsp
CP 850 Scandinavian dictionary	47	scandict
CP 850 Scandinavian no case preference	48	scannocp
Binary sort	50	binary
Latin-1 English, French, German distionary	51	dict
Latin-1 English, French, German no case	52	nocase
Latin-1 English, French, German no case preference	53	nocasep

Description	Collation ID	Collation Name
Latin-1, English, French, German no accent	54	noaccent
Latin-1 Spanish dictionary	55	espdict
Latin-1 Spanish no case	56	espnocs
Latin-1 Spanish no accent	57	espnoac
ISO 8859-5 Russian dictionary	58	rusdict
ISO 8859-5 Cyrillic dictionary	63	cyrdict
ISO 8859-9 Turkish dictionary	72	turdict
Shift-JIS binary order	259	sjisbin

Note: These examples were created using isql and the -Jutf8 flag. For more information about isql refer to using isql in the Sybase reference manuals.

Example:

```
CREATE
 TABLE test_table(
       column01 UNICHAR(10) NOT NULL
)
go

INSERT
  INTO test_table(
       column01
)
SELECT "aab"
go

INSERT
  INTO test_table(
       column01
)
SELECT "aac"
go

SELECT column01
  FROM test_table
 ORDER
    BY SORTKEY(column01, "dict") ASC
go
```

```
aab
aac


SELECT column01
  FROM test_table
 ORDER
    BY SORTKEY(column01, "thaidict") ASC
go
aab
aac
```

SOUNDEX

Usage: The function SOUNDEX is used to generate a four character string representing the way an expression sounds.

Syntax: SOUNDEX(Character Expression)

Example:

```
SELECT SOUNDEX("putnam")
go
P355
```

SPACE

Usage: The function SPACE is used to replicate an integer number of spaces.

Syntax: SPACE

Example:

```
SELECT "AB" + SPACE(5) + "C"
go
AB     C
```

SQUARE

Usage: The function SQUARE is used to raise a numeric value to the power of 2 as a float.

Syntax: SQUARE(Numeric Expression)

Example:
```
SELECT SQUARE(2)
go
4
```

SQRT

Usage: The function SQRT is used raise a numeric value to the power of ½ as a float.

Syntax: SQRT(Numeric Expression)

Example:
```
SELECT SQRT(4)
go
2
```

STR_REPLACE

Usage: The function STR_REPLACE is used to replace all occurrences a character expression with another contained in some character expression.

Syntax: STR_REPLACE(Char Expression, Match Char Expression, Replace Char Expression)

Example:
```
SELECT STR_REPLACE("ABCDEF", "BCD", "EE")
go
AEEEF
```

STUFF

Usage: The function STUFF is used to remove a specified number of characters from a character expression and inserting a new character expression in that location. The location is specified positionally as the number of characters from the left and how many characters to remove. The new character expression is inserted just after the number of characters from the left specified.

Syntax: STUFF(Character Expression, Integer Characters from Left, Integer Characters to Remove, Insertion Char Expression)

Example:

```
SELECT STUFF("ACDE", 2, 2, "G")
go
AGE
```

SUBSTRING

Usage: The function SUBSTRING is used to get a character string from another character string. This is done positionally by specifying the number of characters from the left and how many characters from that position to pull to the right.

Syntax: SUBSTRING(Character Expression, Integer Characters from Left, Integer Character to Pull from Left Position)

Example:

```
SELECT SUBSTRING("ABCDEFG", 1, 2)
go
AB
```

SUM

Usage: The function SUM is used to generate the total of all values in a numeric column.

Syntax: SUM(Numeric COLNAME)

Example:

```
SELECT SUM(column_2)
  FROM table
```

```
go
10000000
```

SUSER_ID

Usage: The function SUSER_ID is used to get your current login id or a specified login name's id.

Syntax: SUSER_ID(<Login Name>)

Example:

```
SELECT SUSER_ID()
go
32
```

SUSER_NAME

Usage: The function SUSER_NAME is used to get your current login name or specified login id's name.

Syntax: SUSER_NAME(<Login ID>)

Example:

```
SELECT SUSER_NAME(32)
go
putnamr
```

TAN

Usage: The TAN function is used to generate the tangent of an angle in radians.

Syntax: TAN(Angle In Radians)

Example:

```
SELECT TAN(PI())
go
0
```

TEMPDB_ID

Usage: The function TEMPDB_ID is used to get the temporary database id your process id is currently assigned, or it used to get the temporary database id of a provided process id.

Syntax: TEMPDB_ID(<ASE Process ID>)

Example:
```
SELECT TEMPDB_ID()
go
2
```

TO_UNICHAR

Usage: The TO_UNICHAR function is the analogue of the CHAR function to get a UNICHAR value of the specified ***integer***.

Syntax: TO_UNICHAR(Integer Expression)

Note: These examples were created using isql and the -Jutf8 flag. For more information about isql refer to using isql in the Sybase reference manuals.

Example:
```
DECLARE @UINT INTEGER

SELECT @UINT = 257

SELECT TO_UNICHAR( @UINT )
go
ā
```

TSEQUAL

Usage: The function TSEQUAL is used to compare to timestamp values as to prevent the update to a record if has been modified since the last timestamp value was stored. The TSEQUAL function should only be used in UPDATE statements. In addition, the WHERE predicate should qualify only one record without the TSEQUAL function.

Syntax: TSEQUAL(timestamp, Saved Timestamp Value)

Example:
```
UPDATE table
   SET column_1 = 5
 WHERE pkid = 20
   AND TSEQUAL(timestamp, 0x0011342300002124)
go
```

UHIGHSURR

Usage: The UHIGHSURR function is used to determine if a UNICODE character string at a specified ***integer*** position is the ***high surrogate half*** of UTF-16 surrogate pair. The function returns a 1 if it is true that the position specified for the UNICODE character string contains the high surrogate half. Otherwise it returns a 0 for false.

Syntax: UHIGHSURR(Unicode Binary, Scan Start Position)

Recall that the range for the ***high surrogate half*** is D800-DBFF.

Note: These examples were created using isql and the -Jutf8 flag. For more information about isql refer to using isql in the Sybase reference manuals.

Example:
```
DECLARE @UNIC BINARY(4)
SELECT @UNIC = 0xd800dc00
SELECT UHIGHSURR( @UNIC, 1 )
go
1
```

ULOWSURR

Usage: The ULOWSURR function is used to determine if a UNICODE character string at a specified ***integer*** position is the ***low surrogate half*** of UTF-16 surrogate pair. The function returns a 1 if it is true that the position specified for the UNICODE character string contains the low surrogate half. Otherwise it returns a 0 for false.

Syntax: ULOWSURR(Unicode Binary, Scan Start Position)

Recall that the range for the ***low surrogate half*** is DC00-DFFF.

Note: These examples were created using isql and the -Jutf8 flag. For more information about isql refer to using isql in the Sybase reference manuals.

Example:

```
DECLARE @UNIC BINARY(4)
SELECT @UNIC = 0xd800dc00
SELECT ULOWSURR( @UNIC, 2 )
go
-----------------------------------------------------------
1
```

UPPER

Usage: The function UPPER is used to convert a character expression to upper case.

Syntax: UPPER(Character Expression)

Example:

```
SELECT UPPER("abc")
go
-----------------------------------------------------------
ABC
```

USCALAR

Usage: The USCALAR function is the analogue of the ASCII function. It is used to get the ***first*** UNICODE scalar from a UNICODE character string. A UNICODE scalar value in ASE is the integer representation of a UNICODE character.

Syntax: USCALAR(Unicode Character)

Note: These examples were created using isql and the -Jutf8 flag. For more information about isql refer to using isql in the Sybase reference manuals.

Example:

```
DECLARE @UCHAR UNICHAR(3)
SELECT @UCHAR = "ABC"
```

```
SELECT USCALAR( @UCHAR )
go
-----------------------------------------------------------------
65
```

USER

Usage: The function USER returns the same information as USER_NAME().

USER_ID

Usage: The function USER_ID is used to get your current user id or a specified user name's id from the current database.

Syntax: USER_ID(<Database User Name>)

Example:

```
SELECT USER_ID()
go
-----------------------------------------------------------------
31
```

U&

Usage: The U& function is used to get a UNICHAR value for the U+***nnnn*** hexadecimal unicode value.

Syntax: U&'***nnnn***'

Note: These examples were created using isql and the -Jutf8 flag. For more information about isql refer to using isql in the Sybase reference manuals.

Example:

```
SELECT U&'\0116'
go
-----------------------------------------------------------------
Ė
```

USER_NAME

Usage: The function USER_NAME is used to get your current user name or a specified user id's name from the current database.

Syntax: USER_NAME(<Database User ID>)

Example:

```
SELECT USER_NAME(31)
go
----------------------------------------------
putnamr
```

YEAR

Usage: The function YEAR is used to get the integer value for the Year out of a date expression.

Syntax: YEAR(Date Expression)

Example:

```
SELECT YEAR("04/05/2004")
go
----------------------------------------------
4
```

Appendix D. Functions

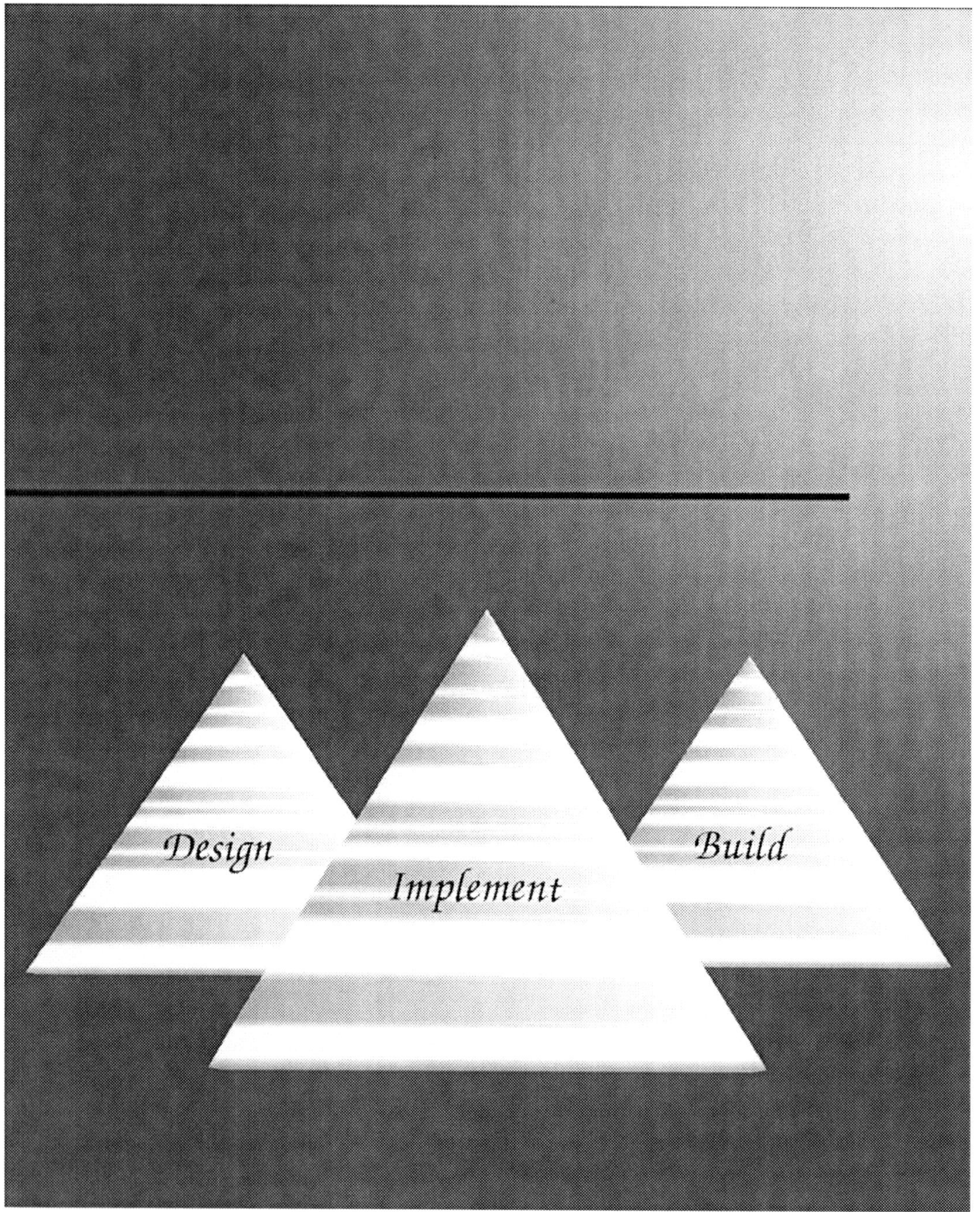
Design
Implement
Build

Appendix E. Global Variables

Sybase ASE provides several useful global variables which we may find very useful to use from time to time.

@@AUTHMECH
A read-only variable that indicates the mechanism used to authenticate the user.

@@BOOTCOUNT
Integer number of times ASE has been rebooted.

@@BOOTTIME
The datetime ASE was last rebooted.

@@CURLOID
The current session's lock owner ID.

@@DATEFIRST
The first day of each week. Where 7 = Sunday.

@@DBTS
The timestamp of the current database.

@@ERROR
The most recent system generated error number.

@@ERRORLOG
The full path to the current ASE errorlog.

@@IDENTITY
Used to get the last value inserted into an identity column.

@@ISOLATION
The current isolation level in effect for your session.

@@LOCK_TIMEOUT
The current lock wait timeout setting in effect.

@@MONITORS_ACTIVE
Reduces the number of messages displayed by **sp_sysmon**.

@@NESTLEVEL
The current nesting level.

@@OPTIONS
The current options in effect.

@@PROCID
The stored procedure/trigger ID of the currently executing procedure.

@@ROWCOUNT
The number of rows affected by the last SQL statement.

@@SERVERNAME
The name of this ASE server.

@@SPID
The current Sybase ASE process ID.

@@SQLSTATUS
The status information from the last CURSOR FETCH statement.

@@TEMPDBID
The temporary database ID your session is assigned.

@@TRANCHAINED
The current transaction chained mode. 0 for unchained and 1 if chained.

@@TRANCOUNT
The current transaction nesting level.

@@TRANSTATE
The state of your transaction after a statement executes.

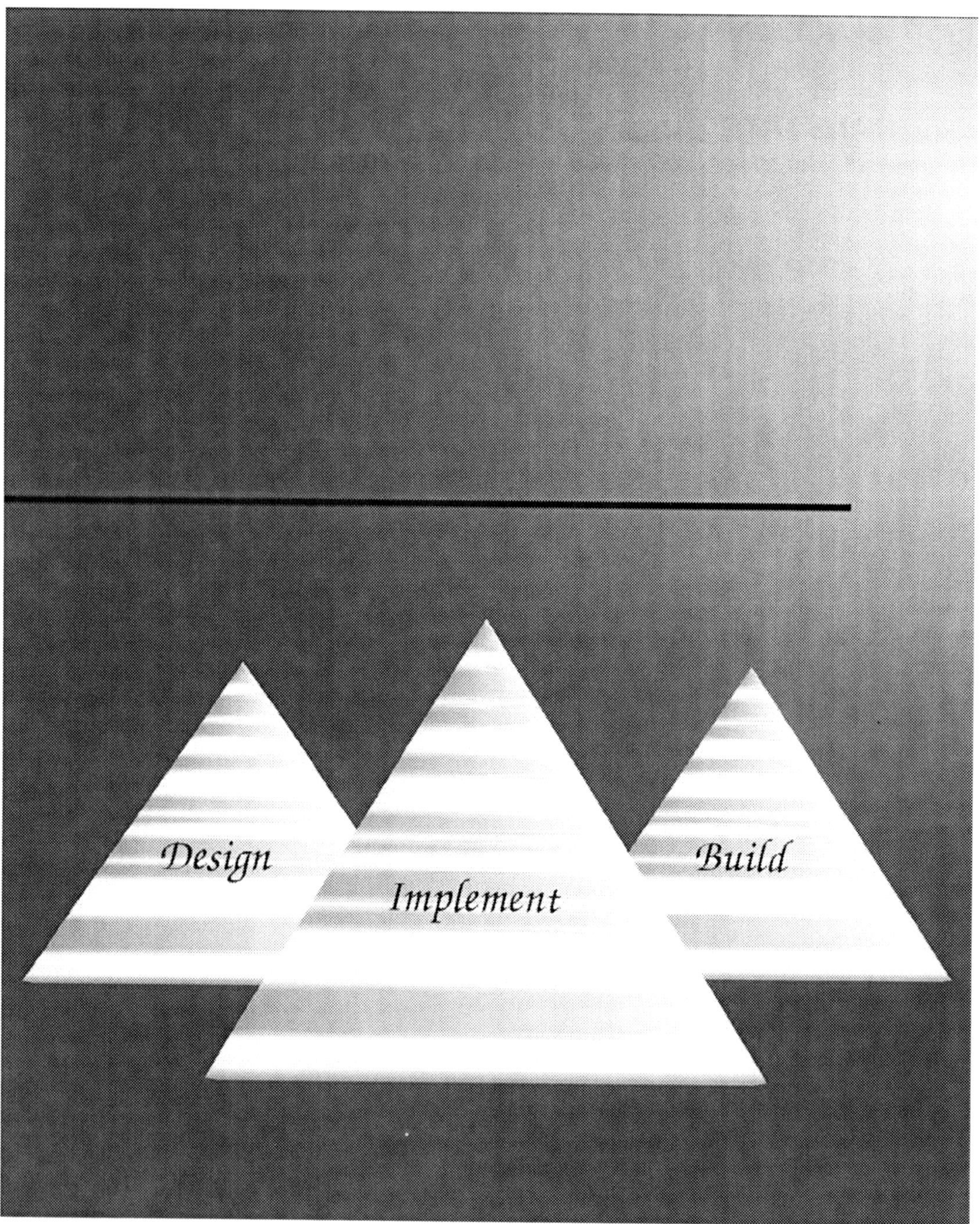
Design
Implement
Build

Appendix F. SET Commands

This is not a complete list of all SET COMMANDs that ASE supports. The ones included here are those which we feel are suitable for developers' needs. Your DBA can help you decide whether you need to run other commands of this nature.

SET ANSINULL <ON | OFF>

Sybase Client Library default is OFF.
ODBC connections default is ON.

To avoid confusion, you should always use IS NULL or IS NOT NULL when checking for nullability. To see what confusion can be caused please review the below table on how Sybase Client Library behaves on certain checks versus how a product which uses ANSI standard “ALWAYS ON” behaves.

ANSINULL State	C1 Value	Comparison	Client Lib	ANSI
OFF	NULL	C1 = NULL	TRUE	UNKNOWN
OFF	***NULL***	***C1 IS NULL***	***TRUE***	***TRUE***
OFF	NULL	C1 != NULL	FALSE	UNKNOWN
OFF	***NULL***	***C1 IS NOT NULL***	***FALSE***	***FALSE***
ON	NULL	C1 = NULL	UNKNOWN	UNKNOWN
ON	***NULL***	***C1 IS NULL***	***TRUE***	***TRUE***
ON	NULL	C1 != NULL	UNKNOWN	UNKNOWN
ON	***NULL***	***C1 IS NOT NULL***	***FALSE***	***FALSE***

When using aggregate functions on columns which can have a NULL value, and SET ANSINULL ON, a warning may be generated stating that a NULL value has been removed from this list. This is ANSI standard behavior and is enabled by default for ODBC connections and disabled by default for Sybase Client Library.

Example:
table

c1	c2
2	1
3	3

4	NULL

```
SET ANSINULL OFF
go

SELECT AVG(c2)
  FROM table
2

SET ANSINULL ON

SELECT AVG(c2)
  FROM table
2
```

Warning - null value eliminated in set function

SET ANSI_PERMISSIONS <ON | OFF>

Default is OFF.

Used to enforce ANSI SQL permissions for delete and update statements.

When OFF, ASE will enforce the following:

UPDATE

- Need to have permission to update the table or permission on the columns which are being updated in the table.

DELETE

- Need to have delete permission on the table.

When ON, ASE will enforce the following:

UPDATE

- Need to have permission to update the table or permission on the columns which are being updated in the table.

- Need to have permission to select from the table or select permission on the columns which are being used in the WHERE predicate.
- Need to have permission to select from the table being updated or be able to select all columns which are being updated.

DELETE

- Need to have delete permission on the table.
- Need to have select permission on the table or select permission on the columns which are being used in the WHERE predicate.

SET ARITHABORT ARITH_OVERFLOW <ON | OFF>

Default value is ON.

When ON, ASE aborts a SQL batch when a arithmetic error occurs. In addition, when a arithmetic error occurs any transaction which is in effect will be aborted as it is part of the SQL batch.

When OFF, ASE will abort the current **statement** in the SQL batch. However, the SQL batch will not be aborted and any transaction which is in effect will still be in effect.

SET ARITHABORT NUMERIC_TRUNCATION <ON | OFF>

Default value is ON.

When ON, ASE will abort any statement which causes a loss of scale to an exact numeric by an implicit datatype conversion. However, the SQL batch will not be aborted and any transaction which is in effect will still be in effect.

When OFF, ASE will go ahead and truncate the results of an exact numeric by an implicit datatype conversion. It will run the query with the truncated results. Nothing will be aborted.

SET ARITHIGNORE ARITH_OVERFLOW <ON | OFF>

Default value is OFF.

When OFF, ASE will display an error message after a division by zero error or a loss of precision has occurred during an implicit datatype conversion.

When ON, ASE will not display an error message after a division by zero error or a loss of precision has occurred during an implicit datatype conversion.

SET CHAINED <ON | OFF>

Default value is OFF.

When OFF and a transaction is not in effect, ASE will wrap all data modification statements with an implicit transaction that will either automatically commit or rollback upon the completion of the command.

When ON and a transaction is not in effect, ASE will begin a transaction before the first data retrieval or data modification statement. The following commands when not in a transaction will automatically start a transaction: delete, fetch, insert, lock table, open, select, and update.

SET CLIENTAPPLNAME <NAME>

Default value is NULL.

A very useful command used to assign a name of up to 30 bytes to the clientapplname column of the sysprocesses table, for your session. This information can be viewed by querying the sysprocesses table.

SET CLIENTHOSTNAME <NAME>

Default value is NULL.

A very useful command used to assign a name of up to 30 bytes to the clienthostname column of the sysprocesses table, for your session. This information can be viewed by querying the sysprocesses table.

SET CLIENTNAME <NAME>

Default value is NULL.

A very useful command used to assign a name of up to 30 bytes to the clientname column of the sysprocesses table, for your session. This information can be viewed by querying the sysprocesses table.

SET CLOSE ON ENDTRAN <ON | OFF>

Default value is OFF.

When OFF, ASE will not automatically close cursors opened during a transaction.

When ON, ASE will automatically close all cursors opened during a transaction.

SET CURSOR ROWS <NUMBER>

Default value is 1.

Specifies the number of rows to return to a Sybase Client Library application for each fetch request.

SET NOCOUNT <ON | OFF>

Default value is OFF.

When OFF, ASE will display how many rows were affected by a statement.

When ON, ASE will not display how many rows were affected by a statement.

SET NOEXEC <ON | OFF>

Default value is OFF.

When OFF, ASE will parse, normalize, optimize, and execute a SQL statement.

When ON, ASE will parse, normalize, and optimize a SQL statement, but will not execute it.

SET PARSEONLY <ON | OFF>

Default value is OFF.

When OFF, ASE will parse, normalize, optimize, and execute a SQL statement.

When ON, ASE will only parse a SQL statement and will not optimize nor execute it.

SET PROXY <LOGIN>

First, in order to be able to proxy to another user account, you must be granted permission. Secondly, changing user accounts is done as a toggle switch. If you change to another account, you must first change back to the original user account before changing to another account.

This is a very powerful command, which allows you to actually become another user in the database. In addition, you will acquire all permissions that that user possesses.

SET ROLE <ROLE | ROLE WITH PASSWD "password "> <ON | OFF>

Used to enable or disable roles which have been granted to you.

SET ROWCOUNT <NUMBER>

Default value is 0, which means it is not in affect.

When non-zero, ASE will stop processing a query after the specified number of rows are affected.

SET SESSION AUTHORIZATION <LOGIN>

ANSI standard method used to changed to a different login account. Identical to SET PROXY.

SET SHOWPLAN <ON | OFF>

Default value is OFF.

When OFF, ASE will not generate a query plan for all submitted SQL.

When ON, ASE will generate the query plan for all submitted SQL.

SET STATISTICS IO <ON | OFF>

Default value is OFF.

When OFF, ASE will not display I/O related statistics.

When ON, ASE will display the following metrics:

- The number of times a table is accessed, aka its scan count.
- The number of logical reads, aka the number of pages accessed in memory.
- The number of physical reads, aka the number of pages accessed off a database device.
- And, the number of buffers which had to be written to disk, aka the total writes.

SET STATISTICS TIME <ON | OFF>

Default value is OFF.

When OFF, ASE will not display the amount of time to parse and compile each command.

When ON, ASE will display the amount of time to parse and compile each command.

SET STRING_RTRUNCATION <ON | OFF>

Default value is OFF.

An error is never raised for an insert or update which truncates only spaces.

When OFF, ASE will not raise a SQLSTATE exception when a insert or update truncates a char, varchar, unichar, or univarchar.

When ON, ASE will raise a SQLSTATE exception when a insert or update truncates a char, varchar, unichar, or univarchar.

SET TEXTSIZE <BYTES>

Default value is 32 kb.

Specifies the how many bytes may be returned by a select statement on an image or text column.

SET TRANSACTION ISOLATION LEVEL <0 | 1 | 2 | 3>

Default value is 1.

Refer to the chapter on isolation levels for more information.

Appendix F. SET Commands

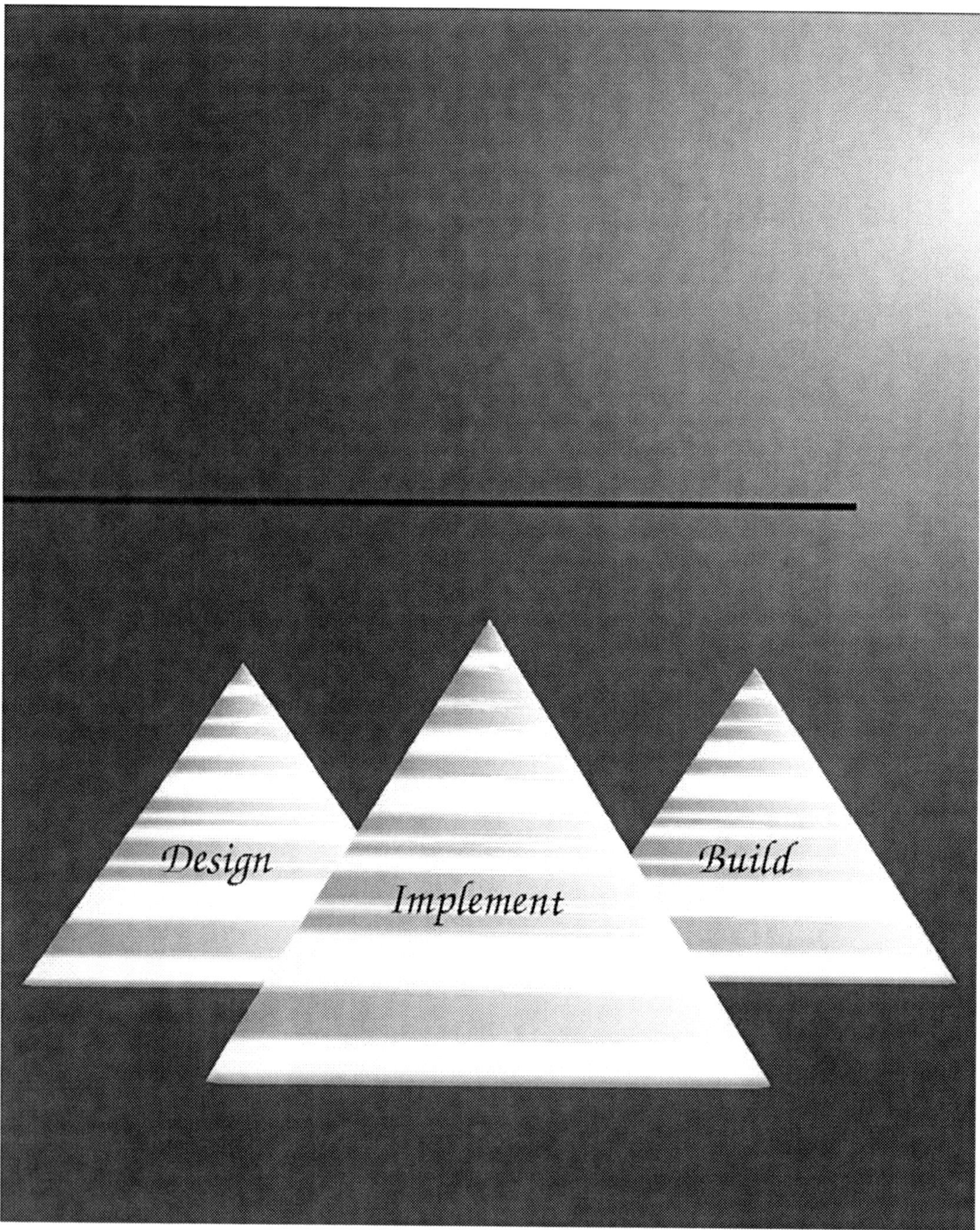
Design
Implement
Build

Appendix G. Catalog Views

The ASE SINF views, System Information views, are very useful for administering the database. Using the views, simple questions such as what permissions are available for a table and what default bindings become very easy. The views are also useful for generating backup information for offline purposes, such as disaster recovery. A schema process has also been developed that plugs into the views to allow for a database schema to be created.

Installation

The SINF must be installed into each database that you wish to use them in. If you will be creating many databases you may find it easier to install the views into the model database. By having the views in model, each database that you create afterwards will automatically get the views. However, keep in mind that by adding objects to model you are increasing its size. I recommend that you allocate an additional 5-10 MB for the model database if you plan create the views there. The benefits that these provide far, far outweigh the fact that you have to install the views into each database.

Package

To create the views you need to install the package sinfvws.sql. This is accomplished by following the below steps.

- Change to the \install\ directory on the cd.
- Locate the file sinfvws.sql
- Install the package by using the isql utility:

```
isql –U<sa> -S<server> -P<pass> -D<db> -n –e –i<sinfvws.sql> -o<output file>
```

- You should review the output file that you named above for errors. If any errors occurred, you will need to correct so that a complete/clean installation is done.

SINF_ALIASES

Definition: Provides information pertaining to aliases created in a database.

Scope: Local Database

Columns:

ALIASING_LOGIN
The login who is aliasing.

ALIASED_LOGIN
The login who is being aliased.

USER_NM
The user name of the login who is being aliased in the database.

SINF_BLOCKS

Definition: Provides information pertaining to blocks on a server.

Scope: Any Database

Columns:

BLKD_LOGIN
The login who is being blocked.

BLKD_SPID
The Sybase process ID of the login which is blocked.

BLKD_CMD
The command being run by BLKD_SPID which is currently blocked.

BLKD_CMD_DBNAME
The database that BLKD_CMD is being executed from.

BLKD_CMD_OBJNAME
The name of the procedure that is being executed by BLKD_SPID.

BLKD_CMD_LINE
The line number in the batch of SQL or procedure that is being executed by BLKD_SPID.

BY_LOGIN
The login which is holding locks causing BLKD_SPID to be blocked.

BY_SPID
The Sybase process ID of the login which is holding locks causing BLKD_SPID to be blocked.

BY_CMD
The command being run by BY_SPID which is causing a block.

BY_CMD_DBNAME
The database that BY_CMD is being executed from.

BY_CMD_OBJNAME
The name of the procedure that is being executed by BY_SPID.

LOCK_IN_DBNAME
The database name where the lock, block is occurring.

LOCK_ON_OBJNAME
The name of object where the lock, block is occurring.

LOCKTYPE
The type of lock causing the block.

CPU_TIME
The cumulative cpu time of the command which is being run by BY_SPID.

PHYS_IO
The cumulative physical IO of the command which is being run by BY_SPID.

SS_BLKD
The number of seconds which BLKD_SPID has been blocked by BY_SPID on LOCK_ON_OBJNAME, LOCKTYPE.

NUMLOCKS
The number of locks which are being held by BY_SPID on LOCK_ON_OBJNAME, LOCKTYPE.

SINF_BOUNDDEFAULT

Definition: Provides information pertaining to defaults that are bound to columns in the database.

Scope: Local Database

Columns:

OWNER
The owner of the table.column to which the default is bound.

OBJNAME
The table to which the column that has the default is bound is part of.

COLNAME
The column which has the default bound.

DEFOWNER
The owner of the bound default.

DEFNAME
The name of the bound default.

SINF_CACHEPOOLS

Definition: Provides information pertaining to cachepools that are part of the ASE data caches.

Scope: Any Database

Columns:

CACHE_NAME
The cache name that the cache pool belongs to.

POOL_NAME
The name and size of the cache pool.

CONFIG_VALUE
The configured size of the cache pool.

RUN_VALUE
The current size of the cache pool.

WASH_SIZE
The size of the wash area in the cache pool.

ASYNC_PF_PCT
The percent of current buffers that may used for asynchronous prefetch requests.

SINF_CACHES

Definition: Provides information pertaining to the caches that are part of ASE.

Scope: Any Database

Columns:

CACHE_NAME
The name of the configured cache.

STATUS
The current state of the cache.

TYPE
The type of cache.

CFG_REPLACE
The configured buffer replacment strategy for the cache.

RUN_REPLACE
The current buffer replacement strategy for the cache.

CFG_VALUE
The configured size of the cache.

RUN_VALUE
The current size of the cache.

SINF_CHKCONSTRAINTS

Definition: Provides information for table and column level check constraints.

Scope: Local Database

Columns:

OWNER
The owner of the check constraint.

OBJNAME
The name of the check constraint.

LVL
Defined level for the check constraint. Table or Column.

TBLCOLID
The colid of the TBLCOLNAME.

TBLCOLNAME
The column name of the TBLOWNER.TBLOBJNAME for this check constraint.

TBLOWNER
The owner of TBLOBJNAME.

TBLOBJNAME
The name of the table that this check constraint is for.

SINF_COLUMNDEFAULT

Definition: Provides information pertaining to defaults created as part of the table definition.

Scope: Local Database

Columns:

OWNER
The owner of the table to which the column belongs.

DEFNAME
The name of the default.

OBJNAME
The name of the table to which the default has been created on.

DEFID
System ID of the default.

COLNAME
The column name for which the default has been created.

TEXT
Definition of the default.

SINF_COLUMNS_1

Definition: Provides information pertaining to columns for views and tables. Resolves the datatype as a user defined datatype.

Scope: Local Database

Columns:

OWNER
The owner of the column.

OBJNAME
The object to which the column belongs.

COLNAME
The name of the column.

DATATYPE
The datatype of the column.

TYPE
The type contained in systypes for the object.

LENGTH
The length or amount of bytes occupied by the column.

PREC
The number of digits in a numeric or decimal.

SCALE
The number of digits to the right of the decimal or the precision of the fractional part of a numeric or decimal.

COLID
The order of the columns for the table or view.

STATUS
The status from syscolumns for the column.

COLTYPE
The type of the object the column belongs to.

SINF_COLUMNS_2

Definition: Provides more detailed information than SINF_COLUMNS_1. In particular, the datatype column is complete and a new column named NULLABILITY is present. Resolves the datatype as a user defined datatype.

Scope: Local Database

Columns:

OWNER
The owner of the column.

OBJNAME
The object to which the column belongs.

COLNAME
The name of the column.

DATATYPE
The datatype of the column.

TYPE
The type contained in systypes for the object.

LENGTH
The length or amount of bytes occupied by the column.

PREC
The number of digits in a numeric or decimal.

SCALE
The number of digits to the right of the decimal or the precision of the fractional part of a numeric or decimal.

COLID
The creation order of the columns for the table or view.

STATUS
The status from syscolumns for the column.

NULLABILITY
States whether or not the column allows nulls.

COLTYPE
The type of the object the column belongs to.

SINF_COMMENTS

Definition: Used to search syscomments for character strings less than 255 bytes.

Scope: Any Database

Columns:

OWNER
The owner of the object.

OBJNAME
The name of the object.

OBJTYPE
The type of object. For example, P = Procedure, D = Default.

OBJID
The Sybase object id in sysobjects for this OWNER.OBJECT.

NOWRAP
The text column from syscomments.

WRAP
Upper half of the text column for a colid and the Lower half of the text column for the next colid.

NOWRAP_HIGHCOLID
The colid for this row.

NOWRAP_LOWCOLID
The colid2 for this row.

WRAP_HIGHCOLID
The next colid for this row.

WRAP_LOWCOLID
The next colid2 for this row.

SINF_DATABASES

Definition: Provides information about databases.

Scope: Any Database

Columns:

DBNAME
The database name.

DBID
The SYSTEM ID of the database name.

SPID
The spid that has the oldest open transaction.

OWNER
The login which created the database.

CREATE_DATE
The date when the database was created.

DUMP_TRAN_DATE
The date of the last successful dump transaction.

OLDEST_TRAN_DATE
The begin time of the oldest open transaction.

OLDEST_TRAN_NAME
The transaction name of the oldest open transaction.

OLDEST_TRAN_OWNER
The owner or login that has the oldest open transaction.

SINF_DATATYPES_1

Definition: Provides information pertaining to user defined and system datatypes.

Scope: Local Database

Columns:

OWNER
The owner of the user defined datatype.

OBJNAME
The name of the user defined datatype.

LENGTH
The length of the system datatype aliased.

PREC
The precision of the system datatype aliased.

SCALE
The scale of the system datatype aliased.

VARIABILITY
A bit indicating whether column is variable length or not. 0=NO VARIATION, 1=VARIABLE

NULLABILITY
A bit indicating whether nulls allowed or not. 0=NOT NULL, 1=NULL

IDENT
A bit indicating whether this is an identity column or not. 1=identity

SYSNAME
The name of the system datatype aliased.

DEFOWNER
The owner of the procedure used to return a default.

DEFOBJNAME
The name of the procedure used to return a default.

CHKOWNER
The owner of the procedure used to check column.

CHKOBJNAME
The name of the procedure used to check column.

UID
The id of the user who created this datatype.

USERTYPE
Internal type associated with a datatype.

TYPE
The physical storage datatype.

HIERARCHY
The datatype precedence when performing mixed mode arithmetic.

PRINTFMT
Currently defined as reserved.

XTYPEID
The internal class id.

XDBID
-1 indicates a class is installed in the system database and -2 indicates the current database.

ACCESSRULE
The OBJID of the access rule in sysobjects and sysprocedures.

SINF_DATATYPES_2

Definition: Provides information pertaining to user defined and system datatypes.

Scope: Local Database

Columns:

OWNER
The owner of the user defined datatype.

OBJNAME
The name of the user defined datatype.

LENGTH
The length of the system datatype aliased.

PREC
The precision of the system datatype aliased.

SCALE
The scale of the system datatype aliased.

VARIABILITY
A bit indicating whether column is variable length or not. 0=NO VARIATION, 1=VARIABLE

NULLABILITY
A bit indicating whether nulls allowed or not. 0=NOT NULL, 1=NULL

IDENT
A bit indicating whether this is an identity column or not. 1=identity

SYSNAME
The name of the system datatype aliased.

DEFOWNER
The owner of the procedure used to return a default.

DEFOBJNAME
The name of the procedure used to return a default.

CHKOWNER
The owner of the procedure used to check column.

CHKOBJNAME
The name of the procedure used to check column.

DATATYPE
The decoded system datatype for user defined datatype.

UID
The id of the user who created this datatype.

USERTYPE
Internal type associated with a datatype.

TYPE
The physical storage datatype.

HIERARCHY
The datatype precedence when performing mixed mode arithmetic.

PRINTFMT
Currently defined as reserved.

XTYPEID
The internal class id.

XDBID
-1 indicates a class is installed in the system database and -2 indicates the current database.

ACCESSRULE
The OBJID of the access rule in sysobjects and sysprocedures.

DATATYPE
The exact datatype created for used defined datatypes.

SINF_DBOPTIONS

Definition: Provides information pertaining to set database options.

Scope: Any Database

Columns:

DBID
The SYSTEM ID of the database.

DBNAME
The database name.

DBOPTION
Any set database option.

SINF_DEFAULTS

Definition: Provides information about defaults.

Scope: Local Database

Columns:

OBJNAME
The name of the default in the database.

OWNER
The owner of the default.

TEXT
The creation text for the default.

COLID
Specifies the order of the text fields in case of long text.

SINF_DEVICES

Definition: Provides information pertaining to devices defined in ASE.

Scope: Any Database

Columns:

SYBNAME
The ASE name for the device.

PHYNAME
The name of the external device.

VDEVNO
The device number used when created.

ALLOC_PAGES
The number of ASE pages allocated for storage on the SYBNAME device.

USED_PAGES
The number of ASE pages allocated to databases for the SYBNAME device.

FREE_PAGES
The number of ASE pages free for allocation to a database for the SYBNAME device.

STATUS
The sysdevices internal status value.

CNTRLTYPE
The controller type for the SYBNAME device.

MIRRORNAME
The name of the mirror device for this SYBNAME device.

DEVICE_TYPE
The type of this SYBNAME device.

DEFAULT_DISK
Whether or not this is a default SYBNAME device for database creations.

LOW
The first virtual ASE page number for a SYBNAME device.

HIGH
The last virtual ASE page number for a SYBNAME device.

SINF_DEVICES_DB_UNUSED

Definition: Provides information pertaining to devices not used for a database.

Scope: Any Database

Columns:

SYBNAME
The ASE name for the device.

PHYNAME
The name of the external device.

VDEVNO
The device number used when created.

ALLOC_PAGES
The number of ASE pages allocated for storage on the SYBNAME device.

USED_PAGES
The number of ASE pages allocated to databases for the SYBNAME device.

FREE_PAGES
The number of ASE pages free for allocation to a database for the SYBNAME device.

STATUS
The sysdevices internal status value.

CNTRLTYPE
The controller type for the SYBNAME device.

MIRRORNAME
The name of the mirror device for this SYBNAME device.

DEVICE_TYPE
The type of this SYBNAME device.

DEFAULT_DISK
Whether or not this is a default SYBNAME device for database creations.

LOW
The first virtual ASE page number for a SYBNAME device.

HIGH
The last virtual ASE page number for a SYBNAME device.

DBNAME
The name of a database ***NOT*** using the SYBNAME device.

SINF_DEVICES_DB_USED

Definition: Provides information pertaining to devices used for a database.

Scope: Any Database

Columns:

SYBNAME
The ASE name for the device.

PHYNAME
The name of the external device.

VDEVNO
The device number used when created.

ALLOC_PAGES
The number of ASE pages allocated for storage on the SYBNAME device.

USED_PAGES
The number of ASE pages allocated to databases for the SYBNAME device.

FREE_PAGES
The number of ASE pages free for allocation to a database for the SYBNAME device.

STATUS
The sysdevices internal status value.

CNTRLTYPE
The controller type for the SYBNAME device.

MIRRORNAME
The name of the mirror device for this SYBNAME device.

DEVICE_TYPE
The type of this SYBNAME device.

DEFAULT_DISK
Whether or not this is a default SYBNAME device for database creations.

LOW
The first virtual ASE page number for a SYBNAME device.

HIGH
The last virtual ASE page number for a SYBNAME device.

DBNAME
The name of a database using the SYBNAME device.

SINF_FKCONSTRAINTS

Definition: Provides information pertaining to foreign key constraints.

Scope: Local Database

Columns:

OWNER
The owner of the column.

OBJNAME
The name of the object the constraint is on.

CONSTRNAME
The name of the constraint created on the OWNER.FK_DB.FK_TB table.

CONSTRID
The id of the constraint created on the OWNER.FK_DB.FK_TB table.

OBJID
The id of the object the constraint is on.

NUMKEYS
The number of key columns for the foreign key.

FK_DB
The database name the foreign key resides.

FK_TB
The name of the table the foreign key resides on.

PK_DB
The database name, where the primary key that this constraint references, resides.

PK_TB
Refers to the table being referenced by this foreign key constraint.

FKEY_1...FKEY_16
The keys in sequence defined for the foreign key constraint.

PKEY_1...PKEY_16
The keys in sequence being referenced as part of this foreign key constraint.

SINF_FKCONSTRAINTS_NO_INDEXES

Definition: Provides information pertaining to foreign key constraints without fully supporting indexes.

Scope: Local Database

Columns:

OWNER
The owner of the column.

OBJNAME
The name of the object the constraint is on.

CONSTRNAME
The name of the constraint created on the OWNER.FK_DB.FK_TB table.

CONSTRID
The id of the constraint created on the OWNER.FK_DB.FK_TB table.

OBJID
The id of the object the constraint is on.

NUMKEYS
The number of key columns for the foreign key.

FK_DB
The database name the foreign key resides.

FK_TB
The name of the table the foreign key resides on.

PK_DB
The database name, where the primary key that this constraint references, resides.

PK_TB
Refers to the table being referenced by this foreign key constraint.

FKEY_1...FKEY_16
The keys in sequence defined for the foreign key constraint.

PKEY_1...PKEY_16
The keys in sequence being referenced as part of this foreign key constraint.

SINF_GROUPS

Definition: Provides information pertaining to groups.

Scope: Local Database

Columns:

GRP_NM
The name of the group in the database.

SINF_GROUP_PERMS

Definition: Provides information pertaining to non-columnar permissions granted to groups.

Scope: Local Database

Columns:

GRP_NM
The name of the group.

OWNER
The owner of OBJNAME.

OBJNAME
The object name which has PERM_NM permission granted to it for GRP_NM.

PERM_NM
The name of the granted permission on OWNER.OBJNAME to GRP_NM.

TYPE
Defines the type of permission for the object. This value may be GRANT or GRANT WITH GRANT OPTION.

SINF_GROUP_COL_PERMS_1

Definition: Provides information pertaining to columnar permissions granted to groups.

Scope: Local Database

Columns:

GRP_NM
The name of the group.

OWNER
The owner of OBJNAME.

OBJNAME
The object name which has PERM_NM permission granted to it for GRP_NM.

PERM_NM
The name of the granted permission on OWNER.OBJNAME to GRP_NM.

COLUMNS
Contains a bitmap of the columns from syscolumns that have permissions granted.

TYPE
Defines the type of permission for the object. This value may be GRANT or GRANT WITH GRANT OPTION.

SINF_GROUP_COL_PERMS_2

Definition: Provides information pertaining to columnar permissions granted to groups.

Scope: Local Database

Columns:

GRP_NM
The name of the group.

OWNER
The owner of OBJNAME.

OBJNAME
The object name which has PERM_NM permission granted to it for GRP_NM.

PERM_NM
The name of the granted permission on OWNER.OBJNAME to GRP_NM.

COLUMNS
Contains a bitmap of the columns from syscolumns that have permissions granted.

TYPE
Defines the type of permission for the object. This value may be GRANT or GRANT WITH GRANT OPTION.

COLUMN
The column which has permissions granted.

SINF_INDEXES

Definition: Provides information pertaining to indexes in a database.

Scope: Local Database

Columns:

OWNER
The owner of the index.

OBJNAME
The table name that the index is storing keys for.

IDXNAME
The name of the index.

INDID
The SYSTEM ID of the index.

ROW_COUNT
The estimated number of rows the object occupies.

MIN_LENGTH
The minimum number of bytes one row occupies.

MAX_LENGTH
The maximum number of bytes that one row occupies.

AVG_LENGTH
The average of MIN_LENGTH and MAX_LENGTH.

STATUS
Taken from status column in sysindexes.

STATUS2
Taken from status2 column in sysindexes

SEGNAME
The segment that the index resides on.

INDEX_PAGES
The number of pages the object allocation is currently across.

MAXROWSPERPAGE
The maximum number of rows to store per page.

RES_PAGE_GAP
After how many pages a page should be left empty for growth.

EXP_ROWSIZE
Specifies the expected number of bytes for a row.

FILL_FACTOR
How much % to fill each page.

IDX_UNIQUE
Specifies whether or not this index is unique.

IDXTYPE
Whether the index is CLUSTERED or NONCLUSTERED.

KEY_1...KEY_20
Displays the index keys in sequence for the index.

KEYO_1...KEYO_20
Shows the ordering the index key was created for. Either ASC or DESC.

CRDATE
The creation date of this index.

SINF_INDEXES_SEG_SPACE

Definition: Provides information pertaining to segment usage for all indexes and text and image data.

Scope: Local Database

Columns:

OWNER
The owner of the index.

OBJNAME
The table name that the index is storing keys for.

IDXNAME
The name of the index.

ROW_COUNT
The estimated record count.

INDEX_PAGES
The amount of space this object occupies.

SEGNAME
The segment which has been defined for future growth of this object.

TOT_SIZE_PAGES
The total number of pages which SEGNAME has the ability to use.

TOT_FREE_PAGES
The total number of pages which are free for SEGNAME and can be used for growth.

SINF_INDEX_CACHE

Definition: Provides information pertaining to cache bindings for indexes in a database.

Scope: Local Database

Columns:

CACHE_NAME
The name of the cache to which the object is bound.

OWNER
The owner of the index.

OBJNAME
The table to which the index belongs.

IDXNAME
The name of the index.

SINF_LOCKS

Definition: Provides information about locks currently be held on the ASE server.

Scope: Data Server

Columns:

LOGIN
The login holding these locks.

SPID
The Sybase process ID of the login holding these locks.

CMD
The command being run by SPID.

CMD_DBNAME
The database that CMD is being executed from.

CMD_OBJNAME
The name of the procedure that is being executed by SPID.

CMD_LINE
The line number in the batch of SQL or procedure that is being executed by SPID.

LOCK_IN_DBNAME
The database name where the lock exists.

LOCK_ON_OBJNAME
The name of object where the lock exists.

LOCKTYPE
The type of lock.

CPU_TIME
The cumulative cpu time of the command which is being run by SPID.

PHYS_IO
The cumulative physical io of the command which is being run by SPID.

NUMLOCKS
The number of locks which are being held by SPID on LOCK_ON_OBJNAME, LOCKTYPE.

SINF_LOGINS

Definition: Provides information about logins on a server.

Scope: Data Server

Columns:

NAME
The login name for the server.

SUID
The System ID for the login name in the server.

STATUS
The syslogins status.

ACCDATE
The last time TOTCPU and TOTIO were cleared.

TOTCPU
Cpu time accumulated for the login.

TOTIO
The I/O accumulated by the login.

SPACELIMIT
Defined as reserved.

TIMELIMIT
Defined as reserved.

RESULTLIMIT
Defined as reserved.

DBNAME
The default database for the login.

PASSWORD
Encrypted password for the login.

LANGUAGE
The user's default language.

PWDATE
The last time the password was changed.

AUDFLAGS
The user's audit setting.

FULLNAME
The fullname of the login.

SRVNAME
The name of the server a pass through connection must be established if the AUTOCONNECT flag is active.

TRIGNAME
Displays the name of the Login Trigger or Stored Procedure for this login. This procedure should be located in the logins default database DBNAME.

SINF_LOGINS_ROLES

Definition: Provides information about role to login mappings on a server.

Scope: Data Server

Columns:

ROLE_NM
The name of a role.

SRID
The server wide role id.

ROLE_PASSWORD
The encrypted password for the role.

LOGIN_NM
The login name.

SUID
The System ID for the login name in the server.

STATUS
Currently defined as unused.

DEFAULT_ROLE
Whether or not this is a default role.

SINF_OBJECTS

Definition: Provides ASE object information.

Scope: Local Database

Columns:

OWNER
The owner of the object.

OBJNAME
The name of the object.

OBJTYPE
The type of object.

USERSTAT
Application-dependent type information.

INDEXDEL
Index delete count.

SYSSTAT
The sysobjects internal status column.

SYSSTAT2
The sysobjects internal status2 column.

DELTRIG
Table ID or Stored procedure ID for a delete trigger.

INSTRIG
Table ID or Stored procedure ID for a insert trigger.

UPDTRIG
Table ID or Stored procedure ID for a update trigger.

SELTRIG
Currently defined as reserved.

CKFIRST
The id of the first check constraint on OBJNAME.

CACHE
Currently defined as reserved.

AUDFLAGS
Mapping the current OBJNAME audit settings.

OBJSPARE
Defined as spare.

VERSIONTS
No definition.

CRDATE
The creation date of OBJNAME.

EXPDATE
Currently defined as reserved.

READ_ONLY
Whether or not OBJNAME is read only.

RI_CONSTRAINT
Whether or not OBJNAME has referential integrity constraint.

FK_CONSTRAINT
Whether or not OBJNAME is a foreign key constraint.

CK_CONSTRAINTS
Whether or not OBJNAME is has check constraints.

SP_CHAINED_MODE
Whether or not OBJNAME is using chained mode.

SP_ANY_MODE
Whether or not OBJNAME is using any mode.

HAS_IDENT
Whether or not OBJNAME has an identity.

NO_VAR_LGTH_COLS
Whether or not OBJNAME has ***NO*** varying length columns.

REMOTE_TBL
Whether or not OBJNAME is a remote table.

PROXY_TBL
Whether or not OBJNAME is a proxy table.

ALLPAGES_TBL
Whether or not OBJNAME is allpages locked.

DATAPAGES_TBL
Whether or not OBJNAME is datapages locked.

DATAROWS_TBL
Whether or not OBJNAME is datarows locked.

PRE_119_TBL
Whether or not OBJNAME has pre-ASE 119 schema.

CLUSTERED_TBL
Whether or not OBJNAME has a clustered index.

EMBD_SQL_PROC
Whether or not OBJNAME is an embedded SQL procedure.

SQLJ_SP
Whether or not OBJNAME is a SQLJ procedure.

ACCESS_RULE
Whether or not OBJNAME has an access rule.

OR_ACCESS_RULE
Whether or not OBJNAME has an or access rule.

SINF_PARTITIONS

Definition: Provides partition information for tables.

Scope: Local Database

Columns:

OWNER
The owner of the table partitioned.

OBJNAME
The table that is partitioned.

PARTITIONID
The ID of the partition.

FIRSTPAGE
The first page of the table in the partition.

CONTROLPAGE
Page number of the control page.

NUM_PAGES
The number of pages in each partition for this object.

SINF_PKCONSTRAINTS

Definition: Provides information pertaining to primary key constraints.

Scope: Local Database

Columns:

OWNER
The owner of table.

OBJNAME
The name of the table.

IDXNAME
The name of the pkconstraint.

INDID
The INDID of the pkconstraint.

STATUS
Status bitmap from sysindexes.

STATUS2
Status bitmap from sysindexes.

SEGNAME
The segment the primary key constraint resides.

KEY_1...KEY_20
The keys that are part of the primary key constraint in order.

KEYO_1...KEYO_20
Contains the ordering the key was created for.

IDXTYPE
The type of index nonclustered or clustered.

ALLOW_DUP_ROWS
Whether or not duplicate rows are allowed.

MAXROWSPERPAGE
The configured max rows per page for the index.

EXPROWSIZE
The expected row size for the index.

FILL_FACTOR
The fill factor configured for the index.

RES_PAGE_GAP
The reserve page gap configured for the index.

STATUS
The status of the command which is being executed.

PHYS_IO
The cumulative amount of physical io for a command.

CPU_TIME
The cumulative amount of CPU time for a command.

MEMUSAGE
The current amount of memory being used by SPID.

BY_SPID
The BY_SPID is the SPID which is blocking this SPID.

BLK_XLOID
Mapped to block_xloid in sysprocesses.

BLKD_SS
The number of seconds this SPID has been blocked.

TRAN_NAME
The name of the transaction being used by SPID.

SYS_ID
Mapped to sys_id in sysprocesses.

SES_ID
Mapped to ses_id in sysprocesses.

SINF_QPLANS

Definition: Gives Query Plans for all Sybase processes which are holding locks.

Scope: ASE Server

Columns:

SPID
The Query plan for this Sybase process.

LOGIN
The Query plan for this login name.

DBNAME
The database that CMD is being executed from.

OBJNAME
The name of the procedure that is being executed.

CMD
The command being run.

CMD_LINE
The line number in the batch of SQL or procedure that is being executed.

CPU_TIME
The cumulative cpu time of the command which is being executed.

PHYS_IO
The cumulative physical io of the command which is being executed.

SINF_QPLANS_BLOCKS

Definition: Gives Query Plans for all Sybase processes which are holding locks and are causing blocking, but are not blocked themselves.

Scope: ASE Server

Columns:

SPID
The Query plan for this Sybase process.

LOGIN
The Query plan for this login name.

DBNAME
The database that CMD is being executed from.

OBJNAME
The name of the procedure that is being executed.

CMD
The command being run.

CMD_LINE
The line number in the batch of SQL or procedure that is being executed.

CPU_TIME
The cumulative cpu time of the command which is being executed.

PHYS_IO
The cumulative physical io of the command which is being executed.

SINF_QPLANS_MAX_CPU

Definition: Gives Query Plans for all Sybase processes which have the greatest amount of cpu time accumulated.

Scope: ASE Server

Columns:

SPID
The Query plan for this Sybase process.

LOGIN
The Query plan for this login name.

DBNAME
The database that CMD is being executed from.

OBJNAME
The name of the procedure that is being executed.

CMD
The command being run.

CMD_LINE
The line number in the batch of SQL or procedure that is being executed.

CPU_TIME
The cumulative cpu time of the command which is being executed.

PHYS_IO
The cumulative physical io of the command which is being executed.

SINF_QPLANS_MAX_PHYS_IO

Definition: Gives Query Plans for all Sybase processes which have the greatest amount of physical io accumulated.

Scope: ASE Server

Columns:

SPID
The Query plan for this Sybase process.

LOGIN
The Query plan for this login name.

DBNAME
The database that CMD is being executed from.

OBJNAME
The name of the procedure that is being executed.

CMD
The command being run.

CMD_LINE
The line number in the batch of SQL or procedure that is being executed.

CPU_TIME
The cumulative cpu time of the command which is being executed.

PHYS_IO
The cumulative physical io of the command which is being executed.

SINF_REP_AGENT_CFGS

Definition: Provides information pertaining to replication agent configuration.

Scope: Local Database

Columns:

DBNAME
The current replication agent database.

CFG_OPTION
The name of the replication agent configuration option.

CFG_VALUE
The configured value for a replication agent configuration option.

SINF_REP_LOG_STATUS

Definition: Provides information pertaining to a replication agents truncation point.

Scope: Local Database

Columns:

DBNAME
The database name for the replication agent.

TOTAL_SIZE_PAGES
The total number of log pages.

USED_LOG_PAGES
The number of log pages which are being used.

FREE_LOG_PAGES
The number of log pages which are free.

VIRTUAL_FIRST_LOG_PAGE
The virtual first log page used for calculations.

VIRTUAL_LAST_LOG_PAGE
The virtual last log page used for calculations.

VIRTUAL_TRUNC_PAGE
The virtual primary truncation page.

VIRTUAL_TRUNC_REP_PAGE
The virtual secondary truncation page.

FIRST_LOG_PAGE
The actual first log page.

UNSCANNED_PAGES
The number pages behind the primary truncation is the secondary truncation point.

TRUNC_LOG_PAGE
The secondary truncation log page.

SINF_REP_LOG_STATUS_1

Definition: Provides information pertaining to a replication agents truncation point.

Scope: Local Database

Columns:

DBNAME
The database name for the replication agent.

TOTAL_SIZE_PAGES
The total number of log pages.

USED_LOG_PAGES
The number of log pages which are being used.

FREE_LOG_PAGES
The number of log pages which are free.

VIRTUAL_FIRST_LOG_PAGE
The virtual first log page used for calculations.

VIRTUAL_LAST_LOG_PAGE
The virtual last log page used for calculations.

VIRTUAL_TRUNC_PAGE
The virtual primary truncation page.

VIRTUAL_TRUNC_REP_PAGE
The virtual secondary truncation page.

FIRST_LOG_PAGE
The actual first log page.

TRUNC_LOG_PAGE
The secondary truncation log page.

SINF_REP_PROCS

Definition: Provides information pertaining to stored procedures that are set to replicate.

Scope: Local Database

Columns:

OWNER
The owner of the configured OBJNAME to replicate.

OBJNAME
The stored procedure configured replicate.

SINF_REP_TABLES

Definition: Provides information pertaining to tables that are set to replicate.

Scope: Local Database

Columns:

OWNER
The owner of the configured OBJNAME to replicate.

OBJNAME
The table configured replicate.

SINF_ROLES

Definition: Provides information pertaining to roles in the database.

Scope: Local Database

Columns:

ROLE_NM
The name of the role in the database.

SINF_ROLE_PERMS

Definition: Provides information pertaining to non-columnar permissions granted to roles in the database.

Scope: Local Database

Columns:

ROLE_NM
The name of the role in the database.

OWNER
The owner of the object which the permission for the role is granted.

OBJNAME
The object which the permission for the role is granted.

PERM_NM
The permission granted on OWNER.OBJNAME to ROLE_NM.

TYPE
Defines the type of permission for the object. This value may be GRANT or GRANT WITH GRANT OPTION.

SINF_ROLE_COL_PERMS_1

Definition: Provides information pertaining to columnar permissions granted to roles.

Scope: Local Database

Columns:

ROLE_NM
The name of the role.

OWNER
The owner of OBJNAME.

OBJNAME
The object name which has PERM_NM permission granted to it for ROLE_NM.

PERM_NM
The name of the granted permission on OWNER.OBJNAME to ROLE_NM.

COLUMNS
Contains a bitmap of the columns from syscolumns that have permissions granted.

TYPE
Defines the type of permission for the object. This value may be GRANT or GRANT WITH GRANT OPTION.

SINF_ROLE_COL_PERMS_2

Definition: Provides information pertaining to columnar permissions granted to roles.

Scope: Local Database

Columns:

ROLE_NM
The name of the role.

OWNER
The owner of OBJNAME.

OBJNAME
The object name which has PERM_NM permission granted to it for ROLE_NM.

PERM_NM
The name of the granted permission on OWNER.OBJNAME to ROLE_NM.

COLUMNS
Contains a bitmap of the columns from syscolumns that have permissions granted.

TYPE
Defines the type of permission for the object. This value may be GRANT or GRANT WITH GRANT OPTION.

COLUMN
The column which has permissions granted.

SINF_RULES

Definition: Provides information about defined rules.

Scope: Local Database

Columns:

OWNER
The owner of the rule.

OBJNAME
The name of the rule.

SINF_SEGMENTS

Definition: Provides information pertaining to segmentation in the database.

Scope: Local Database

Columns:

SEGNAME
The name of the segment in the database.

SYBDEVNAME
The name of the logical Sybase defined as begin part of the collection.

SIZE_PAGES
The amount of space alloted to the segment for the ASE device.

FREE_PAGES
The amount of alloted free space in pages for the segment and ASE device.

SINF_SEGMENTS_DEV_SUM

Definition: Provides segment grouping information by device.

Scope: Local Database

Columns:

SYBDEVNAME
The name of the ASE device.

TOT_SIZE_PAGES
The amount of total space alloted to the database in pages for the ASE device.

TOT_FREE_PAGES
The amount of total free space in pages for the ASE device.

SINF_SEGMENTS_SEG_SUM

Definition: Provides segment grouping information by segment.

Scope: Local Database

Columns:

SEGNAME
The name of the segment.

TOT_SIZE_PAGES
The amount of total space alloted to the database in pages for the segment.

TOT_FREE_PAGES
The amount of total free space in pages for the segment.

SINF_SERVERS

Definition: Provides information regarding servers which have been added.

Scope: Local Database

Columns:

SRVID
The ASE server id for this server.

SRVNAME
The name of the server within ASE.

SRVNETNAME
The name of the server outside of ASE.

SRVTYPE
The type of server.

SRVOPTS
What options are enabled.

TIMEOUTS
Whether timeouts are enabled or not.

SINF_SRVR_CFG

Definition: Provides information pertaining to the data servers configuration parameters.

Scope: Data Server

Columns:

PARAMETER
The name of the configuration parameter.

DEFAULT_VALUE
The data servers default configuration value.

MEMORY_USED
The amount of memory used due to the current run value.

CONFIG_VALUE
The currently configured value for the config parameter.

RUN_VALUE
The currently being used value for the config parameter.

SINF_STATS_HIST_STEPS

Definition: Provides information regarding the statistics and the number of histogram steps.

Scope: Local Database

Columns:

OWNER
The owner of the object.

OBJNAME
The name of the object.

COLNAME
The name of the column.

REQ_HIST_STEPS
The number histogram steps which were requested for the column.

ACT_HIST_STEPS
The actual number of histogram steps for the column.

SINF_STATS_INDEXES

Definition: Provides information regarding statistics for tables and indexes.

Scope: Local Database

Columns:

OWNER
The owner of the object.

OBJNAME
The name of the object.

IDXNAME
The index name of the object.

SEGNAME
The segment which the object's current growth is specified.

IDXTYPE
The type of index.

INDID
The index id.

IDX_HEIGHT
The height of the index.

LOCK_SCHEME
The locking scheme for this object.

NUM_PAGES
The number of pages used by this object.

ROW_COUNT
The estimated row count for this object.

OAM_PAGES
The number of oam pages used by this object.

AVG_ROW_SIZE
The estimated average row size for this object.

EXT_CRCNT
The number of extents allocated when the object was created.

EXT_CNT
The estimated number of extents used by the object.

ROWS_PER_PAGE
The current number of rows per page for this object.

OPT_NUM_PAGES
The estimated number of rows which could fit per page for this object.

OPT_NUM_EXTS
The estimated number of extents which this object could occupy.

WASTED_PAGES
The estimated number of empty page space.

WASTED_EXTS
The estimated number of empty extent space.

FROW_CNT
The forwarded row count.

DROW_CNT
The deleted row count.

REORG_MIN_MAX
The estimated maximum amount of time to reorg this object.

REORG_MIN_MED
The estimated average amount of time to reorg this object.

REORG_MIN_MIN
The estimated minimum amount of time to reorg this object.

DATA_PGE_CLSTR_RATIO
The data page cluster ratio.

DATA_ROW_CLSTR_RATIO
The data row cluster ratio.

IDX_PGE_CLSTR_RATIO
The index page cluster ratio.

LARGE_IO_EFF
The large I/O efficiency.

SPACE_UTIL_EFF
The space utilization efficiency.

SINF_SYSCOLUMNS_1

Definition: Provides information pertaining to columns for views and tables. Resolves the datatype as a server defined datatype.

Scope: Local Database

Columns:

OWNER
The owner of the column.

OBJNAME
The object to which the column belongs.

COLNAME
The name of the column.

DATATYPE
The datatype of the column.

TYPE
The type contained in systypes for the object.

LENGTH
The length or amount of bytes occupied by the column.

PREC
The number of digits in a numeric or decimal.

SCALE
The number of digits to the right of the decimal or the precision of the fractional part of a numeric or decimal.

COLID
The column order for the column.

STATUS
The status from syscolumns for the column.

COLTYPE

The type of the object the column belongs to.

SINF_SYSCOLUMNS_2

Definition: Provides more detailed information than SINF_COLUMNS_1. In particular, the datatype column is complete and a new column named NULLABILITY is present. Resolves the datatype as a server defined datatype.

Scope: Local Database

Columns:

OWNER
The owner of the column.

OBJNAME
The object to which the column belongs.

COLNAME
The name of the column.

DATATYPE
The datatype of the column.

TYPE
The type contained in systypes for the object.

LENGTH
The length or amount of bytes occupied by the column.

PREC
The number of digits in a numeric or decimal.

SCALE
The number of digits to the right of the decimal or the precision of the fractional part of a numeric or decimal.

STATUS
The status from syscolumns for the column.

COLID
The creation order of the columns for the object.

NULLABILITY
States whether or not the column allows nulls.

COLTYPE
The type of the object the column belongs to.

SINF_TABLES

Definition: Provides information pertaining to tables in the database.

Scope: Local Database

Columns:

OWNER
The owner of the table.

OBJNAME
The name of the table.

IDXNAME
The name of the allpages clustered index for the table if one exists, else the table name.

INDID
The indid of IDXNAME.

STATUS
The sysindexes status for this object.

STATUS2
The sysindexes status2 for this object.

SYSTAT
The sysobjects status for this object.

SYSTAT2
The sysobjects status2 for this object.

FILL_FACTOR
The fill factor percent set for the table.

RES_PAGE_GAP
The reserve page gap setting for the object.

EXP_ROWSIZE
The expected row size setting for the object.

MAXROWSPERPAGE
The max rows per page setting for this object.

MIN_LENGTH
The minimum number of bytes one row occupies.

MAX_LENGTH
The maximum number of bytes that one row occupies.

AVG_LENGTH
The average of MIN_LENGTH and MAX_LENGTH.

SEGNAME
The segment where the objects growth will occur.

LOCK_SCHEME
Specifies the locking scheme for the object.

DATA_PAGES
The number of pages the object allocation is currently across.

ROW_COUNT
The estimated number of rows the object occupies.

SINF_TABLES_SEG_SPACE

Definition: Provides information pertaining to segment usage for all tables.

Scope: Local Database

Columns:

OWNER
The owner of the table.

OBJNAME
The name of the object.

ROW_COUNT
The estimated record count.

DATA_PAGES
The amount of space this object occupies.

SEGNAME
The segment which has been defined for future growth of this object.

TOT_SIZE_PAGES
The total number of pages which SEGNAME has the ability to use.

TOT_FREE_PAGES
The total number of pages which are free for SEGNAME and can be used for growth.

SINF_TABLE_CACHE

Definition: Provides information about cache bindings for tables.

Scope: Local Database

Columns:

CACHE_NAME
The name of the cache.

OWNER
The owner of the table.

OBJNAME
The name of the table bound to the cache.

SINF_USAGES

Definition: Provides information about device allocation for the server.

Scope: Data Server

Columns:

VDEVNO
The virtual device number for the device used in this allocation.

SYBNAME
The logical assigned Sybase identifier for the physical name.

PHYNAME
The name of the physical device allocated to Sybase.

DBNAME
The dbname that has this allocation.

DBID
The dbid that has this allocation.

SEGMAP
The segments that comprise this allocation.

SEG_TYPE
User Defined, Defined in a user defined segment
Data Only, Used in a data only segment. Default and/or System.
Log Only, Contains only the databases transaction log.

SIZE_PAGES
The size in pages of this allocation.

FREE_PAGES
The number of free pages for the DBNAME allocation.

DEFAULT_DISK
Whether or not a default disk.

DISK_TYPE
The type of disk.

DISK_MIRRORED
Whether or not disk is mirrored.

DEVICE_SIDE
Side of mirror. Primary or secondary.

MIRROR_ENABLED
Whether mirror is active or not.

STATUS
Status for the device from sysdevices.

CNTRLTYPE
The controller type from sysdevices for this device.

MIRRORNAME
The name of the mirror for this allocation.

LSTART
The Sybase allocation start for a database and allocation.

SINF_USERS

Definition: Provides information about users in the database.

Scope: Local Database

Columns:

LOGIN
The login name associated with the user.

USR_NM
The user name in the database for the login.

GRP_NM
The group name in addition to public, that user has.

SINF_USER_PERMS

Definition: Provides information about non-columnar permissions a user has in the database.

Scope: Local Database

Columns:

USR_NM
The user name with the returned permissions.

OWNER
The owner of the object which has permissions granted.

OBJNAME
The object which has permissions granted to it.

PERM_NM
The name of the permission granted to the user.

GRP_NM
What group the user is in.

TYPE
Defines the type of permission for the object. This value may be GRANT or GRANT WITH GRANT OPTION.

SINF_USER_COL_PERMS_1

Definition: Provides information pertaining to columnar permissions granted to users.

Scope: Local Database

Columns:

USR_NM
The name of the user.

OWNER
The owner of OBJNAME.

OBJNAME
The object name which has PERM_NM permission granted to it for GRP_NM.

PERM_NM
The name of the granted permission on OWNER.OBJNAME to GRP_NM.

GRP_NM
The name of the group.

COLUMNS
Contains a bitmap of the columns from syscolumns that have permissions granted.

TYPE
Defines the type of permission for the object. This value may be GRANT or GRANT WITH GRANT OPTION.

SINF_USER_COL_PERMS_2

Definition: Provides information pertaining to columnar permissions granted to users.

Scope: Local Database

Columns:

USR_NM
The name of the user.

OWNER
The owner of OBJNAME.

OBJNAME
The object name which has PERM_NM permission granted to it for GRP_NM.

PERM_NM
The name of the granted permission on OWNER.OBJNAME to GRP_NM.

GRP_NM
The name of the group.

COLUMNS
Contains a bitmap of the columns from syscolumns that have permissions granted.

TYPE
Defines the type of permission for the object. This value may be GRANT or GRANT WITH GRANT OPTION.

COLUMN
The column which has permissions granted.

What Questions Can I Ask

You tell me... What would you like to ask?

How do I determine what ALIASES I have defined in a database?

Example (ALIASES):

```
SELECT ALIASING_LOGIN,
       ALIASED_LOGIN,
       USER_NM
  FROM SINF_ALIASES
go
```

How do I determine what BLOCKS exist on the system?

Example (BLOCKS):

```
SELECT *
  FROM SINF_BLOCKS
go
```

How do I determine what BLOCKS exist for a process?

Example (BLOCKS FOR PROCESS):

```
SELECT *
  FROM SINF_BLOCKS
 WHERE BY_SPID = <spid>
go
```

How do I determine what BLOCKS exist on an object?

Example (BLOCKS ON OBJECT):

```
SELECT *
  FROM SINF_BLOCKS
 WHERE LOCK_ON_OBJNAME = <object name>
go
```

How do I determine what columns have defaults bound to them?

Example (BOUNDDEFAULT):

```
SELECT *
  FROM SINF_BOUNDDEFAULT
go
```

How do I determine what default is bound to a particular column?

Example (BOUNDDEFAULT ON COLUMN):

```
SELECT *
  FROM SINF_BOUNDDEFAULT
 WHERE OWNER = <object owner>
   AND OBJNAME = <object name>
   AND COLNAME = <column name>
go
```

How do I determine what cachepools and configuration the tempdb_cache cache has assigned to it?

Example (CACHEPOOLS):

```
SELECT *
  FROM SINF_CACHEPOOLS
 WHERE CACHE_NAME = "tempdb_cache"
go
```

How do I determine what caches exist on my system and their configuration?

Example (CACHES):

```
SELECT *
  FROM SINF_CACHES
go
```

How do I determine what check constraint is on a particular column?

Example (CHKCONSTRAINTS):

```
SELECT *
  FROM SINF_CHKCONSTRAINTS
 WHERE TBLOWNER = <object owner>
   AND TBLOBJNAME = <object name>
   AND TBLCOLNAME = <column name>
go
```

How do I determine what default was created on a column as part of the CREATE TABLE or ALTER TABLE commands?

Example (COLUMNDEFAULT):

```
SELECT *
  FROM SINF_COLUMNDEFAULT
 WHERE OWNER = <object owner>
   AND OBJNAME = <object name>
   AND COLNAME = <column name>
go
```

How do I determine what objects in the database have a column with the name of column01 and the datatype for the column at the user defined datatype level?

Example (COLUMNS_2):

```
SELECT OWNER,
       OBJNAME,
       COLNAME,
       COLTYPE,
       DATATYPE
  FROM SINF_COLUMNS_2
 WHERE COLNAME = "column01"
go
```

How do I locate procedures which contain a given string?

Example (COMMENTS):

```
SELECT OWNER,
       OBJNAME
```

```
  FROM SINF_COMMENTS
 WHERE NOWRAP LIKE "%STRING%"
    OR WRAP LIKE "%STRING%"
go
```

How do I determine what the oldest open transaction is for a particular database?

Example (DATABASES):

```
SELECT *
  FROM SINF_DATABASES
 WHERE DBNAME = <database name>
go
```

How do I determine what user defined datatypes are defined in this database and their system datatype?

Example (DATATYPES_2):

```
SELECT OWNER,
       OBJNAME,
       VARIABILITY,
       NULLABILITY,
       IDENT,
       SYSNAME,
       DATATYPE
  FROM SINF_DATATYPES_2
 WHERE USERTYPE > 99
go
```

How do I determine what options a database has enabled?

Example (DBOPTIONS):

```
SELECT DBOPTION
  FROM SINF_DBOPTIONS
 WHERE DBNAME = <database name>
go
```

How do I determine what defaults exist in this database?

Example (DEFAULTS):

```
SELECT *
  FROM SINF_DEFAULTS
go
```

How do I determine what devices have been created for this ASE Server?

Example (DEVICES):

```
SELECT *
  FROM SINF_DEVICES
go
```

How do I determine what devices are NOT used for a database?

Example (DEVICES_DB_UNUSED):

```
SELECT *
  FROM SINF_DEVICES_DB_UNUSED
 WHERE DBNAME = <database name>
go
```

How do I determine what devices are used for a database?

Example (DEVICES_DB_USED):

```
SELECT *
  FROM SINF_DEVICES_DB_USED
 WHERE DBNAME = <database name>
go
```

How do I determine what foreign key constraints exist for this database?

Example (FKCONSTRAINTS):

```
SELECT *
  FROM SINF_FKCONSTRAINTS
go
```

How do I determine what objects reference this object for this database?

Example (FKCONSTRAINTS):

```
SELECT *
  FROM SINF_FKCONSTRAINTS
 WHERE PK_TB = <referenced object name>
go
```

How do I determine if all foreign key constraints in this database have indexes defined about their columns?

Example (FKCONSTRAINTS_NO_INDEXES):

```
SELECT *
  FROM SINF_FKCONSTRAINTS_NO_INDEXES
go
```

How do I determine what groups exist in this database?

Example (GROUPS):

```
SELECT *
  FROM SINF_GROUPS
go
```

How do I determine what GROUP permissions exist for an object in this database?

Example (GROUP_PERMS):

```
SELECT *
  FROM SINF_GROUP_PERMS
 WHERE OWNER = <object owner>
   AND OBJNAME = <object name>
go
```

How do I determine what GROUP permissions exist for a column in this database?

Example (GROUP_COL_PERMS_2):

```
SELECT *
  FROM SINF_GROUP_COL_PERMS_2
```

```
 WHERE COLNAME = <column name>
go
```

How do I determine what INDEXES exist for an object in this database?

Example (INDEXES):

```
SELECT *
  FROM SINF_INDEXES
 WHERE OWNER = <object owner>
   AND OBJNAME = <object name>
go
```

How do I determine the space which an index is occupying?

Example (INDEXES_SEG_SPACE):

```
SELECT *
  FROM SINF_INDEXES_SEG_SPACE
 WHERE OWNER = <object owner>
   AND OBJNAME = <object name>
   AND IDXNAME = <index name>
go
```

How do I determine what cache an index is bound?

Example (INDEX_CACHE):

```
SELECT *
  FROM SINF_INDEX_CACHE
 WHERE OWNER = <object owner>
   AND OBJNAME = <object name>
   AND IDXNAME = <index name>
go
```

How do I determine what locks a process is using on the system?

Example (LOCKS):

```
SELECT *
  FROM SINF_LOCKS
 WHERE SPID = <process ID>
go
```

How do I determine login information about a particular Sybase login?

Example (LOGINS):

```
SELECT *
  FROM SINF_LOGINS
 WHERE NAME = <login name>
go
```

How do I determine what ROLES a login has mapped to it?

Example (LOGINS_ROLES):

```
SELECT *
  FROM SINF_LOGINS_ROLES
 WHERE LOGIN_NM = <login name>
go
```

How do I determine what objects exists in a database?

Example (OBJECTS):

```
SELECT *
  FROM SINF_OBJECTS
go
```

How do I determine the Query Plan for all processes which are holding locks?

Example (QPLANS):

```
SELECT *
  FROM SINF_QPLANS
go
```

How do I determine the Query Plan for a particular Sybase process ID?

Example (QPLANS):

```
SELECT *
  FROM SINF_QPLANS
 WHERE SPID = <process ID>
go
```

How do I determine the Query Plan for the processes which have accumulated the greatest amount of cumulative CPU time and are currently holding locks?

Example (QPLANS_MAX_CPU):

```
SELECT *
  FROM SINF_QPLANS_MAX_CPU
go
```

How do I determine the Query Plan for the processes which have accumulated the greatest amount of cumulative Physical IO and are currently holding locks?

Example (QPLANS_MAX_PHYS_IO):

```
SELECT *
  FROM SINF_QPLANS_MAX_PHYS_IO
go
```

How do I determine the Query Plan for the processes which are causing blocking and are not being blocked themselves?

Example (QPLANS_BLOCKS):

```
SELECT *
  FROM SINF_QPLANS_BLOCKS
go
```

How do I determine the partition count for an object an the number of pages in each partition of an object?

Example (PARTITIONS):

```
SELECT *
  FROM SINF_PARTITIONS
 WHERE OWNER = <object owner>
   AND OBJNAME = <object name>
go
```

How do I determine what primary key constraints exist for this database?

Example (PKCONSTRAINTS):

```
SELECT *
  FROM SINF_PKCONSTRAINTS
go
```

How do I determine what temporary database I am using?

Example (PROCESSES):

```
SELECT *
  FROM SINF_PROCESSES
 WHERE SPID = @@SPID
go
```

How do I determine if a process which appears constantly in recv sleep is executing any commands? Help, because they are causing blocking and I want to determine if this connection is likely dead or not. First off, the BATCH_ID is a sequential INTEGER that whenever a process executes an SQL batch it is increased. Thus, if you query SINF_PROCESSES several times for the BATCH_ID and it is increasing or for that matter changing the process is executing commands. You should also look at the LOGGED_IN_DT to determine if the process has disconnected and a new process has connected.

Example (PROCESSES):

```
SELECT SPID,
       LOGGED_IN_DT,
       BATCH_ID
  FROM SINF_PROCESSES
 WHERE SPID = < SPECIFIED SPID >
go
```

How do I determine the replication agent configuration for this database?

Example (REP_AGENT_CFGS):

```
SELECT *
  FROM SINF_REP_AGENT_CFGS
go
```

How do I determine the primary truncation point, secondary truncation point, and unscanned pages for the log within this database.

Example (REP_LOG_STATUS_1):

```
SELECT *
  FROM SINF_REP_LOG_STATUS_1
go
```

How do I determine what procedures in this database are marked for function delivery?

Example (REP_PROCS):

```
SELECT *
  FROM SINF_REP_PROCS
go
```

How do I determine what tables are marked for replication within this database?

Example (REP_TABLES):

```
SELECT *
  FROM SINF_REP_TABLES
go
```

How do I determine what ROLES exist on this server?

Example (ROLES):

```
SELECT *
  FROM SINF_ROLES
go
```

How do I determine what ROLE permissions an object has for this database?

Example (ROLE_PERMS):

```
SELECT *
  FROM SINF_ROLE_PERMS
 WHERE OWNER = <object owner>
   AND OBJNAME = <object name>
go
```

How do I determine what ROLE permissions a column has for this database?

Example (ROLE_COL_PERMS_2):

```
SELECT *
  FROM SINF_ROLE_COL_PERMS_2
 WHERE COLNAME = <column name>
go
```

How do I determine what RULES exist for this database?

Example (RULES):

```
SELECT *
  FROM SINF_RULES
go
```

How do I determine what SEGMENTS exists for this database?

Example (SEGMENTS):

```
SELECT *
  FROM SINF_SEGMENTS
go
```

How do I determine the space allocation by device for this database?

Example (SEGMENTS_DEV_SUM):

```
SELECT *
  FROM SINF_SEGMENTS_DEV_SUM
go
```

How do I determine the space allocation for a segment for this database?

Example (SEGMENTS_SEG_SUM):

```
SELECT *
  FROM SINF_SEGMENTS_SEG_SUM
go
```

How do I determine what servers I have defined on this server?

Example (SERVERS):

```
SELECT *
  FROM SINF_SERVERS
go
```

How do I determine what the procedure cache size is configured for on this server?

Example (SRVR_CFG):

```
SELECT *
  FROM SINF_SRVR_CFG
 WHERE PARAMETER = "procedure cache size"
go
```

How do I determine what server configuration parameters contain the word remote?

Example (SRVR_CFG):

```
SELECT *
  FROM SINF_SRVR_CFG
 WHERE PARAMETER LIKE "%remote%"
go
```

How do I determine the actual and requested histogram steps for a column for an object in this database?

Example (STATS_HIST_STEPS):

```
SELECT *
  FROM SINF_STATS_HIST_STEPS
 WHERE OWNER = <object owner>
   AND OBJNAME = <object name>
   AND COLNAME = <column name>
go
```

How do I determine the statistics for a particular object or index?

Example (STATS_INDEXES):

```
SELECT *
  FROM SINF_STATS_INDEXES
 WHERE OWNER = <object owner>
   AND OBJNAME = <object name>
go
```

How do I determine, and in COLID order, the columns for a particular object mapped to only system defined datatypes?

Example (SYSCOLUMNS_2):

```
SELECT *
  FROM SINF_SYSCOLUMNS_2
 WHERE OWNER = <object owner>
   AND OBJNAME = <object name>
 ORDER
    BY OWNER ASC,
       OBJNAME ASC,
       COLID ASC
go
```

How do I determine information about a particular table in this database?

Example (TABLES):

```
SELECT *
  FROM SINF_TABLES
 WHERE OWNER = <table owner>
   AND OBJNAME = <table name>
go
```

How do I determine how much space an object is using on a particular segment?

Example (TABLES_SEG_SPACE):

```
SELECT *
  FROM SINF_TABLES_SEG_SPACE
 WHERE OWNER = <table owner>
   AND OBJNAME = <table name>
go
```

How do I determine what cache a table has been bound?

Example (TABLE_CACHE):

```
SELECT *
  FROM SINF_TABLE_CACHE
 WHERE OWNER = <table owner>
   AND OBJNAME = <table name>
go
```

How do I determine what databases are using device fragments?

Example (USAGES):

```
SELECT *
  FROM SINF_USAGES
go
```

How do I determine what users exist for this database?

Example (USERS):

```
SELECT *
  FROM SINF_USERS
go
```

How do I determine what object permissions a user has in this database?

Example (USER_PERMS):

```
SELECT *
  FROM SINF_USER_PERMS
 WHERE USR_NM = <user name>
go
```

How do I determine what column level permissions a user has in this database?

Example (USER_COL_PERMS_2):

```
SELECT *
  FROM SINF_USER_COL_PERMS_2
 WHERE USR_NM = <user name>
go
```

Appendix G. Catalog Views

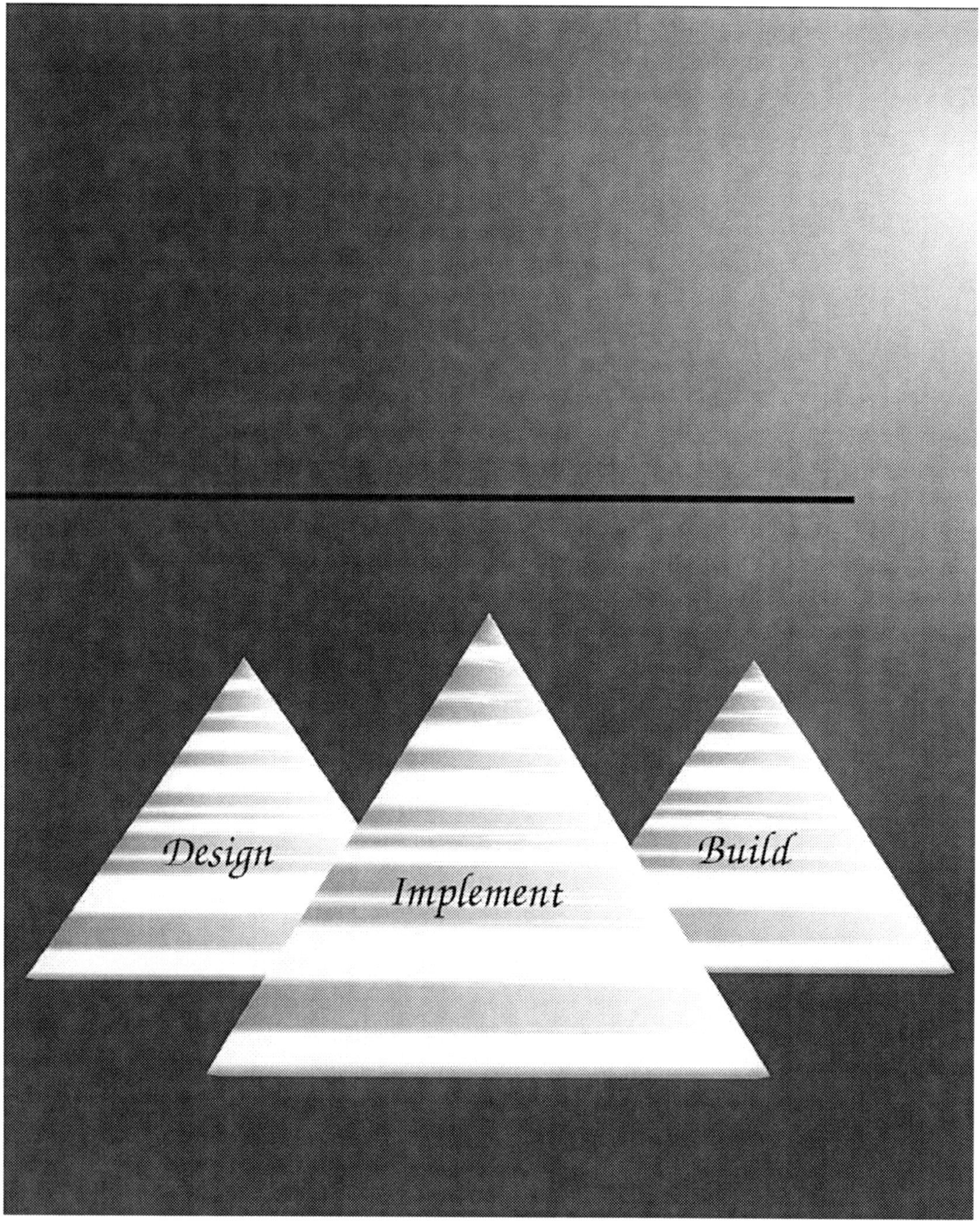
Design
Implement
Build

Appendix H. Sending Mail

The following scripts can be used to generate emails and web reports for events using Sybase XP_SERVER from within ASE.

Unix Script

You will need to edit the below unix shell script for you environment.

```
#!/bin/sh

########################################################################
##
## Author: Ryan Putnam
##
## Intent: Generates Email Messages/Attachments
##
## Return: RETCODE
##
## Revise: Created June 25, 2003
##
########################################################################
########################
## SETUP ENVIRONMENT ##
########################

trap 'rm /tmp/*.$$ 1>/dev/null 2>&1' EXIT INT QUIT KILL TERM

########################
## LOAD FUNCTIONS    ##
########################

typeset opt SRVR_NM EMAIL_GRP_NM EMAIL_MSG_ID MSG_TRANS

while getopts :s:g:m:t:r: opt
do
case $opt in
(s) SRVR_NM="$OPTARG";;
(g) EMAIL_GRP_NM="$OPTARG";;
(m) EMAIL_MSG_ID="$OPTARG";;
(t) MSG_TRANS="${OPTARG}";;
(r) EMAIL_RPT_ID="${OPTARG}";;
(/?)
```

```
print "Unknown option: '-${OPTARG}' given to $0"
exit 1
;;
esac
done

#######################
## PARM VALIDATIONS  ##
#######################
[ ! "${SRVR_NM}" ] && print "SERVER -s MUST BE SPECIFIED" && exit 1
[ ! "${EMAIL_GRP_NM}" ] && print "EMAIL_GRP_NM -g MUST BE SPECIFIED" && exit
1
if [ ! "${EMAIL_MSG_ID}" -a ! "${EMAIL_RPT_ID}" ];then
   print "EITHER SPECIFY EMAIL_MSG_ID -m OR EMAIL_RPT_ID -r"
   exit 1
fi

#######################
## LOAD FUNCTIONS    ##
#######################
autoload setusrpwd

#######################
## MAINLINE          ##
#######################

HOST="`hostname -s`"

## GET ALL EMAIL ADDRESSES FOR THIS GROUP
isql -U${SQLUSR} -P${SQLPWD} -S${SRVR_NM} -w20000 <<EOF \
   | sed "1,2d" >/tmp/email_add.$$
SET NOCOUNT ON
go
SELECT email_usr_nm_id
  FROM svrprf01.dbo.email_grp_usr
 WHERE email_grp_nm_id = "${EMAIL_GRP_NM}"
go
EOF

if [ "${EMAIL_MSG_ID}" ];then
## GET THE EMAIL MESSAGE FOR THIS MSG_ID
isql -U${SQLUSR} -P${SQLPWD} -S${SRVR_NM} -w20000 <<EOF \
   | sed "1,2d" >/tmp/email_msg.$$
SET NOCOUNT ON
go
SELECT email_msg_txt
  FROM svrprf01.dbo.email_msg
 WHERE email_msg_id = "${EMAIL_MSG_ID}"
```

```
go
EOF

if [ "${MSG_TRANS}" ];then
TRSTRING=`print "${MSG_TRANS}" \
 | awk 'BEGIN {FS=":"; OFS=" "}
       {
          print $1,$2,$3,$4,$5,$6,$7,$8,$9,$10,$11,$12,$13,$14
       }'`

typeset -i COUNTER=1
for loop in `echo ${TRSTRING}`
do
   if (( $COUNTER == 1 ));then
      MINPARM="${loop}"
   else
      MINSTR="${loop}"

      cat /tmp/email_msg.$$ \
       | sed -e "s/${MINPARM}/${MINSTR}/g" >/tmp/email_msg_2.$$
      mv /tmp/email_msg_2.$$ /tmp/email_msg.$$

      typeset -i COUNTER=0
   fi

   (( COUNTER = $COUNTER + 1 ))
done

## GET LAST ONE
      cat /tmp/email_msg.$$ \
       | sed -e "s/${MINPARM}/${MINSTR}/g" >/tmp/email_msg_2.$$
      mv /tmp/email_msg_2.$$ /tmp/email_msg.$$
fi
fi

if [ "${EMAIL_RPT_ID}" ];then
## GET THE EMAIL REPORT FOR THIS RPT ID
isql -U${SQLUSR} -P${SQLPWD} -S${SRVR_NM} -w20000 <<EOF \
   | sed "1,2d" \
   | awk 'BEGIN {FS="<EOL>";OFS="<EOL>"}
        {
           print $1
        }' >/tmp/email_rpt_hdg.$$
SET NOCOUNT ON
go
SELECT "<td>" + email_rpt_hdg1 + "</td>" +
       CASE
          WHEN email_rpt_hdg2 IS NOT NULL
```

```
        THEN "<td>" + email_rpt_hdg2 + "</td>"
   END +
   CASE
      WHEN email_rpt_hdg3 IS NOT NULL
         THEN "<td>" + email_rpt_hdg3 + "</td>"
   END +
   CASE
      WHEN email_rpt_hdg4 IS NOT NULL
         THEN "<td>" + email_rpt_hdg4 + "</td>"
   END +
   CASE
      WHEN email_rpt_hdg5 IS NOT NULL
         THEN "<td>" + email_rpt_hdg5 + "</td>"
   END +
   CASE
      WHEN email_rpt_hdg6 IS NOT NULL
         THEN "<td>" + email_rpt_hdg6 + "</td>"
   END +
   CASE
      WHEN email_rpt_hdg7 IS NOT NULL
         THEN "<td>" + email_rpt_hdg7 + "</td>"
   END +
   CASE
      WHEN email_rpt_hdg8 IS NOT NULL
         THEN "<td>" + email_rpt_hdg8 + "</td>"
   END +
   CASE
      WHEN email_rpt_hdg9 IS NOT NULL
         THEN "<td>" + email_rpt_hdg9 + "</td>"
   END +
   CASE
      WHEN email_rpt_hdg10 IS NOT NULL
         THEN "<td>" + email_rpt_hdg10 + "</td>"
   END +
   CASE
      WHEN email_rpt_hdg11 IS NOT NULL
         THEN "<td>" + email_rpt_hdg11 + "</td>"
   END +
   CASE
      WHEN email_rpt_hdg12 IS NOT NULL
         THEN "<td>" + email_rpt_hdg12 + "</td>"
   END +
   CASE
      WHEN email_rpt_hdg13 IS NOT NULL
         THEN "<td>" + email_rpt_hdg13 + "</td>"
   END +
   CASE
      WHEN email_rpt_hdg14 IS NOT NULL
```

```
            THEN "<td>" + email_rpt_hdg14 + "</td>"
      END +
      CASE
         WHEN email_rpt_hdg15 IS NOT NULL
            THEN "<td>" + email_rpt_hdg15 + "</td>"
      END +
      CASE
         WHEN email_rpt_hdg16 IS NOT NULL
            THEN "<td>" + email_rpt_hdg16 + "</td>"
      END +
      CASE
         WHEN email_rpt_hdg17 IS NOT NULL
            THEN "<td>" + email_rpt_hdg17 + "</td>"
      END +
      CASE
         WHEN email_rpt_hdg18 IS NOT NULL
            THEN "<td>" + email_rpt_hdg18 + "</td>"
      END +
      CASE
         WHEN email_rpt_hdg19 IS NOT NULL
            THEN "<td>" + email_rpt_hdg19 + "</td>"
      END +
      "<EOL>"
  FROM svrprf01.dbo.email_rpt
 WHERE email_rpt_id = "${EMAIL_RPT_ID}"
go
EOF

isql -U${SQLUSR} -P${SQLPWD} -S${SRVR_NM} -w20000 <<EOF \
   | sed "1,2d" \
   | awk 'BEGIN {FS="<EOL>";OFS="<EOL>"}
        {
           print $1
        }' >/tmp/email_rpt_txt.$$
SET NOCOUNT ON
go
SELECT "</tr><td>" + email_rpt_col1 + "</td>" +
      CASE
         WHEN email_rpt_col2 IS NOT NULL
            THEN "<td>" + email_rpt_col2 + "</td>"
      END +
      CASE
         WHEN email_rpt_col3 IS NOT NULL
            THEN "<td>" + email_rpt_col3 + "</td>"
      END +
      CASE
         WHEN email_rpt_col4 IS NOT NULL
            THEN "<td>" + email_rpt_col4 + "</td>"
```

```
    END +
    CASE
       WHEN email_rpt_col5 IS NOT NULL
          THEN "<td>" + email_rpt_col5 + "</td>"
    END +
    CASE
       WHEN email_rpt_col6 IS NOT NULL
          THEN "<td>" + email_rpt_col6 + "</td>"
    END +
    CASE
       WHEN email_rpt_col7 IS NOT NULL
          THEN "<td>" + email_rpt_col7 + "</td>"
    END +
    CASE
       WHEN email_rpt_col8 IS NOT NULL
          THEN "<td>" + email_rpt_col8 + "</td>"
    END +
    CASE
       WHEN email_rpt_col9 IS NOT NULL
          THEN "<td>" + email_rpt_col9 + "</td>"
    END +
    CASE
       WHEN email_rpt_col10 IS NOT NULL
          THEN "<td>" + email_rpt_col10 + "</td>"
    END +
    CASE
       WHEN email_rpt_col11 IS NOT NULL
          THEN "<td>" + email_rpt_col11 + "</td>"
    END +
    CASE
       WHEN email_rpt_col12 IS NOT NULL
          THEN "<td>" + email_rpt_col12 + "</td>"
    END +
    CASE
       WHEN email_rpt_col13 IS NOT NULL
          THEN "<td>" + email_rpt_col13 + "</td>"
    END +
    CASE
       WHEN email_rpt_col14 IS NOT NULL
          THEN "<td>" + email_rpt_col14 + "</td>"
    END +
    CASE
       WHEN email_rpt_col15 IS NOT NULL
          THEN "<td>" + email_rpt_col15 + "</td>"
    END +
    CASE
       WHEN email_rpt_col16 IS NOT NULL
          THEN "<td>" + email_rpt_col16 + "</td>"
```

```
      END +
      CASE
         WHEN email_rpt_col17 IS NOT NULL
            THEN "<td>" + email_rpt_col17 + "</td>"
      END +
      CASE
         WHEN email_rpt_col18 IS NOT NULL
            THEN "<td>" + email_rpt_col18 + "</td>"
      END +
      CASE
         WHEN email_rpt_col19 IS NOT NULL
            THEN "<td>" + email_rpt_col19 + "</td>"
      END +
      "<EOL>"
  FROM svrprf01.dbo.email_rpt_txt
 WHERE email_rpt_id = "${EMAIL_RPT_ID}"
 ORDER
    BY email_rpt_id ASC,
      email_rpt_seq_id ASC
go
DELETE svrprf01.dbo.email_rpt_txt
  FROM svrprf01.dbo.email_rpt_txt
 WHERE email_rpt_id = "${EMAIL_RPT_ID}"
go
EOF

## OKAY LETS BUILD THE HTML REPORT NOW
print '<html>' >/tmp/${EMAIL_RPT_ID}.$$
print '<BODY TEXT="BLACK" BGCOLOR="WHITE" link="BLUE" vlink="BLUE"
alink="BLUE">' >>/tmp/${EMAIL_RPT_ID}.$$
print "<H1><center>`[ -f /tmp/email_msg.$$ ] && cat /
tmp/email_msg.$$`</center></H1>" >>/tmp/${EMAIL_RPT_ID}.$$
print '<table border="2" cellpadding="2" cellspacing="0">' >>/tmp/$
{EMAIL_RPT_ID}.$$
print '<tr>' >>/tmp/${EMAIL_RPT_ID}.$$
cat /tmp/email_rpt_hdg.$$ >>/tmp/${EMAIL_RPT_ID}.$$
cat /tmp/email_rpt_txt.$$ >>/tmp/${EMAIL_RPT_ID}.$$
print '</tr>' >>/tmp/${EMAIL_RPT_ID}.$$
print '</table>' >>/tmp/${EMAIL_RPT_ID}.$$
print '</BODY>' >>/tmp/${EMAIL_RPT_ID}.$$
print '</HTML>' >>/tmp/${EMAIL_RPT_ID}.$$

## OKAY LETS PREPARE THE MIME DOCUMENT (THAT IS THE ATTACHMENT)
[ -f /tmp/email_msg.$$ ] && mv /tmp/email_msg.$$ /tmp/email_msg2.$$
print "Mime-Version: 1.0" >/tmp/email_msg.$$
print "Content-Type: text/plain" >>/tmp/email_msg.$$
print "Attached Is Report ${EMAIL_RPT_ID} Please Review" >>/tmp/email_msg.$$
```

```
[ -f /tmp/email_msg2.$$ ] && cat /tmp/email_msg2.$$ >>/tmp/email_msg.$$
print "" >>/tmp/email_msg.$$

uuencode /tmp/${EMAIL_RPT_ID}.$$ ${EMAIL_RPT_ID}.html >/tmp/email_attach.$$

cat /tmp/email_attach.$$ >>/tmp/email_msg.$$

fi

## EMAIL MESSAGE AND GENEREATE HISTORY
while read V_EMAIL filler
do
      mail -s "MESSAGE FROM ${HOST}.${SRVR_NM}" ${V_EMAIL}
</tmp/email_msg.$$
        print "`date +'%m%d%y %H%M%S'`: ${V_EMAIL}: PARMS -s${SRVR_NM} -g
${EMAIL_GRP_NM} -m${EMAIL_MSG_ID}" >>./emailer.log
done < /tmp/email_add.$$

exit 0
```

ASE Setup

You will need to configure the xp_server. Afterwards, they will need to create these objects.

Database

Create a database named svrprf01 for 100-MB data and 20-MB log.

Tables

Create the following tables, indexes, and constraints in the svrprf01 database.

```
USE svrprf01
go

CREATE
 TABLE dbo.email_grp(
       email_grp_nm_id CHAR(8) NOT NULL,
       udt_ts DATETIME NOT NULL,
       udt_prc_id VARCHAR(30) NOT NULL
)
LOCK Allpages ON 'default'
go
```

```
CREATE
 TABLE dbo.email_grp_usr(
       email_grp_nm_id CHAR(8) NOT NULL,
       email_usr_nm_id VARCHAR(90) NOT NULL,
       udt_ts DATETIME NOT NULL,
       udt_prc_id VARCHAR(30)NOT NULL
)
LOCK Allpages ON 'default'
go

CREATE
 TABLE dbo.email_usr(
       email_usr_nm_id VARCHAR(90) NOT NULL,
       udt_ts DATETIME NOT NULL,
       udt_prc_id VARCHAR(30) NOT NULL
)
LOCK Allpages ON 'default'
go

CREATE
 TABLE dbo.email_msg(
       email_msg_id CHAR(8) NOT NULL,
       email_msg_txt VARCHAR(255) NOT NULL,
       udt_ts DATETIME NOT NULL,
       udt_prc_id VARCHAR(30) NOT NULL
)
LOCK Allpages ON 'default'
go

CREATE
 TABLE dbo.email_rpt(
       email_rpt_id CHAR(8) NOT NULL,
       email_rpt_hdg1 VARCHAR(50) NOT NULL,
       email_rpt_hdg2 VARCHAR(50) NULL,
       email_rpt_hdg3 VARCHAR(50) NULL,
       email_rpt_hdg4 VARCHAR(50) NULL,
       email_rpt_hdg5 VARCHAR(50) NULL,
       email_rpt_hdg6 VARCHAR(50) NULL,
       email_rpt_hdg7 VARCHAR(50) NULL,
       email_rpt_hdg8 VARCHAR(50) NULL,
       email_rpt_hdg9 VARCHAR(50) NULL,
       email_rpt_hdg10 VARCHAR(50) NULL,
       email_rpt_hdg11 VARCHAR(50) NULL,
       email_rpt_hdg12 VARCHAR(50) NULL,
       email_rpt_hdg13 VARCHAR(50) NULL,
       email_rpt_hdg14 VARCHAR(50) NULL,
       email_rpt_hdg15 VARCHAR(50) NULL,
       email_rpt_hdg16 VARCHAR(50) NULL,
```

```
        email_rpt_hdg17 VARCHAR(50) NULL,
        email_rpt_hdg18 VARCHAR(50) NULL,
        email_rpt_hdg19 VARCHAR(50) NULL,
        udt_ts DATETIME NOT NULL,
        udt_prc_id VARCHAR(30) NOT NULL
)
LOCK Allpages ON 'default'
go

CREATE
 TABLE dbo.email_rpt_txt(
        email_rpt_id CHAR(8) NOT NULL,
        email_rpt_seq_id NUMERIC(12,0) IDENTITY,
        email_rpt_col1 VARCHAR(50) NOT NULL,
        email_rpt_col2 VARCHAR(50) NULL,
        email_rpt_col3 VARCHAR(50) NULL,
        email_rpt_col4 VARCHAR(50) NULL,
        email_rpt_col5 VARCHAR(50) NULL,
        email_rpt_col6 VARCHAR(50) NULL,
        email_rpt_col7 VARCHAR(50) NULL,
        email_rpt_col8 VARCHAR(50) NULL,
        email_rpt_col9 VARCHAR(50) NULL,
        email_rpt_col10 VARCHAR(50) NULL,
        email_rpt_col11 VARCHAR(50) NULL,
        email_rpt_col12 VARCHAR(50) NULL,
        email_rpt_col13 VARCHAR(50) NULL,
        email_rpt_col14 VARCHAR(50) NULL,
        email_rpt_col15 VARCHAR(50) NULL,
        email_rpt_col16 VARCHAR(50) NULL,
        email_rpt_col17 VARCHAR(50) NULL,
        email_rpt_col18 VARCHAR(50) NULL,
        email_rpt_col19 VARCHAR(50) NULL,
        udt_ts DATETIME NOT NULL,
        udt_prc_id VARCHAR(30) NOT NULL
)
LOCK Datarows ON 'default'
go

ALTER TABLE email_grp
ADD CONSTRAINT email_grp_nm_id_clu
PRIMARY KEY CLUSTERED
( email_grp_nm_id ASC )
ON 'default'
go

ALTER TABLE email_grp_usr
ADD CONSTRAINT email_usr_grp_clu
PRIMARY KEY CLUSTERED
```

```
( email_grp_nm_id ASC, email_usr_nm_id ASC )
ON 'default'
go

ALTER TABLE email_msg
ADD CONSTRAINT email_msg_clu
PRIMARY KEY CLUSTERED
( email_msg_id ASC )
ON 'default'
go

ALTER TABLE email_rpt
ADD CONSTRAINT email_rpt_ix1
PRIMARY KEY CLUSTERED
( email_rpt_id ASC )
ON 'default'
go

ALTER TABLE email_rpt_txt
ADD CONSTRAINT email_rpt_txt_ix1
PRIMARY KEY CLUSTERED
( email_rpt_id ASC, email_rpt_seq_id ASC )
ON 'default'
go

ALTER TABLE email_usr
ADD CONSTRAINT email_usr_clu
PRIMARY KEY CLUSTERED
( email_usr_nm_id ASC )
ON 'default'
go

CREATE NONCLUSTERED INDEX email_grp_usr_nc2
ON email_grp_usr
( email_grp_nm_id ASC )
ON 'default'
go

CREATE NONCLUSTERED INDEX email_usr_grp_nc1
ON email_grp_usr
( email_usr_nm_id ASC )
ON 'default'
go

CREATE UNIQUE NONCLUSTERED INDEX mon_field_dsc_nc1
ON mon_field_dsc
( field_nm ASC )
ON 'default'
```

```
go

ALTER TABLE email_grp_usr
ADD CONSTRAINT email_grp@email_grp_usr
FOREIGN KEY (email_grp_nm_id)
REFERENCES svrprf01.dbo.email_grp (email_grp_nm_id)
go

ALTER TABLE email_grp_usr
ADD CONSTRAINT email_usr@email_grp_usr
FOREIGN KEY (email_usr_nm_id)
REFERENCES svrprf01.dbo.email_usr (email_usr_nm_id)
go

ALTER TABLE email_rpt_txt
ADD CONSTRAINT email_rpt_txt@email_rpt
FOREIGN KEY (email_rpt_id)
REFERENCES svrprf01.dbo.email_rpt (email_rpt_id)
go
```

Procedure

Create the below stored procedure in the sybsystemprocs database.

```
USE sybsystemprocs
go

CREATE PROCEDURE sp_email(
       @email_grp_nm_id CHAR(8),
       @email_msg_id CHAR(8),
       @email_tr_str VARCHAR(128) = NULL,
       @email_rpt_id CHAR(8) = NULL
)
AS
BEGIN
   DECLARE @cmds VARCHAR(255)

   SELECT @cmds = "/mdba/scripts/emailer.ksh -s" + @@SERVERNAME
                + " -g" + @email_grp_nm_id
                + " -m" + @email_msg_id

   IF @email_rpt_id IS NOT NULL
      SELECT @cmds = @cmds + " -r" + @email_rpt_id

   IF @email_tr_str IS NOT NULL
      SELECT @cmds = @cmds + " -t" + @email_tr_str
```

```
   EXEC xp_cmdshell @cmds, no_output
END
go
```

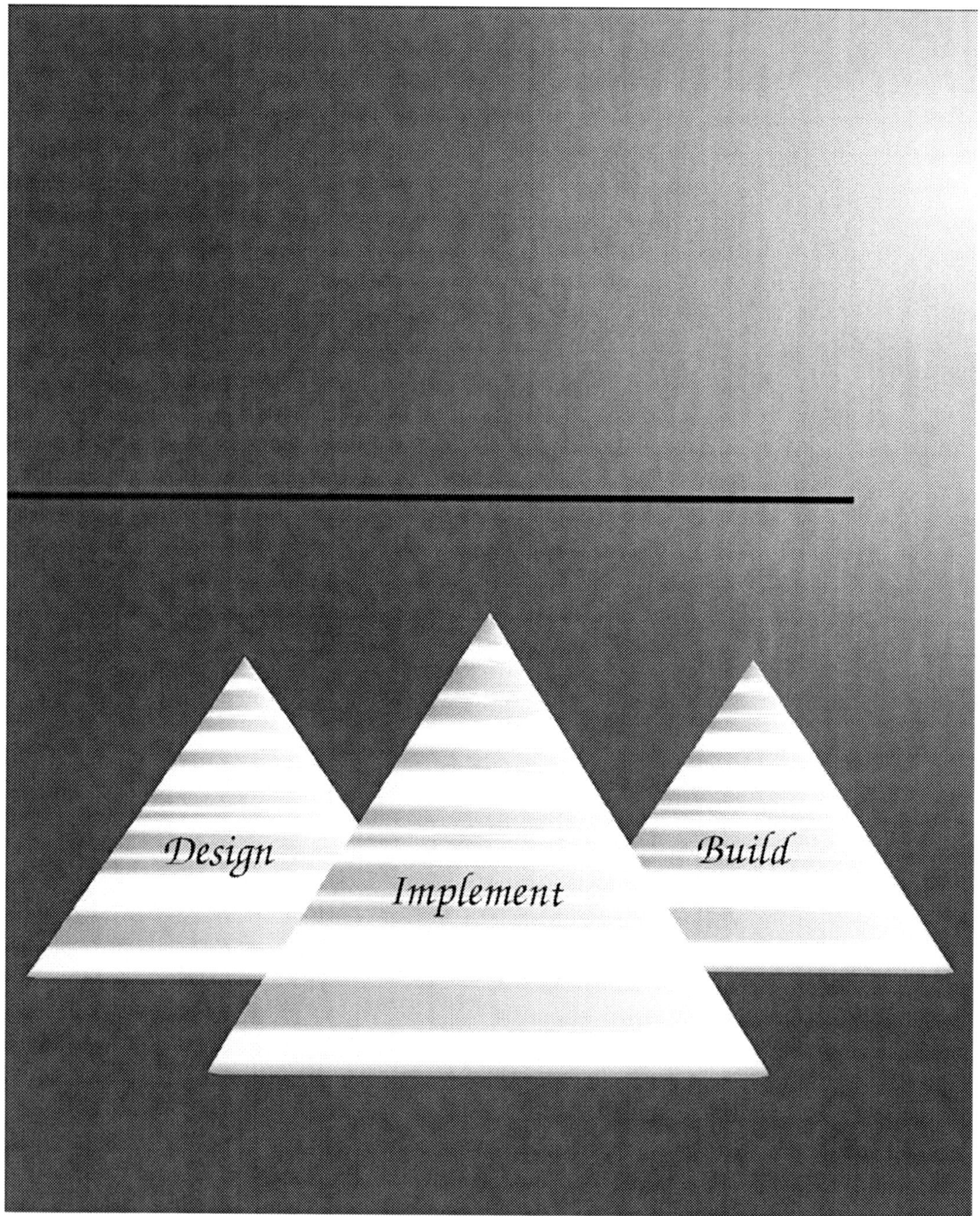
Design
Implement
Build

Appendix I. Determine Fragmentation

The following Korn Shell script frag.ksh is used to determine table and index fragmentation.

```
#!/bin/ksh
#-------------------------------------------------------------------------
#
# Procedure:          frag.ksh
#
# Description:        Identify table and index fragmentation in a database
#
# Parameters:         server_name database name
#
#-------------------------------------------------------------------------
# Vers|   Date   | Who | DA | Description
#-----+--------+-----+----
+---------------------------------------------------
# 1.0 |20/03/04|  MT |    | Initial Version
#-------------------------------------------------------------------------
#
#
# Main section of script
#
SQL_SERVER=$1
DATABASE=$2

if [[ -z ${SQL_SERVER} ]]
then
   echo "Abort: $0 failed. No server name specified on command line"
   exit 1
fi

if [[ -z ${DATABASE} ]]
then
   echo "Abort: $0 failed. No database name specified on command
   line"
   exit 1
fi

ENVFILE=$HOME/${SQL_SERVER}/dba/bin/environment.ksh
```

```
if [[ -f $ENVFILE ]]
then
   . $ENVFILE
else
   echo "Abort: $0 failed. No environment file ( $ENVFILE ) found"
   exit 1
fi

USERNAME="sa"; export USERNAME
FILE_NAME=`basename $0 .ksh`
#
PASSWORD=$(get_password.ksh $SQL_SERVER $USERNAME)
if [ $? != 0 ]
then
   echo "Abort: $0 failed. Query for Sybase password failed"
   exit 1
#
fi

IN_FILE="${LOGDIR}/${SQL_SERVER}_${FILE_NAME}_${DATABASE}.sql"
[ -f ${IN_FILE} ] && rm -f ${IN_FILE}

LOG_FILE="${LOGDIR}/${SQL_SERVER}_${FILE_NAME}_${DATABASE}.log"
[ -f ${LOG_FILE} ] && rm -f ${LOG_FILE}

RESULT_FILE="${LOGDIR}/${SQL_SERVER}_${FILE_NAME}_${DATABASE}.result"
[ -f ${RESULT_FILE} ] && rm -f ${RESULT_FILE}

BCP_FILE="${LOGDIR}/${SQL_SERVER}_${FILE_NAME}_${DATABASE}.bcp"
[ -f ${BCP_FILE} ] && rm -f ${BCP_FILE}

WORK_FILE="${LOGDIR}/${SQL_SERVER}_${FILE_NAME}_${DATABASE}.wrk"
REPORT_FILE="${LOGDIR}/${SQL_SERVER}_${FILE_NAME}_${DATABASE}.report"
[ -f ${REPORT_FILE} ] && rm -f ${REPORT_FILE}

#
echo `date` " ""======= Started $0 analysis =======" >> ${LOG_FILE}
echo `date` " ""======= Creating a list of tables and their size in database
${DATABASE} =======" >> ${LOG_FILE}
#
isql -U${USERNAME} -P${PASSWORD} -S${SQL_SERVER} -w1000 -X << ! > ${IN_FILE}
USE ${DATABASE}
go
SELECT 'USE ${DATABASE} ' + CONVERT(CHAR(1), 0x0A) + 'go'
SELECT 'sp_spaceused ' + name + CONVERT(CHAR(1), 0x0A) + 'go'
  FROM sysobjects
 WHERE type = "U"
--and name = 'syaudit'
```

```
ORDER
   BY name
go
exit
!

#
# get rid of 'rows affected' crap from ${IN_FILE}
#
cat ${IN_FILE} | egrep -i -v 'row' > temp.sql
mv temp.sql ${IN_FILE}
#
echo `date` " ""======= Ordering tables according to their size in O/S and
creating a bcp file =======" >> ${LOG_FILE}

echo "work file is ${WORK_FILE}" >> ${LOG_FILE}

isql -U${USERNAME} -P${PASSWORD} -S${SQL_SERVER} -X -w1000 < ${IN_FILE} >
${WORK_FILE}

cat ${WORK_FILE} | grep -i kb|sort +1nr +0 |awk '{printf "Table %-25s has %
10s rows and is %10s KB\n",$1,$2,$3}' > temp.sql

mv temp.sql ${WORK_FILE}
[ -f ${IN_FILE} ] && rm -f ${IN_FILE}

#
cat ${WORK_FILE} |grep 'Table'|awk '{print $2,"       ",$4," ",$8}' >
${BCP_FILE}

echo `date` " ""======= bcp file created OK =======" >> ${LOG_FILE}
isql -U${USERNAME} -P${PASSWORD} -S${SQL_SERVER} -X  -w1000 -b << ! >
${WORK_FILE}
USE tempdb
go
IF EXISTS(SELECT 1
            FROM sysobjects
           WHERE name = '${DATABASE}_tmp'
             AND type = 'U')
BEGIN
   DROP TABLE ${DATABASE}_tmp
END
go
CREATE TABLE ${DATABASE}_tmp(
   name VARCHAR(30) NOT NULL,
   records INT NOT NULL,
   size INT NOT NULL
)
```

```
go
exit
!

#
### now bcp in tempdb..${DATABASE}_tmp
#
echo `date` " ""======= Bcping in the ordered table list into tempdb table
=======" >> ${LOG_FILE}

bcp tempdb..${DATABASE}_tmp in ${BCP_FILE} -c  -S${SQL_SERVER} -U${USERNAME}
-P${PASSWORD} >> ${LOG_FILE}

#
isql -U${USERNAME} -P${PASSWORD} -S${SQL_SERVER} -X  -w1000 -b << ! >
${WORK_FILE}
USE tempdb
go
IF EXISTS(SELECT 1
            FROM sysobjects
           WHERE name = '${DATABASE}_big_tables'
             AND type = 'U')
BEGIN
   DROP TABLE ${DATABASE}_big_tables
END
go
CREATE TABLE ${DATABASE}_big_tables(
   table_league NUMERIC(10,0) IDENTITY,
   name VARCHAR(30) NOT NULL
)
go
INSERT
  INTO ${DATABASE}_big_tables
SELECT name
  FROM tempdb..${DATABASE}_tmp
 WHERE name NOT LIKE 'rs[_]%'          -- exclude replication stuff
go
IF EXISTS(SELECT 1
            FROM sysobjects
           WHERE name = '${DATABASE}_indexes'
             AND type = 'U')
BEGIN
   DROP TABLE ${DATABASE}_indexes
END
go
CREATE TABLE ${DATABASE}_indexes(
   name VARCHAR(30) NOT NULL,
   index_name VARCHAR(30) NOT NULL,
```

```
   records INT NOT NULL,
   size INT NOT NULL,
   table_type CHAR(3) NOT NULL,
   index_type VARCHAR(15) NOT NULL)
go
INSERT
  INTO ${DATABASE}_indexes
SELECT t.name,
       i.name,
       records,
       size,
       'unk',
       'non-clustered'
  FROM tempdb..${DATABASE}_tmp t,
       ${DATABASE}..sysobjects o,
       ${DATABASE}..sysindexes i
 WHERE t.name = o.name
   AND o.id = i.id
   AND i.indid > 0
   AND t.name NOT LIKE 'rs[_]%'          -- exclude replication stuff
 ORDER
    BY t.name
go
UPDATE ${DATABASE}_indexes
   SET index_type = 'clustered'
  FROM ${DATABASE}_indexes t,
       ${DATABASE}..sysindexes i
 WHERE t.index_name = i.name
   AND (i.indid = 1
       OR (i.indid > 1
          AND i.status2&512 = 512))
go
UPDATE ${DATABASE}_indexes
   SET table_type = 'APL'
  FROM ${DATABASE}_indexes t,
       ${DATABASE}..sysobjects o
 WHERE t.name = o.name
   AND o.type = 'U'
   AND (o.sysstat2 & 57344 = 0
        OR o.sysstat2 & 57344 = 8192)
go
UPDATE ${DATABASE}_indexes
   SET table_type = 'DPL'
  FROM ${DATABASE}_indexes t,
       ${DATABASE}..sysobjects o
 WHERE t.name = o.name
   AND o.type = 'U'
   AND o.sysstat2 & 57344 = 16384
```

```
go
UPDATE ${DATABASE}_indexes
   SET table_type = 'DOL'
  FROM ${DATABASE}_indexes t,
       ${DATABASE}..sysobjects o
 WHERE t.name = o.name
   AND o.type = 'U'
   AND o.sysstat2 & 57344 = 32768
go
exit
!

echo `date` " ""======= Creating a sql file to work out fragmentation for
different tables =======" >> ${LOG_FILE}
[ -f ${IN_FILE} ] && rm -f ${IN_FILE}

cat >> $IN_FILE << !
set nocount on
go
--select 'table     index  table_type   index_type   dpcr   ipcr   drcr
sput   lgio'
go
!

isql -U${USERNAME} -P${PASSWORD} -S${SQL_SERVER} -w1000 -X -h -b << ! >>
${IN_FILE}
USE tempdb
go
SELECT 'USE ${DATABASE}' + CONVERT(CHAR(1),0x0A) + 'go'
SELECT 'SELECT "' +
       name + '         ' +
       index_name + '         ' +
       CONVERT(CHAR(10),records) + '         ' +
       CONVERT(CHAR(10),size) + '         ' +
       table_type + '         ' +
       index_type + '         "' +
       ',DERIVED_STAT("'+name+'","'+index_name+'","dpcr")' +
       ',DERIVED_STAT("'+name+'","'+index_name+'","ipcr")' +
       ',DERIVED_STAT("'+name+'","'+index_name+'","drcr")' +
       ',DERIVED_STAT("'+name+'","'+index_name+'","sput")' +
       ',DERIVED_STAT("'+name+'","'+index_name+'","lgio")' +
       CONVERT(CHAR(1),0x0A)+'go'
  FROM ${DATABASE}_indexes
go
exit
!

#
```

```
# get rid of 'rows affected' crap from ${IN_FILE}
#
cat ${IN_FILE} | egrep -i -v 'affected|--' > temp.sql
mv temp.sql ${IN_FILE}

#
isql -U${USERNAME} -P${PASSWORD} -S${SQL_SERVER} -X -w1000 -b -h <
${IN_FILE} > ${RESULT_FILE}

#
echo `date` " ""======= Creating tempdb..${DATABASE}_final table which will
hold all the required info  =======" >> ${LOG_FILE}

isql -U${USERNAME} -P${PASSWORD} -S${SQL_SERVER} -w1000 -X -b << ! >
${WORK_FILE}
USE tempdb
go
IF EXISTS(SELECT 1
            FROM sysobjects
           WHERE name = '${DATABASE}_final'
             AND type = 'U')
BEGIN
   DROP TABLE ${DATABASE}_final
END
go
SELECT *
  INTO ${DATABASE}_final
  FROM ${DATABASE}_indexes
 WHERE 1 = 2
go
ALTER TABLE ${DATABASE}_final
ADD dpcr FLOAT NULL,
    ipcr FLOAT NULL,
    drcr FLOAT NULL,
    sput FLOAT NULL,
    lgio FLOAT NULL
go
exit
!

[ -f ${WORK_FILE} ] && rm -f ${WORK_FILE}
cat ${RESULT_FILE} |
  {
  while read table index_name records size table_type index_type dpcr ipcr
drcr sput lgio
  do
       isql -U${USERNAME} -P${PASSWORD} -S${SQL_SERVER} -w1000 -X -b -h << !
>> ${WORK_FILE}
```

```
USE tempdb
go
SET NOCOUNT ON
go
INSERT
  INTO ${DATABASE}_final
VALUES("${table}",
       "${index_name}",
       ${records},
       ${size},
       "${table_type}",
       "${index_type}",
       ${dpcr},
       ${ipcr},
       ${drcr},
       ${sput},
       ${lgio}
)
go
exit
!
  done
  }

echo `date` " ""======= Creating report file ${LOGDIR}/{SQL_SERVER}_$
{FILE_NAME}_${DATABASE}.report  =======" >> ${LOG_FILE}

isql -U${USERNAME} -P${PASSWORD} -S${SQL_SERVER} -X  -w1000 << ! >
${REPORT_FILE}
USE tempdb
go
SET NOCOUNT ON
go
CREATE UNIQUE CLUSTERED INDEX ${DATABASE}_final_idx1
ON ${DATABASE}_final(name,index_name)
go
SELECT name,
       table_type,
       records,
       index_name,
       index_type
  INTO #final
  FROM ${DATABASE}_final
 WHERE 1 = 2
go
ALTER TABLE #final
ADD action VARCHAR(20) NULL
go
```

```
DECLARE @records INT,
        @limits FLOAT

SELECT @records = 50000
SELECT @limits = 0.90

INSERT #final
SELECT name,
       table_type,
       records,
       index_name,
       index_type,
       "reorg"
  FROM ${DATABASE}_final
 WHERE table_type = 'DOL'
   AND index_type = 'clustered'
   AND records > @records
   AND dpcr < @limits

INSERT #final
SELECT name,
       table_type,
       records,
       index_name,
       index_type,
       "reorg"
  FROM ${DATABASE}_final
 WHERE table_type = 'DOL'
   AND index_type = 'non-clustered'
   AND records > @records
   AND ipcr < @limits

INSERT #final
SELECT name,
       table_type,
       records,
       index_name,
       index_type,
       "Rebuild the index"
  FROM ${DATABASE}_final
 WHERE table_type = 'APL'
   AND index_type = 'clustered'
   AND records > @records
   AND sput < @limits

PRINT ""

INSERT #final
```

```
SELECT name,
       table_type,
       records,
       index_name,
       index_type,
       "Rebuild the index"
  FROM ${DATABASE}_final
 WHERE table_type = 'APL'
   AND index_type = 'non-clustered'
   AND records > @records
   AND sput < @limits

SELECT "Fragmentation analysis for database ${DATABASE} on " +
       CONVERT (CHAR(25),GETDATE(),100)

PRINT ''
PRINT 'Suggested table list for defragging'
PRINT ''

SELECT DISTINCT
       name,
       table_type,
       records,
       action
  FROM #final
 ORDER
    BY records DESC

PRINT ''
PRINT 'Detailed table and index list for defragging'
PRINT ''

SELECT *
  FROM #final
 ORDER
    BY records DESC

PRINT ''
PRINT "Terminology used"
PRINT "DOL ==>  data-only-locked"
PRINT "APL ==>  all-pages-locked"
PRINT "dpcr ==> data-page-cluster-ratio"
PRINT "ipcr ==> index-page-cluster-ratio"
PRINT "drcr ==> data-row-cluster-ratio"
PRINT "sput ==> space utilization"
PRINT "lgio ==> Large io efficiency"
PRINT "In general the closer the parameter to 1 the better it is"
```

```
PRINT ""
PRINT 'table type ==> DOL and index type ==> clustered, watch =====> dpcr'
SELECT name,
       index_name,
       records,
       dpcr,
       ipcr
  FROM ${DATABASE}_final
 WHERE index_type = 'clustered'
   AND table_type = 'DOL'
   AND records > 10000
 ORDER
    BY records DESC
go
PRINT ""
PRINT 'table_type = DOL and index_type = non-clustered, watch ====> ipcr &
sput'
SELECT name,
       index_name,
       records,
       ipcr,
       sput
  FROM ${DATABASE}_final
 WHERE index_type = 'non-clustered'
   AND table_type = 'DOL'
   AND records > 10000
 ORDER
    BY records DESC
go
PRINT ""
PRINT 'table_type = APL and index_type = clustered, watch  ====> sput &
lgio'
SELECT name,
       index_name,
       records,
       sput,
       lgio
  FROM ${DATABASE}_final
 WHERE index_type = 'clustered'
   AND table_type = 'APL'
   AND records > 10000
 ORDER
    BY records DESC
go
PRINT ""
PRINT 'table_type = APL and index_type = non-clustered watch  ====> sput'
SELECT name,
       index_name,
```

```
       records,
       sput,
       lgio
  FROM ${DATABASE}_final
 WHERE index_type = 'non-clustered'
   AND table_type = 'APL'
   AND records > 10000
go
exit
!

echo `date` " ""======= Finished $0 analysis =======" >> ${LOG_FILE}
msg="`date` Fragmentation report for ${DATABASE} on ${SQL_SERVER}"
cat ${REPORT_FILE}|/usr/bin/mailx -s "${msg}" ${SUPPORT}
```

Appendix I. Determine Fragmentation

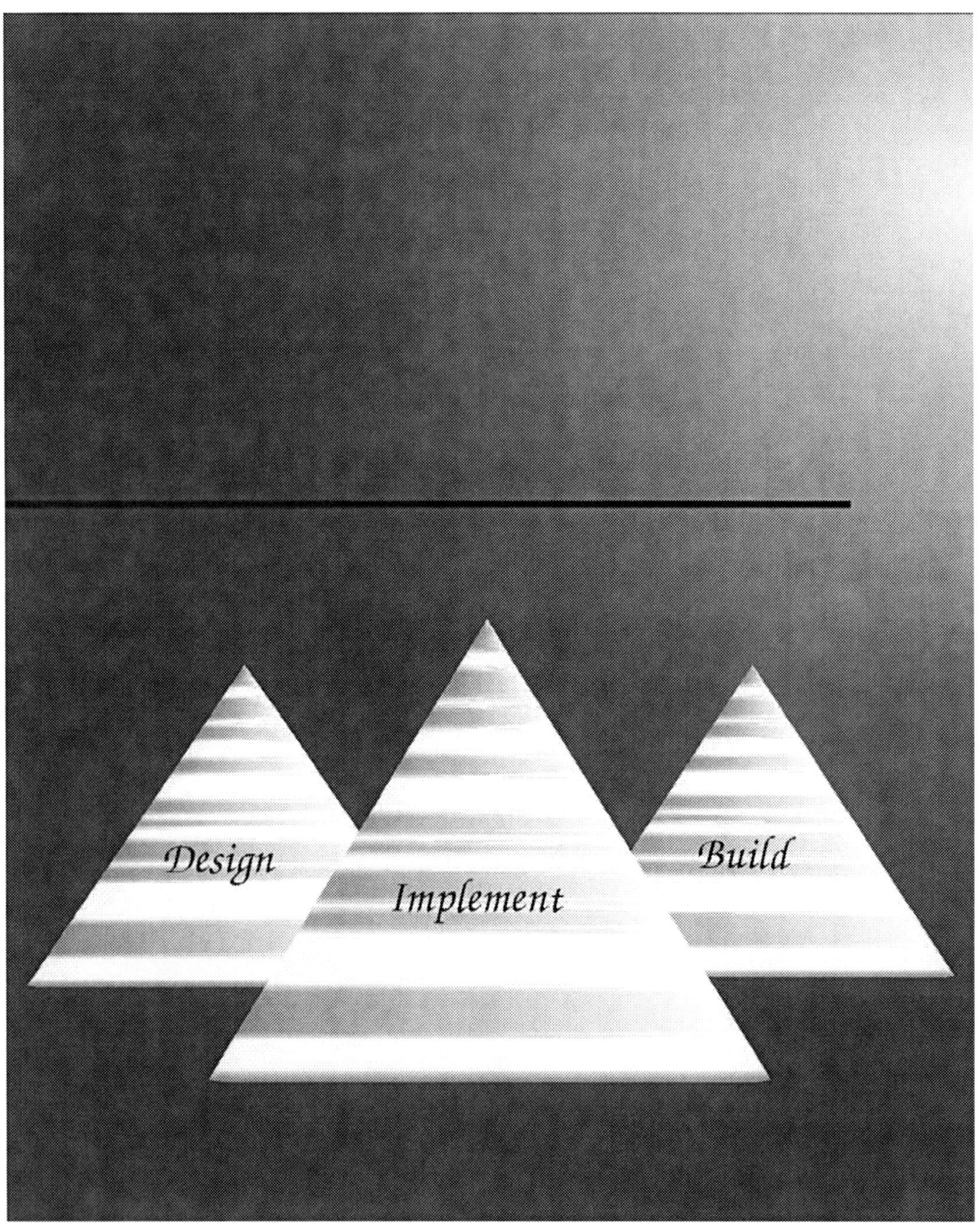
Design
Implement
Build

References

Listed below are materials which we used as references for writing this book. We included many of the examples and diagrams from these manuals. These manuals are generally available from Sybase Inc. in http://www.sybase.com/support/manuals

- Sybase 11.5 Manuals
- Sybase 11.9 Manuals
- Sybase 12.0 Manuals
- Sybase 12.5 Manuals
- Sybase 12.5.1 Manuals
- Sybase 12.5.2 Manuals

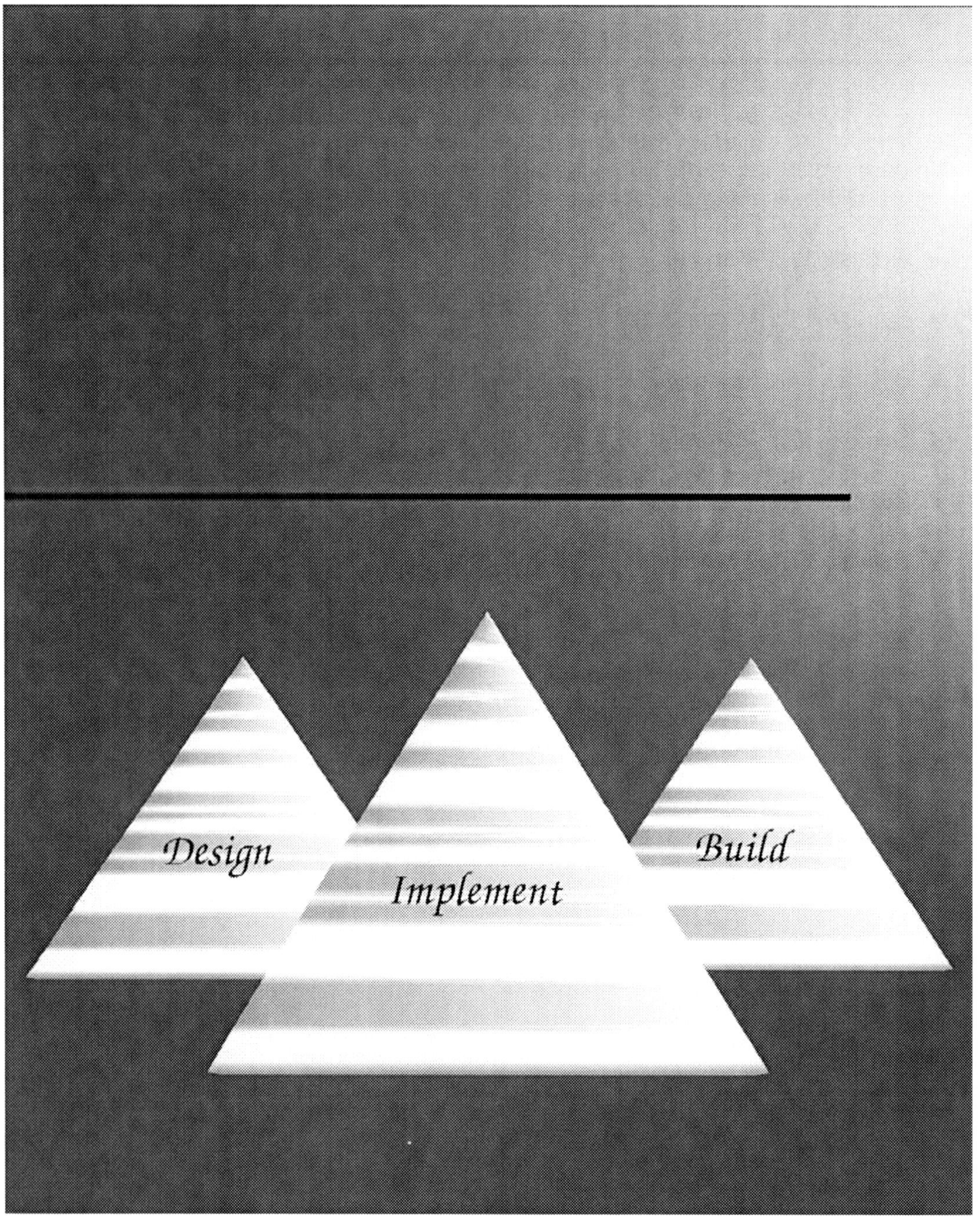
Design
Implement
Build

Index

C

G

R

S

Printed in the United States
138377LV00003B/14/A

9 780975 969304